Women and Religion in Medieval and Renaissance Italy

WOMEN IN CULTURE AND SOCIETY
A series edited by Catharine R. Stimpson

Women and Religion in Medieval and Renaissance Italy

Edited by
Daniel Bornstein and Roberto Rusconi

Translated by
Margery J. Schneider

THE UNIVERSITY OF CHICAGO PRESS
CHICAGO AND LONDON

DANIEL BORNSTEIN is assistant professor of history at Texas A&M University.
ROBERT RUSCONI is professor of Church history at the University of L'Aquila.

The University of Chicago Press, Chicago 60637
The University of Chicago Press, Ltd., London
© 1996 by The University of Chicago
All rights reserved. Published 1996
Printed in the United States of America
05 04 03 02 01 00 99 98 97 96   5 4 3 2 1

ISBN (cloth): 0-226-06637-1
ISBN (paper): 0-226-06639-8

Originally published as *Mistiche e devote nell'Italia
tardomedievale,* © Liguori Editore, Srl, 1992

Library of Congress Cataloging-in-Publication Data

Mistiche e devote nell'Italia tardomedievale. English
    Women and religion in medieval and Renaissance Italy / edited by
Daniel Bornstein and Roberto Rusconi ; translated by Margery J. Schneider.
        p.   cm.
    Includes bibliographical references and index.
    ISBN 0-226-06637-1. — ISBN 0-226-06639-8 (pbk.)
    1. Women in Christianity—Italy—History.   2. Women mystics—Italy—
History.   3. Spirituality—Italy—History.   4. Spirituality—Catholic Church—
History.   5. Monasticism and religious orders for women—Italy—History—
Middle Ages,   600–1500.   6. Christian women saints—Italy—History.
7. Catholic Church—Italy—History.   8. Italy—Church history—476–1400.
9. Italy—Church history—15th century.   I. Bornstein, Daniel Ethan, 1950–.
II. Rusconi, Roberto.   III. Title.
BX1544.M5713   1996
282'.082—dc20   95-44343
                        CIP

Visualize an August day over six centuries ago in Italy, that most beautiful of places. Clare of Montefalco, the revered leader of a convent, is dying. She is only forty years old. Immediately after her death, the sisters of the order open up the body of their abbess. They find in her heart "the symbols of Christ's Passion: the crucifix, the whip, the pillar, the crown of thorns, the three nails, the lance, and the rod with the sponge" (p. 105).

Today, many citizens of a secular age would seek to demystify such a scene. They might suggest that the sisters were the victims of a collective hallucination or that the sisters, consciously or unconsciously, were rewriting the findings of their autopsy in order to enhance the spirituality of their leader. Indeed, in 1881, after a tortuous process, the Roman Catholic Church finally canonized Clare of Montefalco. *Women and Religion in Medieval and Renaissance Italy* asks us to do more than engage in demystifying acts. This wonderful collection of essays compels us to exercise our historical imagination and intelligence in order to understand a time and place where the sacred was a part of everyday, secular life. Doing so, the book raises fundamental historical and contemporary questions about religion.

Because *Women and Religion* focuses on women in northern and central Italy from the twelfth to the sixteenth centuries, it also raises fundamental questions about women and gender during a crucial historical period. These essays explore a paradox. Italian women lacked political, legal, familial, and religious authority. They could not become priests or higher ecclesiastical figures. Nevertheless, in a society in which the Roman Catholic Church was powerful and omnipresent, women were extraordinarily active, influential, and creative religious figures. Not only did they assume spiritual and moral leadership within the home. They were public figures, often charismatically so, whether they were oblates, laywomen who followed a religious life; members of a religious order; or erenites, holy recluses. They imitated and embodied Christ-like virtues. They prayed, worked, tended the suffering, were poor and penitent. They saw visions and welcomed miracles. They founded their own religious groups outside of established orders. They inspired cults and biographies. A significant number of these women, like Catherine of Siena or Clare of Montefalco, became saints. If the Roman Catholic Church did not permit them to preach from the pulpit, they preached with their bodies and deeds.

Women seem to have been at their most active, influential, and creative when established authorities, including ecclesiastical authority, were in disarray, even chaos. When social equilibrium returned, religious life was regularized, women reined in. In brief, late medieval and early modern Italian women are a complex example of the exercise of the powers of the weak. These powers are energetic, fertile, resilient, and limited.

Women and Religion in Medieval and Renaissance Italy both draws upon and bountifully increases the studies of women and spirituality that have become available since the late 1960s. These explorations cultivate several overlapping areas—the ways in which religious institutions construct and represent gender; the roles of women within orthodox religious institutions; the roles of women within heterodox religious groups; and the contributions of women to theology, be it orthodox or heterodox. In addition, the editors of this book, Daniel Bornstein and Roberto Rusconi, working as international collaborators, are bringing a group of strong Italian scholars to the attention of English-speaking audiences. We have a lot to learn from our Italian colleagues. As Bornstein points out, these scholars differ amongst themselves, but they tend to be rigorous empiricists who examine the stucture and processes of institutions such as the Catholic Church; the function of religion within its social, political, and economic context; and the ways in which institutions work at a specific location. *Women and Religion* is not only scrupulous in its fidelity to the demands of empirical historiography. The societies and individuals that the book gives us are dramatic, vivid, living in secular time but craving to live in sacred time, to taste miracles.

As a citizen of a secular society in which various religions flex formidable powers, I occasionally play a mind game and imagine myself as a young woman in a less secular society. I wonder what forms my piety might then have taken. Would I have found myself in a convent or in a women's community that an oblate had established in order to serve God in a different way? What would I have spotted if I had opened the ribcage of Clare of Montefalco and seen her just-stopped heart? *Women and Religion in Medieval and Renaissance Italy* feeds such imaginings. Far more important, this book feeds our need for history, for the indispensable narratives about the days of the past that people wring from hard, scrupulous, and humanistic work and then offer to us for our active contemplation.

Catharine R. Stimpson
Rutgers University (on leave)
Director, Fellows Program,
MacArthur Foundation

This volume is a new edition, rather than a simple translation, of *Mistiche e devote nell'Italia tardomedievale* (Naples, 1992). In fact, both the English and Italian editions were conceived from the outset with distinct publics in mind. For the Italian edition, we included essays by Fernanda Sorelli on the hagiographic writings of Tommaso d'Antonio Caffarini and by Gabriella Zarri on court prophetesses that had previously appeared in French but not in Italian. For this edition, those essays have been replaced by one by Sorelli that focuses more on the holy woman than on her male biographer, and by Zarri's fullest treatment of the living saints of the early sixteenth century. A few pages that were cut from the essays by Chiara Frugoni and Enrico Menestò in the Italian have been restored for this edition; some material from Anna Benvenuti's notes has been integrated into the text of her essay; and Zarri's abundant notes have been condensed somewhat. The scholarly apparatus has been updated in several cases—most notably, the citations in Menestò's essay have been changed to reflect the publication of the canonization proceedings for Clare of Montefalco—and a serious (though unsystematic) effort has been made to provide references to English translations. All of these editorial changes have been reviewed and approved by the authors.

Daniel Bornstein's introductory essay, which closed the Italian edition, has been restored to its original place and thoroughly revised to reflect developments in the field since it was originally drafted. Roberto Rusconi has contributed a new afterword, written especially for the English edition, in which he indicates some particularly compelling directions for future research.

In short, in the expectation that this book will be used both by specialists in the field and by students who do not read Italian, we have tried to make this collection as up-to-date and accessible as possible, while retaining the ample citations from original sources and references to the secondary literature.

Preparing this collection has been a long and demanding project, and transatlantic collaboration has involved some notable problems of communication and coordination; but our spirits and the Italian infrastructure have survived the test. We are grateful to Texas A&M University for helping with the translation costs and to the Fondazione Ezio Franceschini in

Florence and the Newberry Library in Chicago for technical assistance at key moments in the preparation of the manuscript.

Daniel Bornstein
Texas A&M University

Roberto Rusconi
Università degli studi dell'Aquila

I

Women and Religion in Late Medieval Italy: History and Historiography

Daniel Bornstein

In the late Middle Ages, women labored under a heavy burden of institutional and ideological disabilities. They were barred from political office; they were hampered by a host of legal restrictions; they were subjected to the authority of their male relatives; they were excluded from institutions of higher education; they were deemed physically, intellectually, and morally inferior to men.[1] Yet from the twelfth century to the sixteen, women assumed public roles of unprecedented prominence in the religious culture of their time.[2]

This was not a case of placating an excluded and powerless group by allowing its members authority over a separate and inconsequential realm of human activity. Church and society were inextricably bound up with one another; and in terms of landed wealth, political power, intellectual eminence, moral prestige, and cultural influence, the Catholic Church was a dominating presence. Ecclesiastical institutions owned approximately a quarter of all wealth.[3] Exercise of church office was one way in which ruling families secured their power; control over appointment to church office was a primary means by which Florence and other great cities extended their control over subject territories.[4] Control over the pulpit meant that clerics, and especially the great preaching orders of Franciscans, Dominicans, and Augustinians, were responsible for cultural mediation and indoctrination on a scale that no other group could match.[5] Ecclesiastical institutions continued to be the leading patrons of the arts, as they had been ever since the fourth century; and even when laymen commissioned works of art, whether for placement in a church or for private devotional use, the form and content of those works were defined by established religious traditions.[6] Active participation in religious life thus offered women access to power in all its forms, power that was otherwise denied them.[7] By carefully exploiting the institutional church (which barred them from the priesthood and from high ecclesiastical office) and by astutely manipulating religious precepts (which were a principal source of the ideology of female inferiority), women were able to carve out for themselves broad areas of influence.

The powers of the weak are nowhere more apparent than in the case of Margaret of Città di Castello.[8] Born blind and deformed in 1287, Margaret was abandoned by her parents when she was around six years old: their prayers for the restoration of her sight had gone unanswered, and so they brought her to Città di Castello to visit the tomb of a Franciscan friar who was famed for his miracles, and simply left here there when he proved powerless to grant their request. She was taken in first by some devout women and then raised by a married couple, who soon recognized her extraordinary piety. From the age of seven she wore a hairshirt; she fasted rigorously, refused to sleep in a bed, and flagellated herself three times a night, cutting her flesh to the bone. She entered a convent, but the lax nuns found her insistent devotions insufferable and soon returned Margaret to her adoptive parents. Finally, at the age of fourteen, she donned the black mantle of a lay penitent affiliated with the Dominican order; this institutional identity permitted her to live in the world rather than retire to a convent, and to dedicate herself to active charity and severe asceticism without being bound to a communal life. From 1301 to her death in 1320, Margaret pursued her personal perfection through chastity, poverty, and humility, while assuming an increasingly public role as sacred protector of Città di Castello. Though blind and illiterate, she was able to teach others the hidden meanings of the psalms; though poor and ailing, she was able to bring aid and comfort to prisoners and paupers and accord miraculous cures to those afflicted with illness. In her prayers on behalf of her community, she played a quasi-priestly role as intercessor between God and humankind. And the reverence she inspired allowed her to intercede effectively between man and man, restoring peace and unity to Città di Castello.

Città di Castello also offered a variety of institutionalized ways in which more ordinary women could display less heroic forms of piety. Giovanna Casagrande, surveying Città di Castello in the late thirteenth century, discovered there four Benedictine abbeys and a fifth convent belonging to the new Benedictine congregation of Santuccia Terebotti, known as "Santucce."[9] There were also three convents of Poor Clares. These Franciscan houses appear to have been rather larger than the Benedictine abbeys; indeed, when one bishop tried to place a woman and her two daughters in one of these convents, the women there objected that their community already housed all the women it could support.[10] A fourth house seems to have adopted the Rule of St. Clare as a matter of convenience, without actually belonging to the order. Another convent followed instead the more flexible Augustinian rule, often adopted by female houses after the Fourth Lateran Council (1215) obliged all monastic institutions to choose one of the existing and approved rules. In addition to these cloistered institutions, there were a number of formally recognized ways in which women could lead a devout life on the fringes of monastic and mendicant communities. "Sisters of penitence," along with male members of the "order of penance," were affiliated with the Franciscan order or, like Margaret, with the Dominicans; lay converts, both male and female, saw to the functioning of convents and monasteries, staffed the civic and ecclesiastical hospitals, and tended the lepers in the town leprosarium.[11] A few solitary anchoresses lived walled in tiny cells attached to a church or sealed in their rooms at home. Last, there were some vaguely defined little groups in which two or three women undertook to live together, sometimes with the explicit stipulation that they not be bound to any rule.[12] It is not always possible to know the exact number of women associated with these various communities or patterns of life, nor is it certain that these groups, culled from a reading of the Bishops' Books of Città di Castello, represent all of the female religious institutions of that city. Still, one can state that at a minimum, 10 percent of the women of Città di Castello pursued a defined religious life under one of its many forms. The picture that emerges from other such soundings is broadly similar in both the variety of forms of religious life and the large number of women who pursued them.[13]

Adherence to one or another of these institutional forms of female religious life entailed the choice of a particular sort of spirituality. The Franciscan ideal of poverty was defended by St. Clare of Assisi and her circle as they resisted well-intentioned papal attempts to endow them with property and guarantee them a secure income.[14] An equally marked and even more contested renunciation of worldly values determined the careers of recluses like Umiliana dei Cerchi, who broke bitterly with their families to find freedom from social ties in a solitary bedroom or the narrow confines of an anchoress's cell.[15] The broader bounds of the cloister guarded the chastity of nuns who pursued a common life of prayer on behalf of the larger community outside the convent walls.[16] Tertiaries, lay converts, and penitents chose to risk their chastity in dangerous engagement with the world, sustaining the poor, caring for the sick, comforting the dying, promoting peace, and performing other works of mercy.[17]

Women could understand their paths of piety in terms of biblical exemplars: the active Martha and her contemplative sister, Mary, the virile Judith, the reformed sinner Mary Magdalene, and the always virgin Mother of God. Often, however, they invoked more proximate models, clustering around revered ladies like Francesca Bussa dei Ponziani in Rome or patterning themselves on women who had, within living memory, demonstrated exemplary sanctity.[18] By the fifteenth century, it was even possible for a married woman like Francesca, a mother and housewife, to be canonized: human marriage and spiritual nuptials were no longer considered mutually exclusive, though married aspirants to holiness did tend to observe conjugal chastity or, like Angela of Foligno, embarked on their spiritual careers only Velut after their spouse's death.[19] Home and family remained an almost insuperable impediment to the truly holy life, as Angela of Foligno made brutally clear when she expressed the "great consolation" she felt at the deaths of her mother, husband, and children, for which she had devoutly prayed.[20]

Increasingly, however, women expressed in words and acts a conviction that it was possible (though never easy) to lead a good and devout, if not holy, life amid the duties, irritations, and pleasures of home and family. It seems often to have been the women of the household who took the lead in domestic devotions and charitable activities, who read pious vernacular literature, cherished and adorned religious figurines, and raised their children with proper reverence for church and clergy. Such domestic pieties may even have been learned from the brides of Christ, for upper-class families sometimes placed their adolescent daughters in convents for a few months, or even years, to be instructed by the nuns.[21] They could also be learned from books, for women were avid collectors, readers, and critics of the vast amount of devotional literature produced in the fourteenth and fifteenth centuries, by authors ranging from Domenico Cavalca to Girolamo Savonarola.[22] His awareness of women's central place in domestic piety led Giovanni Dominici to direct at a devout Florentine laywoman letters of spiritual counsel, a work of mystical theology, and a manual on childrearing and household management.[23] But however they had acquired their cultural formation, in decorating their homes as in listening to sermons, making confession, and receiving the eucharist, perfectly ordinary women were constant consumers of the sacred.

This vision of women exercising deliberate choices within the range of available options and despite social and cultural constraints runs contrary to received wisdom, which holds that women were pawns manipulated by men in the sociopolitical game of marriage alliances, and that those who were too ugly or too expensive to marry off were dumped in whatever convent would take them.[24] There is doubtless more than a little truth in this; discerning the power of these pawns requires acute insight and careful attention to nuance—and paradox. Denied access to the institutions of higher education and sources of human learning, women served as conduits of divine wisdom; their very ability to speak wisely without human instruction was taken as proof of their miraculous converse with God.[25] Legally subordinated, politically excluded, socially limited, ideologically disdained, women at least held the power of refusal: the Poor Clares and anchoresses of Città di Castello resisted episcopal interference, just as St. Clare herself rejected papal provisions for her well-being.[26] Women exercised vigorously the one form of authority they enjoyed: sacred charisma.[27] They received mystic insights, spoke as prophets and visionaries, interceded for their communities, counseled princes and popes.[28] These holy women may seem to be reduced to the status of religious objects, like breathing icons or living relics collected by calculatedly pious rulers; but theirs is a world in which paintings of the Madonna weep and speak, images of the crucified Jesus bleed and turn, and objects become agents.

Understanding the circulation of images and ideas in this world involves a complex cultural hermeneutic. Much attention has been lavished on the construction and presentation of role models for women. Authors of spiritual tracts advised women on everything from how to pray to how to dress. Preachers defined the character and duties of the good housewife, and sacramental confession saw to it that their words were heeded.[29] Hagiographers praised the exceptional virtues of holy women, while artists depicted the supremely humble and obedient Mother of God and a bevy of other handmaidens of the Lord.[30] That these models were crafted by men for women should not blind us to the active role of women in generating these models or the manifold ambiguities inherent in the process of modeling.[31]

Nowhere is this clearer than in the case of St. Catherine of Siena and her circle.[32] At an early age, Catherine attracted widespread criticism for her rejection of both marriage and cloister in favor of the life of a Dominican tertiary; she then aroused the suspicion of the Dominican order with her mystical experiences and prophetic pronouncements. This disturbingly unusual woman was accordingly placed under the guidance of Raymond of Capua, a mature and well-born Dominican with a sound education and ample experience in the spiritual direction of women. Yet their roles were soon reversed: the father confessor became the spiritual child of his charge, a shift found also in the lives of Angela of Foligno and other holy women.[33] Raymond decided that this uneducated daughter of a Sienese dyer bore comparison with the greatest saints of the Catholic Church; he submitted himself to Catherine's correction and instruction, propagated her teaching, encouraged her pastoral activities, defended her against her detractors, both male and female, and presented her to the world as a model of sanctity.

When he fit her into the saintly mold, he was performing the standard work of hagiographers; but he was also responding to Catherine's firm injunction that her secretaries polish and purify her utterances, removing from them anything that did not serve her church.[34] The result of Raymond's labors was a *vita* of the saint that was faithful to her desires and to the memories of her companions, yet too long to be read easily and too extraordinary to be imitated humanly. Raymond's associates promptly produced Latin supplements and abridgements, vernacular versions, and more accessible patterns for emulation.[35] And so they hatched an astonishing brood of new Catherines: women who elected her manner of life and assumed her role of stigmatized visionary and prophet, and women who merely admired her and in their own far more measured lives of piety and austerity translated the inimitable Catherine into something any good woman could copy.[36] Men, too, adopted Catherine as model and mentor. Raymond of Capua believed that it was Catherine's spiritual patronage that determined his election as master general of the Dominicans; Cardinal Giovanni Dominici testified that her intercession had miraculously cured his stutter, thus enabling him to pursue his calling as a preacher.[37] They and other highly placed churchmen acknowledged her as their spiritual guide and adopted her as the inspirational model for their reformation of the Dominican order. In this manner, from a position of structural weakness and ideological subordination, Catherine was able to exercise a profound influence on religious beliefs and ecclesiastical institutions.[38]

This openness to female influence, and to experimentation with novel religious roles and unconventional devotional attitudes, may have been due in part to cracks in ecclesiastical structures. It was during the long decades of the Avignon papacy and of the Great Schism, when the validity of any particular religious authority was rendered doubtful first by the removal of the papacy from its proper seat and then by the spectacle of two (and later three) competing hierarchies, that women like St. Catherine of Siena, St. Birgitta of Sweden, and other lesser figures were able to emerge as vociferous protagonists of religious life.[39] It was when the male hierarchy was in obvious disarray that prominent churchmen were most willing to listen to strange voices, disregard decorum and timeworn proprieties, and concede to these women a place at (or near) the altar. An altarpiece was dedicated to Margaret of Cortona around the beginning of the Avignon papacy, though she was not canonized until 1728, some 400 years later; around 1400, in the midst of the Great Schism, the Venetian convent of Corpus Christi was adorned with a painting of Giovanna of Florence, Catherine of Siena, Margaret of Città di Castello, Vanna and Daniela of Orvieto—five Dominican tertiaries, all crowned with the golden rays of the beatified, though none of them had been recognized by the church.[40] The restoration of institutional order meant a rejection of eccentric female models, a remasculinization of religious images. Only around 1500, when the Wars of Italy again threw ecclesiastical and political institutions into crisis, was a new generation of female prophets and visionaries able to gather an attentive and responsive audience—for a few brief years, until their exuberant voices, too, were stilled with the return of peace and stability after 1530.[41]

THESE REMARKABLE female presences (and absences) in the religious culture of late medieval Europe have become a major focus of research only in recent years.[42] Of course, occasional studies dedicated to women and religion had appeared earlier. By far the most significant of these is Herbert Grundmann's magisterial *Religiöse Bewegungen im Mittelalter,* which has been called "the most important work on twelfth- and thirteenth-century religion in the past fifty years."[43] In this compelling work of synthesis, Grundmann argued that the vibrant and variegated religious developments of the twelfth and thirteenth centuries were all part of a single vast religious movement. This movement took many forms—the proliferation of wandering preachers and hermits, the reform of existing monastic orders and the foundation of new ones, the establishment of chapters of regular canons, the widespread diffusion of dualist and pauperist heresies, the inception of the mendicant orders, a search for new forms of religious life and new modes of religious expression—but it all sprang from a single impulse: the desire to restore the primacy of apostolic poverty and evangelical preaching. Grundmann thus rejected Marxist-inspired interpretations of religious dissent, insisting that orthodox and heterodox developments were all part of a unitary movement and that the driving force behind this movement was essentially spiritual rather than socioeconomic.

Women shared equally with men in this spiritual awakening. Indeed, their prominent involvement in all its aspects characterized the religious revival of the twelfth and thirteenth centuries and even constituted, according to Grundmann, a distinctive women's religious movement. The forms taken by this women's movement spanned the entire gamut of religious developments. Women flocked to the new monastic orders in such numbers that the Cistercians and Premonstratensians felt compelled to limit the number of nunneries, but they also stood out as teachers of heresy and followers of heretical movements. Women pursued lives of solitary sanctity as hermits or anchoresses and formed devout communities as beguines. They cultivated theological wisdom and philosophical learning at the great nunnery of

Helfta, and austere simplicity among the early followers of St. Francis of Assisi.

Under Grundmann's influence, the women's religious movement of the Middle Ages became a commonplace of medieval historiography, but not an object of further investigation. The only aspect of this movement to draw much attention was the emergence of the beguines: devout laywomen who joined together to lead a pious life in common, dedicating themselves to prayer, charity, and chastity while refusing to be bound by formal monastic vows. In some cities of northwestern Europe, these communities of pious women formed separate neighborhoods, shaping the urban fabric; even when their residences remained scattered throughout the city, their social presence was inescapable. There were at least two or three hundred beguines in Strasburg around 1300, when the population of that city was roughly twenty thousand; in Cologne, which was slightly larger than Strasburg, as many as fifteen hundred women lived in more than 150 beguine houses. The Great Beguinage of Ghent constituted a city within the city, with its walls and moats, two churches, eighteen convents, and hundred houses, its brewery and infirmary. Historians have examined the social composition and economic structure of these communities, their theological underpinnings and ecclesiastical implications, and the novel opportunities for holiness in this world and within marriage that developed in and around beguine groups.[44] But because the striking growth of beguine communities was peculiar to one corner of Europe, the continental scope of the women's religious movement of the Middle Ages was gradually lost from view.

In the last two decades, historians have finally risen to Grundmann's challenge, and studies of women and religion have proliferated. Some of the early efforts were directed at making sources more available: in 1978, Carla Casagrande published a collection of thirteenth-century sermons directed at women, and the following year, Elizabeth Petroff contributed translations of the biographies of four holy women, prefaced by an extended essay on female saints in thirteenth-century Italy.[45] André Vauchez then published his monumental analysis of late medieval canonization proceedings, in which he gives great prominence to the question of female sanctity.[46] In the very year that Caroline Walker Bynum published *Jesus as Mother,* which did so much to add precision to our understanding of the feminization of religious language in the later Middle Ages, Donald Weinstein and Rudolph M. Bell presented a statistical analysis of seven centuries of sainthood that amply confirmed and broadened Vauchez's perceptions on the importance of female sanctity: "Nothing so clearly divided the ranks of the saints," they concluded, "as gender."[47]

Exactly how female sanctity differed from male has been the burden of a number of important recent studies. Weinstein and Bell themselves proposed a distinction between a "masculine type" of saint—"holder of temporal or ecclesiastical power, missionary to the heathen and fiery preacher of the word, champion of public morality, heroic defender of his virtue"—and another type, characterized by "penitential asceticism, private prayer, mystical communion with the Godhead, and charity." They suggested that this latter type should be termed "androgynous" rather than female, since both men and women can be found who fit that pattern.[48] Yet there appear to be a number of traits that, while found in both male and female aspirants to a life of special piety, seem to mark women's religious outlook with particular force.

One is a concern with food and flesh, whether expressed in the extreme fasting, sometimes to the point of death, that Bell explored in *Holy Anorexia,* or the broader range of food practices and related ideas expounded in Bynum's brilliant *Holy Feast and Holy Fast.*[49] Women took the lead in promoting devotion to the eucharist; Juliana of Cornillon gave the new feast of Corpus Christi its initial impulse, and beguines helped propagate it.[50] Subsisting exclusively or almost exclusively on the consecrated host was a characteristically female miracle, just as drinking pus was a characteristically female way of expressing triumph over the body. The theological identification of woman with carnality meant that images and ritualized gestures of eating and not-eating were especially prominent in women's devotional acts and religious language.

Another aspect of this religiosity is the affective piety that encouraged the believer to develop a personal, emotional attachment to Jesus. Affective piety was not an exclusive preserve of devout women. It was cultivated and promoted by men such as Anselm of Canterbury and Bernard of Clairvaux; it was a man, St. Francis of Assisi, who offered the premier example of identification with the suffering person of Jesus, and growing numbers of men followed his lead and embraced an intensely emotional devotional style.[51] But affective piety was presented to women as a devotional mode peculiarly suited to female capacities, as these were understood in the late Middle Ages. Women, with their weak intellects and strong passions, were encouraged to meditate on the most intimately human and grippingly immediate moments in the life of Jesus: his birth, suffering, and death.[52] To the extent that men came to share these devotional modes, the Middle Ages may even have witnessed, as Richard Kieckhefer suggests, "a feminization of male piety, as men began to adopt the extreme fervor previously reserved for women."[53] But here, too, as in Weinstein and Bell's identification of an "androgynous" rather than female model of sanctity, efforts to isolate some form of piety as distinctively female have proven problematic, and those problems have been further complicated by the difficulty of moving from the biological category "female" to the cultural one "feminine." Once we know what features—such as a propensity for visions or a predilection for certain forms of eucharistic devotion—characterize the religious experience of women in particular times and places, it will be possible to move persuasively from a phenomenology of female experience to a typology of feminine piety. Until then, it would be wise to keep in mind the reservations about the very existence of "feminine" piety that Clarissa W. Atkinson voiced in her study of Margery Kempe.[54]

Still, as Atkinson notes, "whether or not piety can be 'masculine' or 'feminine,' ways of living are certainly dictated by gender."[55] Women were barred from the priesthood by church law; they were discouraged from the eremitical life by social custom and by the risks attendant on living alone in the wilderness. On the other hand, although no forms of life were exclusively reserved to women by law or custom, there were certain ones in which they came to predominate. Before 1200, monks vastly outnumbered nuns; in the thirteenth century the sex ratio of cloistered religious became more equal; and by 1500 cloistered nuns outnumbered monks in various parts of Europe.[56] Among those not bound by formal monastic vows, the female presence was even more striking: the beguines were far more numerous than their male counterparts, the beghards. Women also predominated among those pursuing solitary lives of devotion shut in a room at home or walled in a cell attached to a church: Ann K. Warren has identified 780 English anchorites between 1100 and 1539, and of those whose gender can be determined, women outnumber men by better than two to one.[57] Clearly, women chose certain forms of life in disproportionate numbers. Why they did so and what those choices signified in the religious culture of late medieval Europe remain to be clarified.

GUIDANCE TOWARD answers to these questions might be found in Italian scholarship on women and religion, whose spectacular growth has paralleled that of research in English. In 1979, Italy hosted a number of major conferences devoted to female religiosity. In Assisi, the International Society of Franciscan Studies sponsored a conference on the women's religious movement and the Franciscans in the thirteenth century; at Todi, the Center for the Study of Medieval Spirituality sponsored one on fourteenth-century female mysticism; a smaller conference organized by the Historical Association of the Val d'Elsa included an early paper on holy women by Anna Benvenuti Papi, who has since emerged as one of the leading experts in this field.[58] Other conferences soon followed: on St. Catherine of Siena in

1980, on Clare of Montefalco in 1981 and again in 1985, on Angela of Foligno in 1985 as well and in 1991, on Filippa Mareri in 1986, and on the entire female religious movement in Umbria in 1982.[59] The Italian propensity for centennial celebrations means that in any given year we are likely to be treated to conferences to honor the anniversary of some saint's birth or conversion or death—or even, as in the case of Colomba of Rieti, the five hundredth anniversary of her arrival in Perugia.[60] This flood shows no sign of abating: by the time the publications celebrating the eighth centennial of the birth of St. Clare of Assisi have begun to subside, it will be time to brace for those in honor of the seventh centennial of the death of Margaret of Cortona. Nor is this scholarly production limited to conference papers. Scores, even hundreds, of articles have appeared: studies of individual holy women, such as Umiliana dei Cerchi or Beatrice d'Este, and of whole shoals of them, like Benvenuti Papi's survey of fourteenth-century anchoresses and Gabriella Zarri's wide-ranging analysis of the living saints of the early Cinquecento; studies of cloistered nuns, of penitents and tertiaries, and of still more informal groupings of pious women; studies of the entanglement of religious teachings and devotional aspirations in the social, political, and economic arenas of female activity.[61] Studies of female religious life make up a large part of what Robert Brentano has called "the beautifully intricate, brilliantly exact, and profoundly thoughtful work of the young ecclesiastical historians for which Italy should now be famous."[62] Yet this tremendous volume of superb scholarship remains largely unknown outside of Italy.

It remains unknown in part because relatively few scholars read Italian.[63] Those who do have tended to concern themselves with social and political history rather than religious topics.[64] And even those specialists who strive to keep themselves informed of current Italian ecclesiastical historiography are likely to be frustrated by the peculiarities of Italian academic publishing. Since Italy has a limited market for scholarly books, Italian historians tend to favor the essay or article. Some of the finest scholarship thus receives very limited diffusion, in the published proceedings of one of Italy's frequent conferences, in catalogs of exhibits such as those commemorating St. Francis of Assisi or Umbrian holy women, in the Festschriften (such as *Viridarium Floridum*) that Italian publishers are still admirably willing to undertake, in specialized series such as "Fonti e ricerche di storia ecclesiastica padovana," and in periodicals such as *Le Venezie francescane*, *Picenum Seraphicum* or the *Quaderni catanesi di studi classici e medievali*, as well as the dozens of better-known journals published by local historical societies and religious orders—and purchased by only a few of the most important university libraries.[65]

This scholarship deserves to be better known in this country not simply because of its precision and sophistication, but because its particular strengths nicely complement American research. Italian ecclesiastical historians, like Italian medievalists in general, are careful to define the institutional structures that provide the essential framework for religious life. Indeed, entire conferences are dedicated to the investigation of ecclesiastical institutions, issuing in volumes heavy with information on the organization, development, and functioning of parishes and dioceses.[66] American scholarship over the last several decades has tended to place much less weight on institutional history. In the work of Caroline Bynum, for instance, the careful distinctions of institutional identity so prominent in her early *Docere Verbo et Exemplo* have been progressively subsumed within the broader categories of gender.[67] Most disturbing, an exclusive focus on gender theory has led, in some extreme cases, to a rejection not simply of other categories of analysis but of historical method itself, replacing the careful sifting of evidence with unsubstantiated assertions, invocations of authority, and appeals to the orthodoxies of postcolonial theory.[68]

Not surprisingly, Italian scholars are also alert to the play of power within institutions, to the contention and struggles for hegemony that often see institutional structures serving unexpected ends. They see these struggles as engaging all areas of human activity—political, economic, and cultural as well as more specifically religious—and so treat religion as fully embedded in society. To be sure, Italy has a thriving community of ecclesiastical historians who write as committed members of one or another branch of the Catholic Church; but there is also a general recognition on the part of secular historians that religion and the church are too important, too central to Italian history, to be uprooted from the social and cultural soil in which they grew and which they fed, and so leading political, economic, social, and intellectual historians—Cinzio Violante, Giovanni Tabacco, Giovanni Miccoli, Ovidio Capitani, and Giorgio Cracco come immediately to mind—have also published major contributions to ecclesiastical history. In order to disclose the interplay of religion, politics, economics, and social order in its full complexity and delineate it with precision, they generally prefer to work within carefully circumscribed geographical limits. They found their local studies on a thorough and intimate familiarity with rich local manuscript collections. And they carefully locate their studies within the rural penumbra of each town, the broader currents of historical development, and the cosmopolitan world of modern scholarship.

All of these strengths are well illustrated by the essays selected for this collection. These essays are spread over northern and central Italy, from Padua and Venice through Tuscany and Umbria to Rome.[69] They cover the period from the beginning of the thirteenth century to the middle of the sixteenth. This period (which corresponds to what Weinstein and Bell have called the era of the northern Italian urban saint) is defined by two attempts to assert stringent hierarchical control over devotional life: the apparent closure attempted by the Fourth Lateran Council (1215), which forbade the founding of new religious orders and decreed that all existing communities must accept one of the approved rules, and the firmer closure enacted by the Council of Trent (1545–63).[70] The contributors trace the evolution of communities of pious women as these groups tried to accommodate their devotional motives and goals to the strictures of the ecclesiastical hierarchy. They explore the relations between exemplary or exceptional holy women, the devout followers that clustered around them, and society at large. They examine the communication of behavioral models in hagiography, preaching, and art. They deal principally with the mendicant orders, rather than the monastic orders or the secular clergy, since it was the mendicants who assumed primary responsibility for the spiritual direction of women and provided the greatest opportunities for the religious activity of women.

This set of essays also helps to define the salient features of a particular current within Italian historical scholarship. The authors of these essays do not form a school in any concrete sense: they studied at different places and under different masters; they teach and conduct research in different settings, and not always at universities. Their work is, however, interwoven by frequent encounters and constant cross-references, for they share similar concerns and approaches. The hallmark of their work is a rigorous empiricism, a patient, exacting accumulation of precise detail. From these hard-edged bits of information, meticulously arranged, an image gradually emerges, an image with acknowledged gaps and blank spaces, but utterly convincing in its overall solidity: a mosaic rather than a sketch. They eschew the currently fashionable genre of microhistory, with its reliance on judicial records and almost voyeuristic fascination with the odd detritus they contain, its relentless search for meaning in tiny clues, and its readiness to extrapolate an entire ocean from a drop of polluted water. At its best, microhistory combines an enthralling reconstruction of quirky individuals and their vanished environments with a sophisticated reflection on the process by which the historian effects that reconstruction.[71] But even at its best, microhistory is necessarily suggestive rather than conclusive, and these careful empiricists refuse to indulge in so much speculation and supposition. For similar reasons, they maintain a certain distance from the serial methods and structural analyses of the so-called Annales school. They are, of course, alert to its achievements, and especially to the work of Jacques Le Goff, André Vauchez, and Christiane Klapisch-Zuber; some, like Anna Benvenuti Papi, have even studied in Paris. But they remain (on the whole) profoundly suspicious of the scale on which the Annales school prefers to operate: large structures, grand comparisons, and long, slow rhythms. For a Rigon or a Sensi, or even for a Zarri, too much precision must be sacrificed, too many inconvenient burrs must be planed smooth, too much empirical truth must be falsified in the pursuit of such global generalizations. Their conviction, rather, is that the broadest questions demand the most exact answers, and that the only way to arrive at those answers is through a scrupulously accurate and thorough perusal of the available documentary sources.

Concern with the primary sources is evident not only in the rich footnotes to these essays, but in the readiness of Italian scholars to dedicate their energies to the demanding task of editing and publishing texts and documents.[72] Thanks to their efforts over the past decade, we now have at our disposal modern critical editions of the *vitae* of Maria of Venice, Elena of Udine, and Angela of Foligno, and of the canonization proceedings for Clare of Montefalco.[73] We can consult the inventories and descriptions of local archives, many of which contain substantial documentation of female religious life, in the series "Archivi dell'Umbria: Inventari e ricerche," published by the Regione dell'Umbria.[74] We can follow the community life and daily activity of religious communities like the convents of Corpus Christi in Venice, Santa Lucia in Foligno, and Monteluce in Perugia, thanks to the publication of their convent chronicles.[75] We can read the "Monastic Hell" of Arcangela Tarabotti, the anguished complaint of a seventeenth-century Venetian woman who was committed to a nunnery against her will, and find there a penetrating critique and ferocious denunciation of the political, ecclesiastical, and familial structures of the patriarchal culture that imposed such a fate on her.[76] The Italians are not alone in their editorial labors: Anne Jacobson Schutte has edited the autobiography of the "failed saint" Cecilia Ferrazzi, and Jacques Dalarun the register of miracles performed by Michelina of Pesaro—though it is worth noting that both of these works were published in Italy.[77] But they have certainly placed all students of female religious life—indeed, all medieval and Renaissance historians—in their debt by providing documentary underpinning for studies ranging from Katherine Gill's on vernacular religious literature to Katharine Park's on autopsy and dissection.[78]

It is our heartfelt hope that this volume will encourage still closer cooperation between American and Italian scholars as they pursue their investigations of women and religion in medieval and early modern Europe. As the many cross-references in their footnotes demonstrate, the contributors to this collection are engaged in a lively and continuing discussion with one another and with the many other Italian scholars whose work could not be included here; we hope that the appearance of this volume will involve them more fully in the similar debates being conducted in English. There are encouraging signs that this has already begun to take place: when the Italian edition of this collection went to press back in 1990, none of our authors had appeared in English; in the intervening years, the first translations of works by Chiara Frugoni and Gabriella Zarri have been published, and Caroline Bynum (whose work has long been read and appreciated by Italian scholars) has made her first appearance in Italian translation.[79] Still, despite the impressive achievements of recent years, it is abundantly clear that many important aspects of the religious experience of medieval women have hardly been touched. In his afterword, Roberto Rusconi identifies some of these lacunae and calls attention to some particularly promising areas for future exploration: the education and cultural formation of women; the circulation of devotional texts for women; the participation of women in confraternities; the role of women as commissioners of works of religious art, and their depiction in those works. Given the complexity of these topics, the richness of Italy's archives and libraries, and the growing sophistication with which these documents are sifted and analyzed, we can surely look forward to many further discoveries and fresh debates in the years to come. *Buon lavoro.*

NOTES

This survey does not pretend to be exhaustive. My aim is to call attention to some of the more important contributions by Italian scholars, define the characteristic traits of those works, and compare their particular strengths with those of a very different American tradition. In preparing these remarks I have benefited from the comments of Diane Owen Hughes, Julius Kirshner, John Marino, Megan Matchinske, Darleen Pryds, Roberto Rusconi, and Margery Schneider, to all of whom I extend heartfelt thanks.

    1. Ian Maclean, *The Renaissance Notion of Woman: A Study in the Fortunes of Scholasticism and Medical Science in European Intellectual Life* (Cambridge, 1980), provides a good introduction to legal, medical, and theological notions of woman. The intersection between law and society is explored in Thomas Kuehn, *Law, Family, and Women: Toward a Legal Anthropology of Renaissance Italy* (Chicago, 1991).

    2. For a helpful overview with a rather different emphasis, see Duane J. Osheim, "The Place of Women in the Late Medieval Italian Church," in *That Gentle Strength: Historical Perspectives on Women in Christianity,* ed. Lynda L. Coon, Katherine J. Haldane, and Elisabeth W. Sommer (Charlottesville, 1990), pp. 79–96. For a survey of the religious culture of late medieval Italy, see Daniel E. Bornstein, *The Bianchi of 1399: Popular Devotion in Late Medieval Italy* (Ithaca, 1993), pp. 8–42.

3. David Herlihy and Christiane Klapisch-Zuber, *Tuscans and Their Families: A Study of the Florentine Catasto of 1427* (New Haven, 1985), p. 94; Maria Serena Mazzi and Sergio Raveggi, *Gli uomini e le cose nelle campagne fiorentine del Quattrocento* (Florence, 1983), pp. 71–72.

4. Roberto Bizzocchi, *Chiesa e potere nella Toscana del Quattrocento*, Annali dell'Istituto storico italo-germanico, monografia 6 (Bologna, 1987); *Strutture ecclesiastiche in Italia e in Germania prima della Riforma*, ed. Paolo Prodi and Peter Johanek, Annali dell'Istituto storico italo-germanico, quaderno 16 (Bologna, 1984); and *La Chiesa e il potere politico dal Medioevo all'età contemporanea*, ed. Giorgio Chittolini and Giovanni Miccoli, Storia d'Italia, Annali 9 (Turin, 1986), especially the essay by Chittolini, "Stati regionali e istituzioni ecclesiastiche nell'Italia centrosettentrionale del Quattrocento," pp. 149–93.

5. In addition to Roberto Rusconi's contribution to this volume, see his "Predicatori e predicazione," in *Intellettuali e potere*, ed. Corrado Vivanti, Storia d'Italia, Annali 4 (Turin, 1981), pp. 951–1035; "De la prédication à la confession: Transmission et contrôle de modèles de comportement au XIIIe siècle," in *Faire croire: Modalités de la diffusion et de la réception des messages religieux du XIIe au XVe siècle*, ed. André Vauchez, Collection de l'École française de Rome, 51 (Rome, 1981), pp. 67–85; "I francescani e la confessione," in *Francescanesimo e vita religiosa dei laici nel Duecento*, Proceedings of the Eighth International Conference of Franciscan Studies (Assisi, 1981), pp. 251–309; "Dal pulpito alla confessione: Modelli di comportamento religioso in Italia tra 1470 circa e 1520 circa," in Prodi and Johanek, *Strutture ecclesiastiche*, pp. 259–315; "'Ordinate confiteri': La confessione dei peccati nelle 'Summae de casibus' e nei manuali per i confessori, metà XII–inizi XIV secolo," in *L'Aveu: Antiquité et Moyen Age* (Rome, 1986), pp. 297–313; "La predicazione: parole in chiesa, parole in piazza," in *Lo spazio letterario del Medioevo*, part 1: *Il Medioevo latino*, ed. Guglielmo Cavallo, Claudio Leonardi, and Enrico Menestò, vol. 2, *La circolazione del testo* (Rome, 1994), pp. 571–603; and his collection of texts, *Predicazione e vita religiosa nella società italiana da Carlo Magno alla Controriforma* (Turin, 1981). Carlo Delcorno, *La predicazione nell'età comunale* (Florence, 1974), offers a more focused selection of texts and a good introduction.

6. Michael Baxandall, *Painting and Experience in Fifteenth-Century Italy* (Oxford, 1972), pp. 40–56; Peter Burke, *The Italian Renaissance: Culture and Society in Italy* (Princeton, 1986), p. 89.

7. When religious life and institutions are taken into consideration, the commonplace distinction between public and private spheres loses much of its sense. See in this connection Diane Owen Hughes, "Invisible Madonnas? The Italian Historiographical Tradition and the Women of Medieval Italy," in *Women in Medieval History and Historiography*, ed. Susan Mosher Stuard (Philadelphia, 1987).

8. "Vita beatae Margaritae virginis de Civitate Castelli," *Analecta Bollandiana* 19 (1900): 21–36; Marie-Hyacinthe Laurent, "La plus ancienne légende de la b. Marguerite de Città di Castello," *Archivum Fratrum Praedicatorum* 10 (1940): 109–31. On Margaret, see Enrico Menestò, "La 'legenda' di Margherita da Città di

Castello," in *Il movimento religioso femminile in Umbria nei secoli XIII–XIV,* ed. Roberto Rusconi (Florence, 1984), pp. 219–37.

9. Giovanna Casagrande, "Forme di vita religiosa femminile nell'area di Città di Castello nel secolo XIII," in Rusconi, *Il movimento religioso femminile in Umbria,* pp. 125–57. On the bishops' registers, see *Chiese e conventi degli ordini mendicanti in Umbria nei secoli XIII–XIV: Gli archivi ecclesiastici di Città di Castello,* ed. Giovanna Casagrande (Perugia, 1989).

10. It is not clear whether this objection was an honest one or merely an excuse for rejecting a prospective member that the community didn't want: later the same year the convent was excommunicated by the bishop for admitting a woman without his permission.

11. Duane J. Osheim, "Conversion, *Conversi,* and the Christian Life in Late Medieval Tuscany," *Speculum* 58 (1983): 368–90; Daniela Rando, "Laicus religiosus: Tra strutture civili ed ecclesiastiche, l'Ospedale di Ogni Santi in Treviso (sec. XIII)," *Studi medievali,* ser. 3, 24 (1983): 617–56; Giuseppina De Sandre Gasparini, "L'assistenza ai lebbrosi nel movimento religioso dei primi decenni del Duecento veronese: Uomini e fatti," in *Viridarium Floridum: Studi di storia veneta offerti dagli allievi a Paolo Sambin,* ed. Maria Chiara Billanovich, Giorgio Cracco, and Antonio Rigon (Padua, 1984), pp. 25–59; *Le carte dei lebbrosi di Verona tra XII e XIII secolo,* ed. Annamaria Rossi Saccomani (Padua, 1989).

12. The striking phrase is "quod nulli regule sunt astricte" (Casagrande, "Forme di vita religiosa femminile," p. 148).

13. For a survey of the well-studied region of Umbria, see "Pietà, povertà, e potere: Donne e religione nell'Umbria tardomedievale," in Enrico Menestò and Roberto Rusconi, *Umbria: La strada delle sante medievali* (Turin, 1991), pp. 5–33, with a useful bibliographical essay on pp. 198–209.

14. Rosalind B. Brooke and Christopher N. L. Brooke, "St. Clare," in *Medieval Women,* ed. Derek Baker (Oxford, 1978), pp. 275–87; *Chiara d'Assisi,* Proceedings of the Twentieth International Conference of Franciscan Studies (Spoleto, 1993); Marco Bartoli, "Chiara testimone di Francesco," *Quaderni catanesi di studi classici e medievali* 1 (1979): 467–98; Bartoli, *Chiara d'Assisi* (Rome, 1989) (translated as *Clare of Assisi* [Quincy, Ill., 1993]); and the essay in this volume by Clara Gennaro.

15. Anna Benvenuti Papi, "Umiliana dei Cerchi: Nascita di un culto nella Firenze del Duecento," *Studi francescani* 77 (1980): 87–117, and "Velut in sepulcro: Cellane e recluse nella tradizione agiografica italiana," in *Culto dei santi, istituzioni, e classi sociali in età preindustriale,* ed. Sofia Boesch Gajano and Lucia Sebastiani (L'Aquila, 1984), pp. 367–455; these essays have been reprinted in Anna Benvenuti Papi, *"In castro poenitentiae": Santità e società femminile nell'Italia medievale* (Rome, 1990), pp. 59–98 and 305–402.

16. Gabriella Zarri, "Monasteri femminili e città, secoli XV–XVIII," in Chittolini and Miccoli, *La Chiesa e il potere politico,* pp. 359–429; Zarri, "Aspetti dello sviluppo degli ordini religiosi in Italia tra Quattro e Cinquecento: Studi e problemi," in Prodi and Johanek, *Strutture ecclesiastiche,* pp. 207–57; Richard C. Trexler, "Le

célibat à la fin du Moyen Age: Les religieuses de Florence," *Annales: Economies, sociétés, civilisations* 27 (1972): 1329–50.

17. The Franciscan Third Order has been the subject of several conferences; see, for instance, *I frati penitenti di San Francesco nella società del Due e Trecento,* ed. Mariano d'Alatri, Proceedings of the Second Conference of Franciscan Studies, Rome, 12–14 October 1976, (Rome, 1977); *Il movimento francescano della penitenza nella società medioevale,* ed. Mariano d'Alatri, Proceedings of the Third Conference of Franciscan Studies, Padua, 25–27 September 1979 (Rome, 1980); *La beata Angelina da Montegiove e il movimento del Terz'Ordine francescano femminile,* ed. Raffaele Pazzelli and Mario Sensi (Rome, 1984); and *Prime manifestazioni di vita comunitaria maschile e femminile nel movimento francescano della penitenza, 1215–1447,* Proceedings of the Conference of Franciscan Studies, Assisi, 30 June–2 July 1981, ed. Raffaele Pazzelli and Lino Temperini (Rome, 1982). See also Robert M. Stewart, *"De illis qui faciunt penitentiam": The Rule of the Secular Franciscan Order: Origins, Development, Interpretation* (Rome, 1991), and Gilles Gérard Meersseman, *Dossier de l'ordre de la pénitence au XIIIe siècle,* 2d ed. (Fribourg, 1982). On the Dominican Third Order, see Fernanda Sorelli, "Per la storia religiosa di Venezia nella prima metà del Quattrocento: Inizi e sviluppi del Terz'Ordine domenicano," in Billanovich, Cracco, and Rigon, *Viridarium Floridum,* pp. 89–114.

18. In addition to the essay by Anna Esposito in this volume, see Arnold Esch, "Tre sante e il loro ambiente sociale a Roma: S. Francesca Romana, S. Brigida di Svezia, e S. Caterina da Siena," in *Atti del Simposio internazionale cateriniano-bernardiniano, Siena, 17–20 aprile 1980,* ed. Domenico Maffei and Paolo Nardi (Siena, 1982), pp. 89–120; and Guy Boanas and Lyndal Roper, "Feminine Piety in Fifteenth-Century Rome: Santa Francesca Romana," in *Disciplines of Faith: Studies in Religion, Politics, and Patriarchy,* ed. Jim Obelkevich, Lyndal Roper, and Raphael Samuel (London, 1987).

19. André Vauchez, *The Laity in the Middle Ages: Religious Beliefs and Devotional Practices,* trans. Margery J. Schneider (Notre Dame, 1993), pp. 185–203; Lucetta Scaraffia, *La santa degli impossibili: Vicende e significato della devozione a Santa Rita* (Turin, 1990).

20. *Il Libro della beata Angela da Foligno,* ed. Ludger Thier and Abele Calufetti (Grottaferrata, 1985), p. 138; Angela of Foligno, *Complete Works,* trans. Paul Lachance (New York, 1993), p. 126. See Anna Benvenuti Papi, "Il modello familiare nell'agiografia fiorentina tra Duecento e Quattrocento: Sviluppo di una negazione (da Umiliana dei Cerchi a Villana delle Botti)," *Nuova DWF* 16 (1981): 80–107; reprinted in Benvenuti Papi, *"In castro poenitentiae,"* pp. 171–203.

21. The importance of this custom is stressed by Anthony Molho, *"Tamquam vere mortua:* Le professioni religiose femminili nella Firenze del tardo medioevo," *Società e storia* 12 (1989): 16–17.

22. Katherine Gill, "Women and the Production of Religious Literature in the Vernacular, 1300–1500," in *Creative Women in Medieval and Early Modern Italy: A Religious and Artistic Renaissance,* ed. E. Ann Matter and John Coakley (Phila-

delphia, 1994), pp. 64–104; Gabriella Zarri, "La vita religiosa femminile tra devozione e chiostro," in her *Le sante vive: Profezie di corte e devozione femminile tra
'400 e '500* (Turin, 1990), pp. 21–50.

23. Giovanni Dominici, *Trattato delle dieci questioni e lettere a madonna
Bartolomea,* ed. Arrigo Levasti (Florence, 1957), and *Regola del governo di cura familiare,* ed. Donato Salvi (Florence, 1860). Some of Giovanni's pedagogical suggestions are discussed by Christiane Klapisch-Zuber, "Holy Dolls: Play and Piety in
Florence in the Quattrocento," in *Women, Family, and Ritual in Renaissance Italy,*
trans. Lydia G. Cochrane (Chicago, 1985), pp. 310–29. Cavalca, Dominici, and
Savonarola all happen to have been Dominicans, and offering spiritual guidance to
women does seem to have been a specialty of that order, but the Dominicans certainly had no monopoly on this area of activity: in the first half of the fourteenth
century, the Augustinian Simone Fidati of Cascia was equally busy writing, translating, and preaching for the women of Florence. See Anna Benvenuti Papi, "Devozioni
private e guide di coscienze femminili nella Firenze del Due-Trecento," *Richerche
storiche* 16 (1987): 565–606; reprinted in Benvenuti Papi, *"In castro poenitentiae,"*
pp. 205–46.

24. This line of interpretation runs from the fourteenth century, when Franco
Sacchetti complained that "the man who has a misshapen or mutilated daughter
gives her to Christ," to the twentieth, when a leading social historian concluded that
"girls who lacked a sufficiently large dowry or physical beauty, and who had slight
hope of finding a husband, were placed in the convents with equal haste" (David
Herlihy, "Some Psychological and Social Roots of Violence in the Tuscan Cities," in
Violence and Civil Disorder in Italian Cities, 1200–1500, ed. Lauro Martines
[Berkeley, 1972], p. 146; Sacchetti is quoted by Iris Origo, *The World of San Bernardino* [New York, 1962], p. 270). It has been questioned by Julius Kirshner and
Anthony Molho, "The Dowry Fund and the Marriage Market in Early Quattrocento
Florence," *Journal of Modern History* 50 (1978): 403–38. Molho, *"Tamquam vere
mortua,"* emphasizes the multiplicity of motives that could lead to religious profession, as well as the difficulty of discerning which one or ones may have been predominant in any one case.

25. Daniel Bornstein, "The Shrine of Santa Maria a Cigoli: Female Visionaries
and Clerical Promoters," *Mélanges de l'École française de Rome, Moyen Age–temps
modernes* 98 (1986): 219–28.

26. Casagrande, "Forme di vita religiosa femminile," pp. 137 and 149–50.

27. André Vauchez, "Les pouvoirs informels dans l'église aux derniers siècles
du Moyen Age: Visionnaires, prophètes, et mystiques," *Mélanges de l'École française de Rome, Moyen Age–temps modernes* 96 (1984): 281–293; translated in
Vauchez, *The Laity in the Middle Ages,* pp. 219–29. See also David Herlihy, "Did
Women Have a Renaissance? A Reconsideration," *Medievalia et Humanistica,* n.s.
13 (1985): 1–22.

28. On relations between saints and their communities, see Menestò and
Rusconi, *Umbria: La strada delle sante medievali;* Chiara Frugoni, "The City and the
'New' Saints," in *City-States in Classical Antiquity and Medieval Italy,* ed. Anthony

Molho, Kurt Raaflaub, and Julia Emlen (Ann Arbor, 1991), pp. 71–88; Jacques Dalarun, *La sainte et la cité: Micheline de Pesaro (†1356), tertiaire franciscaine*, Collection de l'École française da Rome, 164 (Rome, 1992); and Franco Cardini, "Agiografia e politica: Margherita da Cortona e le vicende di una città inquieta," *Studi francescani* 76 (1979): 127–36. On female prophets, see Gabriella Zarri, "Pietà e profezia alle corti padane: Le pie consigliere dei principi," in *Il Rinascimento nelle corti padane: Società e cultura* (Bari, 1977), pp. 201–37; and Adriana Valerio, *Domenica da Paradiso: Profezia e politica in una mistica del Rinascimento* (Spoleto, 1992).

29. In addition to the essays of Roberto Rusconi cited above in note 5, see Maria Giuseppina Muzzarelli, "'Contra mundanas vanitates et pompas': Aspetti della lotta contro i lussi nell'Italia del XV secolo," *Rivista di storia della Chiesa in Italia* 40 (1986): 371–90.

30. For good introductions to hagiographic scholarship, see *Saints and Their Cults: Studies in Religious Sociology, Folklore, and History*, ed. Stephen Wilson (Cambridge, 1983), and *Agiografia altomedioevale*, ed. Sofia Boesch Gajano (Bologna, 1976). On the iconography of holy women, see *Sante e beate umbre tra il XIII e il XIV secolo: Chiara d'Assisi, Agnese d'Assisi, Margherita da Cortona, Angela da Foligno, Chiara da Montefalco, Margherita da Città di Castello. Mostra iconografica* (Foligno, 1986). A comprehensive survey of the iconography of St. Catherine is gradually becoming available: Lidia Bianchi and Diega Giunta, *Iconografia di S. Caterina da Siena*, vol. 1, *L'immagine* (Rome, 1988), with two more volumes promised. On the interplay between images and visions of holy women, see various essays by Chiara Frugoni: "Su un 'immaginario' possibile di Margherita da Città di Castello," in Rusconi, *Il movimento religioso femminile in Umbria*, pp. 203–16; "Il linguaggio dell'iconografia e delle visioni," in Gajano and Sebastiani, *Culto dei santi, istituzioni, e classi sociali*, pp. 527–36; and her contribution to this volume. For the employment of images in religious instruction, see Jeffrey F. Hamburger, "The Use of Images in the Pastoral Care of Nuns: The Case of Heinrich Suso and the Dominicans," *Art Bulletin* 71 (1989): 20–46; "The Visual and the Visionary: The Image in Late Medieval Monastic Devotions," *Viator* 20 (1989): 161–82; and *The Rothschild Canticles: Art and Mysticism in Flanders and the Rhineland circa 1300* (New Haven, 1991).

31. Gill, "Women and the Production of Religious Literature," explores the dynamics by which a female audience shaped texts by male authors.

32. Many of the principal sources for St. Catherine of Siena are now available in English: Raymond of Capua, *The Life of Catherine of Siena*, trans. Conleth Kearns (Dublin, 1980); *I, Catherine: Selected Writings of St. Catherine of Siena*, trans. Kenelm Foster and Mary John Ronayne (London, 1980); Catherine of Siena, *The Dialogue*, trans. Suzanne Noffke (New York, 1980); and *The Prayers of Catherine of Siena*, trans. Suzanne Noffke (New York, 1983).

33. John Coakley, "Friars as Confidants of Holy Women in Medieval Dominican Hagiography," in *Images of Sainthood in Medieval Europe*, ed. Renate Blumenfeld-Kosinski and Timea Szell (Ithaca, 1991), pp. 222–46.

34. See Catherine's last letter to Raymond (*I, Catherine,* p. 270).

35. The central figure in this production was Tommaso d'Antonio Caffarini of Siena, on whom see Fernanda Sorelli, "La production hagiographique du dominicain Tommaso Caffarini: Exemples de sainteté, sens, et visées d'une propagande," in Vauchez, *Faire croire,* pp. 189–200; and Oriana Visani, "Nota su Tommaso d'Antonio Nacci Caffarini," *Rivista di storia e letteratura religiosa* 9 (1973): 277–97.

36. See the essays in this volume by Sorelli and Zarri. One could add to the list of "new Catherines" the seventeenth-century nun Benedetta Carlini, whose self-fashioning on the pattern of Catherine is hardly explored in Judith C. Brown, *Immodest Acts: The Life of a Lesbian Nun in Renaissance Italy* (New York and Oxford, 1986).

37. Raymond of Capua, *Life of Catherine,* pp. 341–42; *Il processo castellano,* ed. Marie-Hyacinthe Laurent, Fontes vitae S. Catharinae Senensis historici, 9 (Milan, 1942), pp. 446–47.

38. Karen Scott, "Catherine of Siena, *Apostola,*" *Church History* 61 (1992): 34–46; "'Io Catarina': Ecclesiastical Politics and Oral Culture in the Letters of Catherine of Siena," in *Dear Sister: Medieval Women and the Epistolary Genre,* ed. Karen Cherewatuk and Ulrike Wiethaus (Philadelphia, 1993), pp. 87–121; "Urban Spaces, Women's Networks, and the Lay Apostolate in the Siena of Catherine Benincasa," in Matter and Coakley, *Creative Women in Medieval and Early Modern Italy,* pp. 105–19.

39. André Vauchez, "Mystical Sanctity at the Time of the Avignon Papacy and the Great Schism," in *The Laity in the Middle Ages,* pp. 231–36; Roberto Rusconi, *L'attesa della fine: Crisi della società, profezia, ed apocalisse in Italia al tempo del Grande Scisma d'Occidente, 1378–1417* (Rome, 1979); *L'attesa dell'età nuova nella spiritualità della fine del Medioevo,* Convegni del Centro di studi sulla spiritualità medievale, 3 (Todi, 1962). On the inverse relationship between political and cultural order and opportunities for women, see Joan Kelly Gadol, "Did Women Have a Renaissance?" in *Becoming Visible: Women in European History,* ed. Renate Bridenthal and Claudia Koonz (Boston, 1977), pp. 137–64; reprinted in Joan Kelly Gadol, *Women, History, and Theory* (Chicago, 1984), pp. 19–50.

40. *Sante e beate umbre tra il XIII e il XIV secolo,* pp. 108–9, 124–25. The painting of the five *mantellate* has been discussed recently by Creighton E. Gilbert, "Tuscan Observants and Painters in Venice, ca. 1400," in *Interpretazioni veneziane: Studi di storia d'arte in onore di Michelangelo Muraro,* ed. David Rosand (Venice, 1984), pp. 109–20, and by Gaudenz Freuler, "Andrea di Bartolo, Fra Tommaso d'Antonio Caffarini, and Sienese Dominicans in Venice," *Art Bulletin* 69 (1987): 570–86. Both Gilbert and Freuler refer to this small panel as an altarpiece, but its size and iconography argue against such a use. William Hood has suggested to me that it resembles the portraits of illustrious members of their order that Dominicans placed in their choirs as a stimulus to greater virtue. The panel painting of Margaret of Cortona, originally placed in the church of Santa Margherita, is now in the Museo Diocesano of Cortona.

41. In addition to the essay by Gabriella Zarri in this collection, see Adriano

Prosperi, "Dalle 'divine madri' ai 'padri spirituali,'" in *Women and Men in Spiritual Culture, XIV–XVII Centuries: A Meeting of South and North,* ed. Elisja Schulte Van Kessel (The Hague, 1986), pp. 71–90. The attention given to female visionaries was part of a general fascination with prophets, monsters, apparitions, and signs, on which see Ottavia Niccoli, *Prophecy and People in Renaissance Italy,* trans. Lydia G. Cochrane (Princeton, 1990).

42. As recently as 1980, Caroline Walker Bynum could write that the spirituality of medieval women had been "surprisingly neglected" (*Jesus as Mother: Studies in the Spirituality of the High Middle Ages* [Berkeley and Los Angeles, 1982], p. 4). Though Bynum's book was not published until 1982, her preface is dated 1980.

43. Herbert Grundmann, *Religiöse Bewegungen im Mittelalter: Untersuchungen über die geschichtlichen Zusammenhänge zwischen der Ketzerei, den Bettelorden, und der religiösen Frauenbewegung im 12. und 13. Jahrhundert und über die geschichtlichen Grundlagen der Deutschen Mystik* (Berlin, 1935; revised edition, Hildesheim, 1961). Whereas an Italian translation of the second edition appeared over twenty years ago (*Movimenti religiosi nel Medioevo* [Bologna, 1974]), an English translation is only now being prepared for publication. The laudatory judgment is that of Caroline Bynum, *Jesus as Mother,* p. 4.

44. Ernest W. McDonnell, *The Beguines and Beghards in Medieval Culture, with Special Emphasis on the Belgian Scene* (New Brunswick, 1954); Dayton Phillips, *Beguines in Medieval Strasburg: A Study of the Social Aspect of Beguine Life* (Stanford, 1941); Carol Neel, "The Origins of the Beguines," *Signs* 14 (1989): 321–41, reprinted in *Sisters and Workers in the Middle Ages,* ed. Judith M. Bennett et al. (Chicago, 1989), pp. 240–60; Brenda M. Bolton, "Mulieres Sanctae," in *Sanctity and Secularity: The Church and the World,* ed. Derek Baker, Studies in Church History, 10 (London, 1973), pp. 77–95; Bolton, "Vitae Matrum: A Further Aspect of the Frauenfrage," in Baker, *Medieval Women,* pp. 253–73; Jean-Claude Schmitt, *Mort d'une hérésie: L'église et les clercs face aux béguires et aux bégards du Rhin supérieur du XIVe au XVe siècle* (Paris: 1978).

45. *Prediche alle donne del secolo XIII,* ed. Carla Casagrande (Milan, 1978); Elizabeth Petroff, *Consolation of the Blessed* (New York, 1979); see also *Idee sulla donna nel Medioevo: Fonti e aspetti giuridici, antropologici, religiosi, sociali, e letterari della condizione femminile,* ed. Maria Consiglia De Matteis (Bologna, 1981). Petroff has since edited another collection on a particular facet of female religious experience: *Medieval Women's Visionary Literature* (New York and Oxford, 1986).

46. André Vauchez, *La sainteté en Occident aux derniers siècles du Moyen Age d'après les procès de canonisation et les documents hagiographiques,* Bibliothèque des Écoles françaises d'Athènes et de Rome, 241 (Rome, 1981).

47. Donald Weinstein and Rudolph M. Bell, *Saints and Society: The Two Worlds of Western Christendom, 1000–1700* (Chicago, 1982), p. 220. See also Pierre Delooz, *Sociologie et canonisations* (Liège, 1969); Anna Benvenuti Papi, "La santità al femminile: Funzioni e rappresentazioni tra Medioevo ed età moderna," in *Les fonctions des saints dans le monde occidental, IIIe–XIIIe siècle,* Collection de l'École française de Rome, 149 (Rome, 1991), pp. 467–88; Michael Goodich, "The

Contours of Female Piety in Later Medieval Hagiography," *Church History* 50 (1981): 20–32; and Goodich, *Vita Perfecta: The Ideal of Sainthood in the Thirteenth Century* (Stuttgart, 1982), pp. 173–85.

48. Weinstein and Bell, *Saints and Society,* p. 237.

49. Rudolph M. Bell, *Holy Anorexia* (Chicago, 1985); Caroline Walker Bynum, *Holy Feast and Holy Fast: The Religious Significance of Food to Medieval Women* (Berkeley and Los Angeles, 1987).

50. André Vauchez, "Eucharistic Devotion and Mystical Union in Late-Medieval Female Mystics," in *The Laity in the Middle Ages,* pp. 237–42; Caroline Walker Bynum, "Women Mystics and Eucharistic Devotion in the Thirteenth Century," *Women's Studies* 11 (1984): 179–214, reprinted in her *Fragmentation and Redemption: Essays on Gender and the Human Body in Medieval Religion* (New York, 1991). See in general Miri Rubin, *Corpus Christi: The Eucharist in Late Medieval Culture* (Cambridge, 1991).

51. On St. Francis and female piety, see now Jacques Dalarun, *Francesco, un passaggio: Donna e donne negli scritti e nelle leggende di Francesco di Assisi* (Rome, 1993).

52. The results could be so moving that they are still being proposed as models for prayer: *Revelations of St. Bridget on the Life and Passion of Our Lord and the Life of His Blessed Mother* (Rockford, Illinois, 1984). In addition to Chiara Frugoni's essay in this volume, see Baxandall, *Painting and Experience,* pp. 40–49, for some acute observations on the connections between meditative prayer, affective piety, and pictorial art.

53. Richard Kieckhefer, *Unquiet Souls: Fourteenth-Century Saints and Their Religious Milieu* (Chicago, 1984), p. 17. See also Katherine Gill's claim that "if clerics offered women a theological education, women offered men a sentimental education in the widest sense" (Gill, "Women and the Production of Religious Literature," p. 85).

54. Clarissa W. Atkinson, *Mystic and Pilgrim: The Book and the World of Margery Kempe* (Ithaca, 1983), pp. 158–59.

55. Ibid., p. 159.

56. Brooke and Brooke, "St. Clare," p. 276. Important recent studies of female monasticism in northern Europe include Sharon K. Elkins, *Holy Women of Twelfth-Century England* (Chapel Hill, 1988), and Penelope D. Johnson, *Equal in Monastic Profession: Religious Women in Medieval France* (Chicago, 1991).

57. Ann K. Warren, *Anchorites and Their Patrons in Medieval England* (Berkeley and Los Angeles, 1985), pp. 18–20. Warren has been criticized for failing to grapple with the importance of gender for the anchorite vocation: see the review by Penelope D. Johnson in *Speculum* 62 (1987): 746–48.

58. *Movimento religioso femminile e francescanesimo nel secolo XIII,* Proceedings of the Seventh Conference of the International Society of Franciscan Studies, Assisi, 11–13 October 1979 (Assisi, 1980); *Temi e problemi nella mistica femminile trecentesca,* Convegni del Centro di studi sulla spiritualità medievale, 20, Todi, 14–17 October 1979 (Todi, 1983); Anna Benvenuti Papi, "Santità femminile nel terri-

torio fiorentino e lucchese: Considerazioni intorno al caso di Verdiana da Castelfiorentino," in *Religiosità e società in Valdelsa nel basso Medioevo,* Proceedings of the San Vivaldo Conference, 29 September 1979 (Società storica della Valdelsa, 1980), pp. 113–44, reprinted in Benvenuti Papi, *"In castro poenitentiae,"* pp. 263–303; Maffei and Nardi, *Atti del Simposio internazionale cateriniano-bernardiniano; Atti del Congresso internazionale di studi cateriniani, Siena-Rome, 24–29 aprile 1980* (Rome, 1981); *S. Chiara da Montefalco e il suo tempo,* ed. Claudio Leonardi and Enrico Menestò, Proceedings of the Fourth Conference of Ecclesiastical History, Spoleto, 28–30 December 1981 (Florence, 1985); *La spiritualità di S. Chiara da Montefalco,* ed. Silvestro Nessi, Proceedings of the First Research Conference, Montefalco, 8–10 August 1985 (Montefalco, 1986); *Vita e spiritualità della beata Angela da Foligno,* ed. Clément Schmitt, Proceedings of the Conference on the Seven Centenary of the Conversion of the Blessed Angela of Foligno, 1285–1985, Foligno, 11–14 December 1985 (Perugia, 1987); *Angela da Foligno, terziaria francescana,* ed. Enrico Menestò, Proceedings of the Historical Conference on the Seventh Centenary of the Blessed Angela of Foligno's Entrance in the Franciscan Third Order, 1291–1991, Foligno, 17–19 November 1991 (Spoleto, 1992); *Santa Filippa Mareri e il monastero di Borgo S. Pietro nella storia del Cicolano,* Proceedings of the Research Conference, Borgo San Pietro, 24–26 October 1986 (Rieti, 1989).

59. Roberto Rusconi, ed., *Il movimento religioso femminile in Umbria.*

60. *Una santa, una città,* ed. Giovanna Casagrande and Enrico Menestò, Proceedings of the Historical Conference on the Fifth Centenary of Columba of Rieti's Arrival in Perugia, 10–12 November 1989 (Spoleto, 1990).

61. Benvenuti Papi, "Umiliana dei Cerchi"; Antonio Rigon, "La santa nobile: Beatrice d'Este (†1226) e il suo primo biografo," in Billanovich, Cracco, and Rigon, *Viridarium Floridum,* pp. 61–87; Benvenuti Papi, "'Velut in sepulcro'"; and the essay by Gabriella Zarri included in this volume. For a survey of some of these publications, see Giovanna Casagrande, "Sante Umbre: Appunti in margine a recenti pubblicazioni," *Benedictina* 33 (1986): 557–71. See also Giancarlo Andenna, "Il monachesimo cluniacense femminile nella 'Provincia Lumbardie' dei secoli XI–XIII: Origini, evoluzione dei rapporti politici con le strutture organizzative dei territori, e problematiche economiche e sociali," in *Cluny in Lombardia,* Proceedings of the Conference Celebrating the Ninth Centenary of the Foundation of the Priory of Pontida, 22-25 April 1977 (Cesena, 1979), pp. 331–81; Giovanna Casagrande, "Il monastero di Santa Giuliana a Perugia nel secolo XIII," *Benedictina* 27 (1980): 509–32; Gabriella Zarri, "I monasteri femminili benedettini nella diocesi di Bologna, secoli XIII–XVII," *Ravennatensia* 9 (1981): 333–71; P. Renée Baernstein, "In Widow's Habit: Women between Convent and Family in Sixteenth-Century Milan," *Sixteenth-Century Journal* 25 (1994): 787–807; and Mario Sensi, "Incarcerate e penitenti a Foligno nella prima metà del Trecento," in *I frati penitenti di San Francesco,* pp. 291–308. For bibliographical guidance to studies on the penitential movement, see Giovanna Casagrande, "Il movimento penitenziale nei secoli del basso Medioevo: Note su alcuni recenti contributi," *Benedictina* 30 (1983): 217–33.

62. Robert Brentano, "Italian Ecclesiastical History: The Sambin Revolution," *Medievalia et Humanistica,* n.s. 14 (1986): 193.

63. For instance, essays in *Maps of Flesh and Light: The Religious Experience of Medieval Women Mystics,* ed. Ulrike Wiethaus (Syracuse, 1993), discuss Italian holy women like Angela of Foligno and Catherine of Siena without any reference to the Italian literature on them. Some scholars who know how to read Italian do not bother to use that knowledge: the comments on writings by Clare of Assisi and Angela of Foligno by Elizabeth Alvilda Petroff, *Body and Soul: Essays on Medieval Women and Mysticism* (New York and Oxford, 1994), show no awareness of recent critical editions and little of current Italian scholarship. Even as fine a scholar as Caroline Walker Bynum does not read Italian, or assumes that her reader will not read it: her essay "Religious Women in the Later Middle Ages," in *Christian Spirituality,* vol. 2, *High Middle Ages and Reformation,* ed. Jill Raitt with Bernard McGinn and John Meyendorff (New York, 1987), pp. 121–39, directs the reader to works in English, French, and German, but not Italian.

64. This has been particularly true of American Florentinists, though there are signs that the situation is changing: senior scholars such as William Bowsky and Gene Brucker have begun to join Richard Trexler is studying the Florentine church (just when Trexler has turned his attention elsewhere), as has a younger generation of scholars such as Daniel R. Lesnick, George Dameron, and David Peterson. This new ecclesiastical history does not, however, touch on women, while American studies of Florentine social history that do bear on women continue to have little to do with religion.

65. See, for example, *Francesco d'Assisi: Storia e arte* (Milan, 1982); *Francesco d'Assisi: Chiese e conventi* (Milan, 1982); *Francesco d'Assisi: Documenti e archivi, codici e biblioteche, miniature* (Milan, 1982); *Sante e beate umbre;* and *Il francescanesimo in Lombardia* (Milan, 1983).

Major contributions to medieval ecclesiastical history in the series "Fonti e richerche di storia ecclesiastica padovana" include Antonio Rigon, *S. Giacomo di Monselice nel Medio Evo, sec. XII–XV: Ospedale, monastero, collegiata* (Padua, 1972); *Statuti di confraternite religiose di Padova nel Medio Evo,* ed. Giuseppina De Sandre Gasparini (Padua, 1974); Pierantonio Gios, *L'attività pastorale del vescovo Pietro Barozzi a Padova, 1487–1507* (Padua, 1977); Giuseppina De Sandre Gasparini, *Contadini, chiesa, confraternita in un paese veneto di bonifica: Villa del Bosco nel Quattrocento* (Padua, 1979); and Antonio Rigon's essay "I laici nella chiesa padovana del Duecento," an excerpt from which appears in this volume.

See also Ugolino Nicolini, "I Minori Osservanti di Monteripido e lo 'scriptorium' delle Clarisse di Monteluce in Perugia nei secoli XV e XVI," *Picenum Seraphicum* 8 (1971): 100–30; Mario Sensi, "Predicazione itinerante a Foligno nel secolo XV," *Picenum Seraphicum* 10 (1973): 139–95; Roberto Rusconi, "La tradizione manoscritta delle opere degli Spirituali nelle biblioteche dei predicatori e dei conventi dell'Osservanza," *Picenum Seraphicum* 12 (1975): 63–137; Marco Bartoli, "Chiara testimone di Francesco," *Quaderni catanesi di studi classici e medievali* 1 (1979):

467–98. That some of these journals now appear only irregularly or have ceased publication entirely makes them that much harder to obtain.

66. *Pievi e parrocchie in Italia nel basso Medioevo, sec. XIII–XV,* Proceedings of the Sixth Conference on the History of the Church in Italy, Florence, 21–25 September 1981 (Rome, 1984); *Vescovi e diocesi in Italia nel Medioevo (sec. XI–XIII),* Proceedings of the Second Conference on the History of the Church in Italy, Rome, 5–9 September 1961 (Padua, 1964); *Vescovi e diocesi in Italia dal XIV alla metà del XVI secolo,* ed. Giuseppina De Sandre Gasparini, Antonio Rigon, Francesco Trolese, and Gian Maria Varanini, Proceedings of the Seventh Conference on the History of the Church in Italy, Brescia, 21–25 September 1987 (Rome, 1990).

67. Caroline Walker Bynum, *Docere Verbo et Exemplo: An Aspect of Twelfth-Century Spirituality,* Harvard Theological Studies, 31 (Missoula, Montana, 1979).

68. Kathleen Biddick, "Genders, Bodies, Borders: Technologies of the Visible," *Speculum* 68 (1993): 389–418.

69. We regret that it was not possible to include an essay on southern Italy; most of the research on women and religion has been done by scholars working on the northern and central portions of the peninsula. For studies of the evolution of ecclesiastical structures in the south, see the essays in *Pievi e parrocchie,* pp. 1061–1185, especially Giovanni Vitolo's concise and lucid contribution "Pievi, parrocchie, e chiese ricettizie in Campania," pp. 1095–1107, as well as Vitolo's *Istituzioni ecclesiastiche e vita religiosa nel Mezzogiorno medievale: Il codice della Confraternita di S. Maria di Montefusco, sec. XII* (Rome, 1982).

70. Weinstein and Bell, *Saints and Society,* pp. 167–68.

71. For instance, Carlo Ginzburg, *The Cheese and the Worms: The Cosmos of a Sixteenth-Century Miller,* trans. John Tedeschi and Anne Tedeschi (Baltimore, 1980); Giovanni Levi, *Inheriting Power: The Story of an Exorcist,* trans. Lydia G. Cochrane (Chicago, 1988); and *Microhistory and the Lost Peoples of Europe,* ed. Edward Muir and Guido Ruggiero (Baltimore, 1991), which contains a good critical appreciation of this approach by Edward Muir, "Introduction: Observing Trifles," pp. vii–xxviii. Rather sharper criticism of microhistorians' use of legal records has been expressed by Thomas Kuehn, "Reading Microhistory: The Example of *Giovanni and Lusanna,*" *Journal of Modern History* 61 (1989): 512–34.

72. They have also, like American scholars, devoted themselves to making texts more accessible to students and scholars alike by preparing modern translations. Special mention should be made of the excellent anthology *Scrittrici mistiche italiane,* ed. Giovanni Pozzi and Claudio Leonardi (Genoa, 1988), and of the Peregrina Translations series from Peregrina Press and the Classics of Western Spirituality series from Paulist Press, which includes the works of Clare of Assisi, Angela of Foligno, Catherine of Siena, and Catherine of Genoa.

73. Fernanda Sorelli, *La santità imitabile: "Leggenda di Maria da Venezia" di Tommaso da Siena,* Deputazione di storia patria per le Venezie, Miscellanea di studi e memorie, 23 (Venice, 1984); *Vita della beata Elena da Udine,* ed. Andrea Tilatti (Udine, 1988); *Il Libro della beata Angela da Foligno,* ed. Ludger Thier and Abele Calufetti (Grottaferrata, 1985); *Il processo di canonizzazione di Chiara da Mon-*

tefalco, ed. Enrico Menestò, Quaderni del Centro per il Collegamento degli studi medievali e umanistici nell' Università di Perugia, 14 (Florence and Perugia, 1984). Not all these editions succeed in meeting the highest standards: see the criticisms leveled at Thier and Calufetti by Enrico Menestò, "Problemi critico-testuali nel 'Liber' della beata Angela," in *Angela da Foligno, terziaria francescana,* pp. 171–75, and by Giovanni Pozzi, *Il libro dell'esperienza* (Milan, 1992), pp. 236–37 and 246.

74. The section "Chiese e conventi degli ordini mendicanti in Umbria nei secoli XIII–XIV: Inventario delle fonti archivistiche e catalogo delle informazioni documentarie" of this series includes the volumes *Gli archivi della Valnerina,* ed. Vittorio Giorgetti (Perugia, 1984); *Gli archivi di Orvieto,* ed. Marilena Rossi Caponeri and Lucio Riccetti (Perugia, 1987); *La serie Protocolli dell'Archivio notarile di Perugia,* ed. Maria Immacolata Bossa (Perugia, 1987); and *Gli archivi ecclesiastici di Città di Castello,* ed. Giovanna Casagrande (Perugia, 1989).

75. Bartolomea Riccoboni, "Cronaca del Corpus Domini" and "Necrologio del Corpus Domini," in Giovanni Dominici, *Lettere spirituali,* ed. Maria-Teresa Casella and Giovanni Pozzi, Spicilegium Friburgense, 13 (Freiburg, 1969), pp. 257–330; *Ricordanze del monastero di S. Lucia O.S.C. in Foligno, cronache 1424–1786,* ed. Angela Emmanuela Scandella (Assisi, 1987); *Memoriale di Monteluce: Cronaca del monastero delle clarisse di Perugia dal 1448 al 1838,* ed. Chiara Augusta Lainati, with an introduction by Ugolino Nicolini (Assisi, 1983).

76. Francesca Medioli, *L' "Inferno monacale" di Arcangela Tarabotti* (Turin, 1990). See also Stefano Andretta, *La venerabile superbia: Ortodossia e trasgressione nella vita di suor Francesca Farnese, 1593–1651* (Turin, 1994).

77. *Cecilia Ferrazzi: Autobiografia di una santa mancata, 1609–1664,* ed. Anne Jacobson Schutte (Bergamo, 1990); *Liber miraculorum,* in Dalarun, *La sainte et la cité,* pp. 175–220. See also Jacques Dalarun, *"Lapsus Linguae": La Légende de Claire de Rimini* (Spoleto, 1994).

78. Gill, "Women and the Production of Religious Literature"; Katharine Park, "The Criminal and the Saintly Body: Autopsy and Dissection in Renaissance Italy," *Renaissance Quarterly* 47 (1994): 1–33, esp. 1–3.

79. Chiara Frugoni, *A Distant City: Images of Urban Experience in the Medieval World,* trans. William McCuaig (Princeton, 1991); Frugoni, "The City and the 'New' Saints"; Gabriella Zarri, "Ursula and Catherine: The Marriage of Virgins in the Sixteenth Century," in Matter and Coakley, *Creative Women in Medieval and Early Modern Italy,* pp. 237–78. Rudolph Bell's *Holy Anorexia* has been translated as *La santa anoressia: Digiuno e misticismo dal Medioevo a oggi* (Rome and Bari, 1987), and an essay by Bynum is included in *Donna e fede: Santità e vita religiosa in Italia,* ed. Lucetta Scaraffia and Gabriella Zarri (Rome and Bari, 1994).

2

A Community of Female Penitents in Thirteenth-Century Padua

Antonio Rigon

Scholars today agree that study of the penitential movement of thirteenth-century Italy will profit from a focus on carefully defined geographical areas and new sorts of documentation. Investigations of this kind seem essential and urgent, not simply because we feel the need to move "from the juridical domain to the existential," as Théophile Desbonnets advocated in his concluding remarks at a recent conference, but especially because they appear to be the only way to move beyond the polemics that have beset the subject of the order of penitence ever since Gilles Gérard Meersseman called into question an age-old and deeply rooted historiographical tradition by denying that St. Francis could be considered the founder of this order.[1] At the same time, it seems equally important to situate the movement of the penitents in the larger context of the spiritual movements of the twelfth and thirteenth centuries, in which the laity asserted the possibility of living in accordance with the Gospels while remaining in the world, and pursued their own Christian vocation in various forms.

Padua provides an especially interesting arena for investigation, since it was the setting for lively and varied manifestations of lay religious life and the home of major monasteries of the mendicant orders.[2] Moreover, in the specific case of the penitents, the city formed part of the organizational structure of the order, as the seat of one of the four provinces (along with Bologna, Milan, and Genoa) in which the penitent brotherhoods of northern Italy were grouped in the second half of the thirteenth century.[3]

Such research presents formidable problems, however. The documentation, consisting of notarial acts scattered in a wide variety of archival collections, is not easily accessible. Moreover, since sources of this kind do not readily yield information about devotional orientation and statutory regulations, the possibilities of probing some of the essential components of the lives of lay groups and confraternities are severely limited. On the other hand, they offer the advantage of providing much concrete data that would otherwise be hard to find: from the number and social origins of the devotees and the penitents to their activities; from the composition and administration of the property of these communities and associations to their relationships with their civil and ecclesiastical setting. In short, these sources contain precisely the kind of information about everyday reality that students of religious movements today seek ever more avidly.[4]

It is from this perspective, using mostly unpublished documents collected through long though not exhaustive investigation, that I propose to examine experiences and forms of religious life among the laity in Padua.

A Female Penitential Community at San Luca

On 9 July 1213, Crescenzio, the priest of the Paduan church of San Luca, leased a plot of land in Padua "with houses" *(cum casis)* from the archpriest and the canons of the cathedral for the sum of fifty lire, and he in turn ceded that plot to Benvenuta, daughter of the late Marosticano, Floria, daughter of the late Xate, and Altisia, daughter of Bongiovanni, who wished to establish a new religious community.[5] We have no information about the social origins of these three women, but we do know that the fifty lire paid to the canons came not "in actual fact from the possessions of the aforementioned church of San Luca, but from their own possessions and from what others had given them (as they asserted) in charity."[6] If in order to obtain the lease they had even turned to charity, it is reasonable to surmise that these women came from rather modest backgrounds, and that they perhaps lacked the dowries that would have allowed them to enter convents.[7] What is certain is that to achieve their aim of devoting themselves to God, they did not join a religious order; instead, they accepted the status of penitents, associating themselves with a movement that precisely in these years, beginning around 1210, was experiencing widespread and vigorous growth among the laity.[8] In the act of taking the lease, in fact, Benvenuta, Floria, and Altisia committed themselves to remain "statu et habitu penitencie," in the condition and habit of penitence, and not transfer their rights except to such persons "que faciant penitenciam et permaneant," who would do penance and reside there. The expression "facere penitentiam," do penance, was in current use in the ecclesiastical language of the time: the three women voluntarily adopted the ascetic regime that the church imposed on public sinners who had been absolved.[9] But as we know, the penitential experience could take various forms.[10] Many female penitents continued to live in their own homes; others lived together in groups.[11] This little group of Paduan women chose the common life, renouncing individual property in the spirit of poverty. All of the possessions that Benvenuta and her companions received in lease had to remain common property: "Let them value and make use of all things together, and they should communally own, hold, possess, build, inhabit, and improve that place, staying and residing in the penitential condition and habit and living the common life."[12] The program obligated not only the three religious women, but extended also to anyone whom they "concorditer et unanimiter," by common and unanimous consent, wished to welcome among their group, and to anyone who might take their places after their deaths. Harmony and unanimity were the ideals on which communal life was founded, and this also explains why at the outset there were no hierarchical distinctions—or at least none that were emphasized—between the three women, who together received the lease and together decided whether to admit new members.[13] The text emphasizes instead the essential elements of the regimen of religious life they freely adopted: residing together, living according to the penitential condition as symbolized and made visible by their change of dress, and remaining faithful to their own decision.[14] The insistently emphasized obligation to "persist" and the oft-repeated duty to not wander from their chosen path highlight the irreversibility of the religious profession of the state of penitence.[15]

If, on the other hand, the lease should be transferred to individuals who proved incapable of respecting the original program, based on the obligation to live, remain, and persist in a life of penitence, the deed would be deemed invalid. Analogously, if any of the women left "a conventu aliarum," for another convent, she would relinquish her rights. If, finally, all of the women resigned, abandoning "vitam comunem, statum et habitum penitencia," the common life, condition, and habit of penitence, they would lose all of their rights and possessions, which would revert "cum toto melioramento," with all improvements, to the church of San Luca.

The relationship of the female penitents with San Luca was of the greatest importance. San Luca was a chapel, a *capella*, that was on its way to becoming a parish, and so the religious experience of the three women evolved in the shadow of a church that was fully enmeshed in the ecclesiastical structures of the city.[16] Benvenuta and the others went to live on a plot of land located in the district that took its name from the church—"in hora predicte ecclesie Sancti Luce"—a plot of land on the public road, bordering the property of a judge and some artisans.[17] There was no mention of a monastery or church or of plans to build one. Like other female religious communities with no formal ties to an order, the three women remained subject to the parish and accepted the spiritual direction of its priests, in this case surely that same priest Crescenzio who had played an important role in the formation of the group.[18] And in fact, he was later venerated as their blessed founder by the nuns of the convent of Santa Cecilia, which, as we shall see, came into existence when the first female community connected to San Luca affiliated itself with Benedictine monasticism.[19]

But in order to grant to the female penitents the plot of land received in lease from the canons, Crescenzio had to obtain the approval of the prior of the collegiate church of Santa Croce of Cervarese, a venerable institution located about fifteen kilometers from the city, to which San Luca was subject.[20] Moreover, he acted with the consent of his fellow priests Mainardo and Gerusalemme, who lived with him at San Luca. Thus in the vicinity of the church, which had several clerics and near which also lived three laymen, mentioned in our document as witnesses, there now assembled three women as well.[21] A composite community was born, divided symmetrically (and perhaps not coincidentally) into three parts, in which the evangelical ideal of the common life that had inspired the religious renaissance of the eleventh and twelfth centuries and still exercised a powerful appeal was lived within each of three groups, juridically distinct (the women even settled at a certain distance from the church) but spiritually united in their common commitment to religious life.[22]

The collegial organization of the priests of San Luca, their dependence from the collegiate church of Santa Croce of Cervarese, and even the involvement of the cathedral chapter all show the enterprise to be clearly in line with the typical experiences of the canonical movement, which, as we know, had encouraged the development of associative forms of religious life for the laity.[23] Lay brothers and sisters, often engaged in nursing activities, lived alongside the collegiate churches of Padua as well.[24] At the cathedral itself we find recorded the presence of a certain brother Rustico of Costozza, called "de poenitentia," the penitent.[25] In his will of 29 May 1274, this brother Rustico named as fiduciary a nun of Santa Cecilia—the very convent that the women of San Luca eventually formed.[26]

By placing themselves under the direction of the parish clergy, these women were sheltered from possible conflicts with ecclesiastical authorities, who, far from frowning upon their enterprise, actually supported it. The archpriest and canons of the cathedral had granted land and houses; somewhat later, on 2 October 1213, the bishop gave his own consent by confirming the agreement.[27]

In conclusion, the experience of this female community in Padua can be considered a characteristic manifestation of the vast penitential phenomenon that burgeoned all over Europe in the second decade of the thirteenth century. In particular, it had certain features in common with the female religious movements that sprang up in central Italy, Lombardy, and northern Europe: the women's initial recourse to charity and their decision to live a religious life outside of a religious order, even if they were associated with groups of canons.[28] Moreover, the female penitents avoided ownership of the land on which they settled, holding it instead in lease. We have no information about any work they may have done, but it is significant that later documents furnish clear indications of work in textiles, especially silk processing.[29]

But the comparison cannot be extended much further, if only because the community evolved quite rapidly in the direction of monasticism. As early as 6 August 1225 Benvenuta, who together with Floria and Altisia had set up the penitential experiment, is mentioned as "abbatissa monasterii Sancte Cecilie de Padua," abbess of the convent of Santa Cecilia of Padua.[30] Just a few years after founding their settlement at San Luca, the female penitents had already switched over to monasticism, creating an autonomous convent, Santa Cecilia.[31] We do not know the exact date of this transformation, but it is certainly significant that when the nuns accepted the Benedictine rule, they joined the reform movement of the "white" monks who in 1224 had established the "ordo sancti Benedicti de Padua," the order of St. Benedict of Padua.[32] The promoter of the movement, the blessed Giordano Forzaté, who had been in contact with the priest Crescenzio, suddenly appeared as the nuns' authoritative guide, and their decision to enter the order was probably due to his influence.[33] In addition, in these years other religious communities that had sprung up outside of the already approved rules were being incorporated in the Benedictine order of Padua, which, subject to the higher jurisdiction of the bishop, dedicated itself to the revaluation of manual labor as an ascetic exercise, the renunciation of feudal jurisdictions, and involvement in works of charity and peacemaking.[34] There were, moreover, no obstacles to the development of a female branch. Indeed, if women could encounter difficulty in being admitted to traditional Benedictine monasteries for financial reasons, they met with growing hostility also on the part of the new orders, including the mendicants, who were reluctant to assume organizational responsibility for and spiritual direction of the female communities.[35] In the "ordo sancti Benedicti de Padua," however, the existence of double monasteries was allowed from the beginning, and there were no hindrances to the development of female monasteries.[36] In fact, women made up a very substantial component of the order, and the number of nuns in their communities far exceeded that of the older female convents in Padua.[37]

The evolution of a community of female penitents into a monastic community testifies to the attraction exercised by the movement of "white" Benedictines, which in incorporating into a Benedictine framework these diverse religious experiences (which sometimes lacked a precise definition in canon law) was essentially following the course of action proposed by the Fourth Lateran Council.[38] However, what interests us here is not so much these transformations, but rather the formation and survival of associations of pious laymen and -women, who led a religious life in the shadow of the monastery while still maintaining their lay status. It was the ideal of penitence (as Vauchez has recently emphasized) that moved these devout persons to gravitate around monasteries—true hotbeds of penitential spirituality—and inspired them to embrace such widely tested and by now traditional forms of life as that of the *conversi*.[39]

NOTES

Originally published in Antonio Rigon, "I laici nella chiesa padovana del Duecento: Conversi, oblati, penitenti," *Contributi alla storia della chiesa padovana nell'età medioevale,* vol. 1, Fonti e ricerche di storia ecclesiastica padovana, 11 (Padua, 1979), pp. 13–20.

1. Théophile Desbonnets, conclusion to *L'ordine della penitenza di San Francesco d'Assisi nel secolo XIII,* ed. Ottaviano Schmucki, Proceedings of the Conference of Franciscan Studies, Assisi, 3–5 July 1972, Collectanea Franciscana, 43 (Rome, 1973), p. 334; Gilles Gérard Meersseman, *Dossier de l'ordre de la pénitence au XIIIe siècle* (Fribourg, 1961), pp. 1–38. A summary of the introduction to Meersseman's volume, with a documentary appendix, has been reprinted with the title of "L'ordine della penitenza nel sec. XIII," in Gilles Gérard Meersseman with Gian Piero Pacini, *Ordo fraternitatis: Confraternite e pietà dei laici nel Medioevo* (Rome, 1977), pp. 355–409. In addition to Desbonnet's statement at the conference cited above, the necessity of local studies was particularly emphasized by Mariano d'Alatri, "'Ordo paenitentium' ed eresia in Italia," in *L'ordine della penitenza di San Francesco,* p. 196. See Attilio Bartoli Langeli's review of these conference proceedings in the *Rivista di storia della Chiesa in Italia* 28 (1974): 239–43, especially p. 243, for the importance of this research for "breaking free from the polemical diatribes, not by resolving them but simply by moving beyond them." The volume *I frati penitenti di San Francesco nella società del Due e Trecento,* ed. Mariano d'Alatri, Proceedings of the Second Conference of Franciscan Studies, Rome, 12–14 October 1976 (Rome, 1977), represents a first concrete step in this direction.

2. On lay religious life in the thirteenth century, see the information in *Statuti di*

confraternite religiose di Padova nel Medio Evo: Testi, studio introduttivo, e cenni storici, ed. Giuseppina De Sandre Gasparini, Fonti e ricerche di storia ecclesiastica padovana, 6 (Padua, 1974), especially the historical notes that preface the edition of the statutes of the individual confraternities. The mendicant convents referred to are principally the Franciscan house of Sant'Antonio and the Dominican house of Sant'Agostino, whose importance, especially for the history of culture, has most recently been emphasized by Girolamo Arnaldi, "Scuole nella Marca Trevigiana e a Venezia nel secolo XIII," in *Storia della cultura veneta dalle origini al Trecento* (Vicenza, 1976), pp. 355–58; Arnaldi, "Le origini dello Studio di Padova: Dalla migrazione del 1222 alla fine del periodo ezzeliniano," in *La Cultura* 15 (1977): 405–8, 416–17, 429–31; and Paolo Marangon, "Il rapporto culturale tra università e ordini mendicanti," *Il Santo* 18 (1978): 129–32. These studies also contain references to earlier works on the subject.

3. Meersseman, *Dossier,* pp. 8, 160–62, 168–76; *Ordo fraternitatis,* pp. 412–17.

4. On the penitents in particular, see the references in the works of Desbonnets and Mariano d'Alatri cited above. Concerning the heretical movements, Ovidio Capitani's remarks in the introduction to the essay collection he edited, *Medioevo ereticale* (Bologna, 1977), p. 7, are of great interest, as are Grado G. Merlo's investigations of heretics in Piedmont, now collected and expanded in *Eretici e inquisitori nella società piemontese del Trecento* (Turin, 1977).

5. Antonio Barzon, *B. Crescenzio da Camposampiero: Il culto pubblico dalla morte al 1850* (Padua, 1941), pp. 7–8, doc. 1, reprinted in the volume containing four of Barzon's essays, *Santi padovani* (Cittadella [Padua], 1975), pp. 153–55, doc. 1. (The following citations come from this document, which I have checked against the original, correcting Barzon on a few points.) The document was also published by Guido Beltrame, *Storia e arte in S. Tomaso M.* (Padua, 1966), pp. 360–65.

6. "De bonis iam dicte ecclesie Sancti Luce in rei veritate, set de suis et aliunde sibi ut dicebatur ex caritate datis."

7. See Meersseman, *Ordo fraternitatis,* p. 282, who suggests that "one reason for the increase in non-cloistered female penitents was probably economic, because many of these women, swept up in the current of lay pietism, did not have dowries large enough to gain admission to convents. At the beginning of the thirteenth century a solution to this social problem was finally found: in Northern Europe, beguine houses arose, and in Italy hospices for penitents."

8. Ibid., p. 451.

9. Ibid., p. 355.

10. On the various categories of penitents, see ibid., pp. 312–13.

11. See ibid., pp. 270, 278–82, 286, 358–59, 374–77.

12. "Hec omnia valeant et possint insimul et comuniter debeant habere, tenere, possidere, heddifficare, habitare et omnem suam utilitatem inibi facere, stantes et comorantes et permanentes statu et habitu penitencie et in vita comuni viventes."

13. On the absence of a "hierarchy of authority" in the penitential confraternities and on their substitution of horizontal and fraternal obligations for vertical and paternalistic fidelity, see Marie-Dominique Chenu, *La théologie au douzième*

siècle (Paris, 1957), pp. 256 and 270; translated as *Nature, Man, and Society in the Twelfth Century: Essays on New Theological Perspectives in the Latin West,* by Jerome Taylor and Lester K. Little (Chicago, 1968), pp. 245 and 262.

14. For the *mutatio habitus,* the change of dress of voluntary penitents as "the exterior sign of their interior moral conversion" and "the emblem of their change of ecclesiastical condition," see Meersseman, *Ordo fraternitatis,* pp. 283–86.

15. Penitents were allowed to abandon their own condition only if they adopted a more austere ascetic regime. See ibid., pp. 310–11.

16. Paolo Sambin, *L'ordinamento parrocchiale di Padova nel Medioevo* (Milan, 1941), pp. 39–40, 79; and on the meaning of the term *capella,* see Sambin's "Note sull'organizzazione parrocchiale in Padova nel sec. XIII," in *Studi di storia ecclesiastica medioevale,* vol. 1 of *Saggi di storia ecclesiastica veneta* (Venice, 1954), p. 4.

17. "Choeret quidem ut dicebatur eidem sedimini ab uno latere videlicet a mane Micheloto fabro Mercurii (?) et Blasii peliparii, a sero Richarde uxoris Aicardini calegarii, a septemtrione Grunerii Egidioli iudicis, a meridie via publica" (Barzon, *Santi padovani,* p. 155). On the territorial boundaries of the parish of San Luca "in civitate" and "in suburbio," and on San Luca as a *capella* of a district with a growing population, see Cesira Gasparotto, "Padova ecclesiastica 1239: Note topografico-storiche," *Fonti e ricerche di storia ecclesiastica padovana* 1 (1967): 121 and 124.

18. On the subjection of female religious communities to the parish, see Herbert Grundmann, *Movimenti religiosi nel Medioevo* (Bologna, 1974), p. 191.

19. See Barzon, *Santi padovani,* pp. 65–75.

20. On the collegiate church of Santa Croce of Cervarese, see Ireneo Daniele, "Parrocchie," in *La diocesi di Padova nel 1972* (Padua, 1973), pp. 197–99; see also L. Marcato, "L'oratorio della Santa Croce in Cervarese (Padova)," *Archeologia veneta* 1 (1978): 157–64.

21. The act was drawn up "coram magistro Bencio, Arloto et Dominigino qui morabantur ad ecclesiam Sancti Luce," among others (Barzon, *Santi padovani,* p. 153).

22. The bibliography on the common life in the religious renaissance of the eleventh and twelfth centuries is enormous; here it is enough to refer to the proceedings of the conference at La Mendola in September 1959, *La vita comune del clero nei secoli XI e XII,* 2 vols. (Milan, 1962). On the development and also on the distinctive characteristics of the forms of communal life among the laity, see Cosimo Damiano Fonseca, "Discorso di apertura," in *I laici nella "societas christiana" dei secoli XI e XII,* Proceedings of the Third Annual Research Seminar, Mendola, 21–27 August 1965 (Milan, 1968), pp. 10–11. See also Chenu, *La théologie,* pp. 233–44 (*Nature, Man, and Society,* pp. 219–30); Meerssemann, *Ordo fraternitatis,* p. 282. The monastery of Santa Cecilia was built on the spot where the women settled. This space is today occupied by a large block of houses, between the Piazza Castello, Via I. Andreini, Via G. Barbarigo, and Via XX Settembre (Gasparotto, "Padova ecclesiastica 1239," p. 120 n. 416).

23. Cosimo Damiano Fonseca, "I conversi nelle comunità canonicali," in *I laici nella "societas christiana,"* pp. 262–305, especially 276–77, 286, 288–89, 295, and 301–4.

24. This was true of the collegiate church of Ognissanti, which had a hospice attached to it. See Gasparotto, "Padova ecclesiastica 1239," pp. 100–104 and the documents citeds there, and Daniele, "Parrochie," pp. 391–93.

25. At least according to Domenico Maria Federici, *Istoria de' Cavalieri gaudenti,* vol. 2 (Venice, 1787), pp. 147–48, doc. 84. However, the original of the document partially edited by Federici (Padua, Archivio capitolare, 18, *Testamenta,* 1, parchment 22) does not identify Brother Rustico as "de poenitentia," but only as "frater Rusticus, qui fuit de Custoza et nunc stat ad maiorem ecclesiam Padue." It is not clear where Federici found the information that Rustico was a penitent.

26. Padua, Archivio capitolare, 18, *Testamenta,* 1, parchment 22; Federici, in *Istoria,* 2: 147–48, doc. 84, does not provide the passage concerning the naming of the fiduciary, Sister Melda (see also Padua, Archivio di Stato, Diplomatico, part. 2678).

27. Barzon, *Santi padovani,* p. 155.

28. On female religious movements in this period, in addition to the fundamental discussion of Grundmann, *Movimenti religiosi,* pp. 147–403, 447–71, see Gottfried Koch, "La donna nel Catarismo e nel Valdismo medioevali," in *Medioevo ereticale,* pp. 245–75. These works contain references to the essential bibliography on the subject.

29. In her will of 10 February 1257, Benvenuta left "totam tellam lini et stope et totum filum" that she had "in salvamento ad Sanctam Ceciliam Padue" for her soul and for her burial at the disposal of the Franciscan friar Amato: Antonio Rigon, "Appunti per lo studio dei rapporti tra Minori e mondo ecclesiastico padovano nel Duecento," in *S. Antonio di Padova fra storia e pietà: Colloquio interdisciplinare su "Il fenomeno antoniano"* (Padua, 1977), p. 186 n. 5. That there were actual workshops in Santa Cecilia is demonstrated by the bequest of thirty grossi "sororibus Gerardine et Mariebone magistre silici seu sete in monasterio Sancte Cecilie de Padua" from Altiborga, wife of Master Zilio the physician (Padua, Archivio di Stato, Diplomatico, part. 4222).

30. Barzon, *Santi padovani,* pp. 155–58.

31. The original composite community that had formed around San Luca did not break up entirely, however. Arloto, who remained at the church with Master Bencio and Dominigino and who in 1221 is still recorded as "fratre Arloto qui moratur ad S. Lucam" (Francesco Scipione Dondi Dall'Orologio, *Dissertazione settima sopra l'istoria ecclesiastica padovana* [Padua, 1813], p. 23, doc. 20), is indicated in 1226 as "frater" of Santa Cecilia (Padua, Archivio di Stato, Diplomatico, part. 1278). In 1229 he appears as procurator of the abbess (Barzon, *Santi padovani,* pp. 158–59), and in 1233, under the name of "frater Arlotus monasterii Sancte Cecilie," he acts in the name of the convent itself to take possession of a piece of land acquired by the abbess (ibid., pp. 159–161).

32. See Antonio Rigon, "Ricerche sull'Ordo Sancti Benedicti de Padua nel XIII secolo," *Rivista di storia della Chiesa in Italia* 29 (1975): 511–35.

33. Barzon, *Santi padovani,* pp. 61–62; Rigon, "Ricerche," pp. 526–27; on Forzaté see Ireneo Daniele, "Forzaté Giordano, beato," in *Bibliotheca Sanctorum,* vol. 5 (Rome, 1965), col. 987–91.

34. See Antonio Rigon, "Ricerche," pp. 511–35, as well as *S. Giacomo di Monselice nel Medio Evo, sec. XII–XV: Ospedale, monastero, collegiata,* Fonti e ricerche di storia ecclesiastica padovana, 4 (Padua, 1972), pp. 81–82, 127–33.

35. See Grundmann, *Movimenti religiosi,* pp. 171–271.

36. In addition to San Benedetto, the first monastery of the order, it is certain that San Giacomo di Pontecorvo, Santa Maria di Porciglia, San Giovanni di Verdara, San Giacomo di Monselice, and Ognissanti were double monasteries; Santa Cecilia, Sant'Agnese di Polverara, and Santa Margherita di Salarola were female houses. In a few cases, it is not clear whether we are dealing with double monasteries or with convents of nuns with a more or less numerous group of lay brothers attached to them. It is certain that for eleven of the twenty-three "white" Benedictine houses listed in the *ordo domorum* published in Giovanni Benedetto Mittarelli and Anselmo Costadoni, *Annales camaldulenses ordinis sancti Benedicti,* vol. 6, app. (Venice, 1761; reprinted Farnborough, 1970), col. 353–54, there is positive proof of the presence of women. On these houses of "white" Benedictines, see the works cited in note 34, as well as Giovanni Brunacci, *Della B. Beatrice d'Este vita antichissima ora la prima volta pubblicata con dissertazioni* (Padua, 1767), pp. 81–86.

37. In fact, throughout the thirteenth century San Pietro and Santo Stefano, the two oldest and most powerful female monasteries, never had more than ten or fifteen nuns. For San Pietro, see C. Denis Tapparello, "Il monastero di S. Pietro di Padova dalle origini alla prima metà del secolo XV: Con una silloge di documenti inediti dal 1172 al 1237" (*tesi di laurea* defended at the Università degli studi di Padova, Facoltà di magistero, academic year 1968–69), 1: 60–61; and for Santo Stefano, see Padua, Archivio di Stato, Archivio Corona, part. 4010, fols. 45r–45v, and part. 4060; Padua, Archivio di Stato, Diplomatico, part. 1276; Padua, Archivio di Stato, S. Stefano, 15, fols. 5v–6r, 15v; 19, fol. 32v. The "white" Benedictine houses, on the other hand, like the other female religious communities established more recently, appear to be more populous. Here are some examples: San Benedetto had fifty-four nuns in 1263 (Padua, Archivio di Stato, Diplomatico, part. 1192); San Giacomo di Monselice had sixty in 1246 (Rigon, *San Giacomo di Monselice,* p. 63); in Santa Margherita di Salarola in 1227 there were thirty-two nuns (Padua, Archivio di Stato, Diplomatico, part. 1306), the same number that we find in San Vito di Piove di Sacco in 1262 (Padua, Archivio di Stato, SS. Vito e Modesto di Piove, 8, parchment 77). Sant'Agata, a female convent closely associated with the "white" Benedictines but not belonging to the order, had sixty nuns in 1264 (Padua, Archivio di Stato, SS. Agata e Cecilia, 3, fols. 14v–15r, and for its relationship with the "white" Benedictines, 91r–91v). These few bits of information obviously need to be compared with others, but they are certainly quite suggestive.

38. On this aspect, see Rigon, "Ricerche," pp. 514, 525–28.

39. See Vauchez's presentation of Meersseman's *Ordo fraternitatis,* in *Rivista di storia della Chiesa in Italia* 32 (1978): 189–90 (English translation, Vauchez, *The Laity in the Middle Ages: Religious Beliefs and Devotional Practices,* by Margery J. Schneider [Notre Dame, 1993], pp. 107–17). There is a vast bibliography on the conversi; for a start, see the works cited in Rigon, *S. Giacomo di Monselice,* p. 39 n. 26.

3

Clare, Agnes, and Their Earliest Followers: From the Poor Ladies of San Damiano to the Poor Clares

Clara Gennaro

The small group of women who gathered around St. Clare of Assisi at San Damiano represents perhaps the richest and certainly the best known wellspring of the larger female religious movement that arose in Italy, as in other European countries, between the end of the twelfth century and the beginning of the thirteenth. Theirs was a restless movement, one that sought and demanded new forms of religious expression and found in the orders then extant neither room nor voice for the yearning that marked it most profoundly. Their story remains in large part hidden and buried, still to be fully studied and discovered, especially as regards its links with the cultural and spiritual growth that women then sought above all within the religious life.

These groups, which were rooted in the reality in which they arose, embarked on a silent life of prayer and humble manual labor, in residences that became places of meeting and evangelical illumination in the very centers of the cities or in their immediate vicinity. The group formed by Clare and her followers certainly sprang from the words and spirit of St. Francis and so sank its roots in ground that was already tilled and sprouting. But it is difficult to determine to what extent the Franciscan order itself was responsible for the rise of the myriad groups of women all over northern and central Italy—whose numbers will strike anyone who glances through the pages of the *Bullarium Franciscanum*. Everything we know suggests that the Franciscans were a catalyst for a movement already in existence; but there is little evidence from the early years of Clare, Agnes, and their companions at San Damiano, evidence that captures the group at the time of its creation and before it took on the form imposed on it by later regulations.

If this is a problem shared by the history of every group whose life was not extinguished at the outset, it is a particularly thorny one for the Damianites, who received their rule from Cardinal Ugolino—in other words, from the outside—after just a few years of existence. Jacques de Vitry was one of the few who mentioned the group of San Damiano in its early period. In his well-known letter written from Genoa in October 1216, this man of the church, sensitive and alert to the religious expressions of his day, described the Minorites as a single coherent phenomenon, characterized by intense religious fervor and strict poverty.[1] Although he made a distinction between the stationary life of the nuns and the mobile existence of the friars, he gave no hint of the specifically monastic or cloistered character that the female movement was soon to take on.

The very word *monasterium,* indicating traditional religious communities, seems to have been dropped or avoided, as in the *Privilegium Paupertatis,* where Gregory IX—perhaps following Innocent III's earlier text— spoke of *vos* and *ecclesia vestra,* "you" and "your church," as Grundmann aptly noted.[2] Men like Jacques de Vitry substituted for it the word *hospitium,* in the clear awareness that they were dealing with a new reality.[3] Chapter 6 of the Rule of St. Clare, whose substance was restated in her Testament, and the testimony of Clare's early companions at her canonization proceedings spell out her original program with remarkable clarity. She pursued an existence based on radical poverty, which she and her companions, like St. Francis, interpreted as sharing the life of the poor through manual labor and accepting the poor's total dependence on others by begging whenever necessary; on a life in common, marked by the quest for unanimity in charity and humility, which was the animating force of the Franciscan movement; on simple, nonintellectual prayer, arising from an interiorization of the Gospel and from a profound sympathy with all creation; and on a loving, serene, and helpful attention to all the suffering and poverty she saw around herself.[4]

The extent to which Clare and her companions were rooted in the realities of life in Assisi is demonstrated by the variegated throng of people who, burdened and afflicted, constantly came to San Damiano seeking help and support. This very attachment also appears in the general conviction that Clare and her nuns had been placed in Assisi to safeguard the city, which, in an event that immediately took on the coloring of legend, they had supposedly rescued from the "Saracens"—that is, from Frederick II's mob of soldiers.[5]

This group, composed of women from the most powerful families of Assisi, was in existence for many years before it felt the need for a rule.[6] The *formula vitae* (form of life) that Francis had given them, and whose most important elements were included in Clare's rule and Testament, placed at the center of the Damianites' program a life lived in accordance with the Gospels and Francis's solicitude for them.[7] Alongside the *Formula vitae* there grew a collection of *observantiae S. Damiani,* based on the experiences of the group and the teachings that St. Francis communicated to them through letters and notes, the "many writings" to which Clare alludes in her Testament.[8]

Francis's contacts with Clare and her nuns were rather intense in the early years, probably before the Rule of Ugolino. Francis supported this small group of women with his presence and his preaching—and how much they cherished his preaching was demonstrated by his decision, recorded in the second *vita* of Thomas of Celano, to express a sermon in an explicitly penitential act rather than in words.[9] He laid out their manner of life, as we stated; he sent them companions without always having thoroughly tested their vocations, as Clare perhaps learned to do better through her experience with communal life. Their relationship was based on their awareness of sharing a common spirit and perfect concord in their literal interpretation of the Gospels. To Francis, Clare was the true "Christian," because no one expressed, lived, and illuminated the Gospels like her. He turned to her and her companions in moments of darkness, when he felt uncertain on the paths to which he was called. Correspondingly, Clare remembered Francis in her Testament as her pillar of strength, her sole consolation besides Christ, and her support. She considered herself his "little plant," created by him in the spirit of Christ in which they both felt themselves rooted.

Francis never believed that the ties linking him and his friars with the women of San Damiano should be extended to the whole movement that sprang from the program lived by Clare and her group. His blunt and absolute rejection of such an idea was in keeping with that of many other religious orders, which considered the spiritual guidance of nuns to be a burden and danger to their own spiritual life.[10] But a more specific reason for his refusal may have been the fear that his Minorites would be transformed into a monastic order, a transformation that such an obligation would cause or at least encourage. In any case, the whole question of Francis's attitude toward the female religious world calls for further, more detailed study.

In their intense but careful relationship with Francis and in their radical manner of living according to Gospels, the Poor Ladies of San Damiano soon became a reference point for groups of women, both already existing and in the process of formation, who desired to live a religious life according to new models. The network of links that sprang up spontaneously between these groups, and that increasingly centered on the Damianites, is of the greatest interest.

Roberto Rusconi has dedicated an important essay to this topic, but I must discuss it briefly here because it sheds light on the essence of these women's life together.[11] Far from remaining closed within the narrow horizons of San Damiano, they maintained such intense relations with other female groups that Clare and her early companions might be said to display the same apostolic impulses as Francis, in their faith in the evangelical regeneration of humanity, which, through their efforts, could also reach the world of women. Clare's companions left San Damiano in a constant stream—as the canonization proceedings themselves attest at various points—to give "form" to convents not only in nearby Tuscany and Umbria, but also in all of northern Italy and, spreading over ever wider circles, in Bohemia, Germany, France, and Spain.

Thus, to mention just a few of these contacts, Balvina founded and became abbess of the convent of Vallegloria in Spello, where Sister Pacifica of Guelfuccio was her companion for one year.[12] Another Balvina, Balvina of Coccorano, was sent to the convent of Arezzo for a year and a half.[13] Clare's sister Agnes established the convent of Monticelli near Florence in 1219, then went on to Verona, Padua, Venice, and Mantua between 1224 and 1238. And according to the chronicle of Nicolaus Glassberger, the convent of Ulm took its origin from San Damiano.[14] As the relevant monastic sources become available, it would be interesting to study the effect of the presence of the sisters of San Damiano on the directions taken by various groups and, among their diverse forms and programs, to ascertain whether the convents formed by Clare's companions were those that followed most closely the life of strict poverty.[15] It is hard to imagine that a strong connection did not exist, for example, between the sisters of San Damiano and those of San Severino di Colperseto, to whom Francis had been especially attached: in a gesture of charming simplicity, he once gave them a little lamb, as Thomas of Celano narrates in the first *vita*, and while staying there he met and converted Pacifico, "who was called the king of verses."[16] In 1231 these women appeared to adhere to a program of rigorous poverty: "renouncing worldly goods for Christ and accepting poverty as their lot, they chose to be sustained by the alms of the faithful"—as Gregory IX said in a bull that sought to provide them with economic assistance by promising an indulgence of forty days to anyone who helped support them.[17]

A document from 1217 seems to confirm that even in the earliest years Clare's group was already spreading to the surrounding areas: it states that Clare herself, along with two companions, Marsebilia and Cristiana, acquired land in Foligno to found a convent, of which Marsebilia was named abbess.[18]

Faced with the great variety, richness, and energy of these groups, the church felt compelled to intervene to provide direction, norms, and a unitary form for a movement that, however heartfelt, could easily seem so disordered and confused as to call into question, among other things, the condition and position of women in the church, and in the religious life in particular. Indeed, the movement appeared to be assuming the dimensions of a new order, when the Fourth Lateran Council had just decreed that no new orders would be permitted.

Thus began the long struggle of Clare and the group at San Damiano to remain faithful to their vision, which they loved with even greater intensity because it was embodied in Francis. Their loyalty to the life to which they felt called merged and united with their allegiance to Francis, as everything Clare wrote clearly demonstrates. If Francis's resolute resistance to requests that he conform to the rules of other religious orders is well known, Clare's tenacious and silent struggle was perhaps even more difficult. It led her to a painful process of excavation, a search for the heart and essence of her vocation, and an effort to distinguish this core from elements that, although they may not have conformed to her feelings and her program, nevertheless did not threaten what she considered to be indispensable.

We should note, by the way, that nothing—neither fasts, nor vigils, nor prayers—so purified Clare as this secret and profound struggle that marked her entire life. As she wrote sometime between 1235 and 1238 in the Second Letter to Agnes of Prague, urging her to share the outlook that she herself unwaveringly maintained, "If anyone would tell you something else or suggest something which would hinder your perfection or seem contrary to your divine vocation, even though you must respect him, do not follow his counsel. But as a poor virgin, embrace the poor Christ."[19] Indeed, Pope Innocent III's concession of the *Privilegium Paupertatis,* the Privilege of Poverty, seems to have coincided with Clare's acceptance of the title of abbess in conformity with the Benedictine rule in 1215 and 1216. Clare had refused that title for three years, a refusal that went beyond the topos, so common in monastic hagiography, of thrice rejecting an appointment, usually as bishop, and revealed that Clare's conception of the religious life differed from that of the Benedictines. But eventually the so-called Constitutions of Ugolino, which attempted to impose a unified structure and set of norms on the various female religious groups, including that of San Damiano, brought them into the broad stream of the Benedictine rule.[20]

It would be wrong to consider these constitutions the result of a brutal, external desire to channel or regiment spontaneous religious experiences. Rather, they originated in a serious effort to enhance and interpret the strongly and fervidly contemplative character of these groups, something a man with Ugolino's fine religious sensibilities could appreciate.

With his constitutions, Ugolino aimed at a thorough renewal of religious life through a radical and rigorous restatement of the most fundamental monastic requirements. First and foremost was the *fuga mundi,* flight from the world, taken in its most literal sense as absolute, physical separation from one's surroundings. The practice of this form of reclusion followed a tradition that had been revived in recent centuries, mostly by solitary individuals but sometimes by groups in search of a distinctly mystical experience. This type of religious life involved a constant ascetic tension, maintained through periods of silence and fasting in accordance with rhythms and modes of procedure that were strictly defined and standardized. It is no coincidence that these characteristics also marked Ugolino's constitutions.

Ugolino's decision to give his support to these new energies was undoubtedly a structural one, the result of his analysis of the religious and ecclesiastical condition of his times, and it represented a constant element of his ecclesiastical policies, especially after he mounted the papal throne as Gregory IX. But is also sprang from his need for a connection with the deepest roots of his own spiritual quest. This provides a key for interpreting his letters to Clare, whom he called "mother of his salvation," and to the nuns of San Damiano, which properly belong to the genre of letters of monastic friendship, as well as his visits to San Damiano, one of which he recalled in one of his most beautiful letters.[21] It also explains Gregory's intense affection for some of the convents that had accepted his rule, such as San Paolo of Spoleto, where he stayed in May 1228 during the struggle with Frederick II in a visit celebrated and commemorated with astonishment and admiration in Thomas of Celano's first *vita.*[22]

Nevertheless, there remains a clear and unmistakable divide between Ugolino's impassioned monastic project and the quest for other forms of expression, both in the realm of spirituality and in terms of models of the religious life, that at least some of these female groups had undertaken, sometimes (as in the case of Clare and her companions at San Damiano) with a very high degree of self-awareness.

The letter from Gregory IX to Agnes of Prague, dated 11 May 1238, clearly shows the differences between Ugolino's language and that of the Franciscan sisters.[23] Reviewing the stages by which the Damianites had developed, he identified his concession and their acceptance of his constitutions as a fundamental step. He compared the solid food of the constitutions with the milk of Francis's *formula vitae,* which the Poor Ladies of San Damiano, in contrast, always considered the essential guide to the life of poverty that they pursued with all their energies.

Nothing illustrates the radical distance between their spiritual lan-

guages so clearly as the theme of cloister. Although it is very difficult to reconstruct Clare's original program without distortion, her writings nevertheless vibrate with its spirit; and for Clare, the need to mandate
separation from the world simply did not arise, since separation came from
the depths of the heart and was expressed as the quest for the silence and
inwardness that would render contemplation more intense and serene.
Francis's guidelines for friars living in a hermitage—as Lainati has discer-
ningly shown—and the way of life that he envisioned for the Porziuncola,
which he wanted to be the center and model for all of the Minorites, provided ample illumination for a secluded life of contemplation, to which
Francis himself was always attracted and to which he had recourse during
the most difficult and exacting periods of his religious exploration and at
the turning points of the order.[24] The times and sequences of silence and
prayer that Francis set for his friars in the hermitage reproduced the characteristic rhythms of monastic life, and so make it difficult to determine
whether the treatment of these matters in Clare's rule was derived from
Francis or Ugolino—or from a common tradition on which both had
drawn. However, a noteworthy and distinctive feature was the presence and
function of the *serviziali,* or sisters who serve outside the monastery, who
were probably modeled on the "brothers-mothers" of Francis's Rule for
Hermitages.[25]

In Clare's Rule the *serviziali* were treated as distinct from the other sisters, although they were not considered inferior to them; and in the early
days, is it not likely that there was the same alternation of functions and
roles that the Rule for Hermitages ordained for the "sons," absorbed in intense and constant prayer, and the "mothers" who watched over them to
keep them from being disturbed or distracted? In any case, for Clare, the
serviziali—a term, with its echoes of the dignity of lowliness, that she must
certainly have preferred to *moniales*—belonged at the heart of the group.
Her attitude toward them was reflected in her special attentions to them,
such as the act of washing their feet, which was reported by several witnesses during her canonization proceedings.[26] She obviously considered
them full-fledged sisters. And in this connection, it is significant that in this
period and the world of the religious orders, in which symbolically charged
clothing indicated the status and identified the condition of the person wearing it, Clare's rule, unlike that of Innocent IV of 1247, expected all the
women to wear the same habit.

In his rule of 1247, which we will discuss at greater length, Innocent IV
recognized that the *serviziali* were an intrinsic part of the Franciscan reality
of the Damianites.[27] Ugolino's constitutions, in contrast, maintained an eloquent silence in this regard: they did speak of *servientes,* but without allud-

ing to any forays from the convent.[28] The presence of the *serviziali* cannot be considered merely functional, an organizational convenience: it was an integral element in the conception of the life of the *sorores minores* and the *forma paupertatis* they followed. This is demonstrated by Clare's well-known admonishment to the *serviziali* as they set out: "When they saw the beautiful flowering and leafy trees they should praise God; and also when they saw the people and the other creatures, they should praise God always and for all things."[29] These words expressed the full intensity of their communion with God's creation and their human surroundings, linked as well with that rootlessness and dispersion in the world so characteristic of Franciscan spirituality. And beyond these structural elements present in the life of the group at San Damiano, a way of feeling and living the flight from the world that differed markedly from Ugolino's concept of claustration can be sensed in the concordant testimony of two of the sisters—Cecilia Cacciaguerra and Balvina of Coccorano—who reported that when Clare learned that "some friars had been martyred in Morocco" (an event that took place in January 1220) "she expressed her desire to go there."[30]

These statements are clear indications of a tension, in Clare as in Francis, between the apostolic/missionary and the contemplative vocations. For a number of essentially sociocultural reasons, Clare embraced and adopted the latter, without, however, ever feeling the need to erect screens to separate herself and her companions from the world that were as rigid as Ugolino's constitutions dictated.

For Cardinal Ugolino, on the other hand, cloister became the keystone of a strictly ascetic, rigidly monastic arrangement, based on "definite rules and measures, definite laws of discipline" (in the words of the prologue to his ordinances), which were intended to shape a strictly regulated life and thereby make possible a profound religious renewal.[31]

Even though Clare realized how foreign the constitutions were to her quest and that of her companions, she accepted them nonetheless, just as she also accepted the Benedictine rule, clinging only to the *forma paupertatis* as the essential nucleus of the evangelical life, the indispensable condition, the crucible in which her ultimate fidelity to her vocation and to Francis would be tested, the path to perfection along which they could not heed the teaching or advice of anyone else (as Francis himself had instructed in his Last Will to the nuns of San Damiano).

Poverty was the richly meaningful symbol of the incarnation of Christ, whom Clare, in the footsteps of Francis and with a particular affective thrill, saw as the "Lord of heaven and earth, laid in a manger."[32] It was the virtue, springing from the same root as "holy humility" and "ineffable charity," "which led Christ to suffer on the wood of the Cross and die thereon the most shameful kind of death."[33] Clare thus concentrated her energies and struggle on this point: it is in the *Privilegium Paupertatis,* originally granted and drafted with his own hand by Pope Innocent III, that one can recognize the firmly rooted principle of *minoritas,* which united her with Francis and made her his "little plant."

Clare won confirmation of the *Privilegium* from Gregory IX, at the beginning of his pontificate. Her early companions were keenly aware of how precious this was to her: when they spoke of it at her canonization proceedings, they vibrated as if they were touching the incandescent and revelatory essence of her life. Beatrice, one of her blood sisters, testified that although Clare's sanctity was revealed in her virginity, humility, diligence in prayer, her disdain for herself, and "in the ardor of her love of God and in her desire for martyrdom," it "was most visible in her love for the Privilege of Poverty."[34] Sister Filippa, the third witness, recalled that Clare "honored the Privilege of Poverty with great reverence and preserved it well and diligently," emphasizing her fear of "losing it."[35] This fear was certainly not unfounded, as the constant and eager pressures for Clare to accept property for herself and her companions demonstrate. Several Damianites testified to this in the canonization proceedings, and the *Legend* itself reported Gregory IX's proposal to release Clare from the vow and Clare's proud response that on no account and never in eternity would she wish to be dispensed from following Christ.[36]

Gregory IX's diffidence about the desire of Clare and her companions for complete poverty was rooted in an established tradition in the church and monastic life, which considered poverty a condition that exposed people to worldly preoccupations and was therefore inimical to those wishing to dedicate themselves to a serious spiritual life. As the pope wrote in 1232 to the nuns of Santa Maria of the "Poor Recluses" in Milan, in endowing them with the property of the hospital of San Biagio in Monza, he was concerned that "their terrible poverty, caused by the abundant wickedness and flagging charity of many people," would (may God forbid) compel the nuns to fall away.[37]

Moreover, his deeply felt concern made him attentive and patient in designing ways to provide for the sustenance of these women who wanted to possess nothing. Thus, when in 1233 a citizen of Siena offered the convent of the poor cloistered nuns of Santa Petronilla his property, which they did not wish to accept, Gregory IX entrusted it to the consuls of the merchants of the city so that they could pass on the income "faithfully . . . for the nuns' use."[38]

Although it is difficult to discern clear phases and cycles in the history of San Damiano—the distinctions that exist all seem to have been imposed from outside, by those who sought to establish forms and norms for the life of the Franciscan sisters—it appears nevertheless that Clare's spiritual tension burned always brighter in an ever more conscious effort to clarify certain points that constituted the heart of the Gospel, which resonated in her as in the voice of Francis.

In her mind, one of the focal points was an open spiritual relationship with Francis's companions, who had to be allowed entry to San Damiano, bringing the bread that she and her companions needed. Clare's insistence on this came from her growing awareness of the limits imposed on the spiritual growth of her group by Ugolino's constitutions and by a rigid interpretation of vigilance in the relationship between the friars and the sisters, which also rested on Gregory IX's reading in *Quo elongati* of the eleventh chapter of the *Regula bullata,* which treated this subject.[39] The unyielding stand taken by Clare and her companions, who were ready to embark on what we today would call a hunger strike, expresses vividly how strongly she felt the need for communication and for a free and open spiritual relationship with the male Franciscans.

But if the San Damiano experience was strongly marked by Ugolino's constitutions, which had shaped from within its manner and rhythms of life, endowing them, at least in part, with a distinctly monastic character, what we know about the 1230s suggests a new urgency in Clare's effort to give the Damianites their own rule, one that would reflect the Franciscan and Minorite spirit of the group.

Clare's beautiful letters to Agnes of Prague shed a particularly revealing light on this tension. In them Clare expressed in exalted terms a mysticism that sprang from the development and melding of a monastic spirituality with her fervid Franciscan roots. These letters also attest to the birth and steady intensification of the spiritual friendship between these two women, with Clare at first a "mother" for Agnes, who was her junior in terms of the spiritual quest, then (in the Fourth Letter, which probably dates from 1253) "mother and daughter"—that is, a relationship in which each felt herself to be the begetter and the begotten of the other.[40] And even if Clare did not spur Agnes in 1238 to ask that she and the group that had formed around her in Prague be released from Ugolino's constitutions in order to live by Francis's *formula vitae*—an effort to win on the periphery, so to speak, a concession that could then be extended to the entire movement—we can certainly say that the spirit and goals that Agnes shared with Clare impelled her to make such a pointed request.[41]

But is was precisely when Pope Innocent IV seemed to recognize, with the bull *Cum omnis* of August 1247, that the Franciscan roots of the Damianite movement could not fit within the Benedictine framework, that Clare realized yet again that she could not accept a rule that was formulated from outside and substantially foreign to the spirit that animated her experience and that of her companions.[42]

In fact, while the Rule of Innocent IV was attentive to other aspects of Franciscanism that she considered marginal (for example, it permitted the *servientes* to maintain limited relations with the outside world, and provided for more intense ties with the Franciscan friars through the common celebration of the divine office in accordance with Franciscan custom and through the spiritual guidance of the nuns entrusted to them), Clare found that it betrayed the very heart of their doctrine: the refusal to have possessions and the acceptance of complete poverty. Clare's last years were thus marked by the drafting of the new rule; and the force of her desire to have it accepted by the church glows in the testimony of Sister Filippa, who said that Clare hoped "that one day she could place the bull [of approval] to her mouth and then die on the next."[43]

This rule, it must be remembered, was the culmination of a long and difficult religious experience that did not always have the freedom to develop according to its own internal impulses. Clare's rule accordingly reflects the various opinions and traditions that influenced the religious life of the Poor Ladies of San Damiano. Yet for Clare it represented the explicit and, I would say, objective confession of her desire that the sisters of San Damiano live in complete conformity with the Franciscan friars. The Franciscan pedigree of her rule is certainly clear: the *Regula bullata* of St. Francis was the foundation for the entire Rule of St. Clare, though its ideas about communal life were presumably derived not only from the Rule of St. Benedict but also from those of Ugolino and Innocent IV. But Clare's own voice is heard most clearly, freely, and fully in the present chapter 6, the central and pivotal point in her rule. Here, love and observance of "most holy poverty" are not simply abstract norms, but rather the guiding light of an entire spiritual itinerary, the heart of their vocation as it was revealed to them by God and illuminated by the words of St. Francis—an inviolable commitment, therefore, that determined their being and their purpose.

Chapter 6 of Clare's rule has the same exalted tone as the Testament of Francis, which Clare undoubtedly had in mind as she wrote. When they reached the climax—the end—of their lives, both Francis and Clare reviewed the fundamental stages of their lives in the light of a lacerating and purifying suffering, indicating their animating passions and final illuminations, and striving to communicate the highest degree of insight they had achieved. Even the language and literary genre differentiate this chapter from the rest of the text and reveal the author's independent spiritual temperament, one that was not timidly closed in by formal regulation, yet still able to translate her living ideals into concrete specifications. But to comprehend the rule from within and understand more deeply the life and animating spirit of her earliest followers, there is no finer source than the splendid record of Clare's canonization proceedings.

The testimony of Clare's companions described her entirely Franciscan governance, acting (as the rule prescribed) as the spiritual mother and servant to her sisters. They recalled the tender care she displayed in her everyday actions, which revealed her concrete and tangible love, her personal attention to each of them, and above all, her mercy. In the rule, Clare stipulated that the abbess has a specific duty to console the afflicted because "if they fail to find in her the means of health, the sickness of despair might overcome the weak."[44] But the energy with which Clare applied this precept is shown in the testimony of Sister Agnes, daughter of Messer Oportulo, who stated that when Clare saw that "one of the sisters was suffering from temptation or tribulation," she would take the unhappy woman aside and in private "console her with tears, sometimes throwing herself at her feet."[45]

The canonization proceedings also indicate the sources that nourished the spiritual life of the sisters. Listening to the Scriptures, especially through sermons, was undoubtedly among the principal ones: the same Sister Agnes testified that "Lady Clare took great delight in hearing the word of God."[46] This trait was also recalled and elaborated by the author of her *vita*.[47] Further evidence of the importance Clare attached to the word of God was her sharp disagreement with Gregory IX on this very subject, which I have already discussed. Here, interestingly enough, we glimpse the beginnings of that need for serious spiritual nourishment that was to lead to the creation of a body of religious literature in the vernacular, originating within the female mendicant orders. Moreover, it reminds us that not only the laity but also the convents—at least those of these new orders—felt ever more acutely the need to draw nearer to the Holy Scriptures, in particular the Gospels, and so expected the preacher to serve essentially as a mediator of the word of God.

The liturgy, which, moreover, was itself based on the word of God, represented another great source of spiritual teaching for Clare and her sisters. Finally, their prayer (as far as one can tell from the testimony of Clare's companions) essentially centered on heartfelt and loving participation in the principal moments in the life of Christ, particularly his Passion.[48] For these women, therefore, the Word, the liturgy, and prayer constituted the living well from which they drew the mystery of Christ. Clare also expressed this profound truth through simple yet evocative gestures, such as the distribution of holy water to the sisters after compline in memory of the water that gushed from the side of the crucified Christ, which is commemorated in the chant of the aspersion during the Easter season.[49]

Here is perhaps their very essence, the sap that flows unobtrusively through the entire existence of Clare and her companions and makes them Franciscans rather than Benedictines: this meaningfulness of all things, the expression—through actions and through words that were measured yet charged and vital—of the mystery of life that they were conscious of living. Thus the sign of the cross, which Clare delighted in making over humble everyday objects, washing the feet of the *serviziali,* which she surely performed in the spirit of that passage from John 13 so dear to Francis as well, waking the nuns in the middle of the night to call them "with certain signs to praise God," all attest to the spiritual tension, present not only in "religious" moments but pervading her every living action, that imbued her life with flavor and meaning.[50]

Innocent IV's acceptance of her rule marked the end of both Clare's life and the difficult process that had shaped the group of San Damiano, through acts of obedience and resistance, into a specifically Franciscan order founded on strict fidelity to poverty. But these women who roamed barefoot throughout northern Italy and as far afield as Spain, France, and Germany, robed in the cord and habit of San Damiano (and thus were known as the *discalceatae, chordulariae,* or *Minoretae*) worried the papacy, and Gregory IX in 1241, Innocent IV in 1250, and Alexander IV in 1257 and 1261 all solicited in ever sharper terms the intervention of ecclesiastical authorities. Could one say that there was no place within the thirteenth-century church for this particular expression of the spirit of the female Franciscan movement?[51]

This question is unavoidable, given the inflexible obligation of strict cloister that Boniface VIII imposed on all female monastics in 1298. The entire population of female nuns, no matter what their spirit and goals, was forced to express itself from behind the grates, within the enclosed space of the cloister.

In this instance as well, the Poor Clares were the order on which the papacy depended for a renewal of female monasticism, which could only arise from a stark and resolute radicality of life, whose meaning and direction, however, were conceived and presented to women exclusively as a contemplative existence protected and safeguarded from contact with their surroundings.[52]

This prospect should be kept in mind, even if the struggle of Clare and her companions is only measured by their fidelity to the purest poverty, which they understood to be a condition of life reduced to its bare essentials and also an attitude of creatureliness and total dependence on the Father.

Clare and her companions were not only the most rigorous and fervent interpreters of the marrow of Francis's message, but also reaffirmed within the thirteenth-century church and society the revolutionary and highly contested value of poverty in all its radicality.

NOTES

Originally published in *Movimento religioso femminile e francescanesimo nel secolo XIII*, Proceedings of the Seventh Conference of the International Society for Franciscan Studies, Assisi, 11–13 October 1979 (Assisi, 1980), pp. 169–91.

    1. R. B. C. Huygens, *Lettres de Jacques de Vitry: Edition critique* (Leyden, 1960), pp. 75–76; translated in *St. Francis of Assisi, Writings and Early Biographies: English Omnibus of the Sources for the Life of St. Francis*, ed. Marion A. Habig (Chicago, 1983), pp. 1608–9.

    2. Herbert Grundmann, *Movimenti religiosi nel Medioevo: Ricerche sui nessi storici tra la eresia, gli ordini mendicanti e il movimento religioso femminile nel XII and XIII secolo e sulle origini storiche della mistica tedesca* (Bologna, 1974), p. 132 n. 149.

    3. Huygens, *Lettres de Jacques de Vitry*, p. 75.

    4. The emphasis on unanimity appears in Francis's final charge to the nuns of San Damiano: "Vivere et humiliter conversari et esse unanimes in charitate" (live and converse humbly, and be of one mind in charity) (*Speculum perfectionis seu S. Francisci Assisiensis Legenda antiquissima auctore frate Leone*, ed. Paul Sabatier [Paris, 1898], chap. 90, pp. 180–81; translated as *Mirror of Perfection* in Habig, *St. Francis of Assisi: Omnibus of Sources*, pp. 1223–24). The song that Francis supposedly wrote for the nuns of San Damiano has been published by Giovanni Boccali, "Canto di esortazione di S. Francesco per le 'Poverelle' di San Damiano," *Collectanea Franciscana* 48 (1978): 5–29; translated as "The Canticle of Exhortation to Saint Clare and Her Sisters" in *Francis and Clare: The Complete Works*, ed. Regis J. Armstrong and Ignatius C. Brady (New York, 1982), pp. 40–41.

    5. Zefferino Lazzeri, "Il processo di canonizzazione di Santa Chiara di Assisi," in *Archivum Franciscanum Historicum* 13 (1920): 491 (witness 18, art. 6).

    6. The high social standing of the early recruits is emphasized by Jacques Guy Bougerol, "Il reclutamento sociale delle Clarisse di Assisi," in *Les ordres mendiants et la ville en Italie centrale, v. 1220–1350*, in *Mélanges de l'Ecole française de Rome, Moyen Age–temps modernes* 89 (1977): 629–32.

    7. Kajetan Esser, *Opuscula sancti patris Francisci Assisiensis*, Bibliotheca Franciscana Ascetica Medii Aevi, 12 (Grottaferrata, 1978), p. 162 (translated as "The Form of Life Given to Saint Clare and Her Sisters" in Armstrong and Brady, *Francis and Clare*, pp. 44–45); "Clarae Regula," chap. 6, lines 2–4, in Giovanni Boccali, *Concordantiae verbales opusculorum S. Francisci et S. Clarae Assisiensium* (Santa Maria degli Angeli, Assisi, 1976), p. 174 (translated as "The Rule of St. Clare" in

Armstrong and Brady, *Francis and Clare*, pp. 218–19); "Clarae Testamentum," lines 29 and 33, in Boccali, *Concordantiae*, pp. 186 and 187 (translated as "The Testament of St. Clare" in Armstrong and Brady, *Francis and Clare*, pp. 226–32, esp. p. 228, 229).

8. "Clarae Testamentum," line 34 (p. 187) (Armstrong and Brady, *Francis and Clare*, p. 229).

9. Thomas of Celano, *Vita secunda S. Francisci*, in *Analecta Franciscana* 10 (1926–41), chap. 157, par. 207; translated in Habig, *St. Francis of Assisi: Omnibus of Sources*, pp. 527–28.

10. On this attitude, see Grundmann, *Movimenti religiosi*.

11. Roberto Rusconi, "L'espansione del francescanesimo femminile nel secolo XIII," in *Movimento religioso femminile e francescanesimo*, pp. 265–313.

12. Lazzeri, "Il processo," pp. 446 (witness 1, art. 15) and 445 (witness 1, art. 14).

13. Ibid., p. 469 (witness 7, art. 11).

14. Nicolaus Glassberger, *Chronica*, in *Analecta Franciscana* 2 (1887): 572.

15. Giancarlo Andenna's very important and detailed analysis of San Pietro di Cavagnetto, near Novara, can serve as a model: "Le Clarisse nel Novarese, 1252–1300," *Archivum Franciscanum Historicum* 67 (1974): 185–267.

16. Thomas of Celano, *Vita prima S. Francisci*, in *Analecta Franciscana* 10 (1926–41), chap. 28, par. 78 (translated in Habig, *St. Francis of Assisi: Omnibus of Sources*, p. 294); *Vita secunda*, chap. 72, par. 106 (Habig, *St. Francis of Assisi: Omnibus of Sources*, pp. 448–50).

17. "Cum igitur dilectae in Christo filiae pauperes Moniales Sancti Salvatoris de Colpressato Sancti Severini terrenam substantiam abnegantes pro Christo, et sufficientam suam in paupertate ponentes Fidelium eleemosynis elegerint sustentari" (*Bullarii Franciscani Epitome*, ed. Conrad Eubel [Quaracchi, 1908], no. 77).

18. Mario Sensi, "Le Clarisse a Foligno nel secolo XIII," in *Collectanea Franciscana* 47 (1977): 349–63.

19. "II Epistula S. Clarae ad Agnetem," lines 17–18, in Boccali, *Concordantiae*, p. 204 (Armstrong and Brady, *Francis and Clare*, p. 197).

20. *Bullarium Franciscanum*, 1: 394–99.

21. Kajetan Esser, "Die Briefe Gregors IX. an die hl. Klara von Assisi," in *Franziskanische Studien* 35 (1953): 274-95. The letter describing his visit to San Damiano, "Ab illa hora" (p. 277), presumably dates from sometime after Easter 1220; it is also the source of the expression "mater salutis suae," referring to Clare.

22. Thomas of Celano, *Vita prima*, part 3, par. 122 (Habig, *St. Francis of Assisi: Omnibus of Sources*, pp. 336–37).

23. *Bullarium Franciscanum*, 1: 243.

24. See Chiara Augusta Lainati's introduction to *Scritti e fonti biografiche di S. Chiara d'Assisi*, section 4 of *Fonti francescane*, vol. 2 (Assisi, 1977), p. 2227.

25. "Regula pro eremitoriis data," in Esser, *Opuscula*, pp. 296–98 (translated in Armstrong and Brady, *Francis and Clare*, p. 147): "Those who wish to live religiously in hermitages should be three brothers or four at the most; two of these

should be mothers and they may have two sons or at least one. The two who are mothers should follow the life of Martha, while the two sons should follow the life of Mary."

26. Lazzeri, "Il processo," pp. 453–54 (witness 3, art. 9) and 475 (witness 10, art. 6).

27. *Bullarium Franciscanum,* 1: 476–83, esp. 482.

28. Ibid., pp. 394–99, esp. p. 396.

29. According to the testimony of Sister Angeluccia de messer Angeleio da Spoleto: Lazzeri, "Il processo," p. 485 (witness 14, art. 9).

30. Ibid., pp. 465 (witness 6, art. 6) and 468 (witness 7, art. 2).

31. *Bullarium Franciscanum,* 1: 395.

32. "IV Epistola S. Clarae ad Agnetem," line 21, in Boccali, *Concordantiae,* p. 214 (translated in Armstrong and Brady, *Francis and Clare,* p. 205).

33. "In hoc autem speculo refulget beata paupertas, sancta humilitas et ineffabilis caritas, sicut per totum speculum poteris cum Dei gratia contemplari" (ibid., line 18 [p. 214]); "In fine vero eiusdem speculi contemplare ineffabilem caritatem, qua pati voluit in crucis stipite et in eodem mori omni mortis genere turpiori" (line 23 [pp. 214–15]) (Armstrong and Brady, *Francis and Clare,* p. 205).

34. Lazzeri, "Il processo," pp. 480–81 (witness 12, art. 6).

35. Ibid., p. 454 (witness 3, art. 14).

36. *Legenda sanctae Clarae virginis,* ed. Francesco Pennacchi (Assisi, 1910), no. 14.

37. "Abundante iniquitate et refrigescente caritate multorum necessitas nimia" (Luke Wadding, *Annales Minorum, 1221–1237,* vol. 2 [Quaracchi, 1931], p. 681).

38. Ibid., p. 687.

39. Herbert Grundmann, "Die bulle 'Quo elongati' Papst Gregors IX," *Archivum Franciscanum Historicum* 54 (1961): 3–25; reprinted in Grundmann, *Ausgewählte Aufsätze,* vol. 1, *Religiöse Bewegungen,* Schriften der Monumenta Germaniae Historica, vol. 25, no. 1 (Stuttgart, 1976), pp. 222–42. The bull appears on pp. 236–42; the passage in question is on pp. 241–42.

40. "IV Epistula," line 4 (p. 213) (Armstrong and Brady, *Francis and Clare,* p. 203).

41. The suggestion of Clare's prompting is cautiously advanced in Heribert Roggen's succinct, lively, and intelligent book *The Spirit of St. Clare,* trans. Paul Joseph Oligny (Chicago, 1971).

42. *Bullarium Franciscanum,* 1: 476–83.

43. Lazzeri, "Il processo," p. 459 (witness 3, art. 32).

44. "Clarae Regula," chap. 4, line 2 (p. 17): "Consoletur afflictas. Sit etiam ultimum refugium tribulatis, ne, si apud, eam remedia defuerint sanitatum, desperationis morbus prevaleat in informis" (translated in Armstrong and Brady, *Francis and Clare,* p. 215).

45. Lazzeri, "Il processo," p. 475 (witness 10, art. 5).

46. Ibid., pp. 475–76 (witness 10, art. 8).

47. *Legenda sanctae Clarae,* chap. 37.

48. Lazzeri, "Il processo," pp. 474 (witness 10, art. 3), 476 (witness 10, art. 10), and 477 (witness 11, art. 2).

49. Ibid., p. 485 (witness 14, art. 8).

50. For Clare's signing of the cross, see ibid., pp. 446–47 (witness 1, art. 16–18), 453 (witness 3, art. 6) and passim; *Legenda sanctae Clarae*, chaps. 32–35. In the *Little Flowers of St. Francis*, Clare's image is linked with the blessing of the loaves of bread in the presence of Gregory IX, during one of the pope's visits to San Damiano, and the miracle of the sign of the cross that remained imprinted on the bread (Habig, *St. Francis of Assisi: Omnibus of Sources*, pp. 1380–82). The eucharistic miracles associated with Clare, such as this one in the *Little Flowers* and another in which breads were multiplied, recounted during her canonization proceedings, demonstrate that those around her were aware of her very intense devotion to the eucharist (see Lazzeri, "Il processo," p. 467 [witness 6, art. 16]). Perhaps this element could enrich and add nuance to the discussion of Clare's sacerdotal behavior, or at least the witnesses' interpretation of it in these terms, over and above the circumstances of the attack of the "Saracens" on San Damiano, in the face of which Clare supposedly carried—or had someone else carry—the holy sacrament (ibid., pp. 471–72 [witness 9, art. 2] and passim).

On Clare's footwashing, see ibid., pp. 453–54 (witness 3, art. 9) and 475 (witness 10, art. 6); and on midnight calls to prayer, p. 449 (witness 2, art. 9).

51. *Bullarium Franciscanum*, 1: 290 and 541–42; 2: 183–84 and 417.

52. On this topic, see, among others, Robert Brentano, *Two Churches: England and Italy in the Thirteenth Century*, 2d ed. (Berkeley and Los Angeles, 1988), pp. 284–85.

4

Anchoresses and Penitents in Thirteenth- and Fourteenth-Century Umbria

Mario Sensi

The female penitential movement in central Italy, which had taken hold with renewed energy at the end of the twelfth century, found its first spokesman and director in Cardinal Ugolino Conti di Segni. This prelate, as papal legate in Tuscia and Lombardy between 1217 and 1219, and then, from 1227, as Pope Gregory IX, supervised the institutional aspects of the female religious movement until his death in 1241.[1]

This movement represented the religious response to a long-term social and political transformation. As a closed peasant civilization gradually became more urban and international, the religious ideal of monastic life gave way to an urban eremitism based directly on the Gospels and the *imitatio Christi*.[2] At its outset, this movement involved primarily members of the ruling classes, the urban patriciate and the lesser nobility, while shopkeepers and artisans remained untouched by religious malaise.[3]

It must be added that this phenomenon took the bishops almost by surprise. In fact, the problem posed by the penitential religious movement had been addressed by the Fourth Lateran Council in 1215. The bishops, who held the right to approve the founding of religious communities within the boundaries of their own dioceses, were henceforth supposed to adhere to the new norms formulated in the canon *Ne nimia religionum diversitas*. This decree expressly forbade anyone in the future from founding a new order; anyone who wished to enter the religious life had to adopt one of the rules that had already been approved by the church.[4] In practice, these decisions should have blocked the penitential religious movement is its infancy.

This is the context in which we must place the actions of Cardinal

Ugolino, his myriad tiny decisions that add up to an entire program. More-over, herein lies the answer to the question of whether in Italy, at the begin-ning of the thirteenth century, there was a female movement comparable to that emerging in northern France, Brabant, the Lower Rhineland, and a little later in Provence.[5]

The Penitential Movement at the Beginning of the Thirteenth Century

Our picture of the female penitential movement in central Italy at the begin-ning of the thirteenth century is derived from a few terse literary sources, most of which have Franciscan resonances, and some archival documents. The most important literary sources are a letter of Jacques de Vitry, written from Genoa in October 1216; the *Life of St. Clare of Assisi,* written by a Franciscan (perhaps Thomas of Celano) and usually dated 1256, which parallels the letter of Jacques de Vitry; and *The Legend of the Three Com-panions,* the most important of the unofficial biographies of St. Francis, which contains statements that echo Thomas of Celano's.[6]

These sources portray three distinct forms taken by the women's move-ment in central Italy: the cenobitic life of moderately cloistered commu-nities; the eremitical life of solitary oblates, recluses, and hermits, whether within the city or outside its walls; and the penitential life followed by women in their own homes, for whom the *Memoriale propositi fratrum et sororum de penitentia* was drafted.[7]

This categorization is confirmed point by point in archival documents. The papers of the convent of Vallegloria, near Spello, make it clear that be-fore it entered the orbit of San Damiano, this distinctive female community was made up of penitents who did not follow any of the approved rules and lived in moderate seclusion, in keeping with the setting of the convent.[8] Documents from 1208 in Spoleto archives relate that a female penitent, probably an oblate of the cathedral church, invoked the *privilegium fori* when a legal action was brought against her.[9] And in the provincial chapter that the Dominicans held in Perugia in 1249 it was decided "that the friars should avoid frequent and conspicuous contact with *bizzoche* . . . and the confessions of *bizzoche* should be heard infrequently."[10] According to Jacques de Vitry, there was no doubt that *bizzoca* was the Italian word for "beguine."[11]

But the few documents that have survived do not allow us to determine the origins of this phenomenon, let alone quantify it. This is a problem that already troubled contemporary observers, but for which they could not find a convincing answer. Thus the chronicler John the Spaniard, who taught in

Bologna in the 1250s, declared that the movement's origins were unknown, and spoke of "female penitents *[pynzocarae]* who just recently arose from the dust," in a sort of spontaneous generation.[12]

Since there was no codified curial procedure for dealing with this pan-European phenomenon, and since the penitential movement and the monastic orders remained aloof from one another, the women's religious movement generated a variety of institutional forms.[13] This is apparent even in the pattern of settlements. In northern Europe, devout women *(religiosae mulieres)* commonly gathered in a single cluster of buildings, a religious city within the secular one: a spiritual stronghold with its own streets, its own town squares, its special buildings for communal life, and small hermitages on a human scale. This was a characteristic Flemish phenomenon, which began in 1233 and soon spread throughout Europe.[14] In Italy, in contrast, particularity and fragmentation prevailed. Each group maintained its individuality, giving rise to a multitude of small convents. By the end of the thirteenth century, the cities of northern and central Italy swarmed with little convents located just outside the walls, forming a sort of protective belt around the city, the religious equivalent of a city wall.[15] This urban design was the result of a long process whose stages can be traced, permitting us, among other things, to perceive some analogies between the women's religious movement in Italy and the beguine movement to the north of the Alps.

Ugolino Conti di Segni and the Transformation of Anchoresses into Nuns

The Franciscans and the Dominicans were the first who had to formulate an institutional response to the demands of the female penitential movement; but their initial reaction was to evade the task. The Chapter General of 1228 prohibited the Dominicans from admitting virgins to the status of penitents too easily.[16] Subsequently, the Dominicans were advised to visit the *domus beghinarum,* the beguine houses, only on rare occasions.[17] For his part, St. Francis had forbidden his friars from accepting vows of obedience from every pious woman who wished to devote herself to God.[18] He made an exception for Clare of Assisi, the "first little plant," to whose community, located in San Damiano, he had given the *forma vitae* before 1217.[19]

Clare's vocation had progressed through two stages considered to be antithetical: Benedictine monasticism and the urban eremitism of the emerging penitential movement.[20] The movement of the Poor Ladies, under Clare's leadership, represented a synthesis that resolved the differences between traditional monasticism and the newer style of semireligious life, the *bizzocaggio.*[21] This leap forward came about through the providential intervention of St. Francis and Cardinal Ugolino. During his legation in Umbria, Ugolino immediately recognized the novelty of the penitential movement and accordingly consulted with Pope Honorius II. Only a summary of his letter has survived, incorporated in the bull that the pope sent to Cardinal Ugolino on 27 August 1218.[22] It tells how "virgins and women" of patrician birth had abandoned the world and withdrawn to "houses . . . in which the inhabitants lived possessing nothing under the sun except for the houses themselves." Since these houses did not yet contain an oratory, they had no standing in ecclesiastical law. But this pauperistic movement enjoyed such great support among the urban aristocracy that many nobles approached the cardinal, as representative of the Roman curia, with offers of land on which to build the chapels of these new communities, which received women of both the noble class and the upper bourgeoisie who were kept from marrying by social constraints. Thus the ruling classes were interested in the penitential movement not only for religious reasons, but also for social and political ones. The laity sought to exempt the movement from ordinary episcopal jurisdiction: this, it seems to me, was their reason for donating lands to the church for the creation of monastic oratories.[23] Episcopal jurisdiction had to be evaded in order to avoid running afoul of the decree *Ne nimia religionum diversitas.* Eager to find a solution that would best meet the desires of the notables in his legation, Cardinal Ugolino sought the pope's counsel. Honorius III departed from the dispositions of the Fourth Lateran Council by granting this new mendicant movement the privilege of exemption; however, he ordered convents with property to pay the bishop an annual fee. On all other matters he granted wide authority to the cardinal legate.[24] On the strength of this mandate, Cardinal Ugolino issued a rule, the *formula vitae,* which institutionalized the movement, transforming the idea of *fuga mundi,* flight from the world, into *reclusio perpetua,* perpetual reclusion, or absolute separation from one's surroundings.[25] And so that the various groups of women would have identical structures and rules, Ugolino entrusted the *Pauperes dominae* to the disciplinary and spiritual care of his chaplains: the Cistercian Fra Ambrogio, still active in Foligno in 1230; Brunetto Oldradi de Carmaniago, active in Milan in 1224; Fra Pacifico, documented in connection with the houses in Milan, Spello, Siena, and Gubbio; Fra Bonaccorso, also documented for Gubbio, in 1226; Frangipane di Vitale of Perugia, procurator for Gregory IX in Spello and Cortona between 1235 and 1237; and Giovanni di San Germano (Cassino), in Spoleto and Todi, between 1236 and 1243.[26] It even seems that some funds were appropriated for the female penitential movement. This would explain the financial operations on behalf of some communities, like Santa Maria "inter Angulos" in Spoleto: according to the text of the episcopal privilege of 1232, this convent of Poor Clares had been built thanks to the munificence of Pope Gregory IX himself, who "de pecunia sua construi fec[er]it," had it built with his own money.[27]

Ugolino's policies, both as cardinal and as pope, aimed at channeling the movement into a single stream and ensuring that the new communities followed a uniform set of regulations. When Pope Gregory IX wrote to the nuns of San Paolo, near Spoleto, in 1227, he reminded them how "while we were still in a lesser office," that is, while he was still a cardinal, "dedicating yourselves totally to God, you delivered yourselves to perpetual seclusion": in other words, upon the request of the cardinal, these nuns accepted the cloistered life. The document goes on to say that this increase in religiosity, which was indicated precisely by the strict cloister now observed in their community, should be accompanied by an increase in liberty. For this reason the pope forbade the bishop from subjecting their convent to ecclesiastical censures.[28] Reclusion and the privilege of exemption were the twin pillars of Cardinal Ugolino's policies, to which after he became pope he added the requirement that every convent have an endowment sufficient to maintain it. His new concern was thus to provide possessions and secure incomes for the convents that lived according to the *formula vitae* he had prescribed.[29] To be sure, the *Privilegium Paupertatis*—the privilege of poverty that was the defining feature of the *observantiae regulares,* the observance of the rule at San Damiano—soon distinguished that convent and all of the others formed on that model, and hence dedicated to the observance of poverty, from the rest of the monastic current commonly referred to as the Order of St. Damian, and later of St. Clare.[30] In fact, this female monastic order might more appropriately be named for Ugolino (or Gregory IX), who organized it. This was even asserted by his first biographer, a curial official who called him the founder of the "dominarum inclusarum" while he was still a cardinal.[31]

In documentary terms, the institutionalization of the female religious movement in the first half of the thirteenth century was signaled by the privilege *Prudentibus virginibus,* sent to all the individual communities that Cardinal Ugolino had managed to bring under his rule.[32] It contained confirmation of their canonical foundation, a model of which Ugolino sent to the bishops, their exemption from ordinary episcopal jurisdiction, and the *formula vitae* that the new or reconstituted community was to follow.[33] This privilege was confirmed by Honorius III in the bull *Sacrosanta romana ecclesia,* in the form, however, of *litterae gratiosae,* which was more generic than the privilege and therefore less binding for the Roman curia.[34] The final stage of this process was reached with the bull *Religiosam vitam eligentibus.* But no community of Poor Clares succeeded in obtaining this broad apostolic privilege from Honorius III; most of them received it from his successor, Gregory IX.[35]

The policies that Cardinal Ugolino promoted at the Roman curia, and then directed himself as pope, bore remarkable fruit: within the arc of a few years, the female penitential movement in central Italy was brought almost entirely under control. Many of the new communities that sprang up as a result of this movement received their institutional structure from Ugolino's *formula vitae*. This explains the sudden appearance of so many communities of Poor Clares in those years, and forces us to rethink the question of how many convents were spawned by the community of San Damiano and in what way—that is, whether they were created by St. Clare herself or by her early companions.[36] To be sure, traditional monasticism, especially the Cistercian order, long continued to be one of the institutional outlets for the female religious movement. Thus, three female Cistercian communities were founded in Perugia between 1218 and 1253; the last of them, Santa Giuliana, was large enough to house up to 121 nuns.[37] In 1258, the congregation "Servarum b. Mariae virginis" was formed in Gubbio: the constitution of this female congregation derived from the Benedictine rule, but with modifications that reflected current developments.[38] Nor did Cardinal Ugolino sweep earlier Benedictine institutions into the Order of St. Damian, as has recently been asserted for San Paolo "inter vineas" in Spoleto, Santa Maria di Vallegloria in Spello, and San Angelo di Panzo in Assisi. In fact, before adopting Ugolino's *formula vitae,* these three institutions were loose associations of penitents that did not follow any of the approved rules.[39] When faced with such groups, the Roman curia sought to bring them under strict control, but without necessarily subjecting the entire penitential movement to Ugolino's *formula vitae.* Assisi itself provides an example. Whatever his reasons may have been, on 13 September 1229, Gregory IX conceded the privilege of exemption from ordinary episcopal jurisdiction to "priorisse et sororibus ecclesie S. Apolinaris in Flan. Asisinat. diocesis," the prioress and sisters of the church of San Apollinare in the diocese of Assisi. And as late as 1264, this community, which has wrongly been regarded as Benedictine from its inception, was headed not by an abbess but by a rectress, a certain Jacoba, who was "domina et rectrix sororum que morantur in loco qui dicitur locus S. Appolenaris," mistress and rectress of the sisters who reside in a place called the home of San Apollinare. In that year, this community—which consisted of sisters, not nuns—acquired some property within the walls of Assisi "ad agendum in eis penitentiam," to use in doing penance. In other words, they built a hermitage, which only later came under the Benedictine rule.[40] This is a clear example of the beguine manner of life, or rather that of the *bizzoche,* for in Italy that was the name given to these quasi-nuns. Moreover, if the papal exemption from ordinary episcopal jurisdiction freed the community from the obligation of adopting one of the approved rules (that is, of being monasticized in accordance with the constitution *Ne nimia religionum diversitas* of 1215), it also allowed the Roman curia to take precautions against any risk of disorder. It is hardly necessary to remind the reader that Jacques de Vitry obtained a similar concession for his beguines from Pope Honorius III in 1216.[41]

However, when faced with groups that refused to submit to episcopal jurisdiction and simultaneously attempted to elude the necessary control of the curia, Gregory IX was implacable, resorting even to suppression. This is what happened in Spoleto to the *bizzoche* community of San Concordio, another group that has erroneously been considered Benedictine: in 1235 Gregory IX ordered his chaplain Giovanni di San Germano to suppress it.[42]

The Vacillating Policies of the Bishops in the Mid Thirteenth Century

During Gregory IX's lifetime, the bishops of Umbria had little independent opportunity to direct the female movement. The surviving documentation contains nothing more than some privileges of canonical institution and exemption modeled after the *specimen* provided by Cardinal Ugolino. But during the pontificate of Innocent IV, direction of the penitential movement passed into the hand of the bishops. Some of them, right down to the Second Council of Lyons in 1274, used Ugolino's *formula vitae* to institutionalize the new groups of penitent women that had taken shape: the *Bullarium Franciscanum* records twelve new convents on which this rule was imposed between 1225 and 1260.[43] But more recent archival research has shown that many other houses were founded in that same period. For example, Oliger's exemplary studies of Città di Castello revealed the existence of four convents of Poor Clares in the thirteenth century and five in the fourteenth century, inspiring him to exclaim that perhaps nowhere else did St. Clare have so many disciples; yet great historians such as Wadding and Gonzaga, and even Sbaraglia's *Bullarium,* mention only a few of these convents, leaving the rest in absolute silence.[44] The same could be said of many other Umbrian cities, such as Foligno, Gubbio, and Todi, where similar studies have produced similar results. However, in towns where it was not possible to found new convents of Poor Clares, usually because of the opposition of established convents, the new groups were institutionalized under either the Benedictine or Augustinian rule and subject to ordinary episcopal jurisdiction. One representative case is the institionalization of various communities founded in precisely these years in the diocese of Spoleto. In 1244

Bartolomeo Accoramboni, bishop of Spoleto—the very person who, a few years later, in 1253, was entrusted by the pope with conducting the canonization proceeding for Clare of Assisi—granted a privilege of canonical foundation to Agnes "the mother superior and to the sisters of the church of Santa Maria of Civitella, in the diocese of Spoleto, of the order of St. Benedict."[45] The privilege, which begins with the words "Ex iniuncto nobis pastoralis officii," repeats word-for-word the privileges granted to convents of Poor Clares, including, for example, that of Santa Maria "Vallis gaudii" in Città di Castello.[46] But in the case of Santa Maria of Civitella (which later moved to Bevagna and took the name of Santa Maria del Monte) the bishop imposed the Benedictine rule, which is professed by that community to this day, and asserted his own jurisdiction over the institution.[47] Ten years later, in 1254, the same bishop institutionalized the noble *bizzoche* who had retired to a hermitage on the hill of San Tommaso, two miles from Spoleto, obliging them to accept the Augustinian rule, observe cloister, and assist the foundlings and poor of the Ospedale Nuovo (or della Stella), the great new urban hospital that was promoted by the bishop himself.[48] The case of Spello, also in the diocese of Spoleto, is no less interesting. On 15 April 1258, Alexander IV granted the abbess of the Clarissan monastery of Vallegloria in Spello the indult *Dignum est,* which stated that the convent could not be compelled to receive or support any new nuns. On 29 May 1259, the same pope ordered the bishop of Spoleto to forbid the building of new monasteries, whether for monks or nuns, in Spello and its territory, which was replete with them: in particular, a new female community would have caused great harm to the convent of Vallegloria. But despite this interdiction, a monk named Riccardo initiated the construction of a new convent for women in Spello, which, on 15 March 1259, Alexander IV ordered the bishop of Nocera Umbra to have destroyed within twenty days.[49] Nevertheless, four years later this disputed community of SS. Filippo and Giacomo came under the apostolic protection of the new pope, Urban IV, whose consistorial bull *Religiosam vitam eligentibus* confirmed it under the Benedictine rule.[50] About one year later, the pope extended the same broad privilege to another Spoletan monastery, Santa Margherita "iuxta Spoletum," though the rule to be observed there was Augustinian.[51]

In the final year of his papacy, Gregory IX's bull *Ad audientiam* had decreed that bishops should take action against the *religio simulata,* the feigned religion of certain women who were passing themselves off as Damianites.[52] Nonetheless, this movement continued to find converts, and eventually even earned papal privileges: on 20 April 1250, Innocent IV announced to some north-Italian bishops that he had abrogated the bulls promulgated in support of the *sorores minores,* who in reality were only unregulated poor women who wandered about with the intention of founding convents of the Order of St. Damian.[53] This had come about because of the indifference of both the bishops and the mendicant orders toward the female penitential movement, which had found new life in this period. At times, their indifference may even have shaded into open hostility, as some of the hagiographic literature seems to indicate. The *legenda* of Umiliana dei Cerchi (†1246) recounts her vain efforts to enter the Poor Clares of Monticelli, which parallel Rose of Viterbo's (†1252) equally futile attempts to join the Poor Clares of her city.[54] And perhaps all too often, behind some of these rejections lay hidden political reasons or even family quarrels.

The Revival of the *Bizzoche* Movement

From shortly after 1250, Umbrian municipal archives record with some frequency the existence of solitary female recluses who were not part of religious communities. We have fairly detailed information concerning one such recluse in Trevi: a woman named Sofia, daughter of the late Bartolo di Bernardo. According to a deposition she made during the canonization proceedings for the blessed Simone da Collazzone, Sofia entered a cell around 1232. Five years later, she had contracted such severe arthritis that she could no longer move, yet she was able to remain in her cell thanks to the help of a companion "que erat in ipso carcere," who was in the same cell. Sofia seems to have had two successive servants or companions, one of whom related during the canonization proceedings of 1252 that she had often accompanied Sofia "ad fenestram carceris," to the cell's window-grate.[55] Sofia evidently observed strict reclusion, while an attendant who lived with her took care of any necessary contact with the outside world. This deposition also reveals that Sofia shared her cell with women who became recluses for a limited period: one of them was a certain Illuminata di Pietro from Montefalco, who spent an entire Lent with Sofia. But this hospitality was purely temporary, and the cell never housed a community of recluses.

The frequent testimentary bequests made in these years in favor of male and female recluses, and of men and women given to the penitential life as *bizzochi* and *bizzoche*, clearly indicate the renewed vigor of this phenomenon. Its range and vitality are demonstrated in two important documents from Perugia: on 26 May 1277, the municipality of Perugia distributed offerings to twenty female and two male recluses living in the Porta Sole and the Porta Eburnea neighborhoods; and on 5 June of the same year, fully thirty-six female and eight male recluses received communal charity.[56] Cells like these, in which a single male recluse or one or two female recluses lived in strict or moderate seclusion, were hard for the bishops to control. But this was, nevertheless, a phenomenon of vast proportions, as is confirmed by the depositions of various experts whose reports were examined at the Second Council of Lyons (1274). They voiced two concerns regarding these women, who lived as religious but did not submit to the bonds of a religious order and a religious community: the risks to their chastity, since they wandered begging through cities or villages and talked at length with any comer, and the threat of heresy. Indeed, the Franciscan Gilbert of Tournai, taking aim at some Parisian groups, complained in his report that beguines passed around religious writings in the vernacular and commentaries on the Bible in French and, worst of all, founded conventicles that were far too perilous: the mere fact that ignorant women would devote themselves to theology was dangerous in its own right.[57]

Scarcely twenty years later, this phenomenon was repeated in the valley of Spoleto, where, toward the end of the thirteenth century, groups of devotees formed around two products of the penitential movement of recluses, Clare of Montefalco and Angela of Foligno.[58] Both these women were representatives of orthodox mysticism, in whose name they embarked on a fierce struggle against the heretical mysticism propagated by the movement of the Free Spirit.[59]

If we can believe the foundation myth of San Rocco of Montefalco, this house of *bizzochi,* which later became one of the cradles of the Franciscan Third Order Regular, was founded by beghards from Provence who were summoned to Montefalco by St. Clare herself.[60] It is certainly true that there were contacts between Provence and the valley of Spoleto: the biography of St. Clare written by Béranger Donadieu of Saint-Affrique mentions the beguine Marguerite of Carcassonne among Clare's followers, and two manuscripts written in Provençal ended up in Assisi and Todi.[61] But the documents that have come to light so far have not sufficiently clarified the connections between the spiritual current in Provence that was headed by Peter John Olivi and the current or currents that inspired the two communities in the valley of Spoleto. The group in Foligno must have excited particular interest, if the visions of Angela of Foligno aroused comment as far away as Paris; and it was in Paris that Ubertino of Casale became so fascinated by the doctrine of the blessed Angela that he radically changed his way of life: "so that from that moment on I would no longer be the same person that I was."[62]

These groups in Foligno and Montefalco display the characteristic yearnings of a movement of *bizzoche* that was Franciscan in outlook, and in scale far greater than any seen before it in the valley of Spoleto. In a few short years at the end of the thirteenth century, there sprang up almost everywhere *monasteria, oratoria, domus ad penitentiam peragendam*— monasteries, oratories, houses for living in penitence—for men and women who had decided "in habitu religionis Domino famulari," to become servants of God in religious habits. In Spoleto and its vicinity, no fewer than thirteen female communities were founded in less than ten years; four others were founded in Foligno, four in Montefalco, two in Bevagna, one in Spello, and so on.[63] These women pursued their sanctification through meditation on the Passion of Christ, penitence, discipline, and almost total reliance on charity for their sustenance—themes that recur constantly in hagiographic literature such as the *legenda* of the life and miracles of St. Margaret of Cortona and the *vita* of St. Clare of Montefalco.[64]

The Second Council of Lyons had left unsolved the problems posed by the movement of the beguines and *bizzoche,* undoubtedly because of the complexity of the phenomenon. Its constitution *Religionum diversitatem nimiam* simply repeated the dispositions concerning mendicant foundations handed down sixty years earlier by the Fourth Lateran Council.[65] Lacking new directives, the Umbrian bishops made various and repeated attempts to institutionalize the penitential movement, especially among women. Many bishops, seeing that the Damianite path was blocked, assigned them the Benedictine or Augustinian rules, with episcopal constitutions and visitors, though without uniting the female movement of the late thirteenth century to the Benedictine or Augustinian orders. Judging by the privileges of canonical erection of those years, the communities institutionalized did not have the option of choosing one rule or the other. In their petitions seeking juridical recognition, the communities indicate the location and the name of the church that they intend to be their canonical seat, but they leave to the bishop the choice of an approved rule, which according to the conciliar provisions a bishop must assign to a community at the time of its canonical erection.[66]

Many of these early female communities, which followed the Augustinian or Benedictine rule but remained under episcopal jurisdiction, have continued to this day to follow diocesan constitutions, without obtaining exemptions and adopting Augustinian or Benedictine customs.[67] But some would-be Damianite women who found themselves subjected to either the Benedictine or Augustinian rule freed themselves from episcopal jurisdiction and joined the Order of the Poor Clares as soon as they managed to obtain the necessary support and requisite permissions. This is what happened in the case of the Augustinians of Santa Maria del Paradiso near Spello and the Benedictines of Santa Margherita of Bevagna, two communities that were canonically erected at the end of the thirteenth century and became part of the Franciscan order by the 1320s.[68]

By the beginning of the fourteenth century, monasticization under the Benedictine or Augustinian rule, which still occurred now and then,[69] had ceased to be a suitable outlet for the *bizzoche* movement, which soon took a different direction. The watershed was the 1298 constitution *Periculoso* and its confirmation by the bull *Apostolicae sedis* of 1309, which imposed perpetual cloister on all nuns.[70]

Closely linked to the law imposing cloister was the urbanization of the convents, a process that lasted more than a century. In order to safeguard their chastity, female communities that until then had devoted themselves to the eremitical life moved to the cities, settling in the outskirts or just within the city walls. In the latter case, their preferred location was near the city gates.[71] Scholars have ascribed a magical or religious significance to this pattern, but the choice was originally dictated by economic reasons and mutual support. Some documents explain these relocations from suburb to city as the result of frequent wars and devastation, which rendered convents insecure; but the decision to relocate to the city was also influenced by the isolation of so many small convents following the imposition of strict cloister. Moreover, changed socioeconomic conditions now deprived them of the male and female oblates who had maintained contact between them and the city.[72]

After the Constitution "Periculoso": Third Orders and Observants

The bull *Sancta Romana* of 1317, which condemned the Fraticelli—that form of Franciscan dissidence so typical of central Italy—also condemned those who claimed to belong to the Third Order of penitents of St. Francis, yet lived in communities. As the bull specified, since this rule did not permit the profession of three vows, "this way of life is in no way to be allowed."[73] But once the law requiring nuns to observe cloister had taken effect, the Rule of Nicholas IV was the only way that new groups of female penitents that were just taking shape could avoid the process of monasticization and its attendant claustration. What is more, those communities that adopted the Rule of Nicholas IV during this period considered themselves to be released from the obligation to request juridical recognition from their own bishops.

Immediately after the condemnations of Pope John XXII, the female penitential movement in Umbria found new life. Reclusion, formerly an elitist phenomenon, had now become distinctly popular and hence enjoyed political support in the Italian cities.[74] Another new development in the movement was the establishment of convent oratories on lands that were exempt from ordinary episcopal jurisdiction, which allowed the women to escape the law imposing cloister and avoid having to adopt one of the approved rules of monastic life. Most chose or adapted the Rule of Nicholas IV. Thus, whereas in the first half of the thirteenth century exemptions granted by the Roman curia had privileged the Damianite order within the female penitential movement, during the fourteenth century an exemption resulting from a juridical expedient furthered the Third Orders, which became the latest institutional outlet for the *bizzoche* movement. This explains why many female communities that were established between 1320 and 1350 constructed their own oratories (the source of the *titulus,* the juridical basis of their foundation) on lands belonging to Roman basilicas or exempt abbeys. In Umbria the protection of the basilica of St. Peter in Rome was invoked by convents like San Bernardo fuori Porta Sole, in Perugia; Santa Maria del Paradiso and San Giovanni delle Rocche, in Assisi; Santa Caterina di Fra Pace, in Foligno; Santa Maria Maddalena, in Trevi; and the female recluses of Norcia, who "had to make an annual payment of 13 pence to the treasury of the hermitage."[75] Among the convents founded under the protection of the Lateran basilica were the hermitage of Giano, the convent of San Giovanni in Spello, and the convent of the Annunziata in Foligno, which undoubtedly followed the Rule of Nicholas IV from its inception in 1347.[76] The abbeys that extended their protection to female establishments in these years included San Pietro of Perugia, on which depended the convents of Santa Maria Annunziata of Monte Corneo, San Giovanni di Colombella, and Santa Maria of Liviano; Santa Maria di Valfabbrica, on which depended the convent of the same name in Perugia; and Santa Maria "in campis," in Foligno, on which the Cistercian convent of Santa Maria di Betlem depended.[77] These devices made it possible for the *christiane, religiose mulieres,* and *sanctimoniales*—in other words, all women who desired to lead a semireligious life—to avoid the obligation of observing cloister while enjoying juridical recognition of their condition as *bizzoche.* Bound by no more than their promise to live a religious life in common, they could own property, were not subject to a vow of obedience, and could return to lay life whenever they wished.

This version of the pious life attracted the attention and the interest of local lords, such as the ruling Trinci family of Foligno. There, the small house erected by Fra Paoluccio Trinci for the Franciscan tertiaries "de Observantia" soon became the convent of the "countesses," or in other words, the noblewomen: yet another option for the elite, a model of the religious life for girls who could not marry, and for young and not-so-young widows.[78] This choice was soon imitated by many daughters of the ruling classes all over central Italy.[79] But this model of religious life, too, was subject to sudden shifts of fashion. Thus when open, uncloistered communities sprang up all over, the nobility, which until then had lavished patronage and financial support on the Third Order, sought a new way to demonstrate its exclusivity. In Foligno, the daughters of the ruling classes displayed their elite identity by joining Santa Lucia, the Observant convent of Poor Clares: in fact, it was from this convent that the Observant movement spread through the Franciscan Second Order in the middle of the fifteenth century.[80] And yet, in less than a century, historical developments came full circle—in a pattern that was nevertheless in perfect harmony with the unfolding of the female penitential movement, constantly in search of its own identity. The ruling classes of Foligno, faced with the fixed number of convents already established in the city and, what is more important, with the rigid Tridentine strictures on the observance of cloister, went back to placing their unmarried or widowed daughters in open communities—the conservatories—which once again were founded thanks to the friendship and support of the Roman curia.[81]

From then on, right down to our own day, the *bizzoche* movement has never faltered. This essay has merely summarized the multiplicity of institutional forms assumed by the most important groups of *bizzoche* that appeared in central Italy in the thirteenth and fourteenth centuries, offshoots of that vast penitential movement of the Middle Ages that continues to invigorate the church. The work of archival excavation has barely begun to uncover the broad contours of this penitential movement, whose continuing vitality is apparent in the many male and female convents still in operation in central Italy, particularly in the valley of Spoleto.

NOTES

Originally published in *Il movimento religioso femminile in Umbria nei secoli XIII–XIV*, ed. Roberto Rusconi, Proceedings of the International Conference on the occasion of the Eighth Centenary of the birth of St. Francis of Assisi, Città di Castello, 27–29 October 1982 (Florence, 1984), pp. 85–113 and 117–21.

1. On the legation of Cardinal Ugolino, see Guido Levi, *Registri dei cardinali Ugolino d'Ostia e Ottaviano degli Ubaldini,* Fonti per la storia d'Italia, 8 (Rome, 1890). On his meeting with St. Francis in Florence, see Edith Pásztor, "San Francesco e il cardinale Ugolino nella 'questione francescana,'" *Collectanea Franciscana* 46 (1976): 209–39. On his relations with St. Clare and her companions, see *Movimento*

religioso femminile e francescanesimo nel secolo XIII, Proceedings of the Seventh Conference of the International Society for Franciscan Studies, Assisi, 11–13 October 1979 (Assisi, 1980).

2. The fundamental work on this vast subject is Herbert Grundmann, *Movimenti religiosi nel Medioevo* (Bologna, 1980), esp. pp. 169–92; but see also Ida Magli, *Gli uomini della penitenza: Lineamenti antropologici del Medioevo italiano* (Milan, 1977), esp. pp. 46–47.

3. Such was the case in Assisi and Rieti: see Jacques-Guy Bougerol, "Il reclutamento sociale delle clarisse di Assisi," *Mélanges de l'Ecole française de Rome, Moyen Age–temps modernes* 89 (1977): 629–32, and Aniceto Chiappini, "S. Filippa Mareri e il suo monastero di Borgo S. Pietro de Molito nel Cicolano," *Miscellanea Francescana* 22 (1921): 65–119. But we lack comparable documentation for other cities, such as Perugia: see *Francesco d'Assisi: Documenti e archivi, codici e biblioteche, miniature* (Milan, 1982), p. 50.

4. "Ne nimia religionum diversitas gravem in ecclesia Dei confusionem inducat, firmiter prohibemus, ne quis de caetero novam religionem inveniat, sed quicumque voluerit ad religionem converti, unam de approbatis assumat. Similiter qui voluerit religiosam domum fundare de novo, regulam et institutionem accipiat de religionibus approbatis" (*Decrees of the Ecumenical Councils,* ed. Giuseppe Alberigo and others; English translation ed. Norman P. Tanner [London and Washington, 1990], p. 242).

5. Out of the vast literature on this subject, one can recommend the following: Alcantara Mens, "L'Ombrie italienne et l'Ombrie brabançonne: Deux courants religieux parallèles d'inspiration commune," *Études franciscaines,* supplement to vol. 17 (1967); Mens, "Beghine, begardi, beghinaggi," in *Dizionario degli Istituti di Perfezione [DIP],* vol. 1 (Rome, 1974), col. 1165–80; Jean-Claude Schmitt, *Mort d'une hérésie: L'église et les clercs face aux béguines et aux bégards du Rhin supérieur du XIVe au XVe siècle* (Paris, 1978); Raoul Manselli, *Spirituali e beghini in Provenza* (Rome, 1959); Pierre Péano, "Manifestations de la vie en commun parmi les tertiaires franciscains de la France méridionale," in *Prime manifestazioni di vita comunitaria maschile e femminile nel movimento francescano della penitenza, 1215–1447,* ed. Raffaele Pazzelli and Lino Temperini, Proceedings of the Conference of Franciscan Studies, 30 June–2 July 1981 (*Analecta T.O.R.* 15, no. 135) (Rome, 1982).

6. R. B. C. Huygens, *Lettres de Jacques de Vitry: Edition critique* (Leyden, 1960). In Letter 1 (pp. 75–76), after an open indictment of the Roman curia— "having resided for some time at the Curia, I found many things that were not at all to my liking"—Jacques de Vitry added: "I nevertheless found consolation in seeing a great number of men and women who renounced all their possessions and left the world for the love of Christ: 'Friars Minor' and 'Sisters Minor,' as they were called. They were held in great esteem by the Lord Pope and the cardinals. . . . The women live near the cities in various hospices and refuges; they live a community life from the work of their hands, but accept no income" (as translated in *St. Francis of Assisi, Writings and Early Biographies: English Omnibus of the Sources for the Life of St. Francis,* ed. Marion A. Habig [Chicago, 1983], p. 1608).

Following the example of St. Clare, "the noble and the illustrious, contemning stately palaces, built for themselves narrow cloisters and deemed it a great glory to live for Christ in sackcloth and ashes. Youths in eager crowds were incited to holy conflict and were spurred on by the heroic example of the weaker sex to spurn the allurements of the flesh. In fine, many already united in marriage bound themselves by the law of continency by mutual consent: the men passed to Orders, the women to the monasteries. . . . Innumerable virgins, moved by the accounts of Clare, not being able to embrace the life of the Cloister, sought to live as religious without a rule in their own homes. . . . The fame of her virtues filled the dwellings of illustrious women; it reached the palaces of duchesses, and even the private apartments of queens. The flower of the nobility stooped to follow in her steps. . . . the new source of heavenly blessing . . . sprung up in the vale of Spoleto [and then] spread far and wide in the world. . . . Cities without number were adorned with monasteries, and even country districts and mountain places were beautified with the dwellings of this celestial institute" (Thomas of Celano, "St. Clare: Founder of the Franciscan Nuns," in *These Splendid Sisters,* ed. James Joseph Walsh [Freeport, New York, 1927; reprinted 1970], pp. 65–66). Engelbert Grau has recently discussed the author of the *Legenda sanctae Clarae* in "Die Schriften der heiligen Klara und die Werke ihrer Biographen," in *Movimento religioso femminile e francescanesimo,* pp. 195–238, esp. 222–31.

"Thus many youths left father and mother and all they possessed to follow the friars and to be clothed in their habit. . . . Not only men but also women and unmarried virgins were fired by the brothers' preaching and, on their advice, entered the prescribed convents *[monasteria reclusa]* to do penance; and one of the brothers [Brother Filippo Longo] was appointed as their visitor and guide. Married men and women, being bound by the marriage vow, were advised by the friars to dedicate themselves to a life of penance in their own houses" (Habig, *St. Francis of Assisi: Omnibus of Sources,* p. 944).

7. Gilles Gérard Meersseman with Gian Piero Pacini, *Ordo fraternitatis: Confraternite e pietà dei laici nel Medioevo,* Italia Sacra 24 (Rome, 1977), pp. 359–63 and 374–77.

8. On this monastery, see Zefferino Lazzeri, "L'antico monastero di Vallegloria vicino a Spello, con appendice di documenti," *La Verna* 9 (1911): 123 ff.

9. In the dispute between the monastery of San Concordio near Spoleto on one side and Lady Berta and a certain Francesco on the other, concerning a piece of land located in Bajano, Lady Berta "citing her privileges, however, said that she was not under the jurisdiction of our [civil] court" (suum tamen privilegium allegando, dicebat in nostra curia [civili] non esse conveniendam) (doc. 15); she had invoked the *privilegium fori* as an "oblate of St. Mary of the diocese of Spoleto" (oblatam sancte Marie Spoletane diocesis) (doc. 17) "where she received penitence" (in qua accipiebat penitentiam) (doc. 16). After a long trial, on 3 November 1208, Egidio, the bishop of Foligno, ordered Lady Berta to return the land (doc. 17); this sentence was confirmed by Innocent III the following year (docs. 18–20). Francesco was likewise ordered to return the piece of land that he held with Lady Berta, but his sentence was

imposed by a civil tribunal (doc. 21). The documents, located in the archive of the cathedral of Spoleto, have been published by Giuseppe Barletta, "Le carte del monastero di S. Concordio di Spoleto, 1064–sec. XIII," *Bollettino della Deputazione di storia patria per l'Umbria* 74 (1977): 265–334, esp. pp. 291–99.

10. "Quod fratres caveant frequentes et notabiles familiaritates bizzocarum . . . bizzocarum autem confessio rarius audiatur" (Thomas Kaeppeli, *Acta capitulorum provincialium provinciae romanae, 1242–1344* [Rome, 1941], pp. 8–10). But in the decisions made by the chapter general in Paris in 1242, the term "beguine" was used to indicate *religiosae mulieres,* religious women; and the term was repeated in the next chapter general, held in Metz in 1251: *Monumenta Ordinis Fratrum Praedicatorum Historica,* vol. 3 (Rome, 1899), pp. 26 and 59. See Grundmann, *Movimenti religiosi,* p. 317 n. 26.

11. Grundmann, *Moviment religiosi,* p. 317 n. 26 and p. 374 n. 48. *Bizzoche,* like beguines, were women who followed a religious life either in common or in their own homes, observing poverty and chastity but without being bound by formal vows.

12. "Pynzocarae quae de pulvere nuperrime surrexerunt" (Meersseman, *Ordo fraternitatis,* pp. 374–75). This is also the source of the clarification that in central Italy "the penitents were called *pinzocheri;* the documents which cite this familiar term translate it into Latin with the word *continentes.*" But see Romana Guarnieri, "Pinzochere," in *DIP,* vol. 6 (Rome, 1980), col. 1722–24.

13. For an overview, see Grundmann, *Movimenti religiosi,* pp. 169–92.

14. Mens, "Beghine, begardi, beghinaggi," col. 1173–74.

15. For a sketch of the movement of the *bizzoche* in Italy, see Guarnieri, "Pinzochere," col. 1721–49; for central Italy, see Mario Sensi, "Incarcerate e penitenti a Foligno nella prima metà del Trecento," in *I frati penitenti di S. Francesco nella società del Due e Trecento,* ed. Mariano d'Alatri, Proceedings of the Second Conference of Franciscan Studies, Rome, 12–14 October 1976 (Rome, 1977), pp. 291–308.

16. Grundmann, *Movimenti religiosi,* p. 263 n. 42. The chapter general of the Cistercians in 1228 contained a similar decision; for the text of the measure, see ibid., p. 258 n. 13.

17. Meersseman, *Ordo fraternitatis,* p. 376.

18. "Nor did he [St. Francis] ever authorize the founding of other convents, although some had been opened during his life through the good offices of others" ("Cronaca di frate Stefano," in *Fonti francescane* [Padua, 1977], p. 2683).

19. Caietanus Esser, "Forma vivendi s. Clarae," *Opuscula sancti patris Francisci Assisiensis,* Bibliotheca Franciscana Ascetica Medii Aevi, 12 (Grottaferrata, 1978), p. 162; translated in *Francis and Clare: The Complete Works,* ed. Regis J. Armstrong and Ignatius C. Brady (New York, 1982), pp. 44–45.

20. On the convent of San Paolo dell'Abbadesse, where Francis placed Clare on 28 March 1211, just after she fled her home, see Marino Bigaroni, "I monasteri benedettini femminili di S. Paolo delle Abbadesse, di S. Apollinare in Assisi e S. Maria di Paradiso prima del Concilio di Trento," in *Aspetti di vita benedettina nella storia di*

Assisi, Atti dell'Accademia Properziana del Subasio, sixth series, no. 5 (Assisi, 1981), pp. 171–231, esp. pp. 173–180. On Sant'Angelo di Panzo, where, according to the testimony of Sister Beatrice di messer Favarone, "St. Francis, Brother Filippo and Brother Bernardo took her [Clare]," see Sensi, "Incarcerate e penitenti," p. 305 n. 41. At the time that Clare arrived there, this place was a cell, a *bizzocaggio.*

21. On the various names given to the female Franciscan movement, see Ignacio Omaechevarria, "Clarisse," in *DIP,* vol. 2 (Rome, 1975), col. 111–17, and "La 'regla' y las reglas de la orden de santa Clara," *Collectanea Franciscana* 46 (1976): 105–110.

22. "Domicilia . . . in quibus vivant nil possidentes sub caelo, exceptis domiciliis ipsius" (*Bullarium Franciscanum,* 1: 1). For related problems, see Livario Oliger, "De origine regularum ordinis sanctae Clarae," *Archivum Franciscanum Historicum* 5 (1912): 181–209 and 413–47, esp. pp. 193–209.

23. The firm decision of these "purest virgins and other women" to withdraw from ordinary episcopal jurisdiction (*correctionem, institutionem et destitutionem*) makes it hard to see this donation of lands to the Roman Church in pauperistic terms, as a rejection of ownership of one's own monastery, an interpretation proposed by Oliger, "De origine regularum," pp. 195 and 197.

24. For a reconstruction of events, see ibid.; for their interpretation, see Raoul Manselli, "La chiesa e il francescanesimo femminile," in *Movimento religioso femminile e francescanesimo,* pp. 239–61.

25. On the problem of seclusion, see Jacques Leclercq, "Clausura,' in *DIP,* vol. 2 (Rome, 1975), col. 1166–83. On *fuga mundi,* see Clara Gennaro's essay in this volume.

26. Oliger provided a first solution to the problem of the visitors, procurators, and chaplains of the Poor Clares (Fra Filippo, Fra Ambrogio, Brunetto Oldradi, and Fra Pacifico) in "De origine regularum," pp. 418–21. For more recent discussions and corrections, see Zefferino Lazzeri, "L'antico monastero di Vallegloria," *La Verna* 10 (1912): 66–67 (on Fra Pacifico, Fra Filippo, and Frangipane); Lazzeri, "De fr. Philippo Longo anno 1244 omnium clarissarum visitatore atque de initio monasteriorum Volaterrarum et Castri Florentini," *Archivum Franciscanum Historicum* 13 (1920): 286–89; Mario Sensi, "Le clarisse a Foligno nel secolo XIII," *Collectanea Franciscana* 47 (1977): 349–63, esp. p. 353 n. 22; Livario Oliger, "Documenta originis clarissarum Civitatis Castelli, Eugubii (a. 1223–1263) nec non statuta monasteriorum Perusiae Civitatisque Castelli (saec. XV) et S. Silvestri Romae (saec. XIII)," *Archivum Franciscanum Historicum* 15 (1922): 71–102, esp. p. 81; Marino Bigaroni, *Montesanto di Todi, da monastero a rocca dell'Albornoz* (Assisi, 1981), pp. 10–16; Roberto Rusconi, "L'espansione del francescanesimo femminile nel secolo XIII," in *Movimento religioso femminile e francescanesimo,* pp. 265–313, esp. pp. 279–82.

27. "When the Most Holy in Christ lord father pope Gregorius IX, inspired by the grace of God, had a convent in honor of the blessed and glorious and always virginal Mary built with his own money in a place called Costa de Cizan . . . " (Spoleto, 17 July 1232; see *Bullarium Franciscanum,* 1: 201, no. 207).

28. "Totaliter Domino vos dicantes claustro perpetuo vos duxeritis includendas" (ibid., p. 32, no. 10).

29. This was done for the convents of Vallegloria in Spello and of Santa Maria "inter Angulos" in Spoleto, to which Pope Gregory IX gave the property of the suppressed abbey of San Silvestro di Collepino, above Spello (see Lazzeri, "L'antico monastero di Vallegloria," pp. 69ff.). This also happened at Todi, where the pope suppressed the abbey of San Leucio and assigned its property to the Poor Clares of Montesanto (Bigaroni, *Montesanto di Todi*, pp. 28ff.). See also Oliger, "De origine regularum," p. 415, who cites the *Vita Gregorii IX papae*, in Ludovico Antonio Muratori, *Rerum Italicarum Scriptores*, vol. 3, part 1 (Milan, 1723), p. 575.

30. The *Privilegium Paupertatis*, already conceded to San Damiano on 17 September 1228 (*Bullarium Franciscanum*, 1: 771), was extended to the convent of Monteluce in Perugia on 16 June 1229 (p. 50) and also perhaps to that of Monticelli in Florence (p. 62).

31. *Vita Gregorii IX papae*, p. 575: "Cuius officii tempore [that is, when he was still Cardinal Ugolino] Poenitentium fratrum et Dominarum inclusarum novos instituit ordines et ad summum usque provexit."

32. *Bullarium Franciscanum*, 1: 3 (Convent of Monticelli in Florence, 27 July 1219); p. 10 (Gattaiola in Lucca, 30 July 1219); p. 11 (Santa Petronilla in Siena, 29 July 1219); p. 13 (Monteluce in Perugia, 29 July 1219).

33. For the *specimen*, see Oliger, "De origine regularum," pp. 196–97, and Bigaroni, *Montesanto di Todi*, p. 11. The text of Cardinal Ugolino's rule is in Luke Wadding, *Annales Minorum*, 3d ed. (Quaracchi, 1931), 1: 347–52; see *Bullarium Franciscanum*, 1: 263 (no. 292) and 394 (no. 113).

34. *Bullarium Franciscanum*, 1: 3, 10, 11, and 13.

35. For example, for the convent of San Paolo in Spoleto, see ibid., pp. 44 and 162. Among the convents that were the objects of a similar bull (which, however, does not appear in the *Bullarium Franciscanum*), one might mention Monteluce in Perugia, 4 November 1229 (see *Francesco d'Assisi: Documenti e archivi*, pp. 22–33). On the need for precise figures and an exact chronology for the female Franciscan settlements, see Rusconi, "L'espansione del francescanesimo femminile," p. 313 n. 171.

36. On the problem of the Damianite "area of influence" and, in particular, on the convent of Carpello in Foligno, which a document from 1217 seems to attribute to St. Clare herself, see Oliger, "De origine regularum," p. 194 n. 3; Sensi, "Le clarisse a Foligno nel sec. XIII," p. 358; Rusconi, "L'espansione del francescanesimo femminile," pp. 274–76.

37. On the community of Santa Giuliana in Perugia, see Angelo Pantoni, "Monasteri sotto la regola benedettina a Perugia e dintorni," in *Benedictina* 8 (1954): 231–56, esp. pp. 242–43.

38. Franco Andrea Dal Pino, "Agiografia servitana nell'opera dei Bollandisti dal 1600 al 1701," *Studi storici O.S.M.* 12 (1962): 150–51 and 182–83; Leandro Novelli, "Due documenti inediti relativi alle monache benedettine dette 'Santuccie,'" *Benedictina* 22 (1975): 189–253. According to chapter 2 of the constitution

this was originally a special *Eigenkloster* of penitents who were oblates of the abbey of San Pietro of Gubbio.

39. See, for example, Oliger, "De origine regularum," p. 207. The surviving archival material, which has been only partially published, does not demonstrate that these communities belonged to the Benedictine order before becoming Damianite. On the other hand, their association with the penitential movement is indicated by the use of terms such as *foeminae, sociae, ancellae Christi, sanctimoniales,* and *reclusae* to designate the women at San Paolo of Spoleto; by their way of life (the women of Panzo were explicitly called recluses); and by their juridical status as oblates (tradition has it that the sisters of Vallegloria of Spello were oblates of the Camaldolese abbey of San Silvestro di Collepino).

40. The two documents have been edited by Bigaroni, "I monasteri benedettini femminili," pp. 208–10.

41. Huygens, *Lettres de Jacques de Vitry,* p. 74: "impetravi, ut liceret mulieribus religiosis non solum in episcopatu Leodi[n]ensi, sed tam in regno quam in imperio in eadem domo simul manere et sese invicem mutuis exhortationibus ad bonum invitare."

42. Spoleto, Archivio del Duomo, parchment 432: Letter from Gregory IX to Giovanni di San Germano to suppress the convent of San Concordio, no date (circa 1235–36); see Luigi Fausti, "Le pergamene dell'Archivio del Duomo di Spoleto," *Archivio per la storia ecclesiastica dell'Umbria* (1917): 287, no. 432. On the monastery, see also Barletta, "Le carte di S. Concordio," pp. 312–20.

43. This subject is examined in Oliger, "De origine regularum," pp. 426–27.

44. Oliger, "Documenta originis clarissarum Civitatis Castelli," p. 78.

45. "Magistre et sororibus ecclesie S. Marie de Civitellis, Spoletane diocesis, Ordinis sancti Benedicti" (Foligno, Archivio del monastero di Santa Maria di Betlem, unnumbered parchment of Bevagna provenance): in Rome, at the Ospedale di Santo Spirito, on 14 June 1244, Bartolomeo, bishop of Spoleto, canonically founds the convent of Santa Maria of Civitella. The parchment original measures 235 mm. by 225 mm. and has a ribbon of red silk whose seal has been lost; the signatures (six priests, four of whom are canons of the diocese of Spoleto) are autographs. The place of redaction results from the fact that Bartolomeo was abbot commendatory of Santo Spirito in Sassia. On Bartolomeo Accoramboni, bishop of Spoleto from 1236 to 1271, see Conrad Eubel, *Hierarchia Catholica Medii Aevi,* vol. 1 (Münster, 1913), p. 485; for the text of the bull *Gloriosus Deus* of 18 October 1253, see *Bullarium Franciscanum,* 1: 684–85.

46. Oliger, "Documenta originis clarissarum Civitatis Castelli," pp. 89–90.

47. Brief mentions are made of the convent of Santa Maria del Monte in Ludovico Iacobilli, *Vite de' santi e beati dell'Umbria,* vol. 3 (Foligno, 1661), p. 313; and Laurent-Henri Cottineau, *Répertoire topo-bibliographique des abbayes et prieurés,* vol. 1 (Macon, 1939), p. 372.

48. Only a part of the *bizzoche* community of San Tommaso moved to the Ospedale della Stella in accordance with the episcopal order. The constitutions that Bishop Bartolomeo drafted for the hospital have been published by Luigi Fausti,

"Degli antichi ospedali di Spoleto," *Atti dell'Accademia spoletina* (1920–22): 48–50.

49. Lazzeri, "L'antico monastero di Vallegloria," pp. 68–72, docs. 55, 57, and 60.

50. Foligno, Archivio del Duomo, parchment A 18; see Michele Faloci Pulignani, *Inventario dell'Archivio del Duomo di Foligno* (Perugia, 1926), no. 18.

51. Spoleto, Archivio dell'Ospedale della Stella (heceforth AOS), in the Archivio del monastero di San Ponziano, parchment 358: *Religiosam vitam eligentibus,* Orvieto (February/March: there is a gap in the date caused by a worm hole before "Kalendis martii"). Pope Urban IV places the convent of Santa Margherita "iuxta Spoletum" under his protection and that of the Holy See: "in primis siquidem statuentes ut ordo canonicus qui secundum Deum et beati Augustini regulam in eadem ecclesia institutus esse dinoscitur perpetuis ibidem temporibus inviolabiliter observetur." The original parchment measures 520 mm. by 610 mm.; this pontifical bull *cum rota* is signed by the pope and sixteen cardinals.

Assigning the Augustinian rule to communities that had not joined either the Dominican or the Augustinian orders had precedents. For example, see Benigno A.L. Van Luijk, *Bullarium ordinis eremitarum S. Augustini: Periodus formationis, 1187–1256* (Würzburg, 1964), pp. 102 and 128, for a case in Parma: before 23 May 1255, the date of the bull *Iustis petentium* addressed to the convent of San Michele of Parma, the bishop had granted the Augustinian rule to these nuns, "qui tunc nullam de approbatis regulis habebatis," who until now observed none of the approved rules. This canonical foundation, which had also been approved by the cardinal legate, was definitively confirmed by the pope himself. For an analogous situation in Constance in 1247, where the convent of Kirchheim was canonically established by the bishop with the Augustinian rule and only later joined the Dominican order, see Grundmann, *Movimenti religiosi,* pp. 342–45.

52. *Bullarium Franciscanum,* 1: 290.

53. Ibid., p. 541; see also Grundmann, *Movimenti religiosi,* p. 280 n. 169.

54. For an interpretation of the *Legenda,* see Anna Benvenuti Papi, "Umiliana dei Cerchi: Nascita di un culto nella Firenze del Dugento," *Studi francescani* 77 (1980): 87–117, and Benvenuti Papi, "Cerchi, Umiliana," in *Dizionario Biografico degli Italiana,* vol. 23 (Rome, 1979), pp. 692–96. On Rose of Viterbo, see Giuseppe Abate, "S. Rosa da Viterbo, terziaria francescana, 1233–1251: Fonti storiche della vita e loro revisione critica," *Miscellanea francescana* 52 (1952): 113–278, and Anna Maria Vacca, *La menta e la croce: S. Rosa da Viterbo* (Rome, 1982).

55. Michele Faloci Pulignani, "Il b. Simone da Collazzone e il suo processo nel 1252," *Miscellanea francescana* 12 (1910): 97–132, esp. pp. 124–25.

56. The texts have been published by Ugolino Nicolini, in "Ricerche sulla sede di fra Raniero Fasani fuori di Porta Sole a Perugia," *Bollettino della Deputazione di storia patria dell'Umbria* 63 (1966): 202 ff. New data on reclusion in Perugia are provided by Giovanna Casagrande, "Note su manifestazioni di vita comunitaria femminile nel movimento penitenziale in Umbria nei secoli XIII, XIV, XV," in Pazzelli and Temperini, *Prime manifestazioni di vita comunitaria,* pp. 459–79, esp.

pp. 463–64, where she publishes a list of male and female recluses who received charitable offerings from the municipality of Perugia on 23 December 1290: fifty-six "sisters" and twelve "brothers" who, judging by their places of residence, belonged to the movement of reclusion.

57. Autbertus Stroick, "Collectio de scandalis Ecclesiae," *Archivum Franciscanum Historicum* 24 (1931): 33–62, esp. p. 61: "sunt apud nos mulieres quae beghinae vocantur et quaedam earum subtilitatibus vigent et novitatibus gaudent. Habent interpretata scripturarum mysteria et in communi idiomate gallicata . . . legunt ea communiter . . . in conventiculis . . . vidi ego, legi et habui Bibliam gallicatam cuius exemplar parisinus publice ponitur a stationariis ad scribendum." See also Antonino Franchi, "Il concilio di Lione II (1274) e la contestazione dei francescani delle Marche," *Picenum Seraphicum* 11 (1974): 53–75, esp. p. 59.

58. We lack detailed studies of these two groups. For Angela, there are some notes in Mario Sensi, "Il movimento francescano della penitenza a Foligno," *Il movimento francescano della penitenza nella società medioevale,* ed. Mariano d'Alatri, Proceedings of the Third Conference of Franciscan Studies, Padua, 25–27 September 1979 (Rome, 1980), pp. 399–445, esp. p. 399; also *Angela da Foligno, terziaria francescana,* ed. Enrico Menestò (Spoleto, 1992). There are brief mentions of the Montefalco group in Silvestro Nessi, "S. Chiara da Montefalco e il francescanesimo," *Miscellanea francescana* 69 (1969): 369–408, esp. pp. 381–91. See also *S. Chiara da Montefalco e il suo tempo,* ed. Claudio Leonardi and Enrico Menestò (Florence, 1985), which includes the essay by Menestò translated for this volume. On the links between these two saintly women and the penitential movement of female recluses, see Sensi, "Incarcerate e penitenti a Foligno," p. 305.

59. For the role of these two women in the struggle against the heresy of the Free Spirit, see Livario Oliger, *De secta spiritus libertatis in Umbria saec. XIV: Disquisitio et documenta* (Rome, 1943); Romana Guarnieri, "Il movimento del libero spirito dalle origini al secolo XVI," *Archivio italiano per la storia della pietà* 4 (Rome, 1964): 353–708, esp. pp. 404–9 and 411; and Guarnieri, "Frères du libre esprit," in *Dictionnaire de spiritualité et mystique,* vol. 5 (Paris, 1964), col. 1264–68, esp. col. 1251–52.

60. Foligno, Biblioteca Comunale, MS F. 116, Raccolta di documenti vari riguardianti Montefalco, fol. 289: "When the blessed Clare of Montefalco heard that the aforesaid religious [lay Franciscan tertiaries] had come to Italy from Toulouse, she greatly wished to meet and confer with them. One of her followers, from the noble family of the Bennati in Montefalco, acted with words and with deeds: through his words he arranged for her to see and speak with these men; through his deeds he gave them a site by his castle of San Rocco, in the district of Montefalco, where a monastery could be built for them, which was accomplished in 1295, three years after the blessed woman and her nuns had received the said rule of the Franciscan Third Order." On San Rocco, see Gabriele Andreozzi, "S. Rocco in Montefalco, la 'Porziuncola' del Terz'Ordine Regolare," *Analecta T.O.R.* 4–5 (1949–50): 208 ff.; and Silvestro Nessi, "Storia e arte delle chiese francescane di Montefalco," *Miscellanea francescana* 62 (1962): 240–44, esp. pp. 240–42.

61. *Vita S. Clarae de Cruce ord. Eremitarum S. Aug. ex codice Montefalconensi, saec. XIV desumpta,* ed. Alfonso Semenza (Vatican City, 1944): "ecce mulier quedam de Carcasona, nomine Margarita, intravit oratorium casu quodam fortuito, non quod ex proposito ad monasterium memoratum venisset" (p. 31); and "Margarita provincialis existens quodam die" (p. 48).

Assisi, Biblioteca della Chiesa Nuova, MS 9. For a description of this codex from the hermitage of the Carceri and written entirely in Provençal, see Arthur Ingrid, *La vida del glorios Sant Frances* (Uppsala, 1955), pp. 3–10. The codex contains on fols. 95v–99r the "Confessione di fede di fra Matteo da Bousigues," edited by Ferdinand-Marie Delorme in "La 'Confessio fidei' du frère Mathieu de Bousigues," *Études franciscaines* 19 (1937): 224–39. Paolino of Venice, bishop of Pozzuoli (1324–44), relates that Mathieu supposedly fled from Béziers with the books of Peter John Olivi and was acclaimed pope at St. Peter's in Rome in 1296 by a band of thirteen women and five beghards. This episode, whether real or invented, is discussed by Diego Zorzi, "Testi inediti francescani in lingua provenzale," in *Miscellanea del Centro di studi medioevali,* Università Cattolica del Sacro Cuore (Milan, 1950), pp. 249–50; and Manselli, *Spirituali e beghini in Provenza,* p. 42. See also M. Roy Harris, *The Occitan Translations of John XII and XIII–XVII from a Fourteenth-Century Franciscan Codex (Assisi, Chiesa Nuova, Ms. 9),* Transactions of the American Philosophical Society, 75 (Philadelphia, 1985).

Todi, Biblioteca Comunale, cod. 128. For a brief description of this Provençal codex with works of Peter John Olivi and references to the relevant bibliography, see *Francesco d'Assisi: Documenti e archivi,* p. 130, n. 64.

62. "Ut iam ex tunc non fuerim ille qui fui" (Ubertino De Casale, *Arbor vitae crucifixae Jesu* [Venice, 1485], chap. 3). On the probable date of the meeting with the blessed Angela, see Michele Faloci Pulignani, *La b. Angela da Foligno: Memorie e documenti* (Gubbio, 1926), pp. 21–25: of the two possible dates, 1284 or 1298, Faloci Pulignani favors the earlier one.

63. Here is the list of convents, with the date of their canonical erection when it is known. In Spoleto: Santa Caterina and Santa Croce "de Colle floris," later known as Santa Croce de Bonazzello sopra Colle Ciciano (1278); San Concordio (1285); Santa Illuminata de Corvellone (1291); Santa Caterina di Colpetroso (1293); Santa Maria Maddalena di Monteluco (1294); Santa Maria della Misericordia "prope Spoletum" (1296); Santa Maria Maddalena "de Capatis" sul Monte Ciciano (1300); Santa Agnese "prope Spoletum," San Giovanni "de Colle Consilii," Santa Elisabetta "de Corvellone"; Santa Lucia "Collis Gratie"; San Ponziano; and San Bartolomeo di Monteluco. In Foligno: Santa Elisabetta; Santa Giuliana (1293?); Santa Maria della Croce (1286); and Santa Maria del popolo. In Montefalco: Santa Maria Maddalena (1269); SS. Maria e Paolo (1288); SS. Benedetto and Agnese di Camiano, later known as del Poggiolo (1288); Santa Croce; and Santa Caterina "de Boctacio," later known as Santa Chiara (1290). In Bevagna: Santa Margherita (1271) and Santa Lucia. In Spello: Santa Maria del Paradiso (1296). This list, however, is merely provisional. Until critical editions of the texts are published, the relevant documentation can be found in the following archives: in Spoleto, section of the Archivio di Stato,

Corporazioni religiose soppresse (henceforth ASS, Corp. rel.); Fondo Ospedale della Stella, Monastero di Ponziano (AOS); and Archivio capitolare del Duomo (ACS); in Foligno, Archivio capitolare del Duomo (ADF), and Monastero di Betlem; in Bevagna, Monastero di S. Margherita; in Montefalco, Monastero di Santa Croce.

A systematic examination of these and other town archives can be expected to yield, among other things, documentation on the civil and ecclesiastical support given to these establishments. Special mention should be made of the patronage extended by Cardinals Napoleone Orsini and Pietro and Giacomo Colonna. All three cardinals had special ties with the convent of Santa Croce in Montefalco (*Vita S. Clarae de Cruce*, pp. 24, 32, and 71–72). Giacomo Colonna acted in support of the convent of Santa Maria Maddalena in Monteluce (ASS, Corp. rel., parchment 25). Cardinal Napoleone Orsini assisted the convent of San Benedetto del Poggiolo in Montefalco (Foligno, Biblioteca Comunale, MS F. 116, fol. 160) and granted privileges to the convents of Santa Maria del Paradiso in Spello (ADF, parchment 31) and the convent of Santa Croce di Colle Fiorito or Colle Ciciano (ASS, Corp. rel., parchment 31). Napoleone Orsini also approved the foundation of a monastery by St. Clare of Rimini during his legation in the Marches: see Giuseppe Garampi, *Memorie ecclesiastiche appartenenti all'istoria e al culto della b. Chiara da Rimini* (Rome, 1755), pp. 341 and 349. Finally, it must be noted that this same Napoleone Orsini was asked by the pope to organize an inquest concerning the miracles of St. Clare of Montefalco, and that Giacomo Colonna approved the writings of the blessed Angela of Foligno: see Livario Oliger, "Fr. Bertrandi de Turre processus contra spirituales Aquitaniae et card. Iacobi de Columna litterae defensoriae Spiritualium Provinciae," *Archivum Franciscanum Historicum* 16 (1923): 331–35.

64. See Mariano d'Alatri, "L'ordine della penitenza nella leggenda di Margherita da Cortona," in Pazzelli and Temperini, *Prime manifestazioni di vita comunitaria*, pp. 68–80; *Vita S. Clarae de Cruce*, pp. 6ff.

65. Mansi, *Sacrorum conciliorum collectio*, 24: 96–97.

66. See, for example, the decree of canonical erection of the convent of San Concordio in Spoleto, in 1285: "requisiti fuerimus ut eisdem personis aliquam de approbatis regulis sub qua vivere possint concedere dignaremur" (ACS, parchment 490). And in the *vita* of St. Clare we read that Giovanna, the first rectress of the hermitage of Bottacio, together with the other recluses, "a dyocesano unam de approbatis regulis petierunt" (*Vita sanctae Clarae de Cruce*, p. 17); while in the writ of canonical erection of this same convent, Bishop Gerardo states: "Pro parte vestra nobis est humiliter supplicatum ut . . . certam regulam et alia, que loco regulato conveniunt vobis de speciali gratia concedere dignaremur." The bull has been published several times: see Silvestro Nessi, *Chiara da Montefalco badessa del monastero di S. Croce, le sue testimonianze, i suoi dicti* (Montefalco, 1981), p. 14.

67. For an example in Foligno, see Mario Sensi, *S. Maria di Betlem a Foligno, monastero di contemplative agostiniane* (Foligno, 1981).

68. After granting the Augustinian nuns of Santa Maria del Paradiso exemption from episcopal jurisdiction, on 20 March 1325, Bartolomeo, bishop of Spoleto, allowed them to join the Order of St. Clare (ACF, parchments 37 and 38), which they

did (Foligno, Biblioteca Iacobilli, codex C.IX.2: *Libro delle entrate e delle uscite del monastero di S. Maria del paradiso o vero monastero del Rosso "Ordinis sancte Clarae," 1385–1462*). One should also note that some communities dedicated to St. Clare nevertheless observed the Benedictine rule, as occurred in Spello (ADF, parchment A.44) and Gubbio: see Ugolino Paris, "S. Francesco, i francescani e la città di Gubbio," *Studi francescani* 13 (1928): 60.

In the bull *Solet annuere* of 1 June 1358, addressed to the "abbatisse et conventui monasterii S. Margarite de Mevania, Ordinis S. Clare, Spoletane diocesis," Innocent VI confirmed all of the privileges, exemptions, and immunities granted by his predecessors to that community, even though it had been erected by the bishop under the Benedictine rule, as stated in the episcopal document of 1271 (Bevagna, Archivio monastico di S. Margherita, unnumbered parchment).

69. Thus, for example, the convent "dominarum de fratellis sive de sacco" was canonically erected in Città di Castello in 1310, and the religious women there requested "tradi sibi regulam Beati Augustini sub cuius observantiam intendunt perpetuo Christo Domino famulari" (Città di Castello, Archivio della Curia vescovile, Registri della Cancelleria vescovile, no. 2, fols. 8 and 14, now published in *Chiese e conventi degli ordini mendicanti in Umbria nei secoli XIII–XIV: Gli archivi ecclesiastici di Città de Castello*, ed. Giovanna Casagrande [Perugia, 1989], pp. 4–5). I am grateful to Dr. Giovanna Casagrande for calling this document to my attention. Similarly, on 30 July 1344, in Trevi, Bartolomeo, bishop of Spoleto, canonically erected the "family convent" of S. Lucia "Sub regula b. Benedicti" (Anselmo Tappi Cesarini, "La bolla di fondazione del monastero di S. Lucia de Trevi," *Benedictina* 10 [1956]: 75–78).

70. Emil Albert Friedberg, *Corpus juris canonici,* vol. 2 (Leipzig, 1922), pp. 1053–54. On the nuns' reactions to the law imposing cloister, see Jean Leclercq, "Il monachesimo femminile nei secoli XII e XIII," in *Movimento religioso femminile e francescanesimo,* pp. 63–99, esp. pp. 85–87. The decretal did not affect the beguines and *bizzoche,* however: on this point, see the acute comments of Garampi, *Memorie ecclesiastiche,* pp. 117–26.

71. The phenomenon has been analyzed for Florence by Richard C. Trexler, "Le célibat à la fin du moyen âge: Les religieuses de Florence," *Annales: Economies, sociétés, civilisations* 27 (1972): 1329–50, esp. p. 1332; for Bologna by Gabriella Zarri, "I monasteri femminili a Bologna fra il XIII e il XVII secolo," *Atti e memorie della Deputazione di storia patria per le province di Romagna* 24 (1973): 133–224, esp. pp. 149–52; and for Foligno by Mario Sensi, "Il movimento francescano della penitenza a Foligno," p. 406 n. 14. On the typically Italian custom of decorating the gates of the city with images of the patron saints, see Garampi, *Memorie ecclesiastiche,* p. 41 n. c; and more recently, Hans Conrad Peyer, *Stadt und Stadtpatron im mittelalterlichen Italien* (Zurich, 1955), p. 19.

72. For Bologna, see Zarri, "Monasteri femminili," pp. 152–53. The documents from Spoleto date from a later period, and concern the final phase of the urbanization process: for instance, on 13 June 1361, Giovanni, bishop of Spoleto, united the convent of Santa Croce di Borgo San Masseo with the "monasterium

S. Lucie Collis Gratie prope Spoletum, diocesis mee Spoletan. propter guerrarum discrimina et civitatis Spoletan. iacturam et discidia que eadem civitas passa est temporibus retroactis" (AOS, parchment 221). Similar reasons are given in a later document, dated 24 June 1404, which concerns the relocation of the nuns of San Ponziano to the city (AOS, parchment 364). For the case of Spello, see Lazzeri, "L'antico monastero di Vallegloria," p. 84, parchment 82.

Adult oblates, whose status is poorly understood, are nonetheless documented throughout the valley of Spoleto and the mountains between Umbria and the Marches. I cite the example of the convent of Santa Caterina di Monteleone: on 19 December 1349, "Petronus Manenthoni Ascari Odi et Jacoba filia olim Leonardi Bartholomei eius uxor de castro Monteleone . . . volentes pro salute animarum ipsorum monasterium dicte ecclesie S. Chaterine ingredi et ibidem perpetuo famulari," in the presence of the abbess, Filippa de Tibertis, "obtulerunt se et eorum bona profitentes stabilitatem, conversionem, obbedientiam et reverentiam secundum regulam monasterii antedicti" (AOS, parchment 141, Monteleone di Spoleto, 19 December 1349). In Foligno, "Thomas Cicchuri de Trevio, habitator civitatis Fulginei, sindacus et procurator dominarum abbatisse, monialium, capituli et conventus monasterii S. Caterine . . . cum presentia, consensu et voluntate Angeli Petroni de Roviglia, oblati dicti monasterii, et ipse Angelus oblatus, nomine dictorum capituli et conventus . . . concessit . . . unam domum olim dicti Angeli et nunc dicti monasterii" (Foligno, section of the Archivio di Stato, Notarile 106, Luca Lilli [1382–83], unnumbered folio, 12 October 1382). Both of these communities were products of the penitential movement. On the oblates of the monastery of San Angelo di Orsano, north of Trevi, see Guglielmo Salvi, "Gli oblati benedettini in Italia, cenni storici," *Rivista storica benedettina* 21 (1952): 89–169, esp. pp. 164–66.

73. "Talis viventi ritus nullatenus sit concessus" (*Bullarium Franciscanum*, 5: 297).

74. On the revival of this phenomenon and especially on the communal protection accorded the movement of reclusion, see Sensi, "Incarcerate e penitenti a Foligno," pp. 288–89.

75. "Debent annuatim pro fundo carceris dare nobis XIII denarios" (Garampi, *Memorie ecclesiastiche*, p. 101 n. c). This list of female institutions, all of which were established between 1320 and 1350, is purely provisional. On the convents in Perugia, see Pantoni, "Monasteri sotto la regola benedettina a Perugia," p. 236; on the convents in Assisi, see Bigaroni, "I monasteri benedettini femminili," p. 194, and Mario Sensi, "Monasteri benedettini in Assisi, insediamenti sul Subasio e abbazia di S. Pietro," in *Aspetti di vita benedettina nella storia de Assisi*, pp. 27–50, esp. 49 n. 90; on the convents of Foligno and Trevi, see Sensi, "Il movimento francescano della penitenza a Foligno," p. 410 n. 23.

76. Giuseppe Fratini, *Biografia del ven. serva di Dio Elisabetta di ser Lallo ispellese* (Foligno, 1882), p. 23, provides a chaotic series of often contradictory accounts under the heading: "Memoirs drawn from ancient parchments and valuable manuscripts at one time found in the archives of the convent of San Giovanni of Spello." Several mentions are made of the protection extended by the Lateran canons

to the hermitages in Giano and Spello; but the loss of these two monastic archives prevents us from verifying these claims. For the convent of the Annunziata in Foligno, see Sensi, "Il movimento della penitenza a Foligno," pp. 406–9.

77. Pantoni, "Monasteri sotto la regola benedettina a Perugia," pp. 244–49; and Sensi, *S. Maria di Betlem a Foligno,* pp. 5–7.

78. See Sensi, "Il movimento francescano della penitenza a Foligno," pp. 400–3.

79. The *Series provinciarum ragusina* of 1385 lists no fewer than twenty congregations of female tertiaries for the province of San Francesco alone: Girolamo Golubovich, *Biblioteca bio-bibliographica della Terra Santa e dell'Oriente francescano,* vol. 2 (Quaracchi, 1913), pp. 254–55. However, for the period that concerns us, we know of only two, one in Foligno and the other in Perugia. On the latter, see Giovanna Casagrande, "Aspetti del Terz'Ordine francescano a Perugia nella seconda metà del secolo XIV e nel XV," in Mariano d'Alatri, *Il movimento francescano della penitenza,* pp. 362–97, esp. pp. 371–75. It is also difficult to distinguish the list of convents that were actually founded by or at least federated with the congregation of the blessed Angelina from those whose constitutions were modeled on the congregation of Foligno without having any actual ties with it. An example of this would be the convent of Santa Cecilia, which was incorrectly thought to have been founded by Angelina herself, though in reality it never had any connection to her. On the important archives of this convent in Città di Castello, see Livario Oliger, "Acta Tifernensia III Ordinis S. Francisci, 1253–1300 et 1456–1599," *Archivum Franciscanum Historicum* 26 (1963): 390–437; and on the problem in general, see Anna Filannino, "La b. Angelina dei Conti di Marsciano e le sue fondazioni," in Pazzelli and Temperini, *Prime manifestazioni di vita comunitaria,* pp. 451–57.

80. In both Foligno and Perugia, the "puellae et mulieres litteratae" of the local ruling classes were the chief promoters of the Observant movement within the Poor Clares. See Stanislao da Campagnola, "Influssi umanistici nel francescanesimo umbro," in *L'Umanesimo umbro,* Proceedings of the Ninth Conference of Umbrian Studies (Gubbio, 1977), pp. 273–305, esp. 298.

For an initial examination of the Foligno convent, see Luciano Canonici, *S. Lucia di Foligno: Storia di un monastero e di un ideale* (Assisi, 1974), pp. 9–12. Historians have generally relied on the account contained in the *cronica* of Sister Caterina Guarnieri da Osimo, dating from the early decades of the sixteenth century, though with some hesitation. For a partial edition of this source, see Michele Faloci Pulignani, "Saggi della Cronaca di suor Caterina Guarnieri da Osimo," *Archivio storico delle Marche e dell'Umbria* 1 (1884): 287–96. It states: "In the year of our Lord 1425, on 22 July, there came from the city of Sulmona, through divine inspiration, the venerable ladies Sister Alexandrina [and four nuns]. These ladies were received by the lords of the city of Foligno, and when they informed the lords of their holy desire to occupy a convent, the lords granted them . . . Santa Lucia . . . and this was the first convent of the observance of the Second Order of St. Clare to be reformed in this area." However, this account seems to be based on the hazy memories of elderly nuns, whose stories were collected. Confirmation for this hypothesis comes from a long, undated draft of a notarial document inserted between two dated deeds, one from 21 October 1414 and the other from 1 December 1414. The text begins: "Scientes monasterium S. Lucie de Fulgineo esse subiectum ad episcopatum Fulginei et volentes dictum monasterium ad strictiorem S. Clare regulam choartare et dictum monasterium pro futuris temporibus nominari monasterium S. Clare," the bishop (who is not named) decreed the exemption of the convent, but reserved for himself an annual payment of one pound of pepper on the feast day of St. Feliciano (Foligno, section of the Archivio di Stato, Notarile 62, Francesco di Antonio [1407–14], fol. 93). Although it is not known whether this privilege of exemption ever took effect, it would have anticipated by no less than eleven years the subsequent privilege that Giacomo, bishop of Foligno, granted to the convent of Santa Lucia on 15 November 1425, which is usually held to mark the beginning of the reform in that convent: see Antonio Fantozzi, "Documenti intorno alla b. Cecilia Coppoli clarissa, 1426–1500," *Archivum Franciscanum Historicum* 19 (1926): 194–225 and 334–84; the text of the 1425 privilege is found on pp. 375–77.

81. The association and oratory of the virgins of Santa Orsola of Foligno, founded by Paola di Alessandro, won juridical recognition on 29 June 1600: "Fifty of the most noble virgins of the city soon took up this habit and this rule without pronouncing binding vows; nevertheless they punctiliously observe chastity and obedience to the aforesaid superiors and their rule and constitutions and are admitted to the habit with the Mother inside the convent, while the others live in their own houses with great devoutness and modesty, an example for the entire city. Paola, the founder, was elected the first rectress and mother superior by all of her nuns and by the bishop of Foligno; she presided for forty-seven years until the end of her life" (Iacobilli, *Vite de' santi e beati dell'Umbria,* vol. 3 [Foligno, 1661], pp. 443–48). The first biographer of the founder of this Ursuline congregation of women was Michelangelo Marcelli, *Vita della Madre Paola da Foligno* (Rome, 1659). For a bibliography about her relationship with Giovanni Battista Vitelli, founder of the Oratorio del Buon Gesù, see Mario Sensi, "Vitelli, Giovanni Battista, servo di Dio," in *Bibliotheca Sanctorum,* vol. 12 (Rome, 1969), pp. 1240–42.

5

Mendicant Friars and Female Pinzochere in Tuscany: From Social Marginality to Models of Sanctity

Anna Benvenuti Papi

The object of this brief survey is not the flower of mysticism, but rather the soil in which its roots were planted. My aim is to illuminate not so much the modes and forms of the privileged relationship between certain women and God as their ties with the world—or more precisely, the world that they, despite their mystical raptures, represented and expressed. From this point of view, the phenomenon of female sanctity in and of itself is more important than its specific mystical realization. This is why we must not merely dwell on the summits, the highest expressions of female sanctity, but rather consider the entire florilegium of female hagiography organized by the mendicant orders in the thirteenth and fourteenth centuries around figures often of moderate or even minor stature, only a few of whom achieved exceptional renown.[1]

The picture that emerges from a survey of Tuscan saints is rich and varied. The first fact to be noted is the relative preponderance of women. As many observers have noted, the thirteenth century saw the flourishing of lay sanctity, a complex phenomenon linked to the world and the problems of the artisan classes, who through the exercise of their trades devised a new formula of sanctification that was codified and perfected in hortatory models by the mendicant orders.[2] Among the ranks of lay saints, women outnumbered men, even if these laywomen were increasingly monasticized, cloaked in religious habits, and assimilated (often in retrospect) as members of some regular community.

These holy women are notable both for their numbers and for their range of institutional affiliations.[3] Vanna of Orvieto, Agnes of Montepulciano, Villana delle Botti, Catherine Benincasa of Siena, Clare Gambacorta of Pisa, Giacomina (or Pina) of Pisa, Maria Mancini, and Margaret of Città di Castello were all associated with the Dominican order—even if in reality this kind of classification has only limited utility and is often of dubious authenticity. Umiliana dei Cerchi, Bartolomea (or Mea) of Siena, and Margaret and Egidia of Cortona belonged to Franciscan circles. The institutional affiliations of some of the other saints are less certain. Aldobrandesca of Siena is said to have been a member of the Humiliati; Angela Chigi, Giulia Della Rena, and Cristiana (Oringa Menabuoi) of Santa Croce were claimed by the Augustinians, though the Franciscans have linked Cristiana with their order, at least spiritually; Bartolommea (or Elisabetta) of Siena, Giuliana Falconieri, Giovanna Soderini, and Catherine of Siena (not the famous St. Catherine Benincasa) belonged to the Servites. Bona of Pisa, Fina of San Gimignano, Gherardesca of Pisa, Giovanna of Signa, Diana Giuntini, Maria of Pisa, Ubaldesca of Calcinaia, Zita of Lucca, Verdiana of Castelfiorentino, and Bonizzella of Siena belong in a separate category: although they had ties with the mendicants, who were often responsible for writing or (what is even more revealing) for revising their *vitae,* these women shared the distinction of belonging to none of the new mendicant orders, despite later and certainly spurious claims to the contrary. Moreover, for many of these female saints, who generally lived between the end of the twelfth century and the middle of the thirteenth, the earliest hagiographic treatment was apparently designed to meet local needs and purposes. Then there were the new orders, like the "Santucce" whose Tuscan ranks included the blessed Filippa Guidoni, or the female Gesuates, founded by Caterina Colombini under the inspiration of her cousin Giovanni. One might also include Cristiana of Santa Croce, mentioned above as an Augustinian, who established a female convent that embodied the communitarian aspirations typical of the *pinzochere* of the second half of the thirteenth century. These problems of classification reveal the limited utility of attempts to subdivide this singular penitential ferment according to schema that are, after all, external to it, such as the question of affiliation with one order or another. Perhaps something could be learned from a study aimed at identifying significant patterns within the hagiographic literature, such as possible differences between the *vitae* composed by Franciscans and those attributed to Dominicans, Servites, Humiliati, and so on. But what truly characterized this female movement as a whole was the massive efflorescence of the Third Orders, itself in good measure a consequence of the establishment and widespread success of the mendicants.

On the whole, the mendicants dominated the hagiographic production. By contrast with the many saints under mendicant influence or at least affected by their spiritual climate, there are few examples of "traditional" monastic sanctity: Berta, the Vallombrosan abbess of Cavriglia; Umiltà and Margaret of Faenza; and Paola of Florence, linked in Camaldolensian accounts to saints of that order; along with Gherardesca of Pisa and her less well documented colleague Maria. Moreover, the traditions concerning these last figures are not very definite, and one has the impression that their penitential experience was closer to the eremitic life chosen by many of the other women mentioned here than it was to any monastic setting. In short, if the production of examples of sanctity reflects pressure from below, originating among the groups of laypeople that gathered around kernels of religious renewal, the massive presence of laywomen and female tertiaries, quite apart from their evolution toward regular or monastic institutions, testifies to the wide diffusion of female penitence, in a range of experiences of which hagiographic portraits represent simply the highest expression. By the same token, the crisis in traditional monastic recruitment is reflected in the exiguous number of nuns promoted to sainthood; and those few marked phases of internal change in the congregations, as we shall see. In Tuscany the new monastic orders did not produce important saints, at least during the period under consideration here. We need only cite the case of the Florentine convent of Poor Clares, where Agnes of Assisi offered an example of sanctity imported from the Umbrian cradle of the Franciscan order and figures like Piccarda Donati were lauded by poets and chroniclers, but not by hagiographers intent on providing hortatory models to likeminded groups eager to receive them.

Holy Women and Marginalized Women

The sheer weight of numbers would certify the importance of female sanctity in this period, but it is also significant that certain *types* of women keep cropping up in the hagiographical writings examined here: widows, orphans, victims of familial breakdown, social disruption, and economic dislocation. Widows like Umiliana dei Cerchi, Aldobrandesca and Bonizzella of Siena, Clare Gambacorta, and Pina (Giacomina) and Maria Mancini of Pisa were not from humble backgrounds—indeed, the families to which they were born or into which they married belonged to the ruling classes of their cities—and the same is true and "voluntary" widows like Umiltà of Faenza or Gherardesca and Maria of Pisa, who persuaded their husbands to ' transform their conjugal unions into rigid continence based on mystical renunciation. But whatever the familial background, widowhood clearly did not bring availability of economic resources or freedom of action. Margaret of Cortona was unique in that the death of her lover left her an "illicit" widow, and also in being born to extreme poverty. Fina of San Gimignano was an invalid; Margaret of Città di Castello was blind and suffered from serious physical disabilities; Verdiana of Castelfiorentino was an orphan; Zita of Lucca, Cristiana of Santa Croce, and Giovanna of Signa were daughters of poor peasants. Beyond any re-evocation of a traditional typology of religious life (in which widows, for example, could have a place), the sanctity of these women emerged almost exclusively in moments of rupture, of destabilization of the ordinary frameworks for female life: the family and its conceptual synonym, the convent.[4]

This destabilization took concrete shape in different forms, depending on whether the setting was a small rural center or a larger urban agglomeration. In the smaller towns, saints typically came from peasant backgrounds and pursued an occupation of some kind.[5] They often became servants, like Zita of Lucca, Cristiana of Santa Croce, Giulia of Certaldo, and Verdiana of Castelfiorentino, though it was not uncommon for them to perform more specialized roles: Margaret of Cortona assisted the noble ladies of her city during childbirth, and Vanna of Orvieto supported herself by working as a seamstress.[6]

Most of these women lacked a stable family setting, whether in their family of origin or their family by marriage. Verdiana was orphaned; Margaret of Città di Castello was abandoned because of her physical deformities; Fina of San Gimignano was disabled by illness.[7] There were occasional exceptions to this rule, such as Agnes of Montepulciano: she is said to have belonged to a noble family, and perhaps for this reason was able to enter a convent.[8] However, in the standard pattern—whose stock features may be due in part to reciprocal appropriation of textual models—after having exercised some humble profession as a girl, the rural saint next entered into voluntary reclusion. Various former servant girls or peasant laborers adopted the eremitical life and retired to individual hermitages, generally a small walled cell flanking a church, where they renounced any kind of activity and entrusted themselves entirely to the generosity of neighbors and devout people.[9] The defining feature of these anchoresses, who were also found sporadically in larger cities, was the public aspect of their penitence, which they exercised for the most part in heavily trafficked areas: streets, bridges, or the center of town.[10] Another recurring motif was their assumption of the role of patron saints, with the concomitant absorption of all the cultural and political values that role embodied for the town and the collectivity that hosted them.

They were female servants who became patron saints after laboring as peasants, watching over flocks, scrupulously managing aristocratic households with their astute stewardship—girls who left isolated towns and moved to the cities, seeking work in the economic capitals of their regions.[11] As their independence developed through the practice of a profession, even the lowliest one in the hierarchy of social values, they showed themselves to be extremely volatile, ready for travel and for dangerous pilgrimages to distant lands. The most adventurous of the holy pilgrims in our Tuscan sample was surely Bona of Pisa, who ventured as far afield as Jerusalem; but Verdiana went to the sanctuary of Santiago di Compostela in Galicia with other women from Castelfiorentino, and Cristiana of Santa Croce undertook a series of very interesting shorter pilgrimages whose most distant goal was the holy mountain of San Michele al Gargano, in Apulia.[12] These women leave an impression of tremendous female mobility, which nevertheless appears to have been limited largely to the marginalized or those who did not share in the stability of the social classes that were comfortably planted, ideologically and structurally, by their relative prosperity.

In the larger urban centers, the phenomenon had other characteristics. There the predominant status within which women achieved sanctity was widowhood, a condition that unified, albeit in a differentiated manner, the variety of their social extractions. In this connection, it is illuminating to read the biography of Umiliana dei Cerchi with an eye to the problem of female destabilization. As a very young widow determined not to reenter the world of marriage to which her father wished to subject her immediately after the death of her husband, Umiliana was seen as a burden on the family's economy, occupying more space in the paternal household than her domestic and social "passivity" merited—her maintenance an unwelcome imposition. Voluntarily sequestered in the tower of her family's palace, she had to fight a newly married male cousin to defend her right to these poor lodgings in a sort of battle between the "active," functional dimension of the family and her own role, considered unproductive and negative.[13] After her father stripped her of her dowry, which covered the expenses of her return to the paternal home, Umiliana lived in the most abject poverty and the most complete economic deprivation in the midst of a quite well-to-do family. In her biography this conflict with her family represents a good part of the ascesis leading to sanctity. Her biographer, who proclaimed Umiliana to be a model of sanctification achieved through the everyday duties of familial and domestic obligations, seems to forget his declared ideological thesis. Perhaps carried away by his own monastic ideals of purity, he ends by so maligning first Umiliana's husband, then her father, and finally her kinsmen as to leave a clear impression that Umiliana was fighting her battle for salvation against them—and against the family in general—as if they were the devil himself.[14] Indeed, the culmination of her efforts was the laborious recovery of her own purity and the final, ideological restoration of her virginity, signaled by her postmortem apparition to a pious woman adorned with the crown of virginity. Thus, in her biographer's deepest conviction, wives and mothers could not aspire to sanctity. Not even continence—a compromise around which the mendicants had rallied the hopes for salvation of laypeople active in the various Third Orders, particularly the Franciscan— enabled them to aspire to saintly perfection.[15] The practice of chastity was the sole route. And as confirmation of this tendency, we can discern in Umiliana's *vita,* alongside the figure of the protagonist, hidden among the witnesses to her miracles or appearing as her spiritual sisters, companions in penance or prayer, the presence of other women who toiled on the road to sanctity. But the ones destined for greatest success were those who were least pressured by domestic and conjugal duties: other widows or young girls who decided to devote themselves to God without taking traditional monastic vows. In other words, they represent further examples of the phenomenon I have referred to as "destabilization," which beset those strata of female society that—whether voluntarily or not—were not fully integrated into family life.

This phenomenon must have been more marked in larger urban centers than in the smaller towns. In the cities, the increasing demographic concentration was beginning to corrode and dissolve the old structures of solidarity— family, lineage, and neighborhood—creating a need for new mechanisms of association. The mendicant orders hurried to meet this need by promoting and expanding a new constellation of associations combining charitable and devotional purposes, intended to organize and incorporate many of the religious, cultural, and often even political requirements of the new citizens. The order of penitence was one of the solutions they offered, and the desire of the female laity to participate in it should not be underestimated. Nevertheless, the predominance of the confraternal element within these associations of penitents tended to privilege male freedom of action in both the organizational structure and internal life of these groups, sharply restricting—and eventually eliminating—female involvement.[16]

Monastic Orders and Penitential Associations

The customary flow toward monastic institutions was reduced as well, paralleled in certain respects by the decline of the feudal fortunes to which they were closely linked. The reformed Benedictine monasteries had long prided themselves on the nobility of their recruits, at least on the female side. In this connection, we can cite a revealing example from Florence: the emblematic figure of the blessed Berta, a Vallombrosan abbess of the twelfth century who supposedly belonged to the noble family of the Cadolingi.[17] When she was entrusted with reorganizing and reforming the convent of Cavriglia, she proved so zealous that many of the nuns refused to accept her ideas of austerity and fled the convent—testifying to the internal decadence of the female congregation of St. Giovanni Gualberto. As abbess of Santa Maria a Mantignano, she made herself disliked by her community, not for insisting on strict observance of the rule, but for failing to defend with the desired firmness the privilege of direct pontifical jurisdiction over the convent, which was challenged by Bishop Pietro, a most ardent advocate of the pre-rogatives of the Florentine church. Unable to restrain the antiepiscopal sentiments of her nuns, the abbess, now close to death and veneration, returned with a small band of followers to her former convent of Cavriglia. Whether this account is true or not, it bears witness to internal difficulties, an inevitable consequence of the financial and administrative problems that beset monastic institutions when the noble classes and holders of vast estates, on whom they relied for support, suffered political and economic setbacks.[18] It was some time before the social circle of this monastic oligarchy expanded; and in the thirteenth century, the success of Umiltà of Faenza's Vallombrosan convent of San Giovanni Evangelista must be considered exceptional, in that her followers were drawn from less aristocratic backgrounds.[19] Only in the fourteenth century do we find figures like the blessed Paola, a Camaldolese nun whose presence (along with that of her spiritual father, the blessed Silvestro, a former wool-carder) shows that persons of more modest social extraction had joined the ranks of Florentine monasticism, which now did not hesitate to seek new members even in the houses of humble spinners.[20]

It is important to note that each of these figures from the world of traditional monasticism evidences, not the spiritual continuity of her community—as could be said of some of the convents of Poor Clares, where almost every abbess was a holy woman—but a period of rupture, reform, and restoration of the austerity of its early days. This need for (and failure of) monastic reform also appears in the life of Margaret of Città di Castello, the blind child abandoned by her parents when a Franciscan friar failed to produce a miraculous cure. She eventually became, as a tertiary, a featured figure in the Dominicans' gallery of saints, but only after having joined an unidentified female monastic community wallowing in lax religious practices, from which she was driven away because of her excessive severity.[21]

Even the new monastic initiatives envisioned by the mendicant orders, having unified the general movement of female penitence, soon ended by proposing yet again the familiar institutions characterized by enclosure and immobility. Moreover, their recruitment was directed toward a specific segment of society: the emerging urban classes, from which they gathered the excess female population.[22] Piccarda Donati may have found her place within the walls of the convent of the Poor Clares of Monticelli—even if it turned out to be only a temporary one—but Umiliana dei Cerchi did not succeed in crossing its threshold.[23] There were many reasons behind the constriction of monastic outlets even among the new communities of female mendicants. One might, for instance, suggest that the restriction of action inherent in monastic enclosure also dampened certain impulses that mendicant propaganda itself had stimulated when it offered women an opportunity for active charitable involvement and devotional practices that found their inspiration more in the bustling Martha than contemplative Mary.[24]

As we have seen, those women who were unable to marry (whether because of their numbers or for some other reason) found only a marginal place within the order of penitence, whose configuration as the order of continence gave preferential treatment to men and, at most, a few married women, while the supply of places in both old and new monastic institutions shrank in direct proportion to the increase in demand from the female population. The only remaining alternative was the reaffirmation of a penitential order for women, in the form of communities rather than confraternities, with which the traditional forms of private penitence could also be associated.[25] The evolution of the female movement in Florence can be illustrated by the thirteenth-century case of Umiliana dei Cerchi, portrayed by her hagiographers as a model for the nascent groups of women that sprang up around the Franciscan church of Santa Croce. These small and less small groups of penitents—known as *pinzochere, vestite, mantellate*—played an important role in the lives of individual mendicant houses, which they often sustained with a constant flow of donations.[26] The area around Santa Croce was filled with houses of penitents, which left an imprint even on the place names in that neighborhood. At the same time, the houses of Dominican tertiaries clustered around the walls of Santa Maria Novella; and in the fourteenth century one of these tertiaries, Villana delle Botti, was honored at an altar in that church as one of the blessed.[27] The new order of the Servites was receptive to female devotion, robing the followers of the blessed Giuliana Falconieri in their habit.[28] Later in the fourteenth century, the Augustinians, who were active in the rehabilitation of another type of outcast, the prostitutes, also encouraged a large movement of *mantellate* at Santo Spirito, echoes of which spread to the surrounding countryside with the blessed Giulia of Certaldo.[29] In Siena, the Humiliati as well produced a saintly tertiary, the blessed Aldobrandesca.[30]

This efflorescence, which took place roughly during the second half of the thirteenth century and the first half of the fourteenth, defines a characteristic urban pattern. In the major cities, despite the increasingly stringent attempts of the various orders to regulate or reduce contacts between the friars and this exuberant outpouring of female devotion (ever an occasion for woes and scandal, as popular stories so clearly indicate), the attentive and varied mendicant apostolate offered individualized and feasible solutions to a number of needs.[31] If Umiliana dei Cerchi, perhaps inhibited by pride of lineage, did not manage to support herself through work, many of those groups of women who found inspiration in her figure and prayed daily in the Franciscan church for her celestial intervention created for themselves a professional niche in the domestic exercise of certain artisanal activities, or formed cooperatives that allowed them to combine the incomes of poor and middle-class widows and, by living together, to resolve their problems of lodging and lead decorous lives, measured by communal rhythms and collective devotional practices.

In the countryside, in contrast, the way the problem posed by women's social integration was configured, its more limited scale, and the late and uneven penetration of the mendicant orders led to a less progressive and differentiated evolution than in the cities. Private forms of female penitence and anchoritism persisted much longer in rural communities; and in the late thirteenth and early fourteenth centuries, they were joined by more or less embryonic nuclei of female tertiaries, often signaled by the founding of organizations dedicated to charity or social assistance.[32] The establishment of female communities with clear monastic vocations, as in the case of Cristiana of Santa Croce, soon became more rigidly subject to episcopal control and was entrusted to the guidance of mendicant institutions.[33]

In point of fact, in rural areas the evolution of these forms of female penitence from the "independent" lay phase to the monastic phase was more rapid, even if the phenomenon itself seems less important in quantitative terms. As in the cities, female penitence was especially associated with the economically weaker social classes, at least in its initial phases.

In the second half of the fourteenth century, along with the emergence of new monastic communities of various affiliations, the Third Orders— each now institutionalized and clearly differentiated from the others— became more exclusively female. Their rules, which from the late thirteenth century had been taking more definite shape under both papal guidance and that of the leadership of the orders, reached their most complete formulation in the course of the fourteenth century.[34] It was no coincidence that Siena was the center around which coalesced not only the finished institutional organization of the Dominican Third Order Regular, but also the new ideological configuration that made it a model for the Observant reform of the Dominican order—both inspired by that extraordinary Dominican tertiary, Catherine of Siena.[35] Clare Gambacorta and another blessed woman, Maria Mancini, soon transformed the convent of regular tertiaries of Pisa into a center for the diffusion of Catherinian mysticism and a new model of monastic life.[36] This institutional crystallization was integrally linked with the first hagiographic "centralization" of the Dominican Third Order through the writings of one of Catherine of Siena's most faithful followers, Raymond of Capua, master general of the order. He drafted biographies of Dominican holy women and was the direct inspiration for the equally important Tommaso Caffarini, whose vernacular writings proclaimed the merits of the status of female penitent to a wider public.[37] The Franciscan Third Order also underwent a similar evolution at roughly the same time, inspired by the figure of Angelina di Montegiove.[38]

Universality and Particularism

Tuscan hagiography of the thirteenth and fourteenth centuries thus offers a picture of female sanctity as being closely tied to a lay population evolving, under the watchful control of the mendicants, from spontaneous movements toward associations that were increasingly institutionalized in monastic or regular forms.

As part of this religious response to social problems, the mendicants performed the complex cultural operation of systemizing and organizing the new florilegium of sanctity. Outside the mendicants' cultural sphere of influence, the *vitae* of female saints were generally elaborated in response to local sponsorship and for local use, in which the dominant value was patronage. These hagiographic exempla typically had resonance only in a limited area, and were crafted (in a process that often involved political motives) to perform a series of "functional" tasks for the community of that town of which the saint was both patron and symbol. Whether the saint symbolized the acquisition of certain communal liberties and jurisdictional independence from episcopal power or instead became the cultural emblem of a town that had lost its autonomy, there was a close connection, a well-defined relationship between a given community and its heavenly patroness. This type of representation actually appeared with some frequency even in the mendicant literature, where one often finds holy patronesses, but it was gradually reshaped by the hagiographical principles to which the new mendicant orders adhered. With their cultural and devotional outlook that went beyond the confines of any single locality—the same outlook that at first had supplemented the old patron saints of the cities with new cults of

Mary or of the cross—the mendicants inevitably introduced more general, if not more universal, characteristics in their hagiography. On occasion, the hagiographic model might be deliberately designed to fit a specific political context—as, for example, Umiliana dei Cerchi and Rose of Viterbo were deployed as part of the ideological mobilization around certain anti-imperial, anti-Ghilbelline, or anti-Cathar polemics—or it might happen to retain some local values and meanings. But these were destined to be subsumed in the universal significance of the proposed model, which , in addition to codifying the particular virtues of a given religious status, often sought to illustrate the excellence of the order to which the hagiographer himself, or those directly responsible for a certain case of sanctity, belonged. Thus, in the oft-cited case of Umiliana, it is easy to discern the apologetic intentions of the hagiographer Vito of Cortona, who sought to demonstrate that the penitential *propositum* constituted a path to perfection fully worthy of coexisting with the other regular institutions; while in the biography of the recluse Margaret of Cortona, praise of the saint's way of life coincided with an exaltation of the Franciscan movement. As her life was presented by her hagiographer, Margaret could also represent the ideological and cultural moment in which Cortona sought and won independence from the rule of the bishop of Arezzo; but her main function in her *vita* is to be "tertia lux in Ordine Francisci," the third light of the Franciscan order.[39] The Dominicans, too, sought to transform the old ties between local female saints and their communities. Thus, once the *vitae* of Vanna of Orvieto and Agnes of Montepulciano had become part of the cultural and devotional patrimony of the regular tertiaries of St. Dominic, organized by Caffarini in Venice, it was no longer possible to find in them traces of their regional identities or original local functions.[40]

In this process, the virtues of the penitential life were presented in the form of standard ascetic and mystical models. Devotional themes recur constantly, from the cult of childhood to devotion for the eucharist or for Christ's wounds, the gift of tears, and so on, following familiar patterns in which the emphasis might shift slightly because of particular cultural and exegetical preferences. Under the impact of this culture, which could well be called hegemonic, all of the characteristics deemed unnecessary to the purposes of the new hagiographic formulations disappeared. So too did those cultural residues, including what might be some revealing survivals of folk beliefs, which had imprinted not only the devotional relationship between the community and its female saint, but the hagiographic fabric itself.[41] Occurring in tandem with this process was the mendicants' creation of anthologies arranged by status and their progressive assimilation of figures who originally did not belong to their orders.[42] The Augustinians, who were an important cultural and ideological presence in both the cities and rural centers, pursued this process of adoption more eagerly than the Franciscans, whose principal collection of dubiously Franciscan biographies appeared later, in the work of Mariano of Florence.[43]

In conclusion, these few examples, drawn from a sample that calls for more extensive and detailed investigation, confirm a well-known aspect of the mendicants' pastoral activity. They intervened in areas of social laceration and disequilibrium, providing capillary guidance, defusing potentially explosive situations, and redirecting devout women toward the disciplined areas of the regular life. Thus the exuberant religious self-affirmation of a female laity that sometimes found its social condition uncomfortable was molded into the organizational structures of the secular Third Orders, opening a fresh path toward the monastic renewal of the regular orders.

NOTES

Originally published in *Temi e problemi nella mistica femminile trecentesca,* Convegni del Centro di studi sulla spiritualità medievale, 20 (Todi, 1983), pp. 109–35.

1. It is obvious that an exhaustive investigation would require far more space than this essay allows. This will not be so much a synthesis—since only work already completed can by synthesized—as a thematic outline of an ongoing research project that, while no longer in its beginning stages, is far from being completed. For further discussion of the phenomenon of female sanctity, see my essay "Penitenza e santità femminile in ambiente cateriniano e bernardiniano," in *Atti del Simposio internazionale cateriniano-bernardiniano, Siena 17–20 aprile 1980,* ed. Domenico Maffei and Paolo Nardi (Siena, 1982), pp. 865–75. (See now the collection of essays by Anna Benvenuti Papi, *"In castro poenitentiae": Santità e società femminile nell'Italia medievale* [Rome, 1990], where this essay appears on pp. 247–59).

2. On medieval models of sanctity, see the numerous works of André Vauchez, particularly *La sainteté en Occident aux derniers siècles du Moyen Age d'après les procès de canonisation et les documents hagiographiques* (Rome, 1981), and his essay "Female Sanctity in the Franciscan Movement," in *The Laity in the Middle Ages: Religious Beliefs and Devotional Practices,* trans. Margery J. Schneider (Notre Dame, 1993), pp. 171–83. On the mendicant organization of lay religious life, see Giovanni Miccoli, "La storia religiosa," in *Storia d'Italia,* vol. 2, part 1 (Turin, 1974), pp. 793–825, esp. pp. 798–808.

3. For biographical detail and bibliographical guidance concerning these women, see the relevant entries in the *Bibliotheca Sanctorum, Dizionario Biografico degli Italiani,* and *Dizionario degli Istituti di Perfezione.*

4. If the vast majority of holy women were uprooted or marginalized (by widowhood if nothing else), there were also some whose social situation was perfectly

normal. Villana delle Botti, for instance, fully enjoyed the middle-class comforts of fourteenth-century Florentine merchants, first in her father's home and then in her husband's. After her sudden conversion from worldly pleasures (which, significantly, followed the tormented years of the middle of the fourteenth century), Villana adopted the penitential practices of the Dominican Third Order. Villana, like her fellow citizen, the Franciscan Umiliana dei Cerchi almost a century before, rejected the family as a highway leading to worldly temptations. However, hers was the only example of sanctity attained without seriously inconveniencing the husband.

5. For some Tuscan examples, see Anna Benvenuti Papi, "Santità femminile nel territorio fiorentino e lucchese: Considerazioni attorno al caso di Verdiana da Castelfiorentino," in *Religiosità e società in Valdelsa nel basso Medioevo*, Proceedings of the San Vivaldo Conference, 29 September 1979 (Florence, 1980), pp. 113–44 (now in Benvenuti Papi, *"In castro poenitentiae,"* pp. 263–303).

6. Giunta Bevegnata, *Legenda de vita et miraculis beatae Margaritae de Cortona,* in *Acta Sanctorum,* February, vol. 3 (Antwerp, 1658), pp. 298–357; Giacomo Scalza, *Leggenda latina della beata Giovanna detta Vanna da Orvieto,* ed. Vincenzo Mareddu (Orvieto, 1853); Thomas Kaeppeli, *Scriptores Ordinis Praedicatorum Medii Aevi,* vol. 2 (Rome, 1975), pp. 340–41.

7. "Vita beatae Margaritae virginis de Civitate Castelli," *Analecta Bollandiana* 19 (1900): 21–36; Marie-Hyacinthe Laurent, "La plus ancienne légende de la b. Marguerite de Città di Castello," *Archivum Fratrum Praedicatorum* 10 (1940): 109–31; Giovanni del Coppo, *Legenda di Santa Fina di San Gemignano,* ed. M. G. Battelli (Florence, 1919); translated as *The Legend of Holy Fina, Virgin of San Gimignano,* by Mildred Blancke Mansfield (1908; reprinted New York, 1966). Fina's illness prevented her from coming to the aid of her mother when she was attacked; and when her mother died, Fina did not mourn.

8. Agnes had an exceptional biographer, Raymond of Capua; see *Acta Sanctorum,* April, vol. 2 (Antwerp, 1675), pp. 791–817. On Agnes, see Abele L. Redigonda, entry "Agnese Segni da Montepulciano," in *Dizionario Biografico degli Italiani,* vol. 1 (Rome, 1960), pp. 438–39. There are other examples of the persistence of the aristocratic tradition in monastic recruitment, albeit in less uniform fashion. Rosanese dei Negusanti, better known as Umiltà, was born to a noble family of Faenza; the elder Berta of Florence was connected with the Cadolingi family; Gherardesca of Pisa belonged to the noble family of the Della Gherardesca. Later, toward the end of the fourteenth century, the blessed Angelina—a descendant of the counts of Marsciano and, according to tradition, the "founder" of the regular Third Order of female Franciscans—enhanced the social standing of the new convents of tertiaries, which had hitherto been less exclusive. Another example of this progressive social improvement of the new monastic institutions is Clare Gambacorta of Pisa, who was also active in the late fourteenth century. This list of tertiaries who remained in the world, rather than entering a convent, included some women of high social and economic extraction; but since, as I have noted, the majority of them were widows, their original family conditions had little effect on their economic and juridical circumstances.

9. Examples include Verdiana of Castelfiorentino, Giovanna of Signa, Giulia of Certaldo, and according to the little we know about her, Diana Giuntini of Santa Maria a Monte. See Benvenuti Papi, "Santità femminile."

10. In addition to Gherardesca of Pisa, who along with her fellow Pisan Maria lived in the twelfth century or the early thirteenth, examples of female eremitism in an urban cultural context must also include, as a sort of late revival, the Florentine case of Apollonia who, with her companion Giana of Montelupo, adopted the penitential paradigm of hermits, residing in a hut on the centrally located Ponte alle Grazie: see Robert Davidsohn, *Forschungen zur älteren Geschichte von Florenz,* vol. 4 (Berlin, 1908), p. 443. This case is highly unusual for the late fourteenth century. Since their cell was in the neighborhood of Santa Croce, perhaps their manner of life had something to do with the movements of spiritual renewal that must have continued to smolder here and there even in the deliberately conservative ranks of the female Franciscan tertiaries.

11. "Famulatura" is the technical term used by the anonymous biographer of Cristiana of Santa Croce to define the domestic service of Oringa Menabuoi in Lucca (who assumed the name Cristiana after her conversion). See Giovanni Lami, "Vita della beata Cristiana fondatrice del monastero di Santa Maria Novella e San Michele Arcangelo nella terra di Santa Croce," *Charitonis et Hippophili Hodeoporici Pars V,* in *Deliciae Eruditorum,* vol. 18 (Florence, 1769), pp. 189–258, esp. p. 197.

12. See Benvenuti Papi, "Santità femminile," pp. 119–23.

13. See Anna Benvenuti Papi, "Umiliana dei Cerchi: Nascita di un culto nella Firenze del Dugento," *Studi francescani* 77 (1980): 87–117 (now in Benvenuti Papi, "*In castro poenitentiae,*" pp. 59–98), which contains full bibliographical and biographical details; see also André Vauchez's interesting comments in "Female Sanctity in the Franciscan Movement," pp. 178–82.

14. It would be useful not only to reflect on the concept of the family and its negative representation in this hagiographic model, but also to consider the characteristic moment of the religious conversion of both husband and wife. In addition to the many more famous or classical examples that could be cited (from St. Isidore the Farmer to St. Louis or, in a minor key, Lucchese of Poggibonsi, with their respective spouses), the cases examined here include the striking experience of Gharardesca of Pisa. She managed to further her own penitential aspirations by convincing her husband, Alferio, to enter the Camaldolensian monastery of San Savino of Pisa, the first step toward her own seclusion in a small cell built next to it. The Camaldolensian tradition played the same part in the more obscure story of another Pisan woman, Maria, who was said to have realized her vocation as anchoress after convincing her husband to enter a monastery. Similarly, the blessed Umiltà of Faenza initially intended to dedicate herself to monastic life along with her husband, Ugolotto (or Ludovico) dei Caccianemici, though she proceeded to fulfill her ascetic aspirations by secluding herself in the customary cell, built for her next to the convent of Sant'Apollinare. Our only example of domestic normality is Villana delle Botti, who, as we have already noted, succeeded in realizing her religious conversion "de-

spite" her family: see Stefano Orlandi, *La beata Villana della Botti, terziaria domeni-cana del secolo XIV* (Florence, 1955).

15. For studies on the penitents, see *L'ordine della penitenza di San Francesco d'Assisi nel secolo XIII*, ed. Ottaviano Schmucki, Proceedings of the Conference of Franciscan Studies, Assisi, 3–5 July 1972, Collectanea Franciscana, 43 (Rome, 1973); *I frati penitenti di S. Francesco nella società del Due e Trecento*, ed. Mariano d'Alatri, Proceedings of the Second Conference of Franciscan Studies (Rome, 1977); *Prime manifestazioni di vita comunitaria maschile e femminile nel movimento francescano della penitenza, 1215–1447*, ed. Raffaele Pazzelli and Lino Temperini, Proceedings of the Conference of Franciscan Studies, 30 June–2 July 1982 (*Analecta T.O.R. 15, no. 135*) (Rome, 1982); and *Il movimento francescano della penitenza nella società medioevale*, ed. Mariano d'Alatri, Proceedings of the Third Conference of Franciscan Studies, Padua, 25–27 September 1979 (Rome, 1980), in particular the studies by Giovanna Casagrande, "Aspetti del Terz'Ordine francescano a Perugia nella seconda metà del secolo XIV e nel XV" (pp. 363–97, esp. pp. 363–71), Mario Sensi, "Il movimento francescano dell penitenza a Foligno" (pp. 399–445), and Antonio Rigon, "I penitenti di San Francesco a Padova nel XIV e XV secolo" (pp. 285–310). See also Rigon, "I laici nella chiesa padovana del duecento: Conversi, oblati, e penitenti," in *Contributi alla storia della chiesa padovana nell'età medievale*, vol. 1 (Padua, 1979), pp. 11–81, a portion of which is translated in this volume. One should also keep in mind the papers on confraternities and penitents in *Ricerche di storia sociale e religiosa* 17/18 (1980).

16. Anna Benvenuti Papi, "I frati della penitenza nella società fiorentina del Due-Trecento," in Mariano d'Alatri, *I frati penitenti di San Francesco nella società del Due e Trecento*, pp. 191–220, esp. p. 205 n. 46 (now in Benvenuti Papi, "*In castro poenitentiae*," pp. 17–57).

17. On the disputed biography of Berta, who has been confused with the many other women of the same name associated with the convents of Cavriglia and Mantignano, see the relevant entries by Sofia Boesch Gajano in *Dizionario Biografico degli Italiani*, vol. 9 (Rome, 1967), pp. 427–29.

18. Sofia Boesch Gajano (see note 17) is inclined to identify the Berta involved in the dispute with the bishop of Florence as a different abbess of Montignano than the Berta we are discussing here, rejecting the identification first proposed by T. De Colle, *Donna Berta e Beata Berta dell'Ordine delle Benedettine Vallombrosane* (Florence, 1900), pp. 16 ff. and accepted by Emiliano Lucchesi, *Santa Berta abbadessa Benedettina Vallombrosana, dei conti Cadolingi signori di Borgonuovo e Settimo* (Florence, 1938; reprint, with notes by Giuseppe Raspini, Prato, 1979).

19. *De S. Humilitate abbatissa ordinis vallumbrosani Florentiae*, in *Acta Sanctorum*, May, vol. 5 (Antwerp, 1685), pp. 203–22; see also *Vita della beata Umiltà faentina*, ed. Francesco Zambrini (Imola, 1849 and 1856), and the Latin sermons attributed to Umiltà and edited by T. Sala, *Sanctae Humilitatis de Faventia: Sermones* (Florence, 1884) (available now in a new edition, *I sermoni di Umiltà da Faenza: Studio e edizione*, ed. Adele Simonetti [Spoleto, 1995], and in English translation as Umiltà of Faenza, *Sermons*, ed. Catherine Mooney [Newburyport, 1992]).

For documentation on the foundation of the two convents in Faenza and Florence, see M. Ercolani, *Vita di S. Umiltà* (Pescia, 1910), and more recently, *Nel VII centenario della fondazione del monastero faentino di S. Umiltà: Miscellanea storico-religiosa* (Faenza, 1966). Umiltà's followers included another blessed woman: Margaret, also from Faenza, who figures in Umiltà's *vita:* see G. Lucchesi, entry "Umiltà da Faenza," in *Dictionnaire d'archéologie chrétienne et de liturgie,* vol. 16, col. 382–84, which lists the abbessess of the two convents that Umiltà founded.

20. Zanobi Tantini, "Vita della beata Paola e del beato fr. Salvestro converso nel monastero degli Angioli di Firenze, il quale fu maestro e precettore della sopradetta beata Paola badessa in S. Margherita," in *Leggende di alcuni santi e beati venerati in Santa Maria degli Angeli di Firenze,* ed. Casimiro Stolfi (Bologna, 1864), pp. 85–129. On female monasticism, see Ida Magli, "Il problema antropologico del monachesimo femminile," in *Enciclopedia delle religioni,* vol. 4 (Florence, 1972), pp. 627–41.

21. "Vita beatae Margaritae virginis de Civitate Castelli," p. 24; Laurent, "La plus ancienne légende de la b. Marguerite de Città di Castello," p. 123.

22. On the Franciscans, see the interesting overview of Roberto Rusconi, "L'espansione del francescanesimo femminile nel secolo XIII," in *Movimento religioso femminile e francescanesimo nel secolo XIII,* Proceedings of the Seventh Conference of the International Society of Franciscan Studies, Assisi, 11–13 October 1979 (Assisi, 1980), pp. 265–313. In the same volume, see also Clara Gennaro's fine paper, "Chiara, Agnese, e le prime consorelle: Dalle "Pauperes dominae" di San Damiano alle Clarisse" (translated in this volume as "Clare, Agnes, and Their Earliest Followers"), which carefully brings out the pressures that led the early female communities inspired by the life and example of St. Francis to evolve in the direction of canonically accepted forms of monastic life.

23. See Zefferino Lazzeri, "Il monastero di Piccarda," *La Verna* 10 (1912–13): 169–81, 266–70, 361–67, 440–58; Lazzeri, "Memorie del monastero di Monticelli," *La Verna* 9 (1911–18): 478–86; Rusconi, "L'espansione del francescanesimo femminile," n. 35. As evidence of the high social extraction characteristic of the early members of female mendicant convents, see the documentation concerning the Florentine convents of the Poor Clares of Monticelli and the Dominican sisters of Santa Maria a Ripoli, in Davidsohn, *Forschungen,* 4: 411–15.

24. Perhaps instead of focusing on the economic system that usually supported monastic seclusion (that is to say, revenues from endowments of land), discussion should be broadened to include work in the female convents among the other activities that involved mixing with the outside world, such as hospital work and domestic aid to the sick: in other words, those elements of active piety that required a mobility not permitted by monastic enclosure. In any case, work was not incompatible with monastic enclosure: the oldest Florentine document on the existence of a *laboratorium* for weaving—a typically female craft—testifies to the fact that in the ninth century this activity had been performed by *converse* in convents: see Robert Davidsohn, *Storia di Firenze,* vol. 1 (Florence, 1972), pp. 137–39. Practiced for the most part by female servants and domestics, it was progressively abandoned in

the convents, or at least no longer exercised directly by the nuns, in keeping with the custom that, in the outside world as well, had led women of the well-to-do classes to give up the loom. This activity was left to the lower classes, until industrial weaving replaced production within families. Spinning long remained the traditional activity of women of the lower classes. It was the means of survival for many female tertiaries, and eventually returned to the convents, at least those that recruited primarily from the lower classes. An example of this comes from the life of the blessed Paola: "Since Sister Paola took much pleasure in crying, her companion Sister Francesca would tell her that she should spin, in order to produce fine wool or flaxen thread. And Sister Paola would go to the window where the other nun placed the spindles full of yarn and, picking up some, would put it among her few spindles and then devote herself to prayer and weeping" (Tantini, *Vita della beata Paola e del beato Salvestro*, p. 96). The original congregation of the Gesuates also sustained itself through work: see Clara Gennaro, "Giovanni Colombini e la sua Brigata," *Bullettino dell'Istituto Storico Italiano per il Medio Evo e Archivio Muratoriano* 81 (1969): 237–71. Many of the holy women discussed here worked in hospitals. In addition to the well-known case of Catherine of Siena, there are the much earlier ones of Ubaldesca da Calcinaia and Margaret of Cortona, who is said to have founded a hospital dedicated to Santa Maria della Misericordia. Aldobrandesca worked in the Sienese hospital of Sant'Andrea (later called the hospital of Sant'Onofrio), and the more obscure Tessa founded the oblates who lent their pious services in the hospital of Santa Maria Nuova in Florence. Female involvement in hospital activities was very common and merits more detailed study.

25. See the brief discussion in Gilles Gérard Meersseman, *Ordo fraternitatis: Confraternite e pietà dei laici nel Medioevo* (Rome, 1977), pp. 374–77.

26. Romana Guarnieri, entry "Pinzochere" in *Dizionario degli Istituti di Perfezione*, vol. 6 (Rome, 1980), col. 1721–49.

27. See Orlandi, *La beata Villana*.

28. Davide M. Montagna, "La 'Legenda' quattrocentesca della beata Giuliana Falconieri," in *Moniales Ordinis Servorum* 2 (1964): 16–28; see also Pedro M. Suarez and Franco Andrea Dal Pino, "Uffici e messe proprie dei santi e beati O.S.M., testo ufficiale con note critiche e bibliografia," *Studi storici dell'Ordini dei Servi di Maria*, vol. 15 (Rome, 1965). For a detailed analysis of the Servite sources pertaining to Giuliana and the other saints of the order, see Franco Andrea Dal Pino, *I Frati Servi di Santa Maria dalle origini all'approvazione*, vol. 1 (Louvain, 1972), pp. 38–39, 238, 444, and 446.

29. Aside from their success with the female public in general—indeed, we have documentation of numerous tertiaries under the guidance of the Augustinians—in the 1330s an important devotional and charitable enterprise inspired by the Augustinian preacher Simone of Cascia was undertaken by the members of the *laudesi* confraternity of Santo Spirito, who championed the project of rehabilitating prostitutes. The women were offered the opportunity of redeeming themselves with the creation of a small convent in which they could spend their lives in prayer, sewing, and weaving. See Davidsohn, *Forschungen*, 4: 422. For bibliographical guidance to the uncer-

tain sources concerning Giulia's life, see my "Santità femminile nel territorio fiorentino e lucchese," pp. 115, 136 n. 21.

30. *Acta Sanctorum,* April, vol. 3 (Venice, 1738), pp. 466–72.

31. Boccaccio wrote some of the most revealing novellas on the subject (*Decameron* IV, 2 and VIII, 3), but Sacchetti, too, added his voice to the chorus of disparagement: Franco Sacchetti, *Trecentonovelle,* ed. Emilio Faccioli (Turin, 1970), pp. 628–32, novella 207. However, perhaps the best expression of the bitter irony with which some contemporaries viewed the Franciscans and their devout female audience is Boccaccio's story of a beguiling widow who uses a Franciscan church as a place of flirtation: Giovanni Boccaccio, *The Corbaccio,* trans. and ed. Anthony K. Cassell (Urbana, 1975), pp. 58–60.

32. Once again I am thinking of Margaret of Cortona, who is credited with founding a hospital; but it may well be that local charitable institutions were linked with these saints only after the fact, as in the case of the hospital of St. Fina in San Gimignano.

33. The monastic community organized by Oringa Menabuoi and dedicated to the Archangel Michael and Santa Maria Novella claimed Franciscan origins; but these Constitutions of Cristiana of Santa Croce were based on the Rule of St. Augustine, probably because of the episcopal review they had to undergo: see Vincenzo Checchi, *Una fondatrice toscana del sec. XIII e le sue costituzioni: Santa Cristiana da Santa Croce sull'Arno* (Florence, 1927). The Augustinian rule was the one most often adopted by female congregations, whatever the terms of their original establishment may have been. The same is true of the congregation of the "Santucce" of Arezzo, whose ranks included Filippa Guidoni. This congregation spread rapidly to a large part of Tuscany; traces of it can be found even in Siena and Florence. On this movement, see Gregorio Penco, *Storia del monachesimo in Italia, dalle origini alla fine del Medioevo* (Rome, 1961), p. 292, and Leandro Novelli, "Due documenti inediti relativi alle monache benedettine dette 'Santuccie,'" *Benedictina* 22 (1975): 189–253. The spread of various forms of female enclosure—which was the direction usually taken by communitarian experiments—must have posed a difficult problem of identification for their contemporaries as well: see Gilles Gérard Meersseman, *Dossier de l'ordre de la pénitence au XIIIe siècle* (Fribourg, 1961), p. 28 n. 2. In Florence alone there were more than thirty congregations in the thirteenth and fourteenth centuries that followed some form of the Augustinian rule and that became affiliated only at a late date, if at all, with the traditional monastic orders: see Davidsohn, *Forschungen,* 4: 415–22.

34. See Meersseman, *Dossier,* pp. 128–56, and more recently, his *Ordo fraternitatis,* 1: 394–401.

35. Although Catherine remained a member of the secular wing of the Dominican Third Order, her activities as a reformer were the stimulus for the "regularization" of the entire institution, a regularization that would be brought to completion by her most inspired followers, such as Clare Gambacorta. On Catherine's role as an ideological watershed in the Dominican penitential movement, see my brief discussion in "Penitenza e santità femminile in ambiente cateriniano e bernardiniano." It is

also worth remembering that the great popularizer of the Dominican Third Order and its early rules was Tommaso Caffarini: see his *Tractatus de Ordine ff. de Poenitentia s. Dominici,* ed. Marie-Hyacinthe Laurent (Siena, 1938).

36. For the blessed Clare Gambacorta, see *Acta Sanctorum,* April, vol. 3 (Paris, 1965), pp. 503–16, and the especially interesting *Lettere della beata Chiara Gambacorta,* ed. Cesare Guasti (Pisa, 1871). Information on Maria Mancini is more sparse: see Niccola Zucchelli, *La beata Chiara Gambacorta ed il convento di San Domenico in Pisa* (Pisa, 1964), pp. 121–28. Clare Gambacorta's function as "the new Catherine" must be understood in relation with that of Giovanni Dominici as "the new Raymond of Capua." On Dominici, see Giorgio Cracco, entry "Banchini, Giovanni," in *Dizionario Biografico degli Italiani,* vol. 5 (Rome, 1963), pp. 657–64.

37. On the hagiographic works of Tommaso Caffarini of Siena and his role in the organization of the Dominican Third Order, see Fernanda Sorelli, "La production hagiographique du dominicain Tommaso Caffarini: Exemples de sainteté, sens et visées d'une propagande," in *Faire croire: Modalités de la diffusion et de la réception des messages religieux du XIIe au XVe siècle,* ed. André Vauchez (Rome, 1981), pp. 189–200; Sorelli, "Per la biografia del Bianco da Siena, Gesuato: Una testimonianza di Tommaso Caffarini (1403)," in *Atti dell'Istituto veneto di scienze lettere ed arti* 136 (1977–78): 529–536, esp. p. 528 n. 1; and her essay in this volume. See also the classic studies of Marie-Hyacinthe Laurent, particularly his preface to Tommaso Caffarini, *Vita di Santa Caterina da Siena,* ed. Giuseppe Tinagli (Siena, 1938), pp. 7–61.

38. Felice Rossetti, *La beata Angelina dei conti di Montegiove* (Siena, 1976); see also Mariano d'Alatri, entry "Francescane della beata Angelina" in *Dizionario degli Istituti di Perfezione,* vol. 4 (Rome, 1976), col. 269–70.

39. Franco Cardini, "Agiografia e politica: Margherita da Cortona e le vicende di una città inquieta," *Studi francescani* 76 (1979): 127–36; Anna Benvenuti Papi, " 'Margherita filia Ierusalem': Santa Margherita da Cortona e il superamento mistico della crociata," in *Toscana e Terrasanta nel Medioevo,* ed. Franco Cardini (Florence, 1982), pp. 117–37 (now in Benvenuti Papi, *"In castro poenitentiae,"* pp. 141–68).

40. See Sorelli, "La production hagiographique," esp. nn. 10–11.

41. In this regard the case of Verdiana of Castelfiorentino is revealing, since the existence of two hagiographic accounts, one written by a Vallombrosan monk in the early fourteenth century and the other elaborated by a Dominican friar in the fifteenth century, makes possible a comparative study. Thus, to remain on the subject of folklore, the first biographer accepted without question the presence of the serpents (which even became her iconographic symbol) in the life of St. Verdiana, while the second felt the need to fit their "obscure" presence into the cultural fabric with which he was more familiar, likening Verdiana to St. Anthony Abbot in order to interpret this extraneous sign. See Benvenuti Papi, "Santità femminile," p. 1 n. 6.

42. For the Franciscans, see Anna Imelda Galletti, "I francescani e il culto dei santi nell'Italia centrale," in *Francescanesimo e vita religiosa dei laici nel '200,* Proceedings of the Eighth Conference of the International Society of Franciscan Studies,

Assisi, 16–18 October 1980 (Assisi, 1981), pp. 313–63. For the Dominicans see the well-known works of Fathers Taurisano and Kaeppeli.

43. For a bibliography on the Augustinians, see Balbino Rano, "Agostiniani," in *Dizionario degli Istituti di Perfezione,* vol. 1 (Rome, 1974), col. 278–381. On Mariano of Florence, see Anastasius Van den Wingaert, "De Tertio Ordine Sancti Francisci iuxta Marianum Florentinum," *Archivum Franciscanum Historicum* 13 (1920): 3–77; Mariano's work has now been published by Massimo D. Papi, "Il Trattato del Terz'Ordine ovvero 'Libro come Santo Francesco istituì et ordinò el Tertio Ordine de Frati et Sore di Penitentia et della dignità et perfectione o vero sanctità sua' di Mariano da Firenze," *Analecta T.O.R.* 18 (1985): 263–588.

6

The Apostolic Canonization Proceedings of Clare of Montefalco, 1318–1319

Enrico Menestò

The canonization proceedings of Clare of Montefalco, with all of their interruptions, lasted a full 572 years, from 1309, the year of the first informational hearing, to 1881. But were it not for her tortuous road to sainthood, with unsuccessful canonization attempts in 1331, 1743, and 1854, Clare may well not have found the success that makes hers an exemplary case in the field of hagiographic studies. Her story has been muddied, in the first place, by the first two interruptions in her canonization proceedings, for reasons that are still not clear to us; second, by the strange fate of the records of the proceedings, which were mislaid several times and only recently rediscovered; and finally by the old argument between Franciscans and Augustinians, who both claim Clare as a spiritual member of their orders. In point of fact, Clare observed the Rule of St. Augustine from 1290 to her death; but this dispute has little bearing on the story of her canonization, since the question of whether she was Franciscan in outlook or instead was ambivalent in her spiritual orientation had no discernible effect on the delineation of a model of sanctity in her canonization proceedings.

Once these fruitless questions are discarded, the records of the fourteenth-century proceedings, which were undoubtedly among the most important and revealing of the entire Middle Ages, can assume their proper place in any attempt to understand and clarify the process through which Clare of Montefalco arrived at sainthood.

I do not intend to reconstruct here all of the historical details of the proceedings; others, in particular Silvestro Nessi, have already done this.[1] I will simply mention the most significant (and familiar) moments of this history, and then move on to an extended and detailed analysis of the text of the medieval proceedings, in order to define with greater precision the image of Clare and the typology of sanctity that is communicated in this source.

The Vicissitudes of the Proceedings

On 17 August 1308, Clare, daughter of Damiano and Giacoma, and second abbess of the convent of Santa Croce of the order of the Hermits of St. Augustine, died in her convent at the age of forty. Immediately after her death, the sisters opened up her body and found in her heart the symbols of Christ's Passion: the crucifix, the whip, the pillar, the crown of thorns, the three nails, the lance, and the rod with the sponge. In her gall bladder they found three globes of equal size, weight, and color, arranged in a triangle as the symbol of the Trinity.

The news of the discovery of these miraculous signs and the resulting popular excitement provoked an immediate reaction from the civic and ecclesiastical authorities. On 22 August, in fact, Gentile dei Giliberti of Spoleto, the *podestà* of Montefalco, intervened with his officials to examine personally the marvelous objects found in Clare's body.[2]

Immediately after this, Béranger of Saint-Affrique, vicar of the bishop of Spoleto, Pietro Paolo Trinci, came to Montefalco to investigate the veracity of the discovery, "burning with indignation" because he suspected that the signs had been planted by the sisters.[3] Theologians, jurists, and physicians were convened for the inspection. An examination of the heart ruled out the possibility of fabrication or artifice. Back in Spoleto, Béranger, disturbed and impressed by what he himself had verified, decided that such an extraordinary event should not be consigned to future oblivion.[4] For this reason, on 18 June 1309, scarcely ten months after Clare's death, he obtained from the bishop of Spoleto permission to open an inquiry into the entire affair. Thus began the first informational hearing on Clare's life and virtues.[5]

The inquest lasted until April of the following year.[6] But since it was necessary to record many putative miracles that Clare had performed after her death, work continued until 1315. Only after 14 October 1316 could Béranger go to Avignon to present the results of the informational hearing to the new pope, John XXII.[7] Once the contents of Béranger's report had been examined and verified under the direction of Cardinal Napoleone Orsini, on 25 October 1317, with the bull *Magna nobis exultationis,* the pope ordered the opening of an apostolic inquest into Clare's life, virtues, and miracles.[8]

This apostolic inquest lasted from 6 September 1318 to July 1319, and its results were immediately conveyed to the pope.[9] When John XXII received the documents, he appointed three cardinals, one of whom was Napoleone Orsini, to examine and report on them to the consistory. But it took an additional ten years to accomplish this, both because there was an enormous amount of documentation and, more important, because it was necessary to reconstitute the commission several times.[10] Cardinals Napoleone Orsini, a member of the commission from the start, Pietro de Arreblayo, and Bertrand de la Tour were the ones who completed (probably in 1330 or 1331) the examination of the depositions and compiled a final report known as the "Report of the Three Cardinals." This report was read in consistory, where it was agreed that the results of the inquest were decisive and that it was therefore possible to proceed with Clare's canonization.[11] But for incidental reasons that remain unclear, the proceedings went no further.

It was not until 1737, one hundred years after Urban VIII had allowed first the Augustinian order and then the diocese of Spoleto to recite the office and the mass with a proper in Clare's honor, that Clement XII ordered the proceedings to resume.[12] But after six years of work, the proceedings inexplicable came to another halt.

More than one hundred years later, the proceedings were taken up for the third time. On 28 August 1846, Pope Pius IX responded affirmatively to the petition of the new postulator of the suit, who requested that a special committee of cardinals be designated to reopen the proceedings. But because of procedural problems, again no progress was made.

However, two decisions made by Pius IX concerning procedures to be followed in canonization hearings made it possible to resume and, finally, to conclude the examination of Clare's case during the pontificate of Leo XIII. When the special commission assembled by the pope decided in favor of canonization, on 11 September 1881, Leo XIII issued the appropriate decree. The solemn celebration took place on 8 December.[13]

The Documentation

Such, in outline, is the tangled history of the canonization of Clare of Montefalco. The original fourteenth-century documentation generated by the initial inquiries and forming the basis of the case's various resumptions presumably included

1. The investigation ordered by the civic authorities of Montefalco on 22 August 1308, regarding the discovery of the symbols of Christ's Passion in Clare's heart.

2. The commission given to Béranger on 18 June 1309 by the bishop of Spoleto to initiate the first informational inquest on Clare's life and virtues.

3. The first informational proceedings on Clare's life and virtues, conducted by Béranger from 1309 to 1315.

4. Pope John XXII's commission to Cardinal Napoleone Orsini to prepare a secret report to the consistory based on Béranger's dossier.

5. The *Prima inquisitio facta in curia,* or first curial inquest, conducted by Cardinal Orsini from 1316 to 1317.

6. The bull *Magna nobis exultationis,* promulgated in Avignon on 25 October 1317 by Pope John XXII.

7. The bull *Dudum vobis,* promulgated in Avignon on 22 March 1318 by Pope John XXII, which settled the economic questions related to the apostolic proceedings.

8. The power of attorney given to Béranger by various bishops and town governments for the apostolic proceedings of 1318.

9. The records of the apostolic proceedings (6 September 1318 to July 1319). The entire dossier consisted of seven books. The first book contained the official documents (items 6–8 above) and the thirty-one *articuli interrogatorii,* the questionnaire prepared by Béranger; in the second were the depositions of the first two witnesses; in the third, the depositions of witnesses 3–37; in the fourth, the depositions of witnesses 38–66; in the fifth, the depositions of witnesses 67–238; in the sixth, the depositions of witnesses 239–486. Evidence presented during the inquest held in the Roman curia by Cardinal Orsini (item 5 above) constituted the seventh book.

10. The report of the three cardinals.

How much of all of this documentation has survived? As we have already said, the fourteenth-century documents, which were last seen and described in 1881 in Rome, were then mislaid. However, two handwritten copies were made in connection with the third resumption of the proceedings in 1846. The first was completed by Francesco Massi, a Vatican scribe, on 24 January 1850, and the second by Gerolamo Angeli, archivist, notary, and chancellor of the Congregation of Rites, on 26 April of the same year. These manuscripts contain approximately two-thirds of the *articuli interrogatorii,* nos. 13–222 (no. 9 above, book 1); part of the deposition of witness 1 (no. 9, book 2); the complete depositions of witnesses 38–238 (no. 9, books 4 and 5), and the beginning of the "Report of the Three Cardinals" (the *relatio processus*).[14]

In 1881, at the conclusion of the fourth and final resumption of the case, after the commission had reached a favorable verdict in the last and decisive stage of the proceedings—that is, the resolution of the "doubts concerning the miracles"—all of the relevant documentation was published. The textual transmission of another very precious portion of the medieval records was thus ensured. The volume included the text of the investigation carried out by the civic authorities of Montefalco on 22 August 1308; *articuli* 128, 130–132, 142–143, 155, 159–161, and 163–189; certain passages from the depositions of witnesses 1, 38, 39, 45, 53, 59, 60, 62, 66, 67, 68, 82, 97, 118, 119, 153, 157, 173, 175, 178, 204, 229, and 231; the "Report of the Three Cardinals" (the *recollectio minor,* or lesser report, without the *probationes testium*); the list of the 35 miracles regarded by these three cardinals as the most significant of the 303 miracles recorded; and finally, the *recollectio super XXXV miraculis,* or report on the 35 miracles, with the *probationes testium.*

The surviving documentation is therefore ample and detailed. However, I will limit my investigation to the records of the apostolic proceedings (1318–19), since they have always been and continue to be considered the most important—perhaps even the only—basis for interpreting and understanding the meaning and value of Clare's experiences in a broad hagiographic perspective. Even Béranger of Saint-Affrique's biography, the other major hagiographic source on Clare, is based largely on the depositions collected during the preliminary phase of the first informational inquest, depositions that may well have been gathered into the apostolic proceedings.

The Sociology and Hagiography of Canonization

Despite their lacunae, the documents from Clare's apostolic proceedings provide an ideal opportunity to study canonized sanctity, since they contain all the components and elements necessary for this type of research. But what interpretive keys should be used in reading and analyzing canonization proceedings?

Over the course of history, official proclamations of sainthood have assumed various forms. For a long time, popular sentiment, free of juridical preoccupations, decided who should be considered a saint. Later, when the church formulated its own system of law, legal criteria came to be applied to the official recognition of sainthood. Canonization thus became a decision made by the competent ecclesiastical authority to grant a public and mandatory cult to someone; and as we know, this was in fact a strictly juridical act.[15]

But in reality this manner of designating saints brings up various problems. We need to analyze how the official declaration of the cult came about, examine the relationship between the official confirmation of the cult and the cult itself, and trace the establishment of the cult, the spontaneous and popular impulses that gave rise to it, and finally the relations between the cult and the saint.[16] In short, we need to bring to light the fundamental stages of the relationship between cult and canonization.

This relationship is crucial to research on canonized sainthood. For one thing, it allows us to grasp the manner in which the canonical proceedings first took shape, whether as the outcome of a meeting of two different mentalities and cultures (folkloric culture, which usually generates the cult, and the culture of the dominant power, the church, which accepts and propagates that cult) or as the unilateral expression of power, which on its own initiative proposes and justifies the cult. What is equally important, it enables us to comprehend the transformations that the hagiographical model undergoes with the passage of time.

It is true that canonization proceedings are of notable importance for social and political history, since they bear witness to a well-defined social setting—that of the people who knew the saints during their lifetimes and then, upon their deaths, worked to win recognition for their cults—and also (as Le Goff would say) to the stratification of mentalities and distribution of intellectual power within that setting.[17] But it is equally true that these proceedings are the sign and the main evidence of the notion of perfection that a given historical period chose to articulate.

If these observations are valid, then canonization proceedings can be interpreted from at least two points of view: the sociological and the purely hagiographical.[18] The latter still seems to be the only way to grasp what is peculiar to a hagiographic text: its historical value as a model of human perfection, or sanctity.[19]

In the words of Pierre Delooz, canonization, and therefore the declaration of sanctity, emerges as "an activity taking place at the confluence of two powerful rivers. One flows from God's people, and the other from the various ecclesiastical authorities. That the second is stronger than the first is beyond question. There is a special reason for this which we have emphasized. The Church authorities are in a position to give strong guidance to the people of God when it makes choices. This is seen particularly in the influence they wield—ideological in character—on the world of ideas."[20] When (for example) Béranger drew up the questionnaire, or *articuli interrogatorii*, on which the testimony on Clare of Montefalco was to be based, he in fact directed and decisively channeled the depositions of the witnesses.[21] By applying a predetermined schema, he sought to obtain from the historical memory of the witnesses confirmation of a legend that was itself taking shape and structure through his direct intervention.

It was Béranger who transformed the life of a woman, a nun, into the life of a saint. He accomplished this despite testimony disputing Clare's sanctity, such as that of the Franciscan Tommaso Boni of Foligno, who, in addition to stating that he suspected that "the symbols in her heart were planted by a nun from Foligno," affirmed that Clare had "two chaplains, one of whom, Brother Jacopo de Cocorano of the Franciscan order, died while in prison for heresy; the other, by the name of Brother Paolo de Burgo, lived in a cell and had a bad reputation."[22] On top of all this, he suggested that Clare's ecstasies were nothing but epileptic fits.[23]

The economic aspect of the canonization proceedings was also subject in some ways to ecclesiastical influence. The proceedings often required substantial sums of money, which not everyone had readily available. Sometimes ecclesiastical authorities intervened directly to reduce the costs, thus smoothing the course of the proceedings. In the case of Clare's canonization, the pope himself settled the issue of finances. With the bull *Dudum vobis* of 22 March 1318, John XXII prohibited the investigators charged with the proceedings from asking the sisters of the convent of Santa Croce for more than two florins a day per person, given their poverty.[24]

Sanctity, like other values, is studied by sociologists in terms of collective images; but its uniqueness lies in the fact that sanctity exists "only as *recollected by others.* [Sociology] is never concerned with sanctity as lived by someone inside a community, but only with a community's recollection of such a person's behavior." The church, in fact, never declares a living person to be a saint: "Only the dead can be saints."[25]

If Clare is today the object of an official cult, it is because she was declared a saint; but this declaration was possible because Clare was held to be a saint in the past, during her lifetime. Thus the memory of the past informs the beatification and canonization proceedings, as it does in Clare's case.

But if the declaration of sainthood is based on the memories of other people, this means that it is subject to the opinions of others. And if one is a saint for other people, some saints—precisely because they are the result of the requirements, needs, and thus of the choices of other people—can be "constructed." This opens up the possibility of distinguishing between real and constructed saints, even if "all saints are more or less *constructed* in that, being necessarily saints *for other people,* they are remodelled in the collective representation which is made of them.[26]

Clare, however, is historically knowable, and so there is no doubt that she is a real saint, many of whose characteristics can be precisely defined.

She is certainly not an invented saint, at least in terms of documentation. Perhaps because of this, the image of Clare in various periods of history (unlike that of many other saints) has generally remained close to the reality attested to by sources contemporary with her life.

The early image of Clare, then, has never been drastically altered to fit changing sociocultural climates and the particular requirements imposed by these changes. Even her iconography, from what I can determine, has remained more or less faithful to the image of the saint in her canonization proceedings and in Béranger's biography. Her iconography is not one of those in which successive collective mentalities have so refashioned the saint that all traces of the original model, the historically definable person, have disappeared.

Popular Opinion and Ecclesiastical Authentication

If it is true that a saint exists only in the eyes of other people, then we must define who these people are. This is the first problem that must be posed in Clare's case as well.

Clare was a saint in the eyes of her brother Francesco and the sisters in her convent, but also for the people of Montefalco, Spoleto, Todi, and Perugia. She was a saint according to the common people, to whom we can add some representatives of a higher social class (doctors, jurists, and notaries), but also according to Cardinals Napoleone Orsini and Giacomo Colonna, Ubertino da Casale, and the Lateran canon Angelo Tignosi.

Acceptance of her sanctity was not limited to a strictly local area, but rather extended to a broad cultural region. And it certainly cannot be said that church officials simply constructed her cult. On the contrary, when Béranger heard that the sisters in the convent claimed to have found the symbols of Christ's Passion in Clare's heart, he hastened to Montefalco, as we said, indignant and eager to punish those responsible for the presumed fraud. It was only after personally verifying that these symbols were not some swindle perpetrated by the sisters that he was transformed from inflexible inquisitor into an impassioned supporter of Clare's sainthood.

But the memories and opinions of other people cannot by themselves create a saint. Public opinion must be transformed into juridical reality. The final decision to grant a public cult does not rest, in fact, with those who prompted and guided the proceedings. Once the preceding "popular sanctification" has been authenticated and public pressure has thereby been recognized as genuine and convincing, it is up to the ecclesiastical authorities, in the person of the pope, to decide whether to elevate a servant of God to the honor of the altars of the universal church. Public pressure is thus necessary but not sufficient for a declaration of sainthood.

In the case of Clare's canonization, as we have seen, the opinions expressed and pressure applied by Béranger and numerous other people were not enough, even when they took the form of a regular and probative sifting of the evidence; in keeping with the judicial norms, official papal approval was required. That is why, having lost the opportunity of winning approval from John XXII and his immediate successors in Avignon (who perhaps had little or no interest in the case of the nun from Montefalco), almost six centuries went by before Clare was solemnly canonized through the initiative of Popes Pius IX and Leo XIII.

According to procedural norms, the period between the recognition of a reputation for sanctity (the preliminary investigation and the apostolic proceedings) and the definitive judgment that imposes a public cult is devoted to an examination of the candidate's heroic exercise of theological and cardinal virtues and of the miracles that occurred through her intercession, whether during her lifetime or after her death.[27] In practice, this means discussion of what are commonly considered to be the special attributes of sainthood.

Where they exist, the *articuli interrogatorii* are usually arranged in such a way as to certify the exemplary exercise of these virtues, to which are added, in the case of professed religious, the observance of the three vows of poverty, chastity, and obedience to the rules of their own orders. In Clare's case as well, the *articuli* prepared by Béranger furnish a virtue-by-virtue description of the saint's behavior, along with attestations of a great many miracles.[28]

Vows, Promises, and Miracles

A sociological and juridical interpretation of canonization proceedings has the merit of reinserting sanctity into its historical context. For one thing, it allows us to define the outlook of a given historical period, which may or may not be the expression of the dominant institutions: that is, it discloses the way that people from various social classes and cultures interpret, accept, or reject individuals or events that are out of the ordinary. What is more, it enables us—almost compels us—to identify the manifestations and characteristic signs of sanctity in public opinion and the collective memory.

Belief in the supernatural and the conviction that it intervenes in the world is one of the characteristics of medieval culture. It is natural, therefore, that miracles, or the *gesta Dei per sanctos*—God's actions through the saints—constitute one of the main manifestations by which the relationship between heaven and earth is made concrete.

But sanctity has other reflections in common attitudes, as Vauchez has amply illustrated.[29] Vows are a prime example. Very often, the intercession of the saint depends on the formulation of a promise, as Clare's proceedings document. Despite its brevity, the oral formula "Sancta Clara adiuva me" (Help me, Saint Clare) is the preparatory element that establishes relations between the holy protectress and the people.[30] This invocation is often accompanied by a promise or a series of promises that constitute the recompense for the grace being requested. Almost always the promise includes a visit to the saint's tomb, often barefoot, sometimes in a hairshirt, occasionally without a shirt.[31]

Vows were made to bring people to the tomb if they were cured.[32] Women in labor promised to bring their newborns, and if the baby was female, to name her for the saint.[33] People pledged to fast or to recite a certain number of paternosters.[34] The material payment promised most often consisted of candles or a certain quantity of wax for the church, the altar, or Clare's tomb.[35] Recipients of miracles offered wax images, sometimes representing the parts of the body that were cured—a head, an arm, a hand, a foot, a stomach—or objects relating to the illness, such as a truss to represent a hernia now cured.[36] Many procured silver thread to tie around the tomb of the saint, some offered money or an unspecified donation; one promised a piece of cloth.[37]

Generally the promises were rather simple in nature, even if they included two, three, or even more of these elements. Sometimes, however, they could be quite detailed, as was that of Puppo, son of Gentile of Spoleto. He sought the recovery of his brother Baldo, who was gravely ill. As recompense, he vowed to go barefoot on a pilgrimage to Clare's tomb and offer a wax image as large as his brother, together with a two-pound wax candle and fifty pounds in Cortonese coinage, which the sisters of Santa Croce could use either to provide a dowry for a girl or to build a new tomb for St. Clare.[38] In other cases the promise was enriched by an additional element: a pledge to do works of charity in thanks for the grace received.[39]

The vow was in itself a sort of binding moral contract. Before making a vow to an intercessor, members of a religious order had to obtain the authorization of their superiors, for the very reason that the contract restricted their freedom.[40] Moreover, many people were firmly convinced that saints punished those who did not respect their vows.[41] Thus it came to be thought that a favor already granted could be revoked if the promise was not fulfilled or faith in the intercessor was inadequate.[42] Greater faults, such as skepticism or derision of supernatural events, were thought to be met with swift and severe punishment.[43]

On the other hand, on some rare occasions there were people who apologized at the outset for seeking grace and reconciled themselves to the possibility that it would be denied, while others hesitated between the understandable desire to be cured and the recognition that suffering had redemptive power.[44] The beneficiary of a divine favor might also promise perpetual fidelity to the intercessor.[45]

These, then, were the vows. But what kinds of miracles were requested? As one might expect, petitions are generally addressed to celestial forces and spirits as sources of cures and protection—in other words, as guardians of health. In fact, saints by their very nature were supposed to be capable of performing cures and intervening in situations in which human forces were powerless. Thus, a certain Palmola of Montefalco claimed that she had turned to St. Clare because she could not find a doctor able to cure her.[46] But the miracle-working power of the saints was not limited to the physical welfare of men and women; sometimes it also enhanced moral well-being. Biagio of Spoleto declared that under Clare's influence "he was transformed into an almost completely different person."[47]

Transformations of Worship

These are not the only reflections of sanctity in popular attitudes. The mechanisms by which they are embedded in the idea of sanctity and the veneration given to saintly intercessors reveal various complex desires, mental forms, and historical and cultural indicators. For instance, the records of Clare's proceedings contain evidence of an interesting change in the history of the cult of the saints that took place, as Vauchez has amply documented, at the end of the thirteenth century and the beginning of the fourteenth.[48]

Up to this time, the cults of new saints did not always have an easy time establishing themselves, since popular piety was reluctant to abandon old intercessors whose effectiveness had already been abundantly demonstrated. This is the rationale behind those dreams and visions in which well-known saints sponsored the new ones and vouched for their sanctity. At the canonization proceedings of St. Thomas Aquinas, for example, a Dominican and a Benedictine both testified to having had visions in which St. Augustine attested to the orthodoxy of Thomas's doctrine.[49]

In the fourteenth century, however, this pattern was inverted: when the faithful had to choose between two intercessors, quite often they invoked the more recent one. Thus Clare of Montefalco seems to have taken the place of

Clare of Assisi in the hearts of the Umbrian faithful. There is at least one telling deposition on this subject: a woman named Simonetta of Perugia recounted that one day while deep in prayer, she had heard a voice suggesting that, if she wished to be cured of a grave illness, she should make a vow to St. Clare. "And this Simonetta thought to herself that she had already made a vow to St. Clare of Assisi at another time, and she did not know of any St. Clare other than that of Assisi. And then the voice responded to her thought, although she had said nothing, saying: 'The St. Clare of whom I speak had a spiritual master alone, not an earthly one . . . and her humanity is as pure as the humanity of St. John, and she is called St. Clare of the Cross.' "[50]

These new saints who replaced the traditional ones were often local figures, who were considered to be more effective protectors since they were closer than those who, however well-established as objects of official cults, were geographically distant. Popular opinion also held that new saints were more responsive to the requests of those who invoked them, since they in some sense needed to gather an abundant group of devout followers around them to consolidate their prestige.[51] Thus Cecco of Montefalco vowed: "Blessed St. Clare, I ask that by your virtues you might free me from this pain; and I promise you that if you do this, I will notify a hundred people."[52]

The Theme of the Crucifixion

The foregoing considerations justify using data gleaned from these canonization proceedings for insights into cultural values during Clare's lifetime and the period immediately following it. The relationship between hagiography and power, like that between hagiography and mentality and, more generally, hagiography and society—in short, the encounter between the ideological impulse at the origin of a hagiographic text and that responsible for its diffusion and development—are all important historiographical concerns. However, our analysis must also come to grips with the problem of sanctity itself, in order to reconstruct, through the life story by which the perfected state was attained, the model of perfection that this story embodies.

If we examine the nature and characteristics of Clare's mystical experiences from this perspective, it seems evident that she embodied a very important stage in the history of Christian spirituality. Not only did Clare, as many witnesses testified, practice the theological and cardinal virtues in an exemplary fashion while possessing other extraordinary qualities. Not only were her actions marked by intense asceticism: mortification, austerity almost to the limits of human strength, fasting, silence, rejection of all forms of pleasure. And not only did her practice of poverty, chastity, obedience, humility, and prayer that often reached a mystical annihilation in God define a striking pattern of behavior,[53] though one that still remained within the tradition of the way of life that characterized the many communities of recluses that sprang up in central Italy at the end of the thirteenth century and the beginning of the fourteenth. Her importance lay above all in the fact that in her the search for mystic union with the crucified Christ attained truly extraordinary strength and fervor. Through her assimilation with Christ in his humanity, of which Clare was ever more concretely conscious, this nun from Montefalco set a standard and exercised an apostolate both within and beyond her community.

Clare's sanctity revealed itself, then, through her exceptional talents. In addition to possessing the gift of prophecy, the ability to read consciences and intuit the hidden thoughts and errors of her interlocutors, she also had an inspired wisdom, which she received from direct visions of God or by means of the Holy Spirit.[54] Her sanctity also revealed itself in visions and ecstasies, and most strongly of all in the intense devotion to the suffering Christ that impelled her to take on herself the passion and death of the incarnate God.[55] Clare joyously welcomed—in fact, she continually sought out—any opportunity to identify herself with Christ dying on the cross.

Whether genuine or not, the miraculous signs found in Clare's heart concretize the intensity with which she lived Jesus' Passion. In their effective reality or symbolic value, they represent the mysterious force of love and of mystic "com-passion." The intensity of her identification was what convinced the saint and those around her that Christ had placed the cross in her heart. In his deposition, her brother Francesco stated that after the apparition of Christ bearing the cross on his shoulders, "she always physically felt the cross in her heart."[56]

The canonization proceedings record an even more meaningful episode on this theme. During her final illness, which was to lead to her death, Clare turned to Sister Giovanna, who was making the sign of the cross over her to chase away the devil, and exclaimed: "Sister, why do you make this sign over me? I have no need of the cross outside me, for I have my Jesus Christ crucified inside my heart."[57] Thus the cross of Christ was mystically rooted in Clare's heart: for this reason the idea of bearing the cross as she followed him remained with her until she died.[58]

The Themes of Mercy and Love

The Passion of Christ was Clare's favorite theological theme.[59] However, the Christocentric nature of her experience also emerges in another theme, which was closely linked to and conceptually dependent on the first: charity and merciful love. Clare represents the woman who wished to imitate Christ at all costs, even in the sense that mystical "compassion," suffering, and the cross are felt to be the sole means of realizing God's love for humankind. In other words, having accepted the cross as the pattern for her own life, Clare follows internally the path leading to the cross, and in so doing she feels herself transformed into her model and embraces his goals: the redemption of her fellow creatures.

For this reason the austerity of her life can be interpreted as the crucifixion of the flesh, which she practiced in an exemplary fashion starting in her infancy. But following Christ does not mean taking mortification as the supreme guiding principle: the highest law is love. And in the truest and most profound sense, Clare's spiritual experience sprang from love. Her brother Francesco testified that she said that "it is not surprising that the soul loves God above all things a hundred times more than its very self. The reason for this is that he is our creator, who created us out of nothing and formed us in his image. Similarly, he is our redeemer, who with his blood redeemed and ransomed us on that harsh cross, on which he died for us and was cruelly killed, suffering disgrace, vituperation, and immense pain. Likewise, he is our governor, who governs and rules over us, and promises eternal life and will give it faithfully without deceit. And therefore, having considered all of these many remarkable things, the soul should love and adore God inseparably from itself, and even spend itself a thousand times, giving itself in all things as much as it can."[60]

For Clare, this love for God and Christ was not a truly contemplative need, which was felt and experienced only in an interior way; rather, it was primarily love and charity for other people, especially the poor and needy. Francesco also related that Clare "demonstrated such charity for her neighbors that she seemed to love her neighbors more than herself, because she offered herself totally and freely as a spiritual and temporal helper to her neighbors—not so much to her sisters, whom she loved as daughters, but to anyone who was needy and was willing to be helped by her. Similarly, she prayed for sinners with all of the fervor of her mind, empathizing with their suffering, lest they be condemned to be separated from Jesus Christ himself."[61]

Out of love and charity, then, the saint was willing to offer herself completely, following the example of Christ's suffering and death.[62] Clare's God was no longer the lofty and splendid God of the early medieval monks, who made his contemplation the goal of their harsh ascetic life and separation from the world, nor was he any longer St. Bernard's God of love, the object of ecstatic union and annihilation. Instead, he was the God-man, whose defining feature was the cross. He was the God of suffering who could be found in the poor and the oppressed and was no longer felt to be so different and distant, but rather seemed almost human and constantly present, a God who could be encountered at every step among other human beings.[63]

Clare's decision to pattern herself on Christ was thus transformed into a missionary and priestly zeal. Significantly, Clare's zeal was shared by the other great female mystics of medieval Italy, and more particularly, Umbria: Clare of Assisi, Angela of Foligno, Margaret of Cortona, and Margaret of Città di Castello.

Clare's Spirituality

The defining feature of Clare's mystical experience thus seems to be an experiential and "affective" spirituality, fully centered on the human reality of Christ.

Clare's spiritual outlook had perhaps already matured before 1290, the year in which her sister Giovanna, the first abbess of the convent of Santa Croce, adopted the Augustinian rule. It developed, that is, in the period spent living in her first cell (located near the hospital of the poor of San Leonardo) and the second (near a little church dedicated to St. Catherine of Alexandria), in contact with and hence influenced by the Franciscans.[64]

This invocation of the Franciscan movement is certainly not meant to reopen the age-old (and pointless) polemic over Clare's supposed affiliation with the Order of St. Francis; nor do I have any intention of denying that she professed the Rule of St. Augustine.[65] It is simply an observation that might explain how themes that had characterized the spiritual experience of Francis came to appear in Clare. On the other hand, the analogies between Franciscan spirituality and that of Clare, which seem to go well beyond a mere Christocentric piety, do not in any way deny her Augustinian quality.[66] Moreover, it is well known how powerfully Augustine and the tradition that sprang from him influenced Franciscan masters.

The originality of Clare's mystical journey thus seems to reside in her fusion, within the setting of her convent and with full respect for its rule, of two distinct yet closely related spiritual traditions: the Augustinian and the Franciscan. It is a complex originality indeed.

Clare was a woman given to meditation, yet at the same time a woman of action. Hers was, in fact, not only a spiritual choice, but also a historical one, in the sense that Clare loved the world itself and the people in it, and displayed and developed this love in the eyes of the world, involving human things and hence history in her mystical journey. "I see that all created things are good," affirmed Clare, "and see nothing as bad except one thing: sin"—demonstrating a profound and entirely Franciscan awareness of living in God the fullness of the world and of history.[67] Her sanctity is thus rooted in history, in a serene and optimistic relation with the world and a complete dedication to other people.

Like Francis, Clare joined together contemplation and apostolic activity; and as in the career of the saint of Assisi, the historical meaning of her choice is closely bound up with its theological meaning. As many of the depositions attest, Clare was often present among the poor, the ill, the leprous; Sister Marina remembered her also as a mediator of the peace between the cities of Trevi and Montefalco.[68]

Equally revealing is the decided opposition she saw between mystical experience and intellectual knowledge of God, considered a source of pride and hence perilous for the soul. In keeping with the declaration of blessed Giles of Assisi that "Paris, Paris itself is destroying the order of St. Francis" and its echo in Jacopone of Todi, who lamented, "In sorrow and grief I see Paris demolish Assisi," Clare turned to her brother Francesco—at that time a young Franciscan friar—saying: "I do not want you to always seek this knowledge, and always weigh this praise critically. And I tell you for my part that I would be happier if you were a layman and cook for the friars in good spirit and devout fervor than if you were a teacher greater than any other."[69]

For Clare, the intellectual moment was not the apex of human and divine experience. Human life finds its peak in an enduring conformity with Christ in his mysteries of redemption and reconciliation, and above all in his Passion and death; and this conformity is achieved more through experience than knowledge.

These, in broad outline, are the lineaments of Clare's sanctity as they appear in the records of her canonization proceedings in 1318–19. These traits do not simply emerge and end in a private and intimate evolution, but reveal themselves also in history, in human and political events, such as the role—clearly documented in the proceedings—that Clare played in exposing and eliminating the sect of the Free Spirit.[70]

Along with sociocultural and historical-ideological meanings, the records of the canonization proceedings thus present a precise and fully realized image of perfection that, for the originality and complexity of its features, can claim to rank as a highpoint in the history of sanctity.

NOTES

Originally published in S. *Chiara da Montefalco e il suo tempo,* ed. Claudio Leonardi and Enrico Menestò (Florence, 1985), pp. 269–301.

1. See Silvestro Nessi, "I processi per la canonizzazione di S. Chiara da Montefalco: Vicende e documenti," *Bollettino della Deputazione di storia patria per l'Umbria* 65 (1968): 103–60. For biographical and bibliographical information on Clare of Montefalco, see Giulia Barone, in *Dizionario Biografico degli Italiani,* vol. 24 (Rome, 1980), pp. 508–12. When this essay was written, the original fourteenth-century records of Clare's canonization proceeding were thought to be lost. On their rediscovery, see Enrico Menestò, "I processi per la canonizzazione di Chiara da Montefalco: A proposito della documentazione trecentesca ritrovata," *Studi medievali,* ser. 3, 23 (1982): 971–1022. See also the critical edition of the proceedings: *Il processo di canonizzazione di Chiara da Montefalco,* ed. Enrico Menestò (Florence, 1984; reprinted Spoleto, 1991). It is from this edition that the citations—originally based on the nineteenth-century copy of the records—are now taken.

2. See *Sacra Rituum Congregatione particulari, eminentissimo ac reverendissimo domino Thoma Maria Martinelli relatore, Spoletana canonizationis b. Clarae de Monte Falco Monialis Ordinis Eremitarum S. Augustini, positio super miraculis* (Rome, 1881) (hereafter simply *Positio super miraculis*), part 3, *Summarium novum,* pp. 51–54; Pietro Tommaso De Töth, *Storia di S. Chiara da Montefalco* (Siena, 1908), pp. 110–11; Nessi, "I processi," pp. 133–35.

3. *Positio super miraculis,* part 3, *Summarium novum,* p. 95.

4. Ibid., part 2, p. 175.

5. Ibid., pp. 12–13.

6. See Battista Piergili da Bevagna, *Vita della b. Chiara detta della Croce da Montefalco dell'Ordine di S. Agostino* (Foligno: Agostino Alterii, 1640), pp. 263–64.

7. For these and later events, see ibid., pp. 265–68.

8. See Isidoro Mosconio, *Compendium de vita, miraculis et revelationibus beatae Clarae de Cruce Montis Falconis oppidi in Umbria* (Bologna: Apud Heredes Ioannis Rossii, 1601), pp. 13–16; Piergili, *Vita della b. Chiara,* pp. 360–61; *Positio super miraculis,* part 2, pp. 22–25; Nessi, "I processi," pp. 136–38.

9. See *Positio super miraculis,* part 2, p. 93.

10. See ibid., pp. 93–94.

11. See Piergili, *Vita della b. Chiara,* p. 271.

12. See *Positio super miraculis,* part 1, p. 13; part 2, pp. 4–6; 9–10.

13. For these final events in the proceedings, in addition to Silvestro Nessi, "I processi," pp. 119–20, see Lorenzo Tardy, *Vita di Santa Chiara da Montefalco* (Rome, 1881), pp. 225–36.

14. The first of these copies is in the Archivio Segreto Vaticano, Sacra Congregazione Riti, Processo 2929. The second is in the Archivio della Postulazione generale Ordinis Sancti Augustini, MS. 43.

15. See Pierre Delooz, "The Social Function of the Canonization of Saints," in

Models of Holiness, ed. Christian Duquoc and Casiano Floristán, Concilium 129 (New York, 1979), pp. 14–15.

16. See *Agiografia altomedievale,* ed. Sofia Boesch Gajano (Bologna, 1976), p. 43.

17. See Jacques Le Goff, *Pour un autre Moyen Age: Temps, travail, et culture en Occident* (Paris, 1977); translated as *Time, Work, and Culture in the Middle Ages* by Arthur Goldhammer (Chicago, 1985).

18. See Pierre Delooz, *Sociologie et canonisations* (Liège, 1969), and "Pour une étude sociologique de la sainteté canonisée dans l'Église catholique," *Archives de sociologie des religions* 13 (1962): 17–43; translated as "Towards a Sociological Study of Canonized Sainthood in the Catholic Church," in *Saints and Their Cults: Studies in Religious Sociology, Folklore, and History,* ed. Stephen Wilson (Cambridge, 1983), pp. 189–216.

19. For this aspect of hagiographic research, see Claudio Leonardi, "Pienezza ecclesiale e santità nella *Vita Gregorii* di Giovanni Diacono," *Renovatio* 12 (1977): 51–66; "From 'Monastic' Holiness to 'Political' Holiness," in Duquoc and Floristán, *Models of Holiness,* pp. 46–55; and "L'agiografia latina dal Tardoantico all'Altomedioevo," in *La cultura in Italia fra Tardo Antico e Alto Medioevo,* Proceedings of the Conference of the National Research Council, Rome, 12–16 November 1979 (Rome, 1981), pp. 643–59.

20. Delooz, "Social Function of Canonization," p. 23.

21. In at least one case, that of Clare's brother Francesco, the deposition was not directly tied to the questionnaire. It thus took a different course from the stereotyped and homogeneous testimony of the other witnesses.

22. Menestò, *Il processo,* p. 435: "illa singna cordis eius fuerunt facta artificiose ab una sorore de Fulgineo"; "duos cappellanos, unum qui fuit mortuus in carcere propter heresim, silicet frater Iacobus de Cocorano ordinis Minorum, alium qui vivit in carcere et dicebatur esse male fame, nomine frater Paulus de Burgo."

23. Ibid.: "cadebat sepe in terram."

24. See Mosconio, *Compendium de vita Clarae,* pp. 16–17; Piergili, *Vita della b. Chiara,* pp. 361–362; *Bullarium Franciscanum,* 5:147; Nessi, "I processi per la canonizzazione di Chiara," pp. 138–39.

25. Delooz, "Towards a Sociological Study of Sainthood," p. 194.

26. Ibid., p. 195.

27. In the case of martyrs, this includes careful scrutiny of their martyrdom.

28. Of the 315 *articuli interrogatorii* prepared by Béranger, nos. 13–50 treat Clare's "heroic virtues" as witnessed both while she lived in her first hermitage (known as that of Damiano from the name of the father of its founder, Clare's sister Giovanna) and while she lived in the new convent of Santa Croce before becoming its abbess in 1291; nos. 51–158 treat Clare's "heroic virtues" and extrardinary qualities from the time of her election as abbess until her death; nos. 159–89 concern the miraculous discovery of the symbols of Christ's Passion in Clare's heart; and nos. 190–221 relate a series of miracles attributed to her intervention.

29. See André Vauchez, *La sainteté en Occident aux derniers siècles du Moyen*

Age d'après les procès de canonisation et les documents hagiographiques (Rome, 1981), pp. 530–58.

30. Menestò, *Il processo,* pp. 262, 366, 409, 430, 488, 489, 490, and 491.

31. Ibid., p. 366: "Sancta Clara adiuva me, et si hoc feceris vissitabo seppulcrum tuum" (see also pp. 309, 361, 371, 374, 387, 421, 444, 445, and 447); p. 387: "et si hoc feceris, veniam discaltiata ad seppulcrum tuum" (see also pp. 304, 374, 378, 382, 417, 422, 444, 451, 455, 458, 464, 478, 479, and 481); p. 304: "quod iret ad locum suum discalciata, cum cillicio"; p. 458: "quod, si eum deliberaret, iret discaltiata ad visitandum corpus eius et sine camisia."

32. Ibid., p. 324: "quod si eam liberaret portarent eam ad locum et sepulcrum suum" (see also pp. 378, 415, 417, and 458).

33. Ibid., p. 388: "et si hoc feceris, ego veniam ad seppulcrum tuum discaltiata et portabo filium quem mihi dederis"; p. 313: "et quia erat pregnans tunc, si pariet filiam feminam promixit sibi imponere nomen sororis Clare predicte."

34. Ibid., p. 395: "et si hoc feceris, ieiunabo diem tuum in pane et aqua" (see also pp. 358, 410, and 432); p. 402: "et ego promicto ad reverentiam tuam dicere centum Pater noster"; pp. 421–22: "et promisit . . . dicere omni die tempore vite sue tria Pater noster."

35. Ibid., p. 389: "vissitabo seppulcrum tuum et portabo unam candelam de media libra"; p. 405: "et si hoc feceris, accingam altarem tuum cera"; p. 377: "et si hoc feceris, accingam altare tuum de cera de labore meo" (see also pp. 313, 361, 368, 378, 388, 426, 431, 451, 455, 465, 487, and 491).

36. Ibid., p. 357: "et ego offeram ad seppulcrum tuum unam ymaginem de cera"; p. 379: "et ego promicto tibi portare unam ymaginem de cera, magnam sicud est predictus puer"; p. 398: "quod si liberaret eum a predictis febribus, ipsa faceret unam ymaginem de cera ad pondus dicti pueri" (see also pp. 304, 311, 313, 351, 357, 362, 374, 375, 399, 410, 473, 481, 492, 499, 502, 503, 505, and 507); p. 369: "et ego promicto tibi mictere unum capud de cera" (see also pp. 402, 433, and 478); p. 513: "Et promixit dare et ponere ad locum et pilum suum unum bracchium cere"; p. 304: "quod si eam liberaret, daret et portaret ad locum suum manum cere" (see also p. 305); p. 421: "et promisit portare unum pedem cereum"; p. 479: "Et dixit quod promisit portare ymaginem stomaci"; p. 385: "et si hoc feceris, portabo unum lumbare de cera ad seppulcrum tuum."

37. Ibid., p. 452: "et promixit ire ad vissitandum corpus eius et cingere pilum uno filo argenteo" (see also pp. 304, 374, 455, and 458); pp. 380–81: "et, si hoc feceris, vissitabo seppulcrum tuum atque portabo tibi XX solidos" (see also p. 358); p. 511: "et si eam liberaret, promisit facere ibi oblationem"; p. 306: "et promixit portare unum pannicellum ad locum et pilum suum" (see also p. 304).

38. Ibid., p. 394: "Sancta Clara, rogo te quod fundes preces meas apud Deum quod reducat ad sanitatem istum fratrem meum et quod respicias ad necessitatem istius families mee quia, si ipse moreretur, esset deserta; et si reduces eum mihi ad sanitatem, ego promicto tibi venire ad domum tuam pedibus decaltiatis uno semel et offeram tibi unam ymaginem ceream, que erit mangna sicut est predictus frater meus, et unum tortitium de duabus libris et L libras denariorum cortonensium pro

maritanda una puella, vel ad voluntatem sororum monasterii pro faciendo seppulcrum dicte s. Clare."

39. Ibid., p. 397: "Sancta Clara virgo pretiosa, rogo te per illas gratias quas
Deus tibi concessit, quod debeas me liberare de ista infirmitate et si me liberaveris,
promicto omni anno in die tui festi dare commedere uni pauperi."

40. Ibid., p. 163: "Dixit etiam quod dicta Ysayas, sicud ipsa testis audivit ab ea,
reconmendavit se et devovit sorori Clare ad suggestionem sororis Iohanne abbatisse,
concedentis sibi licentiam de voto." See also p. 301: "Et tunc in nocte illa devovit se et
reconmendavit ipsi beate Clare orans et dicens quod si ipsa liberaret eum, ipse testis
semper in vigilia diey mortis sue ieiunaret et quod si posset habere licentiam a prelato
suo semper adesset illi monasterio et caneret ibi missam pro eius reverentia."

41. Ibid., pp. 305–6: "Et hec infirmitas duravit annis tribus per intervalla temporis, quia non semper habebat dictam infirmitatem. Et infra dictum tempus devovit
se Deo et beate Clare predicte et promixit portare manus cereas et ire ad visitandum
corpus suum, et postea stetit per annos duos quod dictam infirmitatem non
habuit. . . . Dixit etiam quod post duos annos etiam supervenit sibi dicta infirmitas
et ipsa credit quod ipsa s. Clara esset indingnata quia non servaret votum. Et tunc
devovit se de novo et promixit portare unum pannicellum ad locum et pilum suum
ultra manus cereas si ipsa liberaret eam a dicta infirmitate."

42. Ibid., pp. 397–99: "Cintia uxor Marcuctii Massericti de Monte Falco . . .
interrogata, respondit et dixit tantum scire quod habet unum filium suum, nomine
Lippulum, qui fuit infirmus febre continua multum graviter, et iam perdiderat loquelam et iam plorabatur ab amicis et consanguineis quasi mortuus. Tunc predicta
testis vovit predictum Lippulum s. Clare quod si liberaret eum a predictis febribus,
ipsa faceret unam ymaginem de cera ad pondus dicti pueri. Et facto voto, dictus puer
sudavit; et hoc fuit VIII die ex quo febres eum arripuerunt et incepit loqui dictus puer.
Et accedens medicus ad predictum infirmum, invenit eum sudantem in die VIII predicta et dixit medicus: 'Iste sudor non est verus terminus.' Sequenti autem die dicta
testis portavit urinam dicto medico, et tunc medicus quando vidit predictam urinam
dixit: 'Iste non potest vivere nisi usque ad tertiam.' Et tunc dicta testis ivit ad ecclesiam dicte s. Clare et recommendavit predictum filium suum dicte s. Clare dicens:
'Sancta Clara, benedicta virgo, rogo te quod liberes filium meum et obstendas tuam
potentiam in eo, ut cum domum rediero inveniam eum sanum et ambulantem.' Et
cum pervenisset dicta testis ad domum, invenit predictum totum melioratum; et vol-
ebat exire de lecto et ambulare, quem mater prohibuit. Tunc quedam sua vicina,
nomine Grana, dixit dicte testi: 'Fatua eras quando tantum affligebaris de filio, quia
non fuit liberatus aliquo miraculo ymmo terminavit et fuit verus terminus.' Et ex hiis
verbis dicta testis cepit credere dicte sue vicine et iam non curabat solvere et ad-
implere votum predictum, cum pauper erat dicta testis tunc, et etiam quia fides quam
habuerat s. Clare cepit propter predicta verba diminuy. Et oedem die dictus puer,
filius dicte testis, cepit perdere loquelam et etiam habere febrem et unam puncturam
in pectore, et vix poterat respirare et erat quasi mortuus. Et tunc dicta testis misit
medico, dicendo quomodo dictus puer sic erat gravatus. Et tunc medicus dixit quasi
disperando de salute dicti Lippuli: 'Dicas quod faciat sibi bonum lectum,' quasi

diceret 'non potest plus evadere.' Et sic intellexit dicta testis et incepit plorare dicta
testis. Tunc quedam sua vicina, nomine Bartholella, dixit eidem testi: 'Redeas ad s.
Claram cum vera fide et non deficias et ita fortiter in fide eius.' Et tunc dicta testis,
puro corde et pura fide et redens se culpabilem quod modicam fidem habuerat in
dicta s. Clara, recomendavit predictum puerum dicte s. Clare quod, si liberaret eum,
adimpleret votum promissum. Et statim fuit melioratus. Et hoc fuit die dominico, de
sero, quasi in media nocte; die vero lune, in tertia, venit quidam suus consanguineus
et invenit dictum puerum quasi totaliter liberatum et dixit dicte testi: 'Iste puer est
liberatus quia terminavit et non propter aliquid aliud.' Tunc dicta testis statim cred-
idit et diminuta est fides in ea. Et statim dictus puer fuit peioratus et arripuit eum
febris et fuit infrigidatus per totum, a capite usque ad pedes, et perdidit loquelam. Et
hoc fuit die lune in vesperis; et videbatur facere tractum. Tunc dicta testis, videns
quod modicam fidem habuerat dicte s. Clare, congnoscens culpam suam dixit: 'Sancta Clara, non respicias ad modicam fidem meam. Ego rogo te per gratias quas Deus
dedit tibi quod liberes filium meum, et ego promicto firmiter solvere quod promisi et
nunquam cespitare a devotione tua.' Et hoc fuit circa primum sonum, de sero, in die
lune. Et statim, emisso voto, iste fuit perfecte liberatus et a febre et a puntura, et loquelam rehabuit. Et in die martis sequentis ambulavit dictus Lippulus per se ipsum,
sine adiutorio et substentaculo." See also pp. 399–400 and 423–24.

43. Ibid., p. 461: "Puppus condam domini Gentilis . . . interrogatus . . . respondit et dixit se hoc scire quod dum esset ipse et alii apud Montem Falcum, iverunt
quidam de Spoleto, et ipse cum eis, ad monasterium Sancte Crucis de Monte Falco,
causa videndi cor suum et alia insingnia paxionis que fuerunt reperta in corde suo, et
cum ipso teste erat Symon ser Gilii de Spoleto; et tunc dompnus Bordonus, sacerdos
de dicto castro, ut credit de ipso, vel alia persona, obstendit eis cor ipsius s. Clare,
volens obstendere insingnia passionis. Quo corde aperto, dictus Symon cepit ridere
et cacchinari et non habuit in devotione qua debebat, ut videbatur, ea que obstende-
bantur. Et exivit tunc subito sanguis de naso in mangna quantitate fortiter. Et tunc
ipse testis et sotii dixerunt ei: 'Captivelle, non vides miraculum quod fecit Deus de te
pro sancta ista? Quomodo non habes fidem in ea et non credis de sanctitate sua et de
hiis?' Et tunc penituit eum et cepit credere et dixit: 'Reducatis mihi ista.' Et tetigit cor
et fuit positus super capud per ipsum dompnum Bordonem, ut credit de ipso dompno
Bordone, et statim sanguis cessavit fluere, cum in veritate, secundum dictum prefati
Symonis, numquam sibi sanguis exivisset de naso, quantumcumque percussus iam
fuisset in naso. Et dixit quod semper postea ipse Symon habuit fidem in ea et revelare
audivit ipsum hoc pro mangno miraculo. Et dixit quod hec fuerunt anno transitus
dicte s. Clare intra unum mensem." See also p. 459.

44. Ibid., p. 318: "Beata Clara, ego rogo te quod per tuam sanctitatem et tua
bona opera tu debeas me liberare, si pro meliori est et esse debet mee anime, alio-
quin miserearis mey et intercede pro me ad Dominum, ut faciat michi misericor-
diam."

45. Ibid., p. 434: "Domine Deus, rogo te quod per merita sororis Clare facias
michi hanc gratiam quod liberes me de ista infirmitate vel da mihi tantum somnum
quod ego non sentiam dictam amputationem pedis mei; et ego ero semper fidelis

tibi"; p. 491: "et si hic feceris, vissitabo seppulcrum tuum et habebo fidem in te"; p. 399: "et ego promicto firmiter solvere quod promisi et nunquam cespitare a devotione tua."

46. Ibid., p. 511: "Libera me de hac infirmitate quia non invenio medicum qui me iuvet de hac infirmitate."

47. Ibid., p. 438: "Mutatus fuit quasi in alium hominem."

48. See Vauchez, *La sainteté*, pp. 154–58.

49. Ibid., p. 153.

50. *Menestò, Il processo*, p. 31: "Et tunc dicta domina Symoneta considerabat in mente sua quod ipsa iam se devoverat alias s. Clare de Assisio, et ipsa nesciebat aliam sanctam Claram quam illam de Assisio. Et tunc illa vox respondit ad cogitatum illius domine quamvis ipsa nichil loqueretur et dixit: 'Sancta Clara de qua ego loquor habuit magistrum spiritualem tantum et non terrenum . . . et eius humanitas est pura sicut humanitas sancti Iohannis, et ipsa vocabatur sancta Clara de cruce.'"

51. See Vauchez, *La sainteté*, p. 156.

52. Menestò *Il processo*, p. 411: "Sancta Clara benedicta, ego rogo te per virtutes tuas quod debeas me liberare ab isto dolore; et ego promicto tibi, si hoc feceris, notificare centum personis." On the same subject, see also the depositions on p. 455: "devovit se Deo et beate Clare quod si liberaret eum a dicto periculo, ipsa iret discaltiata et portaret ad cingendum pilum suum de candelis seu filo argenteo et publicaret miraculum quam citius posset"; and p. 312: "Si facias michi istam gratiam, ego faciam isstud miraculum scribi et predicari."

53. See *articuli interrogatorii* 13–45, 51–61, 65, 69–73, 75–85, 104, and 106–58, and the corresponding responses of witnesses 1, 38, 39, 45, 46, 67, 82, 214, 215, 216, 231, and 234; also Vauchez, *La sainteté*, p. 404. Clare's insistence on the ascetic value of work (*art.* 55), which was also linked in fundamental ways with charity, was noteworthy. In fact, Clare was always ready to perform any service. When she became abbess, she refused any title and insisted on being called by her given name (Menestò, *Il processo*, p. 184); she continued to work in the garden and the kitchen, clean the house, and tend old and ill sisters, and on many occasions she kneaded the clay used to stop up the cracks in the oven where the food was cooked. Many witnesses testified that she carried out her functions as abbess by submitting to the will of God as expressed through the will of the sisters. While respecting and responding to the sisters' wishes, Clare perfected the internal organization of the convent: she decreed that some lay sisters or servants should take turns attending to the duties outside of the convent—visiting the sick, bringing food and necessary supplies to the poor, going shopping, and so on—and that the rest would observe strict cloister; she determined the rotations within the various offices and forbade the sisters to go alone to the grate or outside the convent; she also determined that the sisters who had the greatest aptitude for prayer would devote more time to it, while the others would dedicate themselves more to manual labor. Clare often instructed and admonished her fellow nuns, not only in the weekly chapters but on all occasions, separately or as a group, as the occasion arose. The result (as we see in *art.* 53) was a continual dialogue, especially on the subject of the fundamental obligations: the love of God, pro-

gress in the virtues based on humility, chastity, and the most meticulous defense of one's virginity in order to reach total unity with God.

54. Her ability to read consciences enabled Clare to discover and denounce the quietist errors of the sect of the Free Spirit, errors that were propounded especially in the preaching of Fra Bentivenga of Gubbio and his followers. See *articuli* 112–14 and the corresponding responses of witnesses 1, 38, 39, and 45.

On Clare's wisdom, see *articuli interrogatorii* 86–103, 105, 125, 126, and 130 and the corresponding responses of witnesses 1, 38, 39, 45, 67, and 82. This faculty enabled Clare to provide learned answers to the most difficult questions that theologians and philosophers could pose to her. The testimony of her brother Francesco is noteworthy: "interrogatus, respondit et dixit se hec scire, videlicet quod ipsa Clara habebat intelligentiam tante virtutis et gratie atque divine sapientie, quod in onnibus videbatur intellectum profundum et profundissimum habere. Sicut, verbigratia, ipsi testi legenti, studenti, et questiones difficiles addiscenti, et illas questiones dicte Clare cum argumentis difficilibus per ordinem explicanti, ipsa cum tanta subtilitate et intelligentie profuditate omnes questiones quascumque ita lucedissime enodabat et solvebat quod dixit dictus testis quod amplius de claritate Scripture accepit de ipsius expossitionibus et responsionibus, quam in quibuscumque scolis vel lectionibus a se ipso factis" (Menestò, *Il processo*, p. 276).

On the source of Clare's wisdom, see ibid., p. 67: "Et ipsa Clara venit ad missam cum illa contritione, et quando fuit ante sanctificationem, subito fuit aperta ei mens sua, quasi aperiretur unum ostium et vidit unam rectitudinem divinam et essentiam divinam rectam, quasi una virga rectissima et videbat et congnoscebat se apodiatam et unitam illi rectitudini et veritati divine, quod videbat Deum in se et se in Deo, et videbat se quasi nihil in Deo respectu infinitatis divine"; pp. 277–78: "et quandocunque loquebatur cum tanta claritate et efficacia influebat et cum fervore et spirituali sapore eruptabat, quod recte Spiritus Sanctus loquebatur in ea, quia conmuniter audientes dicebat se spiritualem gratiam ab ipsa Clara luminis et intelligentie recepisse. Et quod eloquentia ipsius esset eloquentia Spiritus Sancti probat dictus testis, quod ipsa Clara dixit sibi testi quod, quando ista ita alta et sublimia proferebat, nunquam antea ordinabat vel cogitabat quomodo loqui deberet, iuxta illud verbum 'Nolite cogitare quomodo aud quid loquamini: dabitur enim vobis in illa hora, quid loquamini, non enim estis vos qui loquimini, sed spiritus Patris qui loquitur in vobis."

55. On Clare's visions, see *art.* 74 (ibid., p. 11): "Item dicit et probare intendit quod sancta Clara predicta retulit, dum vivebat, anno XV ante suum obitum et tunc corporis infirmitate gravata, quod in quadam visione et revelatione per Dei gratiam sibi facta, videbat unum montem pulcherrimum, de quo splendor maximus emicabat, et in illo monte erat gloria sanctorum. Et de illo loco audivit et fuit revelatum ipsi sancte Clare, quod ipsa sancta Clara deberet stare in mundo per XV dies et postea venire illuc ad gloriam sanctorum predictam. Et tunc in eadem visione seu revelatione videbat ipsa sancta Clara et congnoscebat et sentiebat etiam corporaliter quod in corpus suum, quod erat infirmitate gravatum, mitebatur desuper a Deo ros suavissimus, qui refrigerabat eam et manna dulcissimum quod confortabat eam etiam corporaliter et spiritualiter." See also the responses to this article by witnesses

39, Sister Tomassa (pp. 205–7), and 45, Clare's brother Francesco (pp. 278–79); and see also pp. 164–65. Although this vision concerned the universal judgment with images of hell and heaven, other apparitions allowed Clare to see "quemdam solem magis fulgentem isto sole quem videmus . . . , quod veniebat a Christo. . . . pedes eius tangebant terram et capud eius tangebat celum; et color eius erat sicud fulgur auri fulgentis" (p. 468); and also "Christus cum cruce in collo seu humero" (p. 294). Sometimes the saint herself was physically and directly at the center of extraordinary apparitions: some witnesses testified that Clare was often surrounded by a strange luminosity: see *articuli* 62–64 and the corresponding responses of witnesses 38 and 39.

On her ecstasies, see Menestò, *Il processo,* pp. 190–91 and 205, among other passages; but in this regard the testimony of Sister Marina (witness 38) is particularly noteworthy: "Interrogata quomodo scit, dixit scire quia pluries et pluries ipsa testis eamdem sanctam Claram vidit in raptibus et presens fuit quando habebat tales raptus. Interrogata quid est raptus, dixit quod de raptu tantum scit, quod credit quod raptus sit intensa et fortis elevatio mentis in Deum. Dixit quod quando aliqua persona est in raptu, nichil sentit, nec percipit sensibus corporis de sensibilibus exterioribus, et quod quando ista entense et fortis elevatio mentis sive ipse raptus cessat, persona sic elevata et rapta manet et surgit consulata et gaudiosa corporaliter et spiritualiter" (pp. 117–18). As Vauchez writes, along with these prodigious events "there was also a whole series of psychosomatic conditions that were described and analyzed with great precision in certain depositions. In the various forms of ecstasy that Clare exhibited, we can thus distinguish *elevatio mentis,* which is simply the 'absence' that resulted from intense contemplation, from the *raptus* characterized by the loss of physical sensations, which defines the period of mystical ascension and expresses the completeness of the amorous union of the soul with God. In rapture the saint remained totally immobile, with hands joined and eyes closed; her face became more luminous and flushed than usual. During these periods onlookers could touch her or even prick her with needles without her showing the slightest reaction. Her body even seemed to levitate, miraculously free of the laws of gravity" (*La sainteté,* pp. 515–16).

Finally, see *articuli interrogatori* 46–50 and 132 and the corresponding responses of witness 1, 38, 39, and 45 on her devotion to the suffering Christ.

56. Menestò, *Il processo,* p. 295: "in corde suo semper sensibilem crucem sensit."

57. Ibid., p. 21; see also pp. 235, 71, 72, 73, and 76.

58. See Matthew 16:24: "If any man would come after me, let him deny himself and take up his cross and follow me."

59. Menestò, *Il processo,* p. 181: "Oh quantus fuit dolor quem Dominus meus Yhesus Christus substinuit pro me! Ego sum digna, si plus possem portare doloribus et infirmitatibus maioribus, omnia habere." See also pp. 193–94 and 258–59.

60. Ibid., p. 274: "quod non est mirum si anima diligit Deum super omnia in centuplo plus quam seipsam; ratio cuius erat, quia ipse est creator noster, qui de nichilo nos creavit, et ad suam inmaginem nos formavit; similiter ipse est redemptor

noster, qui nos suo sanguine redemit et reconperavit in cruce durissima, in qua cum opprobriis, vituperiis et immensis doloribus pro nobis mortuus fuit et crudeliter occisus, similiter ipse est gubernator noster, qui nos gubernat et regit, et vitam eternam promictit, et fideliter sine falatia dabit. Et ideo hiis onnibus et tamtis et talibus consideratis debet anima ipsum Deum inseparabiliter diligere et amare, et etiam se milies inpendere et dare in omnibus sicud potest."

61. Ibid., p. 274: "habebat caritatem ad proximum, in tantum quod videbatur proximum diligere amplius quam se ipsam, quia se in adiutorio spirituali et temporali proximo totaliter et liberaliter exhibebat, non tantum suis sororibus, quas diligebat ut filias, sed quibuscumque indigentibus et ab ipsa iuvari volentibus. Similiter et toto fervore mentis orabat pro peccatoribus, eis cum doloribus conpatiendo, ne ab ipso Iesu Christo divisi dampnarentur."

62. Ibid., p. 274: "Similiter [Clara] dicebat quod ex amore et caritate anima unitur Deo et fit unum cum ipso in volunptate, quia tanta est amicitia Dey ad animam et anime ad Deum ex caritate, quod quicquid Deus vult, vult anima sic unita, et quidquid vult talis anima, vult etiam Deus ipse; et propter hoc non est mirum si anima, ex amore et caritate quam habet ad Deum, vult milies mori, si oporteret, antequam ab ipso dividi vel deiungi vellet. Unde dicebat quod non est mirum quod anima dicat quod nec mors, nec vita, nec aliqua creatura possit eam separare a Deo; immo omnis mors, et onnis dolor, et onnis tribulatio, quam pro ipso sufferre posset, esset sibi dulcissima."

63. This is also true of St. Francis. See Claudio Leonardi, "L'eredità di Francesco d'Assisi," in *Francesco d'Assisi: Documenti e archivi, codici e biblioteche, miniature* (Milan, 1982), p. 113.

64. In this connection, see the interesting study of Attilio Bartoli Langeli, "I penitenti a Spoleto," in *L'ordine della penitenza di San Francesco d'Assisi nel secolo XIII,* ed. Ottaviano Schmucki, Proceedings of the Conference of Franciscan Studies, Assisi, 3–5 July 1972, Collectanea Franciscana, 43 (Rome, 1973), pp. 303–30.

65. In the official records pertaining to the canonization proceedings, Clare is always identified as "Ordinis sancti Augustini." What is more, with the official inclusion of the convent of Santa Croce in the Augustinian order shortly after Clare's death, the saint could also be deemed juridically a member of that order.

66. Nor is it denied by the special devotion that Clare felt for St. Francis, which is clearly attested in the records of the canonization proceedings. According to the testimony of Sister Tomassa and Sister Giovanna, shortly before dying Clare exclaimed: "Ego non possum plus stare, vos quid facitis? Non facitis aliquid. Ecce tota vita eterna paratur pro me, quia me vult, et sanctus Franciscus et omnes sancti venerunt pro ducendo me secum, quia Dominus Yhesus Christus me vult. Et ecce Madonna cum virginibus" (Menestò, *Il processo,* p. 236; see also p. 78). A certain Caratenuta of Spoleto told how "quadam nocte dum diceret sua Pater noster coram crucifixo et cogitaret de factis s. Clare predicte et examinatione et inquisitione que fiebat de canoniçatione sua, sompnus aliquantulum cepit eam; et in illo pauco sompno fuit sibi dictum et sonitum in auribus suis quod quedam vox dixit sibi quod

s. Clara predicta tenuerat vitam sancti Francisci et quod ivit post vitam Yhesu Christi" (p. 458).

67. Ibid., p. 22; but see also pp. 237 and 336.

68. Ibid., p. 228.

69. *Dicta Beati Aegidii Assisiensis* (Quaracchi, 1939), p. 91: "Parisius, Parisius ipse destruis ordinem sancti Francisci." Iacopone da Todi, *Laude,* ed. Franco Mancini (Bari, 1974), p. 293 (lauda 91, v. 2): "Mal vedemo Parisi, che àne destrutt'Asisi" (Jacopone da Todi, *The Laude,* trans. Serge and Elizabeth Hughes [New York, 1982], p. 123). Menestò, *Il processo,* p. 272: "Nollem quod tu curares semper de ista sientia, et de ista extollencia semper disceptares. Et dico tibi pro parte mea quod maiorem consolationem haberem si tu esses laicus et coquinarius fratrum cum uno bono spiritu et fervore devotionis, quam si esses de quibuscunque lectoribus unus maior."

70. See *articuli interrogatorii* numbers 112–16 and the responses given by witnesses 1, 38, 39, and 45; and Livario Oliger, *De secta spiritus libertatis in Umbria saec. XIV: Disquisitio et documenta* (Rome, 1943). On the movement of the Free Spirit, see Romana Guarnieri, "Il movimento del libero spirito dalle origini al sec. XVI," *Archivio italiano per la storia della pietà* 4 (1964): 353–708; Guarnieri, "Frères du libre esprit," in *Dictionnaire de spiritualité ascétique et mystique,* vol. 5 (Paris, 1964), col. 1241–68; Guarnieri, "Fratelli del libero spirito," in *Dizionario degli Istituti di Perfezione,* vol. 4 (Rome, 1977), col. 633–52.

7

Female Mystics, Visions, and Iconography

Chiara Frugoni

"Many persons discuss mental activity in terms of meditation and contemplation," wrote Ugo Panciera in his guide to meditation, the *Trattato della perfezione della mentale azione*. "Perfect mental activity is the way to attain perfect meditation and contemplation . . . through the exercise of imagination, which must be so powerful that its object remains vibrantly present to the bodily senses. . . . When the mind first begins . . . to think about Christ, he appears to the mind and imagination in written form. He next appears as an outline. In the third stage he appears as an outline with shading; in the fourth stage, tinted with colors and flesh tones; and in the fifth stage he appears in the flesh and fully rounded."[1]

Reflecting on a text or an image thus allows the imagination to construct, out of the supply of figurative and textual echoes stored in the memory, a new mental image that becomes ever clearer, like a film exposed to the image or text that was the starting point of the meditation, until it acquires an emotional and affective charge that can make it come to life. Through this intense process of visualization, introspection arrives at the climax of mystical experience, the desired true encounter with the divine. The vision constitutes a genre that expresses experiences that otherwise would be incommunicable, and therefore describes them in terms that are always essentially figurative.

As Richard of St. Victor said, "This, I believe, is why Rachel (that is, Reason) has her maidservant—or Imagination—produce children before she herself gives birth; because it is pleasant to hold in the memory, if only by imagining them, things which one is not yet capable of apprehending through reason. As everyone knows, this is the first step by which one can begin to contemplate the invisible."[2]

One day, suffering from a raging fever, Agnes of Montepulciano saw the Virgin "seated on her throne of majesty," surrounded by angelic musicians who "seemed to fan the air with lovely cloths, as is commonly done for those burning up from the heat." Even though Mary had not asked for such service, "Agnes conceived all this in order to indicate her refreshment," comments her biographer with penetrating understanding of how thoroughly the saint identified with the Virgin, whom she longed to see and who finally appeared to her in the iconographic form of the Virgin enthroned with angels.[3]

When Mary intercedes with her son, according to Gherardesca of Pisa, "she removes from her head the crown, which angels reverently receive and keep."[4] Here, the image is that of a Madonna over whose head two angels hold a crown suspended in the air (fig. 1), as if a painting long pondered had come to life, like a freeze-frame springing back into motion.

A delightful childhood memory of Clare of Montefalco was the product of a similar mental transformation. When she was a little girl, in the convent, Clare saw the Virgin with Jesus, a child just Clare's age, under her mantle. Seeing that Clare wished to play, Mary urged her son to stop clinging to her, but he rushed back to his mother.[5] The source of this vision, with its charming quality of the daydream of a child who still longs for her home and her games, was a glycophilous icon like the one presently in the National Gallery of Perugia (fig. 2).

This "mental imaging," which is at once an act of memory and a means of communicating mystical experiences, may then in turn leave its imprint on the texts themselves, shaping the production of further meanings. This occurs, for instance, when metaphors are transformed into visions. In a passage in the *vita* of Clare of Montefalco, that saint, in the throes of a grave spiritual crisis, saw herself assailed by the virtues and vices. Every virtue and vice, "each with its own distinctive properties, hurled itself upon Clare in this vision." The battle finally ended with the victory of the virtues; "but in this conflict she received such knowledge and learning that she could respond ably to anyone who sought to learn about the virtues and vices, their properties, or anything else."[6] The well-known literary and artistic theme of the Psychomachia, in which moral concepts are represented through personification, here acquired the force of an image and event, becoming a part of the saint's vision.[7] The recollection of this event then seems to have formed the basis of a new vision—though here her biographer's reflections also played some part. After her death, Clare appeared to a companion draped in a red mantle "on which the virtues of the virgin Clare were displayed as in pictorial narratives."[8] To my mind, this illustrated robe is a visual echo of the earlier victorious battle.

Clare also appeared to the friar who had preached her funeral sermon and was perturbed by the audience's reaction to his effusive praise of her, which they found excessive: "And after the aforesaid friar had reposed on his pillow for a while, Clare sat down on the pillow and, placing one hand and arm between the pillow and the neck of the friar, who was sleeping lightly, with the other hand tapped the friar sweetly and gently on his cheek, saying, 'Look now and see if I am beautiful.'"[9] Clare sought to reassure her apologist not only by appearing beautiful, but also by displaying her gratitude in a tangible gesture of simple affection. This encounter seems to have been shaped by a verse from the Song of Solomon (8:3), where the exultant bride exclaims: "O that his left hand were under my head, and that his right hand embraced me!"[10] But the textual reference to the wife's tender caress is superimposed on a visual reference to the Virgin's heartbreaking embrace of her dead son, lying on his sepulchre as if it were a bed (as we can see, for example, in the small panel painting reproduced in figure 3). The Virgin leans over Christ's face with its eyes closed, like those of the friar "who was sleeping lightly"; one hand reaches under his neck, while the other embraces his chest. In this case, we cannot determine the sequence of the scriptural and iconographical influences that formed this episode. I would prefer to speak of a simultaneous reception of stimuli from two repertories, whose distinct origins are clearly recognizable despite their fusion here.

These last two examples raise a problem that I would rather not discuss at length: the narratives of Clare's postmortem apparitions were obviously composed not by the mystic herself, but by her biographer. But I think this difficulty is minimized if we presume a fundamental harmony between these mystics and their biographers, who were almost always their confessors: their frequent contacts would have led to a natural confluence of thought. We should also keep in mind that the female mystic's mental outlook resembled that of her public, making it possible for those around her to receive, rework, or create stories analogous to those to which they listened so devoutly.[11]

At a more rudimentary level of projection, it was not the figure in a long-pondered painting that animated the mental transposition of a vision, but rather the material object itself, the panel or sculpture, that suddenly came to life and filled with impassioned meanings. The long list we could easily make of crucifixes that bleed or speak, display their sores or offer their wounds to be kissed, of tormented and weeping Virgins, testifies to an almost obligatory experience in the life of a mystic and confirms the crucial importance of images for ascesis.[12]

For example, Giacomo Bianconi received some money from his mother to buy clothes. He went to Perugia and instead used some of the money to "have a wooden image of the Crucifix made," which he placed in the church of the friars in Bevagna—to the great annoyance of his mother, who complained that he had lied to her.[13] One day, as Giacomo prayed more intensely than usual before this image, seeking some sign of salvation, he suddenly heard a voice reply: " 'Let this blood be a sign and a certitude for you.' Suddenly fresh blood and water gushed from the side of the crucifix onto the supplicant's face and the front of his cloak, just like the water boys often spurt from straws"—an amusing image from everyday life.[14] With the rest of the money received from his mother, Giacomo commissioned an image of the Virgin. When the moment of his death drew near, Jesus, Mary, St. Dominic, and St. George appeared to him. Each one explained the reason for his or her presence. While the two saints had come because of the habit Giacomo wore and the pious efforts he had made to enlarge the church of San Giorgio, Christ explained: "We will be present at your death . . . because you gave money to clothe my statue and to make an image of my mother."[15] I will not dwell here on the utilitarianism of this passage, which is typical of a faith whose impulses and rewards could be quantified. Instead, the important point to note is that dedicating one's life and sustaining an important public construction project are assigned the same ethical value as having two cult objects made.

The vitality of the model that this mystic's life offered to his public is evident in the most widely diffused woodcut book of the late fifteenth century: that "iconographical crystallization of the Christian death," the *Ars moriendi*.[16] In the final woodcut, which shows how the good death should take place, we see Christ on the cross, the Virgin, and saints and angels gathered around someone's deathbed (fig. 4). The text comments: the dying person invokes the intercession of Mary, the apostles, the angels, and the saints, "especially, however, those whom in his former state of good health he had venerated and esteemed, and whose images, along with the image of the crucifix and the blessed Virgin Mary, were present before him."[17] This might be termed the "mass marketing" of the mystical experience: what in Giacomo Bianconi's biography was presented as a vision and a supreme gift has become a regular devotional practice; the mysterious encounter with heaven's inhabitants has given way to their representation in painted or sculpted images.

Mystics of both sexes were particularly attentive to images drawn from their everyday experiences, the seedbed for their interior meditations. Even changes in the standard iconography were faithfully noted in their visions. When the blessed Aldobrandesca was meditating one day on Christ's

Passion, she felt an overwhelming desire to see the nails and "soon thereafter an angel came to her, displaying three bloody nails, one of which was larger than the others, perhaps because it had served to fasten both feet."[18] The "memory" of this vision remained so firmly implanted in her that she promptly made an identical nail from a branch in her garden. This, explains her biographer, is why Aldobrandesca is often depicted in votive paintings holding a nail in her hand. Similarly, St. Rita is portrayed with a thorn in her hand—the thorn that she felt pierce her head at the climax of her own impassioned meditation.[19]

Three nails were also found (along with the other symbols of the Passion) in the heart of Clare of Montefalco, and naturally, the one for the feet was larger than the other two.[20] The three nails were first mentioned in the *Meditations on Christ's Passion* by the Pseudo-Bonaventure, and they received their first artistic representation at nearly the same time (1260), in Nicola Pisano's Crucifixion on the pulpit of the baptistry in Pisa.[21] This felicitous iconographic innovation spread through Italy, especially Tuscany, and supplanted the earlier portrayal with four nails because the new triangular schema placed the wounded body in greater tension, emphasizing Christ's agony. It was an effective illustration of the new emotional force with which the Passion was charged, in a line leading from St. Anselm and St. Bernard to the Franciscans.[22]

The new manner of representing Christ's Ascension by showing only the feet, as if the rest of the body were already "off-stage" (perhaps influenced by the theatrical machinery of the mystery plays, which became common starting in the thirteenth century), seems to have influenced a passage in the *vita* of the blessed Villana.[23] Certain female recluses testified that they had had a vision of the recently deceased Villana hovering in the air. At first they took her to be the Virgin, but then recognized her as that woman "with whom they had shared so many devout conversations. . . . However, when they wished to embrace her most holy feet, they saw her rise ever higher into the air and vanish from their sight."[24]

The Resurrection, too, began to be depicted as if it were caught in the act—an iconography unknown before the twelfth century, which pictorially filled a space previously left open to the imagination.[25] Now, instead of the empty sepulchre, we see the figure of Christ hovering in the air: the mystery is rendered visible and concrete, a token of the desire to participate emotively in the miracle as it unfolds.

Even a new architectural feature—the column upon which the Virgin Annunciate was leaning when surprised by the angel (as in Lippo Vanni's fresco, reproduced in figure 5)—is registered in the Annunciation "witnessed" by Gherardesca of Pisa: Mary "was leaning against a column, engaged in devout prayer."[26] This detail also appears in the *Meditations* of Pseudo-Bonaventure, though in connection instead with the Nativity.[27]

Why were images so important for mystical experience? In addition to what I have already said—that mystic ascesis unfolds through visions and hence through images—I believe that the social status of these saints was also a factor. Female mystics, unlike their male counterparts, did not usually modify their lay status: they were and remained laywomen, at most formalizing their religious zeal by joining one of the Third Orders. They were almost always married and had children, which to my mind explains their preference for an affective exegesis, their predilection for the themes of the Christ child and the Crucifixion, and their extreme sensitivity to the damage done to the Savior's body during the Passion.[28] Marriage and motherhood, however, constituted the prehistory of their mystical experiences, a past they thoroughly renounced.[29] As Lapo Mazzei noted of Birgitta of Sweden, "Widowhood was the time of her greatest perfection."[30] Even if the biographies of female saints were consciously presented as paradigms on which the faithful could model their lives (as their prologues often stated explicitly), the church, speaking through biographers who were invariably churchmen and often the confessors of these saints, could not conceive of ordinary Christians as anything other than imperfect monks.[31] The pastoral guidance offered the laity proved incapable of bridging the gulf between the Christian family and ascetic perfection. When human affections and ties with husbands and children were suppressed—only to resurface violently as troubling temptations—the only love still possible was that sublimated in the unreal and constant condition of mystical marriage, of union and annihilation in Christ.[32] But mystical marriage was experienced with a concreteness of perception and sensation to be expected from women whose bodies had known these impulses and acts. The lives of female saints were thus lay models for laypeople—and that was an audience, as Jacques de Vitry stated, to whom "one must preach differently than to clerics. . . . Laypeople have to be shown everything concretely, as if it were right under their eyes."[33] Precisely because the people fed on images and not books— they attended church, observed paintings, and listened to their exposition in sermons, but did not read the Bible for themselves—the substance of their spiritual life came from this world of images. And in this connection, it is worth noting that pulpits sculpted with stories from the Gospels proliferated with the spread of the new orders of preaching friars.

In his brief treatise on contemplation, the *Trattatello della contemplazione,* which was incorporated in the vernacular version of the *Meditations,* the Pseudo-Bonaventure emphasized that "contemplation of the life of Christ in human terms, because it concerns bodily existence, is recommended as suitable for the unsophisticated and not for the perfect," while "the higher contemplation . . . that is, that concerning the heavenly court and God's majesty . . . is reserved exclusively for the perfect."[34] The church's distrust of believers who turned to the sacred texts without its mediation is too familiar to require much comment.[35] As Jacopo Passavanti said, "Layfolk and unlettered people have other obligations: it is enough for them to have a general knowledge of the commandments of the law, the articles of the faith, the sacraments of the Church, sins, ecclesiastical ordinances, and the doctrine of the Holy Gospel, such as they require for their salvation and receive from their priests and from preachers of the Scriptures and the faith. They should not try to be overly sophisticated, nor should they wade too deeply in the sea of the Scriptures."[36] This distrust was exacerbated whenever laymen tried to preach, and grew sharper still in the case of laywomen, who were expressly forbidden to preach.[37]

The habitual use of images was thus a characteristic feature of the laity. One might even say that being a married woman with a family virtually guaranteed this orientation. "The need to look after a family is no less important than frequent prayer," admonished Giovanni Dominici, while St. Bernardino of Siena affirmed that "the primary religious duty of married women is to be good wives, which means good and thrifty managers of the household."[38] Since this limited even further the physical space allowed women in particular for their religious activities, their silent meditations would normally take place at home, before their domestic altars—which in the fourteenth century acquired a remarkable and unexpected diffusion. In his *Regola del governo di cura familiare,* a collection of advice on family management addressed to one of his female penitents, Giovanni Dominici recommended arranging some altars in the home so that the children could look after them and decorate them on feast days (which, among other things, would accustom them to church altarpieces, blackened by smoke).[39] Attention thus came to center on domestic intimacy, in a sort of private chapel.

Female mystics were often uneducated—or at least their biographers sought to emphasize the similarities between their models and the public to which they were presented. They were generally capable only of reciting the Lord's Prayer and the Creed or, in the case of young Clare of Montefalco, the canonical hours according to the usage of unlettered nuns—that is, those who did not know Latin.[40] When they happened to possess great learning, this was presented as an ineffable divine gift; and if learning was openly desired and pursued, the miraculous gift of the vision was lost.[41] Throughout her eleven years of impassioned studies and intense social intercourse with cardinals and bishops, Clare of Montefalco was bitterly tormented by her inability to encounter God: "She lacked her usual light of revelations and peace of soul."[42] When she realized that she had to abandon herself entirely to God's will and renounce her burning desire for knowledge, the comforting visions returned.

The religious practices of female mystics depended primarily on memorization, and the use of images served a similar mnemonic function.[43] According to Thomas Aquinas, the purpose of art was "first of all to instruct the ignorant and secondly to keep the mystery of the incarnation and the examples of the saints more firmly in our memory"—precisely the concerns of female mystics.[44] In one vision of the blessed Aldobrandesca of Siena, the infant Jesus vanished at the very moment of the embrace she had longed for; although she tried "to keep his exact likeness in her imagination," everything disappeared. On another occasion, while meditating on Christ's Passion in front of a crucifix (an image that was an essential aid to her reflection), she felt the need to taste the blood she saw flowing from his side: "As she focused intently on Christ and the image of the crucifix, she saw a single drop of blood issue from the image's side." She received it on her lips and tasted its extraordinary delicacy and sweetness. "To commemorate this divine grace," she commissioned a painting (probably resembling the Deposition from the Cross reproduced in figure 6) of "the Virgin Mary, holding in her arms the body of her son removed from the cross, with her mouth touching the wound in his side."[45] Note that in the icon it is not Aldobrandesca who drinks Christ's blood, but the Madonna. This substitution is noteworthy, for it reveals a specific mental process. Devotion and respect have restored Christ to the arms of his true mother; but since we know that this votive painting was intended to commemorate Aldobrandesca's kiss, we can have some idea of the pictorial medium's power of suggestion: it enables the mystic who contemplates it, and who feels the need to contemplate it in order to retain the emotional charge of the vision, to conjure up the scene so clearly that she can identify with and even take the place of the Virgin. Here is the reason behind the commission and the importance evidently ascribed to the image.

In her account of her own life, whose language pulses with underlying violence despite being filtered through the Latin of her confessor, Angela of Foligno recalled: "Whenever I saw the Passion of Christ depicted, I could hardly bear it, and I would come down with a fever and fall sick. My companion, as a result, hid paintings of the Passion or did her best to keep them out of my sight."[46] So great was her excitement upon seeing the Passion of Christ performed in the piazza in front of Santa Maria that she felt that her soul "had indeed entered at that moment within the side of Christ. All sadness was gone and my joy was so great that nothing can be said about it."[47]

She recalled how one day, while meditating on the nails of Christ, she was overcome by sorrow: "I bent over and sat down; and I stretched out my arms on the ground and inclined my head on them. Then Christ showed me his throat and his arms." Suddenly "my former sorrow was transformed into a joy so intense that I can say nothing about it. . . . Such also was the beauty of Christ's throat or neck that I concluded it must be divine."[48]

Here, in the fervor of her mystic exaltation, Angela has taken the place of the Virgin, almost as if she had invaded a painting of the Pietà.[49] Holding the supine body of Christ on her lap, Angela dwells upon his throat, that beautiful throat that she saw obsessively even in the host.[50] The erotic violence of this reflection—in a woman who had not hesitated to extinguish the flames of her youthful passions by applying real fire to her "shameful parts"—was not simply the consequence of repression (even if this was particularly marked in these women), but an aspect of that potent condensation of feelings that enabled her to pass beyond the shadows and reach heights of sublimity and deification.[51]

Angela similarly drew on iconographic language to express her emotional reaction to seeing Francis as a second Christ and her jealous desire to reach the same level of perfection. One day Angela entered the basilica of San Francesco in Assisi, and there "I saw a stained-glass window depicting St. Francis being closely held by Christ. I heard him telling me: 'Thus I will hold you closely to me. . . . You are holding the ring of my love. From now on you are engaged to me.'"[52]

Everything that I have said to this point indicates how important images were as an aid to mystical meditation, and so it is no surprise that an icon or crucifix was often the focal point of an episode either narrated in words or represented visually. Thus, the dying Angela of Foligno identified herself with the iconography of the Dormition of the Virgin (fig. 7), as she saw Christ appear to her and reassure her: "Come to me, my beloved. . . . I do not entrust to either the angels or any other saints the task of bringing you to me. I will come for you in person and I will take you with me."[53] St. Catherine of Alexandria, the mystic bride of Christ and saint of the medieval *Conversio*, is often depicted in paintings and sculptures as converted by a hermit who shows her an icon of the Virgin.[54] St. Bonaventure is portrayed holding a small picture of Christ crucified on the tree of life, the *Lignum vitae* that provided the title for Bonaventure's famous work.[55] St. Rose of Viterbo went about the city to convert sinners clutching to her breast a small painting of the Virgin in Majesty.[56] When Clare of Rimini had a vision ordering her to enlarge her cell so that it could accommodate more companions, she too received a small Virgin in Majesty as a gift from heaven.[57] Clare also relived the Passion in public, having herself beaten in the town square with her hands bound behind her back, in keeping with the iconography of Christ at the column.[58] The orphan Vanna of Orvieto answered some mocking children by bringing them into a church where, "pointing to a certain angel painted on the wall, she said, 'You shall learn that this angel is my mother.'"[59] It was common for visions to be triggered by an icon or crucifix before which the saint prayed or at which she gazed intensely: Christ and the saints appeared to the seven-year-old St. Catherine of Siena "just like she had seen them depicted in churches."[60] Accounts of visions often concluded with concrete gifts: the little cross worn on the neck of the baby Jesus was given to Agnes of Montepulciano, the Virgin's girdle went to St. Thomas, a staff and a book to St. Dominic, and a robe to his companion Reginald.[61] The image of Christ crucified, with its corporeal solidity, satisfied the mystic's need for a tangible sign of the divine; like the relic, it witnessed to the living presence of the sacred. Thus, St. Rose of Viterbo told Christ: "I would like to have from you an icon that would contain your exact likeness so that through it, by holding your keepsake and image in my bodily arms and in my heart, I may often find comfort in it."[62]

At times, it was instead the piety of the faithful that sought (or was encouraged to seek) to collect tokens of saints' visions. Tiny misshapen Margaret of Città di Castello, for instance, whose blindness seemed to heighten her powers of visual concentration, always had "in her mind and mouth the parturition of the glorious Virgin, the nativity of Christ, Joseph's assistance"—and it is touching to find this as the dominant theme in someone whose deformities had caused her to be rejected and abandoned by her own parents.[63] After her death, from her heart—the locus of her affective exegesis—fell "three small stones, imprinted with different images." Thanks to the eager interpretive efforts of the friars, who had already exhumed her heart to display it to the faithful in a golden vessel, the first stone was seen to portray the Virgin wearing a golden crown, the second "a small child in a cradle surrounded by flocks," and the third "the image of a bald man with a white beard and a golden mantle on his shoulders [that is, the standard iconographical features of St. Joseph] and next to him a kneeling woman dressed in a Dominican habit. . . . On the side of this stone was sculpted the shining white dove . . . by whose mediation Mary had conceived her son."[64] It was in effect a tiny crèche that the bystanders longed to see, the crèche that Margaret had constructed in her heart. But they also wanted to see included the figure of the saint herself, so that they could pay reverent homage not only to the Holy Family but also to Margaret, the object of their affections. The saint was a faithful mediator of their veneration for the Christ child, and her little kneeling figure—an image that epitomized its devout audience—reassuringly invited their identification.

FIGURE 1. *Madonna of Humility,* mid fourteenth century. Pinacoteca Nazionale, Siena

FIGURE 2. *Madonna and Child* (detail), late thirteenth century, northern Umbria. Galleria Nazionale, Perugia

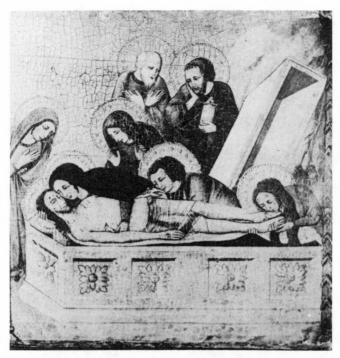

FIGURE 3. Master of 1310,
Deposition in the Tomb. Museo
Vaticano, Vatican City

FIGURE 4. *The Good Death*,
ca. 1470. From the *Ars moriendi*,
fol. cvii, Bibliothèque Nationale,
Paris

FIGURE 5. Lippo Vanni, *Annunciation* (detail), mid fourteenth century. Cloister of the church of San Domenico, Siena

FIGURE 6. *Deposition from the Cross*, ca. 1310–20, Umbria. From the *Speculum humanae salvationis*, Bibliothèque de l'Arsenal, Paris

FIGURE 7. Pietro Cavallini,
Dormition of the Virgin (detail),
1295. Santa Maria in Trastevere,
Rome

FIGURE 8. First Master of Santa
Chiara da Montefalco, *Clare with
Christ Bearing the Cross,* 1333.
Chapel of Santa Chiara,
Montefalco

FIGURE 9.   Maso di Banco, *Last Judgment,* mid fourteenth century. Bardi di
Vernio Chapel, Santa Croce, Florence

FIGURE 10. Follower of Daddi, *Mary at the Sepulchre,* second half of the fourteenth century. Statens Museum for Kunst, Copenhagen

FIGURE 11. Late follower of Lorenzetti, *Altarpiece* (detail), late fourteenth century. Museo Civico Vetrario, Murano

The heart of Clare of Montefalco was found to contain instead *all* the instruments of the Passion—and all murmurs of doubt were soon silenced.[65] Each object reflected a thorough awareness of contemporary iconography, carefully observed: the nails were thus three in number, with elongated and rounded heads; the cross was T-shaped, with a small swelling designating the head of the dying Christ tilted to the right; the scourge, still flecked with clots of blood, had knotted cords and a strap by which to hang it; at the base of the column was a slender crown bristling with thorns; and so on.[66] What is noteworthy here, I think, is the effort to interpret, even to the point of forcing a meaning: the faithful did not at first see the whip, but rather a nerve or tendon that split into five smaller tendons, each one of which had protuberances at regular intervals "as if knots had been tied in the cords of a whip or scourge."[67] This exegesis by "as if," constantly iterated, was what had guided Clare when she experienced mealtime in the refectory as a repetition of the Passion: the bread became the sponge; the water turned into bile, vinegar, and the tears of Christ; the food was his wounds. Clare's mental images crystallized around real, concrete objects, which formed the core of her interior vision: "She focused her meditation so strongly on the bitterness of Christ's Passion that most of what she apprehended through her physical senses reflected his sufferings."[68] From this interior spiritual iconography capable of finding in a glass of water an echo of the feelings evoked by the tears painted on the faces of so many crucifixes, we pass, in the devout veneration of the symbols of the Passion found in Clare's heart, to a materialization of that spiritual iconography. The tendons with their reddish spots like clots of blood, once interpreted, are seen to be really a miniature scourge, an object for devotion and ready-made relic. The fresco depicting Clare before Christ is not only a faithful representation of a passage from her *vita*, but also a "devotional" picture (fig. 8): a handsome young Christ bearing a cross "similar in form and equal in size to the true cross on which he had been crucified" tells Clare that he is seeking the right place to plant this cross, and that the only one he had found was this, adding "if you wish to be my daughter, you must die on the cross."[69] Clare thus learned that she had been chosen: this vision laid the foundation for the formation in her heart of the signs of the Passion. The fresco both invites us to venerate the saint and suggests that the cross shifted from Christ's back to Clare's is the cross of all humankind. But this simply translates a written message into an image, and the scene was not reproduced elsewhere.

Other illustrations, however, were repeated many times; and sometimes a successful visualization managed to establish a new iconography, permanently modifying the earlier tradition. Such was the case with St. Birgitta of Sweden's meditations on the Nativity.[70] The traditional Byzantine iconography, which portrayed the Virgin lying in bed, exhausted by the pain of childbirth and seemingly unmindful of Jesus, had already been modified by Giotto, who in the Scrovegni chapel depicted Mary, reclining on the bed, taking the baby in her arms to place him in the manger. The tenderness and affection of this scene, which invites a new kind of emotional involvement on the part of the viewer, was further heightened in a painting by Taddeo Gaddi: not only does the kneeling Virgin gaze maternally at her divine son, but Joseph too, no longer aloof and distant, prays before the tiny newborn child in the manger.[71] But it was in Birgitta's meditations that the details of the nativity, described point by point with the sensibility of a mystic and mother, acquired clear and enduring form. Here, too, the writings of the Pseudo-Bonaventure and, earlier, of St. Matilda and St. Bernard had given the tradition an initial impulse, just as the motif of the cow and donkey kneeling before the baby Jesus was appropriated from the *Golden Legend* to enrich the saint's meditations.[72] But the point to emphasize is that the essentials of the new iconographic formula, whose details were immediately fixed and widely diffused, rest on the words of St. Birgitta; and the clay figures in our crèches follow them to this day.

In Bethlehem, where Birgitta had gone in pilgrimage, Mary reenacted for her, as promised, the birth of Christ—an idea that I think may have been suggested by the saint's familiarity with mystery plays. In a grotto, illuminated by a candle held by the elderly Joseph, appeared Mary, her blond hair falling over her shoulders; by her side lay her white cloak, her shoes (removed like Moses' before the burning bush), and the swaddling clothes for the baby. Mary knelt and began to pray, and the child was born "in ictu oculi," in the blink of an eye, resplendent with wondrous light. Then the Virgin, "with bowed head and joined hands, adored the child with great dignity and reverence and said to him: 'Welcome, my god, my lord, and my son.'" While angels sang, she cuddled the child, who was shivering with cold, easily severed the umbilical cord, and swathed him. "When these things were done the old man entered and, throwing himself to the ground on bended knees, adored the child with joyful prayer." The image condensed these temporal phases, placing Mary and Joseph immediately together, kneeling symmetrically on either side of the child, who thereby becomes the visual focal point for their adoration and ours.[73] The Byzantine treatment of the Nativity, which presented a realistic account of childbirth (naturally, with midwives bustling around the Virgin and her newborn child), has here become a scene of adoration of the divine child, whose birth began the process of redemption. The allusion to the Resurrection would become more explicit in the Renaissance use of a sarcophagus-like cradle.[74]

But in the fourteenth century, a period dominated by preoccupation with personal salvation, this new iconography had already taken hold—an iconography that made it possible, taking the words and gestures of the two worshipers as a model, to repeat their prayer, their request for aid and comfort.

Thus far I have sought to explore the mystic's relationship with images. Mystics relied on images to inspire visions and used them as a kind of linguistic vehicle to define and communicate experiences that were otherwise ineffable. Mystics also created and diffused images to illustrate their innovative meditations, and in so doing had a definite impact on their social surroundings. At this point I would like to consider the model of behavior implicit in the representation of the mystic, male or female, rapt in vision or engaged in fervent prayer, or flanked by other saints from whom the mystic was distinguished by his or her visionary gift.

The little icons and personal altars that were an increasingly common furnishing in fourteenth-century homes often presented, in addition to the traditional scenes of the Gospel narratives, a new image fraught with internal contradictions: the Pietà, a representation of both death (with eyes shut and arms and body still gripped in death's embrace) and the triumph over death. I will not linger over the origins of this subject, noting simply that as early as the twelfth century we can find a tendency to show Christ and Mary as a separate group in depictions of the Deposition: Mary takes Joseph of Arimathea's place in receiving her son from the cross, or she alone embraces Christ's body laid on the sarcophagus, while the apostles and Mary Magdalene cluster at his feet.[75] A definite narrative has been transformed into a devotional image, whether the Virgin appears bent over Christ's body in a final embrace or contemplating his corpse laid on her lap, or—as in the Ecce Homo—resting her cheek against that of her son, a living cadaver half-risen from his tomb. Especially in this last category (from which the figure of Mary may even disappear) Christ becomes a paradoxical image of non-human death. Every narrative possibility is canceled, leaving the viewer only a contemplative immersion in an atemporal representation.[76]

Indeed, a spatial and temporal break had already taken place in the solitary encounter of (for instance) St. Francis at the foot of the cross, where the *where* and *when* of the story are negated. But in this case, the presence of the saintly mediator between Christ's Passion and that of all humankind allows the spectator to insert human time within the circle of divine time. In the Ecce Homo, Christ, having survived death though still suffering abundantly—not triumphant and hieratic as in Byzantine crucifixes, nor sprawled on the ground in the sleep of death as in so many older Western Lamentations—opens the possibility of an identification through human conversion, a human relationship.[77] This more subjective and personal religiosity had many facets, each of which reflected a corresponding shift in the history of mentalities. The representation of a universal and otherworldly judgment that "prefigures the hierarchical vision of the Beyond" gives way to the representation of an individual judgment; Christ enthroned on the rainbow has returned to this earth to judge not souls, but the dead—even a single member of the Bardi family (fig. 9)—who as they are resurrected are captured in individualized postures that express the extreme emotional tension of the moment.[78] Christ does not look at his elect but rather turns his gaze on the spectators, involving them directly. The gigantic figures of Jesus and Mary in apses and cupolas are replaced by little altars and altarpieces, cross-shaped crucifixion panels, in which the image of devout donor or mediating saint opens the way to a more personal and private approach. Old Testament stories no longer have the popularity they once enjoyed; it is above all the earthly lives of Jesus and Mary that are depicted, drawing largely on the Apocrypha, the *Golden Legend,* and the *Meditations on the Life of Christ.*[79] Scenes of Jesus' childhood illustrate the domestic and intimate side of daily life, emphasizing the importance of family ties.[80] At the same time, the constant concentration on the representation of the Holy Family brings into focus the private world, the household, the human family, leading to the discovery of that figure missing from the medieval heart, the child; and the anachronistic details of the setting—the jugs, tablecloths, and clothing—link the scene represented all the more closely with daily life. This humanization of the divine fostered images in which new sentiments of tenderness, compassion, and pity blossomed and grew: lyrical scenes, devoid of action, but which established an affective relationship with the viewer. In addition to the Pietà, we see the solitary Christ bearing the cross, Mary weeping as she follows her son with his heavy burden, Mary Magdalene despairing at Calvary (a violently emotional scene, propagated chiefly by the Franciscans), the solitude of Judas (first shown isolated in his despair by Taddeo Gaddi), and the Virgin swooning on the sealed sepulchre (fig. 10)—a rare subject that is nonetheless emblematic of the quest for new scenes of emotivity.[81]

On the other hand, this subjective relationship with the divine involved a more personalized sacral patronage. The saints, each of whom specialized in a particular area, interceded for the individual donor, not for sinful humankind. The mantle of the Virgin of Mercy gave shelter to confraternities—those great commissioners of "private" banners and altarpieces—or to members of religious orders, or to donors and their families, but not to Christendom as a whole.[82] The sacred image itself was broken down into the elements that had the greatest emotional impact: the symbols of Christ's

Passion, the hand that slapped him, the mouth that spit on him. Or else the source of those feelings was isolated and put on display: Christ's heart glows on his breast, or is even proffered to the faithful in his hand—as it was to mystics like St. Catherine, who proceeded to exchange hearts with Jesus.[83]

But the church, as the repository of the universal doctrine of salvation, also offered grand decorative programs of a doctrinal and theological character, often elaborated by Dominicans, to propagate its teachings: the vices and virtues, the works of mercy, and the seven sacraments. In Giotto's bell-tower in Florence, where so much space is dedicated to the lay values of a city already fully conscious of its greatness, the seven sacraments (including the strikingly novel representation of the eucharist) are a forceful reminder that salvation is only possible through the divine grace promised by the church. Frescoes reflect and celebrate the official stance of the church. An obvious example is the triumph of the Dominican order in the Spanish Chapel at Santa Maria Novella, with its clear identification of the enemies to persecute, from the infidel to the heretic; but one might also think of the various other triumphs of St. Thomas Aquinas or of St. Francis, and the diffusion, in portrayals of the life of St. Francis, of the scene in which the pope approves the rule, thereby channeling the order and assigning it its place within the church.

The same impulse can be discerned at work in subjects that at first sight might seem remote from it: the Virgin of Humility, seated on the ground with her Son; and the Annunciation, in an iconography that emphasizes yet again Mary's humility and submission to the divine will. The church urged resignation and acceptance on the part of the laity and at the same time displayed its authority, which entailed observing its precepts.[84] On both sides there is a sort of retreat to fortified positions: the church asked for conformity and claimed that it alone could grant salvation, without any further desire for renewal or radical reform; the laity withdrew into the interiority of their own consciences, encouraged to constantly deepen their feeings. Religion tended to be equated with sentiment, "or rather, a specific sentimental moment that did not seem to demand that it be grounded firmly in the ordinary setting of daily life."[85]

Mystical experience, which is always a privileged and personal vocation dominated by the emotions of the encounter with God, was thus truly a model for society, but an unattainable paradigm for life. Care of the sick in hospitals and help for the poor, the needy, and fallen women, which were so often associated with the progress of spiritual ascesis, were seen as a means of conforming ever more closely to the divine calling, to which they were always subordinated. Charitable activity was not the result of calculated efforts to solve a problem, but merely the response to a personal need. This is why the acts of repulsive self-humiliation to which (for instance) Angela of Foligno subjected herself in caring for lepers reveal a desire to sublimate herself *through* the leper rather than a willingness to open herself *to* the leper.[86] Edifying revulsion served to reinforce that feeling and the sense of distance she felt in the face of the sores and mutilations of the ill.

And yet the mystic's close contact with her city, not only through such works of charity but also through the attraction exerted by exceptional personalities, could not help but leave its mark. It sparked a desire for advice and instruction of a not purely doctrinal nature: in Venice people flocked to see Clare of Rimini, "coming and going like ants."[87] Holy women such as Clare of Montefalco and Angela of Foligno were very often endowed with penetrating prophetic insight—the counterpart to their capacity for introspection—which enabled them to see into people's hearts, inducing them to confession, repentance, and good deeds but also identifying sinners and heretics; and these insights were supported, guided, and confirmed by their visions.[88] Mystics were frequently in touch with the souls in purgatory, encouraged in this by a sensibility that tended to make even what had slipped away and passed beyond human time seem near, tangible, and alive.[89]

I would like to emphasize that the relationship between female saints and their followers was not based exclusively, or even primarily, on direct accounts of their mystical experiences: if such had been the case, their effect on the lives of their contemporaries would have been negligible, since their experiences were often communicable only through negations and hyperboles. It was instead through their *vitae,* often written by their confessors, that female mystics reached a wider audience of the devout, for the *vitae* filtered and transformed their specifically mystical language into a continuous narrative, couched in terms of everyday experience and thereby rendered accessible. Furthermore, the female mystics were civic, local, homegrown, and contemporaneous saints. Franco Sacchetti, for example, frowned on "these new saints" who "made people lose faith in the old ones" and "who, barely beatified and not even canonized, have monopolized the veneration reserved for God and the Virgin." "The Dominicans in the city of Florence . . . have the blessed Villana, who was my neighbor, and was a Florentine girl who went around dressed like any other girl, and they celebrate her and neglect St. Dominic. . . . And the people all chase after novelties rather than pay heed to St. Augustine and St. Benedict, because all new things are pleasing.[90]

Since these biographies presented a model of life that was inimitable as a whole, only the most domestic aspects were absorbed and copied: a turning in on oneself; a desire for solitary prayer in the quiet of one's own room, which for that purpose was decorated with little altars and crucifixes, concrete and personalized reference points for one's own piety, one's own yearning for salvation and individual perfection; the prayer gestures and devotional practices that so many *vitae* did not fail to highlight and even (as in the popular pamphlet *How St. Dominic Prayed*) to propagate.[91]

But the devout also longed to have their own magical encounters with the divine, their personal contact with the sacred. Thus arose the proliferation of ex-voto images, eloquent testimonies to miracles that had touched them personally.[92] What strikes me as the most important feature of these ex-votos is that through them individuals were asking the community that assembled in the church or sanctuary where the painting was exhibited to recognize the importance of an extremely private moment, their brush with the divine. And just as the Virgin mediated between humankind and God, here the female mystics, whose miracles while alive were a first installment of their postmortem ones, acted to intercede, protect, and save. The devout, who commissioned wax figures representing themselves or the parts of their bodies restored to health and placed them on the altar for the pious edification of the faithful, believed that their personal experience, because it had been touched in passing by the divine, was a suitable object for meditation, a model and hope for other acts of saving grace. Like a scrap of robe or a piece of veil still imbued with the sanctity of the body it had clothed, these wax images, little paintings, and crutches rendered no longer necessary were relics, precious remnants of a numinous encounter. These encounters were made domestic and familiar by the countless images depicting holy female mystics in their chambers, in solitary meditation before crucifixes or votive images (fig. 11), demonstrating both the gestures and the modes of contrition and prayer.[93]

Here, too, lie the origins of the *santino*, that little picture of a pious praying figure absorbed in mystical converse and divine vision—the souvenir of a death that touched us or of our own personal encounter with God on the day of confirmation or first communion, which may suddenly come rushing back to us with the unexpected rediscovery of a forgotten bookmark.

NOTES

Originally published in *Temi e problemi nella mistica femminile trecentesca*, Convegni del Centro di studi sulla spiritualità medievale, 20 (Todi, 1983), pp. 139–79.

1. Arrigo Levasti, *I mistici del '200 e del '300* (Milan, 1960), p. 273. On the

"ubiquitous visionary imagination" that dominated the medieval perception of reality, see Carolly Erickson, *The Medieval Vision: Essays in Vision and Perception* (New York, 1976), esp. pp. 3–28. My references will be limited to those works most directly relevant to the topic. For more complete biographical guidance on each of the mystics discussed, see the *Bibliotheca Sanctorum, Lexikon der christlichen Ikonographie, Dizionario Biografico degli Italiani, Bibliotheca Hagiographica latina,* and Massimo Petrocchi, *Storia della spiritualità italiana,* vol. 1 (Rome, 1978).

2. "Haec, ut arbitror, est causa cur Rachel prius liberos habeat de ancilla quam generet de seipsa; quia dulce est ei saltem imaginando eorum memoriam retinere, quorum intelligentiam nondum valet ratiocinando apprehendere. . . . Hanc esse primam viam omni ingredienti ad invisibilium contemplationem nemo ignorat" (Richard of St. Victor, "De praeparatione animi ad contemplationem, liber dictus Benjamin minor," *Patrologia latina,* 196:10.

3. Raymond of Capua, *Vita,* in *Acta Sanctorum,* April, vol. 2 (Antwerp, 1675), p. 800: "vidit gloriosam virginem Dei Matrem in sede maiestatis suae sedere, et coram eo Angelorum multitudinem sibi assistentium: quorum quidam ante faciem eius gloriosam quibusdam pulcherrimis manutergiis auram excitare videbantur, prout consuetum est nimio calore ferventibus fieri. . . . Scimus enim Reginam caeli aurae refrigerio non indigere, nec vocis consonantia opus habere: sed omnia illa propter Agnetem sunt figurata, ad suum refrigerium demonstrandum." I cite this rather than the more recent edition of Uga Boscaglia (Florence, 1954), because even if that is based on a codex of Montepulciano "which reproduces the older one, not autograph but considered authentic, preserved among the sealed relics of the saint" (p. 4), Boscaglia provides only an Italian translation of it.

4. *Vita,* in *Acta Sanctorum,* May, vol. 7 (Antwerp, 1688), p. 172: "sublevat sibi coronam de capite, quam angeli reverenter suscipiunt et conservant."

5. Pietro Tommaso De Töth, *Storia di S. Chiara da Montefalco secondo un antico documento dell'anno 1308* (Siena, 1908), p. 9.

6. "In isto autem conflictu tantam recepit scientiam et doctrinam quod cuicumque petenti scivisset de vitiis et virtutibus ac de eorum proprietatibus et quibuscumque aliis sufficientissime respondere" (ibid., p. 26).

7. Adolf Katzenellenbogen, *Allegories of the Virtues and Vices in Mediaeval Art* (London, 1939; reprint, New York, 1964).

8. "In quo virtutes Clarae virginis apparebant quasi essent istoriatae ibidem" (De Töth, *Storia di S. Chiara,* p. 128).

9. "Et post modum cum dictus frater appodiatus existeret ad cervical, Clara super cervical predictum se posuit ad sedendum, et inter collum fratris, qui leviter obdormierat et cervical manum suam et brachium interponens, cum manu altera percussit fratrem dulciter et leviter in superiori maxilla dicens 'inspice modo et vide si sum pulchra'" (ibid., p. 107).

10. The friar's reply, in words taken from the Song of Solomon (4:7), confirms this interpretation: "respondit verbum illud quod pro themate secunde predicationis antea assumpserat et ore loquendo dixit: 'Tota pulcra es amica mea, et macula non est in te'" (ibid., p. 108).

11. To cite just one example drawn from the life of Clare of Montefalco: when Clare was a child, the Virgin appeared to her bearing the baby Jesus "sub clamide"; after Clare's death, the Virgin appeared to an abbess of the convent of San Nicola of Norcia carrying the saint "sub sua clamide" (ibid., pp. 9–10 and 120).

12. For instance, one day while Clare of Rimini was praying before an altar "in which there was a small panel painting depicting Christ our Lord, she heard a voice that spoke to her" (Giuseppe Garampi, *Memorie ecclesiastiche appartenenti all'istoria e al culto della B. Chiara di Rimini* [Rome, 1755], pp. 70–71). The *vita* of Agnes of Montepulciano (p. 794) says: "Dum enim quadam vice, puella Deo devota coram imaginem Crucifixi devotius oraret; in tantum eam arripuit amor Sponsi sui, quod relicta terra tam alte fuit corpus suum purissimum sublevatum in aere, quod ipsi imagini supra altare in eminenti loco positae se pari situ coniunxit." Aldobrandesca of Siena drank a drop of blood she saw spurt from the side of Christ while she was meditating before the crucifix (*Vita,* in *Acta Sanctorum,* April, vol. 3 [Antwerp, 1675], p. 470). Giacomo Bianconi experienced the same miracle (*Vita,* in *Acta Sanctorum,* August, vol. 4 [Antwerp, 1739], p. 732). After forgiving the murderer of his father, who had thrown himself at his feet "expansis manibus in modum Crucis," Giovanni Gualberto entered a church: "Crucem eiusdem ecclesiae caput sibi flectere contuetur, quasi gratias eidem redderet" (*Vita,* in *Acta Sanctorum,* July, vol. 3 [Antwerp, 1723], p. 343). Following instructions received from Christ himself in a vision, Bona of Pisa had a cross made from the iron chain she wore, and when it was completed she saw a drop of Christ's blood fall on it (*Vita,* in *Acta Sanctorum,* May, vol. 7 [Antwerp, 1688], p. 157). On another occasion she bowed and crossed herself before the church of San Sepolcro, where there was a painted image of Christ: "imago eadem, versa vice se totam inclinans B. Bonae, extensa manu benedixit eamdem" (p. 148). On these aspects of medieval religiosity, see *Faire croire: Modalités de la diffusion et de la réception des messages religieux du XIIe au XVe siècle,* ed. André Vauchez (Rome, 1981).

13. Giacomo replied that Christ was his clothing, and that in keeping with Paul's injunction (Romans 13:14) he had "put on the Lord Jesus Christ": "Cum esset Mevaniae beatus Jacobus, a matre sua pecunias petivit pro indumentis emendis. Accepta ergo aliquali pecunia, Perusium ivit, et imaginem Crucifixi ligneam fabricari fecit. Cum autem Mevaniam detulisset, et in ecclesia Fratrum collocasset, dixit mater eius: Quare mihi dixisti mendacium, ut pro indumento pecuniam peteres, et Crucifixum fecisti? Cui ille: Mater mea, mendacium non fuit hoc, quia Christus indumentum est, ut dicit Apostolus: Induimini Dominum Jesum Christum" (*Vita* of Giacomo Bianconi, pp. 731–32).

14. " 'Sanguis iste sit tibi signum et certitudo.' Statim de latere Crucifixi sanguis vivus fluxit et aqua in faciem eius et anteriorem cappae ipsius partem orantis, quemadmodum pueri cum cannula aquam projicere solent" (ibid., p. 732). The echo of Longinus and his cure is obvious.

15. "Et quia tu pro mea imagine tuam dedisti pecuniam indumenti, et pro imagine similiter Matris meae fecisti; Georgius vero, quia eius ecclesiam ampliasti; Do-

minicus, quia habitum ipsius et Ordinem suscepisti, ideo in transitu tuo praesentes erimus" (ibid.)

16. Alberto Tenenti, *La vie et la mort à travers l'art du XVe siècle* (Paris, 1952), pp. 49–50.

17. "Specialius tamen illos quos vel quas prius sanus in veneracione habuit et dilexit, quorum ymagines cum ymagine crucifixi et beate virginis Mariae ei presententur" (in ibid., pp. 119–20).

18. "Mox Angelus adfuit, tres ei clavos sanguineos exhibens; quorum unus ceteris grandior, forte quia utrique pedi configendo servire debuerat" (*Vita* of Aldobrandesca of Siena, p. 469). Gherardesca of Pisa had a similar vision: Christ appeared to her holding "pedes coniunctos uti tenuit in cruce afflixos, sanguine de plagis manante"; and stirred by a desperate impulse she wanted "proprio ore de pedibus clavum extrahere" in order to thrust it into her own flesh (*Vita* of Gherardesca of Pisa, p. 177).

19. Adolfo Morini, "La cassa funebre di S. Rita da Cascia," *Archivio per la storia ecclesiastica dell'Umbria* 3 (1916): 75–80 and the figure facing p. 76.

20. De Töth, *Storia di S. Chiara*, pp. 102–3.

21. *Meditaciones de passione Christi olim Sancto Bonaventurae attributae*, ed. Sister M. Jordan Stallings (Washington, D. C., 1965), p. 112. The passage is also cited by Giorgio Petrocchi, *Scrittori religiosi del Duecento* (Florence, 1975), pp. 93–94, with a thorough bibliography on p. 25. This text was probably written by Giovanni de' Cauli, one of the earliest followers of St. Francis: Giorgio Petrocchi, *Ascesi e mistica trecentesca* (Florence, 1957), p. 78. For other early depictions of the three nails, see Evelyn Sandberg-Vavalà, *La croce dipinta italiana* (Verona, 1929; reprinted Rome, 1980), 1:89 and 115.

22. Cuthbert Butler, *Western Mysticism* (New York, 1967). According to Butler, the spread of the teachings of Pseudo-Dionysus in the twelfth century signaled a profound transformation in mystical experience, introducing new "passional" elements (visions, intense emotionalism, psycho-physical upheavals, stigmata) foreign to the religious tradition that ran from St. Augustine and Gregory the Great to St. Bernard, according to which contemplative activity was a goal attainable by all and not restricted to a privileged few, the natural and unexceptional climax of a committed spiritual life. On both the problems with this thesis and its enduring vitality, see David Knowles's introduction, which carefully recounts the work's tortuous composition. I would like to emphasize one fact that strikes me as very important for defining the difference between the "old" and "new" mysticism of Butler's interpretation: until St. Bernard, mystical ecstasies were not accompanied by physical phenomena, but only by mental ones. In Bernard's words, "Thus, then, the Bridegroom-Word, though he has several times entered into me, has never made his coming apparent to my sight, hearing, or touch. . . . In the reformation and renewal of the spirit of my mind, that is, of my inward man, I have perceived in some degree the loveliness of His beauty" (Bernard of Clairvaux, "Sermones in Cantica Canti-

corum," sermo 74, *Patrologia latina,* vol. 183, cols. 1141–42; translated in Butler, *Western Mysticism,* p. 101).

23. Entry "Himmelfahrt Christi," *Lexikon der christlichen Ikonographie,* ed. Engelbert Kirschbaum (Freiburg, 1979), vol. 2, cols. 274–75. In one of his stories, Franco Sacchetti described how the Ascension was dramatized in the church of the Carmine in Florence, in an elaborate performance in which one could see "our Lord rising aloft on a rope" (Franco Sacchetti, *Opere,* ed. Aldo Borlenghi [Milan, 1957], novella 72, p. 237). This passage is cited by Frederick Antal, *Florentine Painting and Its Social Background: The Bourgeois Republic Before Cosimo de' Medici's Advent to Power, XIV and Early XV Centuries* (Cambridge, 1986), p. 154 n. 13.

24. "Asserebant nocte ipsa in oratione vigilantibus, magna cum luce ac odoris fragrantia mulierem quamdam ornatu regio astitisse, quasi duobus cubitis a terra elevatam. Quam licet primo intuitu beatam dei genitricem crederent. Diligentius observantes, electam dei Villanam esse decernunt, cum qua devotissimum sepius contubernium illis extiterat. Verum quia interrogata sepius numquid ipsam foret, respondisse perhibetur. Ego nunc in celis margarita non amplius villana vocor. Cum igitur vellent eius sanctissimos tenere pedes elevari illam in aera vident continueque magis ab eorum subtrahi conspectibus" (Stefano Orlandi, *La beata Villana terziaria domenicana fiorentina del secolo XIV* [Florence, 1955], pp. 86–87).

25. Otto Pächt, *The Rise of Pictorial Narrative in Twelfth Century England* (Oxford, 1962), pp. 41–42 and 55–56.

26. "Incumbebat columnae, manens in oratione devota" (*Vita* of Gherardesca of Pisa, p. 167).

27. Henrik Cornell, *The Iconography of the Nativity of Christ* (Uppsala, 1924), p. 35.

28. A short list of married female mystics would include Aldobrandesca of Siena, a tertiary in the order of the Humiliati; Umiltà of Faenza, who bore two sons who predeceased her before becoming a Vallombrosan nun; Chiara Agolanti of Rimini, an Augustinian nun; Villana delle Botti, a Dominican tertiary at Santa Maria Novella in Florence and mother of one son; Angela of Foligno, a Franciscan tertiary whose husband and children predeceased her; Gherardesca of Pisa, a Camaldolensian nun; Michelina of Pesaro, a Franciscan tertiary whose one son predeceased her; Birgitta of Sweden, mother of eight children and later a nun in the Order of the Holy Savior, which she founded; Margaret of Cortona, a Franciscan tertiary whose son became a friar in that order.

29. Angela of Foligno declared that after the deaths of her mother, her husband, and her children, she "felt a great consolation," since this was the only way that "my heart would always be within God's heart, and God's heart always within mine" (*Il Libro della beata Angela da Foligno,* ed. Ludger Thier and Abele Calufetti [Grottaferrata, 1985], p. 138; translation from Angela of Foligno, *Complete Works,* trans. Paul Lachance [New York, 1993], p. 126). Michelina of Pesaro reluctantly accepted her companion's suggestion that she pray God for her son's death so that she might be liberated from that earthly love (*Vita* of Michelina of Pesaro, in *Acta Sanctorum,* June, vol. 4 [Paris and Rome, 1867], p. 777).

30. Cited by Giovanni Miccoli, "La storia religiosa," in *Storia d'Italia*, vol. 2, *Dalla caduta dell'Impero romano al secolo XVIII* (Turin, 1974), p. 862.

31. The biographer of Clare of Rimini began his work by declaring: "This is the life of the blessed Clare of Rimini, who was an example for all flighty women" (Garampi, *Memorie ecclesiastiche*, p. 1; the *Vita della beata Chiara di Rimino* is found on pp. 1–76). The *vita* of the blessed Villana was written "for the instruction of the faithful" (Orlandi, *La beata Villana*, p. 76). Angela of Foligno wanted to show that it was possible to reach Christ despite all obstacles: indeed, as her biographer Arnaldo wrote in the first prologue of his *vita,* God deliberately selected this "mulierem saecularis status, mundo obligatam, viro, filiis, divitiis irretitam, scientia simplicem, viribus impotentem" (*Vita,* in *Acta Sanctorum,* January, vol. 1 [Antwerp, 1643], p. 186).

32. For example, Aldobrandesca of Siena was tempted by the devil "frequenti coniugalium deliciarum recordatione" (*Vita* of Aldobrandesca of Siena, p. 469). At the beginning of her conversion, Angela of Foligno felt that her old vices were still alive in her (like a hanged man who remains alive while he dangles on the rope, as she put it) and that vices formerly absent were starting to take root (*Il Libro della beata Angela da Foligno,* p. 338; *Complete Works,* p. 197).

On mystical marriage with Christ, see Reginald Grégoire, "Il matrimonio mistico," in *Il matrimonio nella società altomedievale* (Spoleto, 1977), pp. 701–95, which goes well beyond the chronological parameters of the early Middle Ages and gives serious consideration to psychoanalytic interpretations of the phenomenon.

33. "Aliter clericis, aliter laicis est predicandum. . . . Quando vero in conventu et congregatione sapientium in latino idiomate loquimur, tunc plura dicere possumus, eo quod ad singularia non oportet descendere; laicis autem oportet quasi ad oculum et sensibiliter omnia demonstrare" (cited by Giovanni Getto, *Letteratura religiosa del Trecento* [Florence, 1967], p. 10).

34. *Prosatori minori del Trecento: Scrittori di religione,* ed. Giuseppe De Luca (Milan and Naples, 1954), p. 1037; Giovanni da San Gimignano, *Meditazioni sulla vita di Gesù Cristo* (Florence, 1931), p. 160.

35. For an overview, see Miccoli, "La storia religiosa," p. 845.

36. Jacopo Passavanti, *Lo specchio di vera penitenza,* ed. Filippo Luigi Polidori (Florence, 1863), p. 279.

37. For example, Giordano da Pisa, *Prediche sulla Genesi recitate in Firenze nel 1304,* ed. Domenico Moreni (Milan, 1839), sermon 31, pp. 195–96: "One should not make everyone into a preacher, and anyone who preaches without permission and without training commits a grave sin. The office of preacher is not entrusted to everyone: first of all, it is absolutely forbidden to all women under all circumstances; and also to all laymen and uneducated and illiterate people . . . because Scripture is weighty and profound and quite difficult to understand, and not suitable for everyone." On this passage, see Miccoli, "La storia religiosa," p. 845.

38. Giovanni Dominici, *Regola del governo di cura familiare,* ed. Donato Salvi (Florence, 1860), p. 55; and Bernardino da Siena, *Prediche volgari sul Campo di Siena, 1427,* ed. Carlo Delcorno (Milan, 1989), p. 501, who added that "if you can

not manage to do what is necessary for your whole family, I will not praise your coming here, because you need to frequent the altars in moderation." On this subject, see Miccoli, "La storia religiosa," p. 872, and the essay by Roberto Rusconi in this volume.

39. Dominici, *Regola del governo di cura familiare*, pp. 133 and 146–47. For commentary on this passage, see Antal, *Florentine Painting*, p. 135, and Carlo Ginzburg, "Folklore, magia, religione," *Storia d'Italia*, vol. 1, *I caratteri originali* (Turin, 1972), pp. 624–25.

40. De Töth, *Storia di S. Chiara*, p. 12; and on this sense of "unlettered," see Miccoli, "La storia religiosa," p. 799. The need for greater learning often surfaced nonetheless; but when it did, it was requested as a divine favor, as if to emphasize the danger of education autonomously pursued. This was true of Margherita of Faenza: *Acta Sanctorum*, August, vol. 5 (Antwerp, 1741), p. 849.

41. One day, when Clare of Montefalco was meditating on the words of the Gospel, with her closed missal by her side, she wished "videre illud verbum tantummodo scriptum, et vix comprimens et cohercens me timore superbie continuissem me ne dictum librum pre nimia siti et amore meis manibus aperirem." In the dream that immediately followed, profound understanding of the Epistles and the Gospels was presented to her as a "delectabilissima" thing, which surpassed all worldly desires. When she awoke, the memory of her joy was accompanied by the certainty "quod nihil predicatur de delectione Dei. Et illi qui predicant non possunt illam predicare, et ea que predicant non intelligunt. Et ita dixerat michi ille qui duxerat me in visione" (De Töth, *Storia di S. Chiara*, pp. 14–15).

42. "Lumen solitum in revelationibus et pacem in anima non habebat" (ibid., pp. 26–27).

43. Sometimes even pious gatherings of women had the same purpose: Clare of Rimini often went to Santa Maria in Muro "to speak pleasantly with certain excellent and noble French ladies . . . in that garden or rather church, where they committed to memory many wise sayings about various holy men and women, fasting, abstinence, and praiseworthy examples" (Garampi, *Memorie ecclesiastiche*, p. 24).

44. Cited by Antal, *Florentine Painting*, p. 276. On the esthetics of St. Thomas, see Rosario Assunto, *La critica d'arte nel pensiero medioevale* (Milan, 1961), pp. 243–54.

45. "Nam in sanctissimo Christi natali datum est eidem videre totum mysteriorum eo die ac nocte gestarum ordinem, cum adoratione Magorum et fuga in Ægyptum. Sed dum in spiritu accurrere nititur, ut divinum infantem stringeret brachiorum amplexu, evanuit visio, et caelesti consolatione plenam reliquit; quam Aldobrandesca cupiens frequenti memoria acceptae gratiae conservare, conata est illius expressam similitudinem imaginando retinere: nec potuit. . . . Dumque in eo atque in imagine Crucifixi haeret defixa, gratiam istam a Jesu et Maria flagitans, guttam unam sanguinis e latere imaginis suae conspexit prorumpere: quam labiis colligens, ineffabilem suavitatem in ore suo sensit: atque in huius beneficii memoriam pingi fecit Virginem Matrem, depositi e cruce filii corpus inter brachia tenentem, ipsique lateris vulnere applicantem os suum" (*Vita* of Aldobrandesca of Siena, p. 470).

46. "Et quando videbam Passionem Christi pictam, vix poteram sustinere, sed capiebat me febris et infirmabar, unde socia mea abscondebat a me picturas Passionis et studebat abscondere" (*Il Libro della beata Angela da Foligno*, p. 152; *Complete Works*, p. 131). On Angela's language, see Evelyn Underhill, "A Franciscan Mystic of the XIII Century: The Blessed Angela of Foligno," in *Franciscan Essays* (Aberdeen, 1912), pp. 89–107.

47. "Anima intravit intus in latus Christi. Et erat non tristitia, immo tanta laetitia quod narrari non potest" (*Il Libro della beata Angela da Foligno*, p. 278; *Complete Works*, p. 176).

48. "Inclinavi me et sedi; et inclinavi caput super brachia mea quae proieceram in terra, et tunc ostendit mihi Christus gulam et brachia. Et tunc prior tristitia conversa est in tantam laetitiam, quod de ea non possum manifestare aliquid. . . . Et erat tanta pulchritudo illius gulae vel gutturis, et quod intelligebam illam pulchritudinem resultare ex deitate" (*Il Libro della beata Angela da Foligno*, pp. 192–94; *Complete Works*, p. 146).

49. In the same way, she substituted herself for the Virgin sprawled on the sepulchre mourning her dead son (see figure 3).

50. *Il Libro della beata Angela da Foligno*, p. 194; *Complete Works*, pp. 146–47.

51. *Il Libro della beata Angela da Foligno*, p. 342; *Complete Works*, p. 198.

52. "Et vidi sanctum Franciscum pictum in sinu Christi, dixit mihi [Christus]: Ita te astrictam tenebo. . . . Tu habes anulum mei amoris et es arrata a me" (*Il Libro della beata Angela da Foligno*, pp. 184 and 188; *Complete Works*, pp. 141 and 143).

53. "Veni dilecta mea. . . . Ego non committam te angelis nec aliis sanctis ut te deducant, sed ego personaliter veniam pro te et assumam te ad me" (*Il Libro della beata Angela da Foligno*, p. 734; *Complete Works*, p. 315).

54. See in general the entry "Caterina d'Alessandria," *Enciclopedia Cattolica* (Florence, 1949), cols. 1138–42, which treats her iconography in col. 1140. Depictions of St. Catherine of Alexandria in this period include the dossal by a close follower of the St. Cecilia Master, in the W. Randolph Hearst Collection, New York, reproduced in George Kaftal, *Iconography of the Saints in Tuscan Painting* (Florence, 1952), fig. 243; the fourteenth-century fresco by Allegretto Nuzi in the church of Santa Maria della Rocca in Offida (Ascoli Piceno), in George Kaftal, *Iconography of the Saints in Central and South Italian Schools of Painting* (Florence, 1965), fig. 282; and the mid-fourteenth-century bas-relief depicting the legend of St. Catherine (now destroyed) in the church of Santa Chiara in Naples, on which see Pietro Toesca, *Il Trecento* (Turin, 1951; reprinted Turin, 1971), p. 340 and figs. 304–5, and Stanislao Fraschetti, "Dei bassorilievi rappresentanti la leggenda di Santa Caterina a Napoli," *L'Arte* 1 (1898): 245–55.

55. Kaftal, *Iconography of the Saints in Central and South Italian Schools of Painting*, col. 288, mentions a painting by Fiorenzo di Lorenzo (1487) in the niche of the church of San Francesco in Perugia and one by Benedetto Bonfigli (1472) in the church of San Francesco in Corciano (Perugia), and reproduces the latter in fig. 255. On the wide diffusion of Bonaventure's *Lignum vitae*, see Zelina Zafarana, "Pietà e

devozione in San Bonaventura," in *San Bonaventura francescano,* Convegni del Centro di studi sulla spiritualità medioevale, 14 (Todi, 1974), p. 142.

56. Giuseppe Abate, "S. Rosa da Viterbo, terziaria francescana, 1233–1251: Fonti storiche della vita e loro revisione critica," *Miscellanea francescana* 52 (1952): 113–278, provides editions of *Vita* I from a thirteenth-century codex and of *Vita* II from the copy in the canonization proceedings of 1457. The passage in question is found in *Vita* I, par. 5 (p. 228). *Vita* II, par. 11 (p. 237), provides further details, and seems to refer to a small dyptich: "Ex tunc autem crucifixi Jesu et Virginis gloriosae imagines semper in suo pectore deferebat." *Vita* I, par. 9 (p. 230), also says that St. Rose sang God's praises through the city "cum croce in manibus." But on the verso of the parchment scroll containing *Vita* I she is not shown holding the Virgin in Majesty, as Abate claims, but rather a palm frond and a book: see the plate facing p. 128.

57. Garampi, *Memorie ecclesiastiche,* p. 41

58. Ibid., pp. 44–47. Clare was emulating a gesture of St. Francis of Assisi: see Bonaventure, *Legenda maior,* 6.2.

59. "Ostenso quodam Angelo depicto in pariete, aiebat: 'Istum Angelum mihi noveritis esse matrem'" (Giacomo Scalza, *Leggenda latina della B. Giovanna detta Vanna d'Orvieto,* ed. Vincenzo Mareddu [Orvieto, 1853], chap. 2, p. 5).

60. Alvaro Grion, *Santa Caterina da Siena, dottrina e fonti* (Brescia, 1953), p. 261.

61. *Vita* of Agnes of Montepulciano, p. 797. For pictures of the gift of the Holy Girdle, see Roberto Longhi, "Ancora su Spinello Aretino," *Paragone* 187 (1965): 52–55 and fig. 26; Kaftal, *Iconography of the Saints in Central and South Italian Schools of Painting,* cols. 1082–90; and Kaftal, *Iconography of the Saints in Tuscan Painting,* cols. 982–84. On the iconography of St. Dominic, see George Kaftal, *St. Dominic in Early Tuscan Painting* (Oxford, 1948).

62. "Vellem unam a vobis habere iconam quae vestri expressam similitudinem contineret; ut per ipsam, memoriale et signaculum vestri in brachiis corporis tenens, et cordis, saepius consoler in ea" (Abate, "S. Rosa da Viterbo," p. 153).

63. "Cuibus (!) chooperabatur frequens et assidua meditatio vite Christi, nam in mente et in ore semper videbatur habere partum Virginis gloriose, Christi nativitatem, Joseph administrationem, de quibus frequentissime loquebatur" (Marie-Hyacinthe Laurent, "La plus ancienne légende de la b. Marguerite de Città di Castello," *Archivum Fratrum Praedicatorum* 10 [1940]: 126).

64. "Extrahunt dictum vas tereum in quo viscera condita fuerant et sepulta. Quo extracto dum dictus frater Nicolaus presentibus suprascriptis et aliis multis incideret canam, ad quam dictum cor pendet, ut purum extraheret, subito ex dicta cana tres lapilli mirabiles exilierunt diversas ymagines impressas habentes. In quorum altero quedam facies cum corona aurea cuiusdam mulieris pulcerime videbatur insculpta, quam quidam interpretati fuerunt efigiem esse beate Marie virginis gloriose cui aficiebatur immensa devocione Margarita beata. In altero vero quidam parvulus videbatur in cunis et pecudes circumquaque, quem Christum vel Christi nativitatem quidam significare dixerunt. In tertio vero lapillo sculpta erat ymago cuiusdam viri calvi cum barba canuta et cum palio aureo super spatullis et coram isto quedam mul-

ier vestita in habitu Predicatorum genuflexa, et hunc beatum Iosep et beatam Marga-
ritam figurare dixerunt. A latere vero dicti lapilli sculpta erat quedam candidissima
columba, quam Spiritum sanctum representare dixerunt, quo mediante Maria Filium concepit" (ibid., p. 128).

65. Doubts had emerged as early as three days after her death: see Silvestro
Nessi, "I processi per la canonizzazione di S. Chiara da Montefalco (vicende e documenti)," *Bollettino della Deputazione di storia patria per l'Umbria* 65, part 2 (1968):
103–5 and 128 n. 1; and the essay by Enrico Menestò in this volume.

66. De Töth, *Storia di S. Chiara da Montefalco*, pp. 97–103.

67. "Ac si nodi in alicuius flagelli seu fruste funiculis essent facti" (ibid., p. 99).

68. "Acerbitati passioni Christi sic suae considerationis intuitum defigebat
quod pro maiori parte quidquid per apprehensionem exteriorum sensuum cog-
noscebat totum ad ipsius amaritudinem reflectebat" (ibid., p. 23).

69. "Similem et equalem in forma et magnitudine vere crucis in qua ipse èxtitit
crucifixus . . . si vis esse filia moriaris in cruce" (ibid., p. 39). On the problem of how
apparitions or dream visions were represented in images in the Middle Ages, see
Hubert Damisch, "Textes et images: Figuration et représentation, le problème de
l'apparition," *Annales: Economies, sociétés, civilisations* 26 (1971): 664–80.

70. Cornell, *Iconography of the Nativity*, pp. 1–44.

71. Ibid., fig. 8.

72. Ibid., pp. 28 and 36.

73. "Inclinato capite et iunctis manibus cum magna honestate et reverentia
adoravit puerum et dixit illi: Bene veneris deus meus, dominus meus et filius
meus. . . . Hiis igitur completis intravit senex, et prosternens se ad terram genibus
flexis adorando eum orabat pre gaudio" (ibid., pp. 9–11, quoting from the *Revelations* of St. Birgitta, vol. 7, chap. 1 and 21–22; translation in Birgitta of Sweden, *Life
and Selected Revelations*, trans. Albert Ryle Kezel [New York, 1990], pp. 202–5).
The early depictions of the Nativity also include the presence of the saint, like Margaret of Città di Castello; but this was later eliminated. For an example from the early
fifteenth century, see the painting attributed to Falconi in the museum of San Matteo
in Pisa: Enzo Carli, *Il museo di Pisa* (Pisa, 1974), plate 19 and pp. 79–80. On the
miniatures illustrating other visions of St. Birgitta, see Carl Nordenfalk, "Saint
Bridget of Sweden as Represented in Illuminated Manuscripts," in *De Artibus
Opuscula XL: Essays in Honor of Erwin Panofsky*, ed. Millard Meiss (New York,
1961), pp. 371–93.

74. See, for instance, the painting by Ghirlandaio discussed by Aby Warburg,
"Le ultime volontà di Francesco Sassetti," *La Rinascita del paganesimo antico* (Flor-
ence, 1966), p. 243 and fig. 72; and for a more general treatment, the entry "Geburt
Christi" in *Lexikon der christlichen Ikonographie*, vol. 2, cols. 86–120.

75. Of the immense bibliography on this subject, the dense article by Erwin
Panofsky is particularly illuminating: "'Imago Pietatis': Ein Beitrag zur Typen-
geschichten des 'Schmerzensmannes' und der 'Maria Mediatrix,'" in *Festschrift für
Max J. Friedländer zum 60. Geburtstage* (Leipzig, 1927), pp. 261–307. More recently, Tadeusz Dobrzenieski has contributed two studies, of which the first is pri-

marily a textual study: "Mediaeval Sources of the Pietà," *Bulletin du Musée National de Varsovie* 8 (1967): 5–25; and "A Gdansk Panel of the *Pitié-de-notre Seigneur*: Notes on the Iconography," *Bulletin du Musée National de Varsovie* 10 (1969): 29–55.

76. Angela of Foligno seems to have fully absorbed this disturbing new imagery. One Holy Saturday, "in a state of ecstasy, she found herself in the sepulcher with Christ. She said she had first of all kissed Christ's breast—and saw that he lay dead, with his eyes closed—then she kissed his mouth, from which, she added, a delightful fragrance emanated, one impossible to describe. This moment lasted only a short while. Afterward, she placed her cheek on Christ's own and he, in turn, placed his hand on her other cheek, pressing her closely to him. At that moment, Christ's faithful one heard him telling her: 'Before I was laid in the sepulcher, I held you this tightly to me.' Even though she understood that it was Christ telling her this, nonetheless she saw him lying there with eyes closed, lips motionless, exactly as he was when he lay dead in the sepulcher. Her joy was immense and indescribable" (*Il Libro della beata Angela da Foligno*, pp. 296–98; *Complete Works*, p. 182).

77. Werner Körte, "Der Ursprung der italienschen Pietà," *Kunstgeschichtliches Jahrbuch der Bibliotheca Hertziana* 1 (1937): 8–18; Georg Swarzenski, "Italienische Quellen der deutschen Pietà," in *Festschrift Heinrich Wölfflin* (Munich, 1924), pp. 127–33.

78. Alberto Tenenti, "L'attesa del giudizio individuale nell'iconografia del Quattrocento," in *L'attesa dell'età nuova nella spiritualità della fine del Medioevo*, Convegni del Centro di studi sulla spiritualità medioevale, 3 (Todi, 1962), pp. 173–93. The discussion of this painting in Antal, *Florentine Painting*, pp. 180 and 220 n. 80, is stimulating, even if the proposed relation between social class and pictorial style seems excessively rigid.

79. Antal, *Florentine Painting*, pp. 144–46.

80. Other common domestic scenes include Anne and Joachim, Anne with two others—["Anna Selbdritt"],—and the nativity of the Virgin.

81. Antal, *Florentine Painting*, fig. 46 (Barna of Siena, Christ carrying the Cross, Frick Collection, New York), fig. 75b (workshop of Niccolò Gerini, Christ carrying the Cross, church of Santa Brigida, Bardino [Savona]), p. 174 and fig. 18 (Taddeo Gaddi, Allegory of the Cross, Santa Croce, Florence), and fig. 27b (follower of Daddi, Mary swooning at the Sepulchre, Statens Museum for Kunst, Copenhagen).

82. Walter Bombe, "Gonfaloni Umbri," *Augusta Perusia* 2 (1907): 1–7.

83. George Kaftal, *St. Catherine in Tuscan Painting* (Oxford, 1949); Jean Leclercq, "Le Sacré-coeur dans la tradition bénédectine au Moyen Age," in *Cor Jesu: Commentationes in litteras Encyclicas Pii XII "Haurietis aquas"* (Rome, 1959), 2:26.

84. The church generally advised resignation in the face of social injustice, when it did not actually support repressive action: Giordano da Pisa deplored the fact that the merchants of the wool guild had managed to have their workers excommunicated for doing an unsatisfactory job. For this and other examples, see Antal, *Florentine Painting*, p. 84.

85. Miccoli, "La storia religiosa," p. 843.

86. After having washed the lepers she drank the foul water and swallowed a scab as if it were the host. (*Il Libro della beata Angela da Foligno,* p. 242; *Complete Works,* p. 163).

87. Garampi, *Memorie ecclesiastiche,* p. 62.

88. See Chiara Frugoni, "The City and the 'New' Saints," in *City-States in Classical Antiquity and Medieval Italy,* ed. Anthony Molho, Kurt Raaflaub, and Julia Emlen (Ann Arbor, 1991), pp. 71–88.

89. Clare of Montefalco, for example, often experienced such visions (De Töth, *Storia di S. Chiara da Montefalco,* pp. 23, 42, 47, 49, and 54). Thanks to the intercession of St. Bona of Pisa, a dying person was spared the pains of purgatory and passed directly to heaven (*Vita* of Bona of Pisa, p. 158). On the social function of visions, see Peter Dinzelbacher, "Die Vision des Mittelalters: Ein geschichtlicher Umriss," *Zeitschrift für Religions- und Geistesgeschichte* 30 (1978): 116–28, esp. 125, which promises a future study on the subject (since published as *Vision und Visionsliteratur im Mittelalter* [Stuttgart, 1981]).

90. Franco Sacchetti, *La Battaglia delle belle donne, Le Lettere, Le Sposizioni di Vangeli,* ed. Alberto Chiari (Bari, 1938), pp. 101–2.

91. Adele Floris, *Come pregava S. Domenico* (Rome, 1947).

92. We still lack a good study of ex-voto images as a source for the history of mentalities. For an introduction to the subject, see Lenz Kriss-Rettenbeck, *Das Votivbild* (Munich, 1958), which contains an extensive bibliography. A group of ex-votos were recently the object of a detailed, intelligent analysis designed to elicit data on the families, social classes, domestic arrangements, illnesses, and religious orientation of their donors (but not the historical origins of ex-votos or the reasons for the sudden popularity): see the issue on popular religion of *Le monde Alpin et Rhodanien* 5 (1977), and in particular the articles by Bernard Cousin, "Ex-voto provenciaux et histoire des mentalités" (pp. 183–212) and Christian Loubet, "Ex-voto de Notre-Dame d'Oropa en Piémont, XVI–XX siècles: Images d'une dévotion populaire" (pp. 213–47).

93. See the representations of Catherine of Siena, Daniela of Orvieto, Elizabeth of Hungary, Margaret of Cortona, and Rose of Viterbo in George Kaftal's iconographic repertories.

8

Imitable Sanctity: The Legend of Maria of Venice

Fernanda Sorelli

With his Italian translations of the *vitae* of Vanna of Orvieto and Margaret of Città di Castello, the Dominican friar Tommaso Caffarini of Siena had acquired the experience needed to write a hagiographic legend himself.[1] He dedicated it to a young Venetian woman in the order of penitence, Maria Sturion, who had been under his spiritual guidance in the years leading up to her death on 28 July 1399.[2] Shortly after that event—we do not know exactly when—Caffarini began the first version of the work, in Latin; this was finished by July 1402, as can be inferred from a reference to it found in the first part of his *Tractatus,* which we know to have been written before that date.[3] The *explicit* of the Italian translation states that it was completed on the Octave of the Assumption in 1403, in the Dominican convent in Chioggia.[4]

When compared with the dramatic stories of other saints, the life of Caffarini's protagonist, Maria Sturion, seems remarkably ordinary. Born around 1379 to a well-to-do, though not noble, Venetian family, she grew into a proper young lady: polite and well-mannered, with a normal interest in worldly display. At the age of fifteen or so, she married a man of similar social background, Giannino della Piazza, and moved into the house of her husband's family. The marriage, however, was not a great success: Maria's husband soon went off to the wars near Mantua, abandoning her to the care of his father. Unhappy with this arrangement, Maria returned to her family home. It was at this point that she began to frequent the Dominican church of SS. Giovanni and Paolo, where she passed her time listening attentively to the sermons of Caffarini, who became her spiritual director and eventually granted her the habit of a Dominican penitent. She did not get to wear it for long: her short life came to an end when she died of the plague in 1399, only twenty years old.[5]

The brief time that elapsed between the events described and Caffarini's narrative elaboration of them, together with his personal acquaintance with Maria and familiarity with her Venetian surroundings, lend considerable immediacy and interest to the *Legend of Maria of Venice*. But apart from what it can tell us about the social framework of Venetian piety, Caffarini's *Legend* is particularly interesting for the hagiographical model it presents. For unlike other works of its genre, the *Legend* is notably silent on the subject of supernatural phenomena, prodigious events, and miracles connected with Maria's presence or intervention.[6] This silence is all the more striking in that Caffarini was certainly not reticent about relating miracles, or what seemed to be miracles, in his other writings.[7]

What, then, could lead Caffarini, and consequently his audience, to think of this young penitent as a saint?[8] What were the foundations of her sanctity? The opening lines of the prologue provide the answer: "her remarkable conversion," "the commendable way she lived her life from that point on," and "her happy death"—that is to say, the events of her life, or rather, the manner in which she conducted herself during her life. We thus need to examine Maria's activities, habits, and outlook in order to understand in what way and to what extent they expressed her adherence to the precepts or directives of the Christian faith, the church, and the Dominican order, as well as her response to the tendencies and promptings of her religious culture.

Caffarini emphasized above all Maria's perfect fulfillment of the two essential commandments, to love God and to love one's neighbor. She understood the love of God, known principally in the person of Jesus Christ, to mean a constant and fervent dedication to carrying out his will, which was revealed to her especially in the preacher's words; a complete and selfless giving of herself in every moment of her active and contemplative existence; the practice of penitence and the joyous acceptance of illness and suffering; and, finally, the quest for martyrdom.[9] She achieved martyrdom not by joining some hypothetical crusade against the Turks—an implausible idea, and one that apparently hardly even crossed her mind—but by dying of the plague, which she perhaps contracted while nursing women of her city who had been infected with the disease.[10] Indeed, Caffarini considered people who endured this disease with equanimity or, not fearing contagion, willingly provided aid to the plague-stricken, to be the equivalent of martyrs: if they died of the plague, they would be cleansed of all sin and welcomed immediately into heaven.[11]

It is to be expected that the protagonist of a work of hagiography would disdain or renounce earthly goods. According to a widely held and deeply rooted belief (which, to be sure, varied somewhat in its expression), the love of God could hardly be separated from renunciation of the world.[12] But in the *Legend* Maria's renunciation never assumed particularly harsh tones, nor did she make any flamboyant or dramatic acts of repudiation—perhaps in part because of the vigilant control exercised by her family and her spiritual director—even if she is described as being quite impatient with life in this world, especially because of the obstacles it places in the path leading to the fullness of "divine dilectation." What is more, certain attitudes or incidents could be classified more appropriately as devotional, rather than contemplative or mystical.[13] These include her attempt to have herself depicted in the act of offering her heart to Christ crucified and her regret when the painter portrayed her proffering it to him with only one hand, her unrelenting repetition of fixed verbal formulas, and her habit of raising her eyes to heaven.

For Maria, love of one's neighbors meant above all concern for their spiritual salvation.[14] She expressed this sort of pious concern for her husband, although he had wronged and abandoned her; for her parents and other members of her family, whom she did not hesitate to admonish, though always with humility; for more distant relatives, to whom she "sent letters and messages to comfort them in Christ"; and for her confessor, who she wished to be a great servant of God and preacher of his word, and "a most ardent zealot for saving souls, even if it meant suffering some terrible martyrdom."[15]

In reality, despite Maria's self-proclaimed readiness to reach out to embrace all of the infidels, her affective life was restricted to a tiny circle. In addition to her family and spiritual director, Maria's world consisted of her brethren and, more important, sisters of the order of penitence, the nuns of Corpus Christi, and the Dominican friars of Venice—whom she venerated in a prudently detatched manner, loving them (in an echo of Romans 8:4) "not according to the flesh, but only according to the spirit," without indulging in any earthly weaknesses.[16] Equally revealing, I think, is the text's overall lack of attention to concrete consequences, or to the practical enactment of the precept by actually performing works of charity. Indeed, Caffarini noted that he himself restrained Maria's charitable impulses, which were expressed mainly in her assistance to the ill, claiming that he had counseled moderation because she was a young and attractive woman.

Maria, who even before her conversion stood out for her good and upright character, was perfect not only in her charity, but in the other theological and cardinal virtues as well.[17] Caffarini describes these standard virtues in customary, generic terms; but his stiff portrait still manages to suggest a woman notable for her modesty, humility, and unusual wisdom.[18] Her reasoning in responding to her mother, the noted preacher Giovanni Dominici, and Caffarini himself was so acute and cogent that it seemed worthy of "a great philosopher of Christ."[19]

Aspiring to reach the highest degree of virtue, Maria undertook to fulfill the vows of poverty, chastity, and obedience. This she did on her own initiative and even before taking the habit of a penitent—and in any case, these vows did not figure in the rule for the order of penitence promulgated in 1285 by the Dominican master general Muñoz of Zamora, and were mandatory only for persons who belonged to religious orders.[20] Obedience and chastity could be exercised fully, and indeed with the unconditional approval of her confessor, who strongly emphasizes her innate purity and almost infantile innocence, offering as evidence her firmness in maintaining her "holy proposition" against the wishes of her husband, during the brief period she returned to live with him after her conversion.[21] But her wish to renounce all possessions, even giving her personal belongings to the poor without informing her family, was considered excessive, or at the very least imprudent, and thus called for a firm application of restraint.[22]

Among Maria's most notable characteristics was the fervor with which she performed ascetic and penitential practices: restricting or depriving herself of clothing, food, and rest, observing silence for long periods, scourging herself with a whip, and wearing hairshirts and a chain under her clothes.[23] She was equally fervent in her devotional practices: assiduous in visiting churches, especially the Dominican church of SS. Giovanni and Paolo, reverent in participating in the rites, unfailingly attentive at sermons, intense and constant in prayer, exemplary in confession and communion.[24] Even her reading and writing were directed toward devout purposes.[25]

But the most unusual and most insistent element in Caffarini's portrait of Maria is her unwavering desire to don the habit of a penitent.[26] This desire throws into relief the unusual nature of her situation. While it is true that her husband had abandoned her, we catch hints that their separation was not complete. However, what most mattered in this context was that she did not have the explicit and formal consent of her husband, which was normally required for admission to the order of penitence.[27]

Her powerful affection for the habit of the *mantellate* testifies to the symbolic value of clothing in late medieval culture, and it is worth noting that in Caffarini's account, the various stages of Maria's story and spiritual progress correspond closely to changes in her manner of dressing.[28] One of the first gestures signifying her conversion was that of stripping from her clothing (which must have been quite sumptuous, given her family's affluence) "every superfluous and vain ornament, with a marvelous fervor of spirit." When she had reached a more advanced stage in her ascent toward perfection, she donned "a white tunic over her hairshirt." This tunic was a sort of foretaste of the habit she so desired, that white tunic with white bands and veil and a black mantle whose reception would mark the consummation of both her spiritual and earthly journeys.[29] Finally, in visions revealing her heavenly glory, she appeared radiant with joy, wearing "the most beautiful habit of St. Dominic" or even "dressed entirely in gold."[30]

In these and in other passages, the *Legend* transparently aims to extol the penitential order to which Maria belonged.[31] But the text also seems to be informed by two other purposes that are no less noteworthy. One, readily apparent even if not stated explicitly, is to present a concrete example of how the rule of Muñoz should be applied: the abstract norm is rendered visible, at least in part, in Caffarini's description of Maria's comportment, thereby making it easier to understand and assimilate. A parallel reading of both the hagiographic and normative sources would be needed to confirm their many points of contact; here it is enough to point out those precepts in the rule that are enacted most clearly in the *Legend*. Obviously, these will not touch on the organizational structure and collective life of the female penitents, since their community in Venice was just taking shape at the time of the events described by Caffarini, but rather the qualities, practices, and behavior expected of each individual.

First of all, one cannot help but notice how perfectly the moral and spiritual image of Maria matches a passage in the first chapter of the rule, which requires that the aspirant be "of honest life and good reputation, and that in no way should she be suspected of any heresy or error, but rather, as a special daughter in Christ of St. Dominic, be an outstanding follower of and zealot for the truth of the Catholic faith, to the limits of her knowledge and power."[32]

Moreover, many of Maria's actions and habits mirror more or less precisely the general content of some of the succeeding chapters, or specific principles contained therein. One thinks, for instance, of chapter 6, "On saying the seven canonical hours," which regulates the frequency of prayer; chapter 8, "On confession and communion," which specifies when members of the order should receive these sacraments; chapter 9, "On observing silence," concerning proper behavior in church; chapter 11, "On fasting," and chapter 12, "On food"; chapter 15, "On visiting and looking after the sick"; and, finally, chapters 13, "On the speech of the sisters and brothers," and 18, "On the office of prioress and of prior," which prescribe for the sisters, especially the young ones, an austere and reserved existence, warning them against doing anything that might "scandalize their neighbors" and having any familiarity with men who were not their close kin and, in addition, "of honest life and honorable reputation." Maria not only observed all these precepts, but often voluntarily extended their application and increased their rigor. For example, whereas the rule prohibited eating meat only on certain days of the week and allowed exemptions from this fast in special circumstances, when Maria was "healthy, she did not eat meat at any time, and even when she was ill, she only ate it when specifically ordered to do so."[33] And while the rule prescribed visiting and nursing only fellow penitents who had taken ill, Maria offered her services to any woman she could find—including slaves, who in general must have inspired much less concern than other people.[34] One might call this a "heroic" interpretation of the rule, which was not in any case a very severe one.

The second and more explicit purpose of the *Legend* is to call attention to the image of Catherine of Siena, as reflected in Maria and refracted through her. But how was this model understood and interpreted? The best, or rather the only, basis for comparison with Caffarini's work is Raymond of Capua's *Life of Catherine of Siena,* and the results are unmistakable: Maria is a shrunken and faded reproduction of a figure who was so exceptional that she could never have been equaled in any case, no matter how faithful the imitation.[35]

Let us set aside any discussion of supernatural manifestations and miraculous events, which were almost completely absent from Maria's life but present very strikingly, both for their quality and their quantity, in Catherine's—and this despite Raymond of Capua's awareness that the recognition of sanctity should be based more on works than on miracles.[36] One can easily note, however, numerous parallels between Maria's comportment and spiritual life and Catherine's, ranging from their youthful expressions of amazing sagacity to their kindly but firm attitudes toward those close to them, from their love of Christ to their acts of charity, from their spontaneous obedience to the three vows to their resolute request for the Dominican habit, from the intensity of their devotional practices to their quest for mortification.

But while nearly everything that Catherine accomplished was extraordinary for its profundity and energy (when it was not outright miraculous), Maria's sphere of action was entirely human, and her perfection remained within limits that could be reached by nearly anyone. Compared to the sweeping gestures and frequent drama that characterized Catherine's bold actions, which could hardly be repressed by the weight of caution and propriety, Maria's behavior and feelings, despite all her undeniable enthusiasm and austerity, cannot help but appear modest and contained.

Thus Caffarini's *Legend*—certainly not unintentionally—served a dual function: it acquainted readers with Catherine (or reminded them of her) and led them to venerate her; and it demonstrated how she could and should be imitated, in concrete and everyday terms, by people (especially women, of course) who were thoroughly ordinary, albeit endowed with a certain religious fervor.

One particularly telling example will suffice to show how Caffarini's mediation functioned. Consider the manner in which Maria, on her confessor's suggestion, absorbed the typically Catherinian image of the mental or interior cell. In Catherine's original formulation as in Raymond of Capua's later interpretation, this image had a purely spiritual meaning, referring to the concentration and tension directed at attaining, through a more vigorous development of one's interior forces, a deeper knowledge of oneself and of God.[37] In the *Legend,* however, it becomes naive and elementary, materializing (so to speak) in a prayer or devout formula that Caffarini transmitted to Maria "written on a certain piece of paper," which she then copied with her own hand and "studied well." Its power was such that it seemed to her that "since she placed herself mentally in that cell, through intellectual meditation, . . . wherever she was or wherever she went, it was as though she were in the presence of Christ and the queen of Heaven and all the angels and saints and the whole court triumphant and militant."[38]

Caffarini's inspirational, propagandistic, and didactic purposes inevitably lend a certain rigidity to Maria's portrait, especially its spiritual aspect, which seems to follow point by point a carefully preconceived pattern. Nevertheless, her character as a whole is endowed with enough concreteness and verisimilitude that one almost seems to catch occasional glimpses of the "real" Maria Sturion through the web of hagiographic conventions and doctrinal and devout references.[39] But there is no sense in pursuing them, for such a problematic project would only be workable if we had some sort of direct evidence regarding Maria or could discover revealing references to her in contemporary sources.

And so we must be content with discussing (as we have been) a figure who is essentially Caffarini's hagiographic creation. It is still worth reflecting on the meaning of a sanctity so unspectacular both in its constituent elements and in its outward manifestations and effects.[40] To be sure, there are a number of allusions to Maria's divine inspiration and prophetic powers, as well as to her vision of the "heavenly host."[41] But these do not amount to very much at all, and seem even less significant when compared with the many kinds of extraordinary phenomena, testifying to a direct and privileged relation with the divine, that were a primary feature of female sanctity, especially in this period.[42] Moreover, the diabolical temptations and interventions so common throughout hagiographic literature—and not only hagiographic literature—are conspicuously absent from the *Legend*.[43]

Maria was indeed an anomaly as a saint. Caffarini's choice may well seem unusual, but in fact it was neither unmotivated nor ill-considered. The idea that the true greatness of the saints did not reside in their miracles but rather in their lives, and that these lives should be examined above all for their exemplary value, had been in circulation for some time, thanks especially to the efforts of the mendicant orders; and specific statements to this effect can be found even in hagiographic texts.[44] Here I will cite only a single passage in the *Life of Catherine of Siena*, which has already been mentioned in passing. In the epilogue, Raymond of Capua discussed with great lucidity the inherently ambiguous nature of wonders and miracles, which do not provide "absolute proof of sanctity," even if they are "an important indication of it, especially if they occur after death"; and he concluded that before declaring someone a saint, the church should pay more attention to the putative saint's accomplishments and behavior while alive than to the miracles attributed to him or her.[45]

This alone was enough to justify writing the *Legend*, for Caffarini must have considered it particularly useful to add to the ranks of noted penitents who had belonged (or were thought to have belonged) to the Dominican order a more contemporary figure, and one that was certainly closer to the experience and outlook of the faithful.[46]

It was also likely (if only as a secondary consideration) that, having lived in Venice for several years and become thoroughly familiar with the local hagiographic traditions, this Sienese friar welcomed an opportunity to showcase a particular form of sanctity—female and Dominican—in a place where both these categories had hitherto been poorly represented.[47]

Among the handful of women in Venice who had entered the order of penitence around 1400 and died without having traded that habit for a monastic one, Maria was perhaps the only serious candidate for the role of protagonist of a hagiographic work that "needed" to be written just then. Certainly she was the most suitable one, because of certain important features of her life story, such as her unhappy marriage and her premature death from the plague, but above all because of the religious values inherent in her behavior, the level of her spiritual qualities, and the intensity of her ties with the Dominicans.

Caffarini's *Legend* thus sketches for us the shadowy image of a would-be mystic, a female saint on a modest scale who lived at the end of the fourteenth century. Or did Maria perhaps represent instead the new image—one even slightly ahead of its time—of an exemplary tertiary, the ideal devout woman of the fifteenth century? A bit of both, I would say, and the real interest of the *Legend* may lie precisely in this ambivalence. With her harsh mortification and pious practices, fervent enthusiasm and bashful poses, the figure of Maria, in its hazy outlines, is to some degree emblematic of the transition from a strong, open, and vibrant spirituality to a meek, repetitive, and retiring religiosity.[48]

NOTES

Originally published in Fernanda Sorelli, *La santità imitabile: "Leggenda di Maria da Venezia" di Tommaso da Siena,* Deputazione di storia patria per le Venezie, Miscellanea di studi e memorie, 23 (Venice, 1984), pp. 22 and 118–33.

1. On Caffarini and his hagiographical writings, see Fernanda Sorelli, "La production hagiographique du dominicain Tommaso Caffarini: Exemples de sainteté, sens et visées d'une propagande," in *Faire croire: Modalités de la diffusion et de la réception des messages religieux du XIIe au XVe siècle,* ed. André Vauchez (Rome, 1981), pp. 189-200, and the works cited there.

2. *Leggenda,* p. 208. (The essential source for Maria's life is Caffarini's *Leggenda di Maria da Venezia,* found on pp. 151–225 of Sorelli, *La santità imitabile.* It will be cited here as *Leggenda.*)

3. Tommaso da Siena "Caffarini," *Tractatus de ordine ff. de paenitentia s. Dominici,* ed. Marie-Hyacinthe Laurent (Florence, 1938), p. 20: "Soror Maria . . . que singulari puritate refulsit in tantum ut per . . . me fratrem Thomam . . . , de dicte sororis vite processu et transitu specialiter informatum, quedam licet compendiosa composita sit legenda." See also p. 54.

4. *Leggenda,* p. 225. On the basis of this *explicit,* Marie-Hyacinthe Laurent asserts bluntly that "Caffarini wrote this legend in 1403" (preface to Tommaso Caffarini, *Vita di Santa Caterina da Siena,* ed. Giuseppe Tinagli [Siena, 1938], p. 41). Both versions are also dated to 1403 by Oriana Visani, "Nota su Tommaso d'Antonio Nacci Caffarini," *Rivista di storia e letteratura religiosa* 9 (1973): 290.

5. [This paragraph has been added by the editors. Sorelli discusses the structure of the text, Maria's family background and social setting, and the religious climate of Venice in portions of her thorough introduction of the *Leggenda di Maria da Venezia* not translated here.]

6. On the meaning of "miracles" in hagiographic sources, see the remarks of Sofia Boesch Gajano, "Il culto dei santi: Filologia, antropologia, e storia," *Studi storici* 23 (1982): 122–35 (with an ample bibliography on the subject).

7. In addition to his works on St. Catherine, see Caffarini's *Historia disciplinae regularis instauratae in coenobiis Venetis ordinis praedicatorum nec non tertii ordinis de poenitentia s. Dominici in civitatem Venetiarum propagati,* in Flaminio Corner, *Ecclesiae Venetae antiquis monumentis nunc etiam primum editis illustratae* (Venice, 1749), dec. 11, 1, pp. 167–234, which recounts various miracles, including an episode in which Caffarini himself was the protagonist. While he was preaching in

174

FERNANDA SORELLI

the Venetian church of St. Apollinaris on the feast day of that saint, "contigit frustum lapideum sive marmoreum, ubi poni consuevit Evangeliorum liber, de columna in qua cum ferro fixum fuerat, prosilire," and it would have fallen with disastrous consequences if Caffarini had not managed to hold it back, despite its weight. This first miracle was followed by a second: there was "quaedam singularis devotionis persona, quae dum haec agerentur, vidit quemdam in habitu pontificali coram me stantem, et reputatum est quod fuerit sanctus Apollinaris, mihi contra praefata pericula benigne et misericorditer occurrens ac adiuvans." For this reason, concluded the author, "concepi ex tunc semper de dicto sancto memoriam facere. Et cum postea ad eius ecclesiam invitarer ad praedicandum, tanquam eidem singulariter obligatus, semper acceptavi laetanter" (pp. 180–81).

8. I use the term "saint" in the broadest sense. In any case, it was only starting in the fourteenth century that the distinction between "saint" and "blessed" "became effective, in that these terms took on precise meanings that they had not previously had in current usage. 'Saint' denoted a person canonized by the Catholic Church, while 'blessed' designated someone upon whom the church had not yet passed judgment. This boundary line, however, was far from rigid" (André Vauchez, *La sainteté en Occident aux derniers siècles du Moyen Age d'après les procès de canonisation et les documents hagiographiques* [Rome, 1981], p. 102; but see in general pp. 99–120). In the Italian version of the *Legend* the term most often used for Maria is "dilecta," or beloved, though the terms "saint" and "blessed" also appear (see pp. 153 and 151).

9. On charity, see *Leggenda,* pp. 181–92. To properly assess the enormous importance that the *Legend* places on charity, in its double expression as love of God and of neighbor, it is helpful to recall that two other Dominican writers with whom Caffarini was thoroughly familiar, Thomas Aquinas and Catherine of Siena, also assign it a fundamental role, although with differing emphases in thought and expression. Particularly helpful on this subject is Giuliana Cavallini, "La dottrina dell'amore in S. Caterina da Siena: Concordanze col pensiero di S. Tommaso d'Aquino," *Divus Thomas* 75 (1972): 369–88; but see also Karen Scott, "'This Is Why I Have Put You among Your Neighbors': St. Bernard's and St. Catherine's Understanding of the Love of God and Neighbor," in *Atti del Simposio internazionale cateriniano-bernardiniano, Siena, 17–20 aprile 1980,* ed. Domenico Maffei and Paolo Nardi (Siena, 1982), pp. 279–94.

On the quest for martyrdom, see *Leggenda,* pp. 162–63. On the role of the mendicant orders in providing women with religious and moral instruction, see *Prediche alle donne del secolo XIII,* ed. Carla Casagrande (Milan, 1978). For interesting evidence about the reception of sermons by the faithful, see Zelina Zafarana, "Per la storia religiosa di Firenze nel Quattrocento: Una raccolta privata di prediche," *Studi medievali,* ser. 3, 9 (1968): 1017–1113.

10. The allusion to the Turks may be explained by the climate of fear rampant in Europe following the battle of Nicopolis on 26 September 1396, where the Turkish army of Bayezid I decisively defeated the Christian forces; but one should also keep in mind Catherine of Siena's insistent calls for a crusade: Franco Cardini, *Le*

crociate tra il mito e la storia (Rome, 1971), pp. 269–73 and 279–84. See also Franco Cardini, "L'idea di crociata in Santa Caterina da Siena," in *Atti del Simposio cateriniano-bernardiniano*, pp. 57–87; Paul Rousset, "L'idée de croisade chez Sainte Catherine de Sienne et chez les théoriciens du XIVe siècle," *Atti del Congresso internazionale di studi cateriniani, Siena-Roma, 24–29 aprile 1980* (Rome, 1981), pp. 362–72; and Anna Benvenuti Papi, "'Margarita filia Jerusalem': Santa Margherita da Cortona e il superamento mistico della crociata," in *Toscana e Terrasanta nel Medioevo,* ed. Franco Cardini (Florence, 1982), pp. 117–37 (now available in Anna Benvenuti Papi, *"In castro poenitentiae": Santità e società femminile nell'Italia medievale* [Rome, 1990], pp. 141–68).

11. There is a similar passage in Caffarini, *Historia disciplinae,* p. 195.

12. *Leggenda,* pp. 159–60.

13. For a precise definition of the term, see A. Fonck, entry "Mystique (théologie)," in *Dictionnaire de théologie catholique,* vol. 10 (Paris, 1929), cols. 2599–2601; cols. 2601–74 provide a description of mystical phenomena. See also the useful anthology edited by Elémire Zolla, *Mistici medievali,* vol. 4 of *I mistici dell'Occidente* (Milan, 1978). On mystics and artistic images, see the essay by Chiara Frugoni in this volume.

14. This is the theme of chapter 10 of the *Legend,* from which I have taken the details that follow. Catherine of Siena's position is presented in Antonio Volpato, "L'onore di Dio e la salute delle anime in S. Caterina," in *Atti del Simposio cateriniano-bernardiniano,* pp. 301–8.

15. Caffarini even has Maria express gratitude to her husband, who, by leaving her, had made it possible for her to feel more closely joined to her "heavenly spouse" and serve him more freely. The *Legend* thus displays a substantially negative valuation of marriage, which was depicted here, as in the majority of late medieval hagiographic texts, as an obstacle to the attainment of Christian perfection. This applies not only to Maria (whose status as an abandoned wife was perhaps not unique, but certainly rare in the typology of late medieval female sanctity), but also to other women who appear in the *Legend:* see, for example, *Leggenda,* p. 213. The tight link between Christian perfection and the state of virginity, especially for women, was part of a well-rooted tradition—as was, for that matter, the unfavorable portrayal of Maria's husband: in addition to Vauchez, *La sainteté,* pp. 442–46, and the works cited there, see Baudouin de Gaiffier, "Intactam sponsam relinquens: A propos de la vie de S. Alexis," *Analecta Bollandiana* 65 (1947): 157–95. On the subject of family and marriage in female hagiography, see Anna Benvenuti Papi, "Umiliana dei Cerchi: Nascita di un culto nella Firenze del Dugento," *Studi francescani* 77 (1980): 87–117; and "Il modello familiare nell'agiografia fiorentina tra Duecento e Quattrocento: Sviluppo di una negazione (da Umiliana dei Cerchi a Villana delle Botti)," *Nuova DWF: Donna, woman, femme* 16 (1981): 80–107, which focuses on two women affiliated with the orders of penitence, one Franciscan and the other Dominican (these essays can now be found in Benvenuti Papi, *"In castro poenitentiae,"* pp. 59–98 and 171–203). See also Robert Brentano, "Catherine of Siena, Margery Kempe, and a caterva virginum," in *Atti del Simposio caterin-*

iano-bernardiniano, pp. 45–55. For the general framework, see John Bugge, *Virginitas: An Essay in the History of a Medieval Ideal* (The Hague, 1975), and the anthology edited by Maria Consiglia De Matteis, *Idee sulla donna nel Medioevo: Fonti e aspetti giuridici, antropologici, religiosi, sociali, e letterari della condizione femminile* (Bologna, 1981).

16. The scruples expressed in the *Legend* are effectively explained and justified by a deliberation approved by the Great Council of Venice on 14 September 1404 (not long after the composition of the *Legend*): "Cum introducta sit consuetudo ab aliquo tempore citra quod mulieres fecerunt sibi licitum eundi ad serviendum in monasteriis religiosorum, pro serviendo infirmis et aliis causis in apparentia honestatis, et talis consuetudo non sit bona per inhonestates et alia mala que sub hoc colore fieri et sequi possent in displicentiam Dei et contra honorem civitatis, vadit pars quod de cetero aliqua mulier queque sit non audeat vel presumat habitare aliqua causa, modo vel forma in aliquo monasterio vel loco fratrum vel monachorum vel aliorum religiosorum ducatus Veneciarum, sub pena standi uno anno in carceribus inferioribus et solvendi libras centum pro qualibet vice qua fuerit contra factum. De qua pena non possit fieri aliqua gratia, suspensio, donum vel declaratio vel remissio, nec revocari presens pars sub pena librarum mille pro quolibet ponente vel consentiente partem in contrarium, et committatur advocatoribus communis ad inquirendum et exequendum predicta contra contrafatientes, habendo partem ut de aliis sui officii. Et si erit accusator per quem sciatur veritas, habeat tertium pene pecuniarie et teneatur de credentia" (Venice, Archivio di Stato, *Maggior Consiglio, Deliberazioni,* reg. 21, *Leona,* 1384–1415, fol. 140r [145r]. On the theme of detachment from earthly affection, including that for one's family, see Benvenuti Papi, "Umiliana dei Cerchi," p. 91, and "Il modello familiare," p. 96.

17. *Leggenda,* pp. 156 and 192, which adds in blandly generic terms that she embodied "the perfection of all of the virtues and beatitudes and gifts and fruits of the Holy Spirit"—a claim that by then was almost obligatory in a hagiographic profile. See Vauchez, *La sainteté,* pp. 608–14.

18. *Leggenda,* p. 164. Whether inside or outside the church, "no one could look her directly in the face," and this withdrawn, shy bearing was offered as a model. Here also, the image presented by Caffarini is closely related to social realities, such as "the practice of isolating young noblewomen once they reached puberty," in keeping with the advice of moralists; in contrast, "lower-class women were more accessible as victims. Important women, in imitation of upper-class mores, were probably more isolated and carefully watched" (Guido Ruggiero, *Violence in Early Renaissance Venice* [New Brunswick, 1980], pp. 76 and 86). See also the exhortations to the nuns of Corpus Christi in Giovanni Dominici, *Lettere spirituali,* ed. Maria-Teresa Casella and Giovanni Pozzi, Spicilegium Friburgense, 13 (Freiburg, 1969), p. 129.

19. *Leggenda,* pp. 159, 176–77, 194–95.

20. Ibid., pp. 171–73. In later years, especially after the recommendations made by the chapter general of Ferrara in 1498, some communities of tertiaries decided to pronounce formal vows and even accept cloister, thus coming to resemble

actual nuns: see Raymond Creytens, entry "Costituzioni domenicane," in *Dizionario degli Istituti di Perfezione*, vol. 3 (Rome, 1976), col. 195–96.

21. See *Leggenda*, pp. 170, 172, and 220. Note the brief and cautious comparison of Maria to the "great Virgin Mary" and the thoroughly conventional one to Mary Magdalene (p. 172). On this subject, see the observations and bibliographic references in Casagrande, *Prediche alle donne*, pp. 11–12 nn. 2–3.

22. On Caffarini's advice, Maria gave all her possessions to her mother, thus becoming "poor in spirit" (*Leggenda*, p. 171). Caffarini's scant and not entirely positive attention to poverty as a form of perfection, and to Maria's effective practice of it, reflects the official attitude of the church ever since the beginning of the fourteenth century, when the concept of "spiritual poverty" was advanced; by 1400 it had spread throughout Christian society. On the reasons behind and expressions of this attitude, see Vauchez, *La sainteté*, pp. 457–60, 476, and 622; on poverty and the poor in general, see Michel Mollat, *The Poor in the Middle Ages*, trans. Arthur Goldhammer (New Haven, 1986).

23. *Leggenda*, pp. 165–66. Maria is explicitly said to be imitating Catherine of Siena, but these forms of mortification were quite common in saints' lives. On the meaning of asceticism in the spirituality of late medieval female mystics, who saw it as a means of reproducing the sufferings of Christ, see Vauchez, *La sainteté*, pp. 474–77. On the specific subject of food deprivation, see Maria Giuseppina Muzzarelli, "Norme di comportamento alimentare nei libri penitenziali," *Quaderni medievali* 13 (1982): 45–80.

24. *Leggenda*, pp. 160–65. On the role of confession in late medieval religious life, see Lester K. Little, "Les techniques de la confession et la confession comme technique," in Vauchez, *Faire croire*, pp. 87–99; and especially the wide-ranging book by Thomas N. Tentler, *Sin and Confession on the Eve of the Reformation* (Princeton, 1977). On communion, see André Vauchez, "Dévotion eucharistique et union mystique chez les saintes de la fin du Moyen Age," in *Atti del Simposio cateriniano-bernardiniano*, pp. 295–300; translated in Vauchez, *The Laity in the Middle Ages: Religious Beliefs and Devotional Practices*, trans. Margery J. Schneider (Notre Dame and London, 1993), pp. 237–242. But Maria's use of communion was essentially devotional, not mystical.

25. See *Leggenda*, pp. 167–71, which also contains remarks on Maria's use of confession and communion. Speaking of Maria's desire to hear sermons, Tommaso specified that this sprang not from "curiosity for knowledge or any other vain thing," but only from her desire to "please God" (p. 162). The idea that education and learning—or even, as in this case, basic instruction—should be exclusively religious in content and purpose was typical of the outlook of the leading exponents of the Dominican Observance: see Giorgio Cracco, "Des saints aux sanctuaires: Hypothèse d'une évolution en terre vénitienne," in Vauchez, *Faire croire*, pp. 287–88. On the relation between education and sanctity, see Vauchez, *La sainteté*, pp. 472–74; and on education for women, see Maria Ludovica Lenzi, *Donne e madonne: L'educazione femminile nel primo Rinascimento italiano* (Turin, 1982).

26. *Leggenda*, pp. 192–200.

27. Some exceptions to this rule seem to have been allowed: "Those women who have husbands should not be allowed to join this association without the permission and consent of their husbands, which consent should be recorded in a formal document; and this should be observed likewise by men who have wives, unless they or one of them has some excuse deemed legitimate in the opinion of reasonable people" (Tommaso da Siena "Caffarini," *Tractatus*, p. 171).

28. See also the observations, in another context, of Chiara Frugoni, *Una lontana città: Sentimenti e immagini nel Medioevo* (Turin, 1983), pp. 113–114; translated as *A Distant City: Images of Urban Experience in the Medieval World* by William McCuaig (Princeton, 1991).

29. For the description of the habit of Dominican penitents, see Tommaso da Siena "Caffarini," *Tractatus*, p. 171.

30. *Leggenda*, pp. 159, 182, 215, 218, 219, and 220. See the interesting comments of Annie Cazenave, "Pulchrum et formosum: Notes sur le sentiment du beau au Moyen Age," in *Etudes sur la sensibilité: Actes du 102e congrès national des sociétés savantes, Limoges, 1977 (Section de philologie et d'histoire jusqu'à 1610)* (Paris, 1979), 2:43–67.

31. The *Legend* states that Maria was loved by all, and that many people "decided to receive the habit of St. Dominic because of their love for her" (*Leggenda*, p. 222; see also pp. 175–76 and 205).

32. Tommaso da Siena "Caffarini," *Tractatus*, pp. 170–78.

33. Ibid., p. 174; *Leggenda*, p. 165: "essendo essa sana, carne non mangiava di nesun tempo et, essendo essa inferma, anco non ne mangiava sença obediençia speçiale."

34. Tommaso da Siena "Caffarini," *Tractatus*, p. 174; *Leggenda*, pp. 183–84. Notice, incidentally, the reference to female slaves, who at that time were particularly numerous in Venice: Benjamin Z. Kedar, *Merchants in Crisis: Genoese and Venetian Men of Affairs and the Fourteenth-Century Depression* (New Haven, 1976), p. 127.

35. Raymond of Capua's work is the only one that provides a full and coherent biographical and spiritual profile of Catherine. Moreover, the fact that the two texts belong to the same genre entails not only similarities in form and structure, but presumably shared intentions and choices on the part of the authors, thus making the two works strictly comparable. Any reading of Catherine's *vita* should take into account that of Sofia Boesch Gajano and Odile Redon, "La *Legenda maior* di Raimondo da Capua, costruzione di una santa," in *Atti del Simposio caterinianobernardiniano*, pp. 15–35.

36. Raimondo da Capua, *S. Caterina da Siena: Vita*, trans. Giuseppe Tinagli (Siena, 1978), pp. 401–3; translated as *The Life of Catherine of Siena* by Conleth Kearns (Dublin, 1980).

37. See, for example, the following passage, from a letter to the nuns of Santa Marta: "I don't think it is possible to have virtue or the fullness of grace without dwelling within the cell of our hearts and soul, where we will gain the treasure that is life for us; I mean the holy abyss that is holy knowledge of ourselves and of God.

From this holy knowledge, dearest sisters, comes the very holy hatred that makes us join ourselves with supreme eternal First Truth, because we recognize that we ourselves are the basest of lies, agents of that which has no being" (Caterina da Siena, *Epistolario,* ed. Eugenio Dupré Theseider, vol. 1 [Rome, 1940], pp. 4–5, with note 6 for possible sources, and 89; translation from *The Letters of St. Catherine of Siena,* trans. Suzanne Noffke, vol. 1 [Binghamton, 1988], p. 38). Raymond says that "inspired by the Holy Spirit," Catherine "built a secret cell in her soul" (Raimondo da Capua, *S. Caterina,* pp. 62–63).

38. *Leggenda,* p. 161: "E questo dicea per una cella mentale, la quale in una certa carta scritta essa avea da me ricevuta et ella di sua mano se l'avea trascritta e bene studiata, per la quale, sì come mentalmente per intellectuale meditaçione in detta cella constituta, le pareva, dounche andasse o stesse, esser come che dinançi a Cristo e a la reina del cielo e tutti li angeli e' santi e a tutta la corte triumphante e militante." Tommaso also discussed the theme of the interior cell in his sermons, as he himself notes in the *Historia disciplinae,* p. 234.

39. "The problem of the relationship between the 'historical saint' and the 'constructed saint' becomes particularly complex in the case of female sanctity," as Boesch Gajano and Redon observe ("La *Legenda maior,"* p. 35). For the terminology they adopt, see Pierre Delooz, *Sociologie et canonisations* (Liège, 1969), p. 7.

40. These effects are noted principally in chapter 16, placed at the end of the *Legend,* where one would normally expect to find a list of miracles. They are summarized effectively in the declaration that Maria's perfection of grace and virtue "that shined particularly in her, more than in all other women . . . not only made her beloved and gracious to others, but also roused them to deeds of virtue" (*Leggenda,* p. 223). For example, the noble Antonio Soranzo "felt himself so strongly attracted by her sanctity that he resolved henceforth never again to eat meat" (p. 211). The case of Maria's contemporary, the Dominican friar Marcolino of Forlì, is somewhat different: a "homo simplex" who was esteemed more by the townspeople than by his fellow friars, his sanctity was demonstrated by the many miracles that occurred after his death. But Giovanni Dominici's opinion of him could also fit Maria: "Ecce quod indocti rapiunt coelum, humiles ad ipsum accedunt, simplices ipsum mercantur, aquirunt pauperes, poenitentes assequuntur" (*Historia disciplinae,* pp. 185–93; the passage cited is on p. 192). On Marcolino, see Vauchez, *La sainteté,* pp. 470–71.

41. *Leggenda,* esp. pp. 186, 193, 196, 197, and 205. At the center of Maria's vision of the heavenly host, which she experienced when she was ill (and so was perhaps the result of feverish delerium, or a dream), was Nicolò of Ravenna, prior of San Domenico di Castello and fervent promoter of the Dominican Observance, who had died in 1398. There are mentions of other visions; but rather than visions that Maria experienced herself, they were ones in which she appeared to other people who had been close to her during her lifetime, while they were either sleeping, praying, or ill (as Caffarini usually, but not always, specifies): see *Leggenda,* pp. 211–21. The "visions" or "raptures" of her friend Orsolina are particularly noteworthy for their many elements typical of the devotion and sensibilities of the period. Visions were a common theme in medieval literature: in addition to Chiara Frugoni's essay in this

volume, see Carolly Erickson, *The Medieval Vision: Essays in Vision and Perception* (New York, 1976); and Peter Dinzelbacher, "Die Visionen des Mittelalters: Ein geschichtlicher Umriss," *Zeitschrift für Religions- und Geistesgeschichte* 30 (1978): 116–28. A wider arc of time is covered by *I linguaggi del sogno,* ed. Vittore Branca, Carlo Ossola, and Salomon Resnik (Florence, 1984); for the Middle Ages, see the contribution by Robert Brentano, "Il sogno di S. Anselmo e lo sviluppo della biografia medievale," pp. 395–406.

42. André Vauchez, "La sainteté mystique en Occident au temps des papes d'Avignon et du Grand Schisme," *Genèse et débuts du Grand Schisme d'Occident, Avignon, 25–28 septembre 1978* (Paris, 1980), pp. 361–68; translated in Vauchez, *The Laity in the Middle Ages,* pp. 231–36.

43. The single exception is a passage that refers, not to Maria, but to another young woman, who, "claiming she saw the devil, asked her mother to say the Credo" (*Leggenda,* p. 218). In contrast, the *Life of Catherine of Siena* is full of references to the devil or demons: see Raimondo da Capua, *S. Caterina,* index entry "Demonio," p. 440. See also the *Vita sanctae Coletae, 1381–1447,* prolegomenis auxerunt Charles Van Corstanje, Yves Cazaux, Johan Decavele, and Albert Derolez (Tielt and Leiden, 1982), illustrated with the expressive miniatures that adorn the copy of the *vita* by Pierre de Vaux in MS 8 of the convent of Bethlehem in Ghent (and especially the images reproduced on pp. 209, 211, 221, 233, 235, and 257). On the often obsessive presence of the devil or demons in female religious sensibility and on its causes, manifestations, and consequences, see the influential, if rather one-sided, interpretation of Marcello Craveri, *Sante e streghe: Biografie e documenti dal XIV al XVII secolo* (Milan, 1980), esp. pp. 7–62.

44. "But even the most fiery sermons would not have managed to hold the attention of the faithful and inspire them to rise to the point of contemplating the merits of God's servants. . . . As good pedagogues, the friars and clergy usually concealed carefully their real opinion, which was that the saints' greatest miracles, if not their only ones, were their deeds" (Vauchez, *La Sainteté,* pp. 619–20; but see in general pp. 583–622). As a result, miraculous, supernatural, and marvelous events continued to have a place in sermons and hagiography, attracting the attention and meeting the expectations of the faithful.

45. Raimondo da Capua, *S. Caterina,* pp. 401–3.

46. Caffarini himself provided a list of female penitents associated with the Dominican order: "Item reperimus in huiusmodi statu etiam postquam sortitus est nomen de penitentia sancti Dominici, non solum . . . fuisse personas caste sive continenter et virtuose viventes, sed adhuc quam plures pre aliis precipue sanctitatis et vite existentes, necnon et aliquas non tantum mentis et corporis castitate seu innocentia baptismali, quam etiam utriusque hominis virginitatis integritate et puritate vigentes." He goes on to praise Vanna and Daniela of Orvieto, Margaret of Città di Castello, Giovanna of Florence, Pina of Pisa, Maria of Venice, and Catherine of Siena (Tommaso da Siena "Caffarini," *Tractatus,* pp. 18–28). On the subject of female sanctity in the penitential orders, see Benvenuti Papi, *"In castro poenitentiae."*

47. See the examples in Giovanni Musolino, Antonio Niero, and Silvio Tra-

montin, *Santi e beati veneziani: Quaranta profili,* Biblioteca agiografica veneziana, 1 (Venice, 1963). Despite the indubitable value of the series that opened with this volume, much remains to be learned about medieval hagiography in Venice; see, however, the review essay by Lia Sbriziolo, "Venezia sacra," *Rivista della storia della Chiesa in Italia* 20 (1966): 451–71.

48. The religious culture of fourteenth- and fifteenth-century Italy is analyzed thoroughly in Giovanni Miccoli, "La storia religiosa," in *Storia d'Italia,* vol. 2, *Dalla caduta dell'Impero romano al secolo XVIII* (Turin, 1974), esp. pp. 825–975. But see also Etienne Delaruelle, E.-R. Labande, and Paul Ourliac, *L'Eglise au temps du Grand Schisme et de la crise conciliaire,* vol. 14 of *Histoire de l'Eglise depuis les origines jusqu'à nos jours,* ed. Augustin Fliche and Victor Martin (Paris, 1964); Giorgio Cracco, "La spiritualità italiana del Tre-Quattrocento: Linee interpretative," *Studia patavina* 18 (1971): 74–116; *The Pursuit of Holiness in Late Medieval and Renaissance Religion,* ed. Charles Trinkaus with Heiko A. Oberman (Leiden, 1974); and Massimo Petrocchi, *Storia della spiritualità italiana,* vol. 1 (Rome, 1978), pp. 59–154.

9

St. Bernardino of Siena, the Wife, and Possessions

Roberto Rusconi

"What is a household without a wife? It's a house of ruin and filth. Your wife gives you children, raises them, takes care of them, and nurses them when they are sick. The whole burden of childrearing falls on the wife. And if you fall sick, she looks after you with faith, love, and charity for both your body and your soul. . . . What's more, I tell you that she's the caretaker and guardian of your possessions. You go out and make money, while she stays home and takes care of things. Sometimes taking care of what has been earned is at least as important as earning it. If you, the husband, make money but have no one to take care of it, the household goes to pieces. Without a wife, your possessions go to wrack and ruin."[1]

These words appear toward the end of the twenty-fifth sermon in the series that Bernardino of Siena delivered in Florence during the Lenten season of 1424. In them, Bernardino delineates with oratorical emphasis, but also with great precision, the moral criteria behind "taking a wife." At the same time, he invokes a social and economic function: the "household management" that, beginning in the mid fourteenth century, was assigned to the wife by spokesmen of mercantile culture from Paolo of Certaldo to Leon Battista Alberti.

In the great series of vernacular sermons that Bernardino delivered between 1424 and 1427 in the two leading cities of Tuscany, Florence and Siena, he introduced the practice of treating from the pulpit, in full detail, themes of marital and familial ethics. Thus, the sequence delivered in Siena in 1427 included a closely linked series of sermons: "How a husband should love his wife, and the wife her husband," "The proper love that should exist between wife and husband," "How marriage should be considered," "How widows should be respected."[2]

Particularly striking is his explicit and programmatic discussion of ethical problems connected with sexual practices, both within marriage and outside of it. "And people say it's shameful to preach about and give advice about these acts and facts. One has to tiptoe around this in confession, so that no one will say that confessors teach how to commit sins; in preaching one says almost nothing on the subject, to avoid the criticism of ignorant people. . . . What are you going to do, Brother Bernardino? If you keep quiet out of fear of yapping half-wits or out of shame or for some other reason, you'll be damned! You are obliged to preach: it is your job to chide people for their vices and sins, and lead them back onto the path to salvation."[3] Within this framework, even the raging sermon denouncing "the abominable sin of cursed sodomy" finds its allotted place.[4]

It would be utterly banal to assert that Bernardino decided to tackle preaching on these themes because he recognized their topicality. However, one can't help but note that his preaching found its own niche by adopting an existing doctrinal inheritance and offering it to a society in the throes of a profound transformation.[5] In order to better understand the origins, purposes, and orientation of Bernardino's preaching and interpret it properly, it is extremely important to grasp the basic familial and matrimonial realities that Bernardino addressed in his sermons. Fortunately, we have available an exhaustive statistical profile of those realities in David Herlihy and Christiane Klapisch's massive study *Tuscans and Their Families,* which presents a detailed cross-section of Tuscan, and especially Florentine, society in the first quarter of the fifteenth century.[6] Without pretending to summarize Herlihy and Klapisch's work, it might be useful to call attention to a few results of their richly informative exposition that bear most directly on the framework of Bernardino's preaching.

By the end of the fourteenth century and in the first decades of the fifteenth, the demographic decline caused by a devastating series of epidemics and famines had eased the pressure of overpopulation and increased notably the readiness of Tuscans to marry.[7] The social consequences of this trend were quite striking, in that it lowered perceptibly the normal age of marriage for women, to fifteen to twenty years, while the median age of marriage for men remained significantly higher—by approximately six years in rural areas and twelve years in the major cities.[8] Cities evidently discouraged men from entering into early marriages because of the economic burdens they entailed for the young.[9]

The male tendency to delay marriage, however, meant the presence, especially in urban centers, of many young men who were barred from any legitimate sexual activity for roughly fifteen years after puberty. This stimulated the more or less covert spread of female prostitution and of sodomy.[10]

At the same time, widows formed a conspicuous element in urban society: in Florence in 1427, one woman out of four was a widow. Whereas in the countryside, the inseparable link between agricultural production and the family unit pressed widows to remarry, in the cities widows found it hard to contract new marriages, and in fact most of them definitively embraced the state of widowhood on the death of their first husband. In addition, one should not forget that those rural widows who did not remarry were drawn to the urban centers and the employment opportunities they offered.[11]

On the whole, the data furnished by Herlihy and Klapisch come together in a pattern indicating the reaggregation of women into a male-dominated domestic group, which coincided with an antifemale juridical reaction evident in the elaboration of norms governing property relations between spouses.[12] This overall trend is the framework for the conceptualization of the family and the attitude toward women shared by the lay moralists and ecclesiastical preachers of Bernardino's day.

MARRIAGE WAS a recurrent theme in Bernardino's preaching, amply documented in the sermons recorded by listeners and carefully rethought by Bernardino himself in the preparation of his first Latin collection of Lenten sermons, *De christiana religione,* redacted between 1429 and 1436.[13] However, in this connection it is essential that we understand the process by which Bernardino crafted his vernacular and Latin sermons, a protracted work in progress whose origins go back to years before the justly famous Italian *reportationes* and the definitive redaction of the Latin opus.

Bernardino's thinking on marital practice was shaped in important ways by the thought and teaching of Peter John Olivi.[14] In fact, between 1420 and 1425 Bernardino copied with his own hand a group of Olivi's *quaestiones super matrimonium,* which he then developed into a draft for a sermon.[15] In this draft, Bernardino sought to remain as faithful as possible to Olivi's exact words, though he incorporated a few observations of his own and added some other sources and examples. However, he carefully steered clear of Olivi's theories about the superiority of virginity to matrimony or about the conception of the sacrament of marriage itself, for which Olivi had been censured by the ecclesiastical authorities.[16]

Bernardino drew amply on Peter John Olivi for that whole area of mat-

rimonial ethics concerning the marriage debt and its circumstances, a subject on which he preached repeatedly: in Padua, during Lent of 1423 (sermon 27, "On sanctifying love"); in Florence, during Lent of 1424 (sermon
24, "On the marriage debt"); in Perugia in 1425 (sermons 18 and 19, "On
marriage"); and in Siena in 1427 (sermon 20, "On the well-ordered love
that should exist between wife and husband").[17]

The way Bernardino read Olivi's matrimonial *quaestiones* and used
them in actual preaching confirms that his principal interest in marital matters, from the very outset, was directed not at dogmatic issues, but exclusively at ethical concerns. He seems to have preached on the topic from this
angle as early as 1419–20, in Milan, taking his cue from the *thema* furnished by the liturgy for that day: "He who loves his wife loves himself"
(Ephesians 5:28). This, at least, is what one surmises from a passing reference, the manuscript containing the outline for that sermon having been
lost.[18]

The notes that form a draft of a sermon for the second Sunday after
Epiphany, jotted down in the *Itinerarium anni*—an autograph manuscript
containing an informal record of Bernardino's activities from 1418 to
1424—also seem to have an occasional character. Starting from the biblical
thema "There was a marriage at Cana in Galilee" (John 2:1), Bernardino
simply refers to the sixth chapter of book 3 of Ubertino of Casale's *Arbor
vitae*.[19] He evidently found little of interest in this point of departure, since
he used it only for sermon 19 in the series given at Siena in 1427.[20]

However, we cannot rule out the possibility that he thought of returning to the wedding at Cana in the final years of his life. In fact, in the years
1433–34, while assembling new theological material in the *Postillae in
Epistolas et Evangelia*, Bernardino crammed the margins and spaces between the lines of John 2:1–11 with numerous notes, taking them in particular from the writings of Peter John Olivi.[21]

For all its complex articulation, Bernardino's work in progress revolves
around a single, well-defined center of gravity. His conception of the family
and of marriage is essentially that current among the Tuscan oligarchy—
mercantile, bourgeois, and urban—at the end of the fourteenth century and
beginning of the fifteenth. The "possessions" of Bernardino's sermons are
nothing other than the "household goods" of Leon Battista Alberti's writings. On the other hand, in proclaiming from the pulpit a social model supplied by the ruling class, Bernardino sought to carve out an ethical arena
within which the institutional church could perform its inescapable function as the purveyor of individual salvation.

Among the Latin sermons that Bernardino never finished writing is one
entitled "On well-ordered, disorderly, and dissolved marriages," whose

redaction certainly preceded the great vernacular sermon cycles of the years 1424–27, and may even date from before 1420.[22] In this text, he thoroughly exploits the traditional literature of Catholic ethics: a glance at the apparatus of the critical edition suffices to show how Bernardino's text is woven out of passages taken from the *Decretum,* the *Decretals,* canonistic and penitential literature such as the *Summae casuum* of the Dominicans Raymond of Peñaforte and Bartolomeo of San Concordio, and some commentaries on the *Sentences* of Peter Lombard—in short, the handbooks of "moral theology" of the time. This doctrinal material, however, is rearranged according to a specific and organic design.

In the first part of this sermon, Bernardino specifies the three *obligationes:* of the husband toward his wife, the wife toward her husband, and of each toward the other.[23] The duties of the husband—to instruct, correct, cohabit, and support—fit within that affirmation of masculine authority that in precisely those early decades of the fifteenth century was being ever more firmly consolidated. In particular, the husband's duty to instruct his wife—placed first in Bernardino's list—finds an exact parallel in the family memoirs, or *ricordanze,* which insist on the need to train the young bride to assume her new responsibilities.[24] The bride's youth (amply confirmed and quantified for Tuscany by Herlihy and Klapisch) is the sociological rationale for making "instruct" precede the husband's other duties.[25] It also explains the urgency with which Bernardino, in his sermons, calls for the instruction of girls (and one notes that Bernardino speaks only of *girls*) before their weddings, even if to his mind this instruction should be concerned essentially with what is licit and illicit in conjugal relations in the strict sense.[26]

The wife's duties toward her husband merely reaffirm the woman's subordinate role: she should respect, serve, obey, and admonish him. However, the reciprocal obligations between husband and wife—affection, fidelity, honor, and the marital debt—allude to two topics of great significance: one for its resonances with humanistic and mercantile culture; the other for Bernardino's reaffirmation of a specifically religious contribution to marital ethics.

As for the first of these terms—affection—recent studies have emphasized the extent to which the revaluation of marriage and family in the *ricordanze* involved a new appreciation of the quality and importance of conjugal love, presented in the tracts of Bernardino's lay contemporaries as the most natural of emotions.[27] In Bernardino's sermons, it appears instead as a duty, or better, as an ordained affection, of which he speaks repeatedly. For instance, the rough draft of a sermon entitled "On jealousy between spouses" in the Budapest manuscript was developed into sermon 30 of the Florentine Lenten cycle for 1425: "On marriage."[28]

It is, however, the second term—the marriage debt—that lies at the heart of Bernardino's matrimonial ethics, as is apparent from the ample attention lavished on it in his sermons. Bernardino, in fact, set himself the programmatic task of eliminating "the crude and foolish ignorance of people concerning the facts of marriage," as he put it at the start of sermon 24 of the Florentine Lenten cycle of 1424.[29] And he reiterated this idea in the prologue to sermon 17, "On proper marital behavior," in his *De christiana religione*, justifying in especially full detail the obligation of every preacher to tackle this subject.[30]

Throughout the passage from his drafts and outlines to the redaction of the Latin text of his sermons and their actual delivery in the vernacular (which differed only superficially, as a consequence of the tremendous oratorical verve that masked the rigid structure of his sermons), Bernardino's exposition of his matrimonial ethic remained constant, and notably arid. It seems tinged with the gray grimness of the approach to the problems of moral and Christian life typical of the handbooks for confessors—and in fact, Bernardino's vernacular sermons were intended to prepare his listeners for sacramental confession.[31]

There is little basis, then, for speaking of a singular "social" analysis that Bernardino applied to marriage. Let us take as an example sermon 46, "On the multitude of ills that follow from vanity," and in particular the passage (art. 3, chap. 2) entitled "How excessive vanity leads many people not to have children."[32]

Oh how many children used to be born, whose conception and birth are now obstructed by vanity! Indeed, because of the great expenditures demanded by the wicked habits of vain wives, many either do not take wives at all or delay taking them, since the costs often devour almost any dowry, no matter how large. Similarly, many parents, since they can't afford to expend such immense dowries on their daughters, keep them sterile (and not on God's account) at home—and would that they were modest and virginal! And what is even more cruel, if they have three or four daughters and are unable to dower them all as they might wish, they lead one or two of the prettier ones to the altar with the largest dowries possible; and the others, especially if they are crippled, lame, blind, or in some other way deformed, they close in a convent like the world's spit and vomit. And if only they were dedicating them to God, rather than the devil! . . .

For these reasons, you do not join in matrimony unbridled youths and men, and wrongly keep older girls at home; and I would rather keep silent than start talking about the terrible consequences. Not only girls, but neither widow nor bride is left unmolested. . . . But what is worse than everything said so far, this spawns and nourishes the horrible and detestable vice of sodomy, which is increasing terribly. Indeed, who can express the shameless deeds into which these lascivious youths—nourished on pleasure, weak, undisciplined and immodest—fling themselves? . . . Once young men have been seized by this pestiferous weakness, they can hardly ever be cured; they consent to marry only reluctantly and after long delay, if ever. And if by chance they do take a wife, they either abuse her or ignore her, and so they produce no children.

This long passage (which is repeated even more vividly here and there in Bernardino's vernacular preaching) is dominated by a thoroughly traditional goal: the purpose of marriage is the procreation of children. What is notable here is not so much that Bernardino's polemical blast at the matrimonial strategies of the Florentine merchant class (ostentatious dowries for some daughters, and relegation of the rest to convents), like that against delayed marriage for men and the moral vices (especially sodomy) that follow from it, lacks an analytical framework: it would be anachronistic to expect one of him. But even more, Bernardino seems completely blind to the institutional, social, and economic roots of the situation, linked as it was with the matrimonial strategies of the merchant class on one side and with salary structures on the other.[33]

This sort of public preaching on morals was a novel development, and there is no doubt that the ample attention given to marriage and related subjects in Bernardino's sermons was very closely bound up with the prominent place that the family occupied in the advice manuals of the early fifteenth century.[34] Driving all this was nothing other than the new marital trend after the demographic catastrophe of the fourteenth century, with the consequent accentuation of the themes of marriage and family in Tuscan society of the early Quattrocento.

Of course, lay moralists wrote for the more restricted circle of those who bought and read books (such as Leon Battista Alberti's *Book of the Family*), while ecclesiastical preachers such as Bernardino generally addressed themselves to the larger crowds in urban centers.[35] But despite their genuine differences in themes and inspiration, both contributed in equal measure to promoting a conception of marriage that could provide ideological cohesion to the process of social restructuring then under way.

If this was truly the purpose of Bernardino's preaching, one can understand the reasons underlying his bitter opposition to the followers of Man-

fredi of Vercelli, whom he attacked in his Florentine Lenten sermons in
1425.[36] When Manfredi preached of the imminent arrival of the Antichrist,
the followers of this Dominican friar took this to imply a radical rejection of
marriage bonds on the eve of the end of time, "under the cover of going
forth to do battle with the Antichrist."[37] In the sermons delivered during
this controversy, Bernardino publicly expounded the traditional canons
governing matrimony, but above all rejected the values inherent in Manfredi's penitential movement as potentially subversive of the social order:
"They also say that the Antichrist is born, and this they assert contrary to
Holy Scripture, which says that neither we nor even the Son of the Virgin,
insofar as he was a man, could know the time and moment of judgment day.
They say the Antichrist is born, so that you will do nothing, and you young
people won't marry and you men won't take wives, and so the population
will decline and become heretics like them."[38]

It is hardly surprising, in short, to discover that Bernardino's conception of the family coincides with the fifteenth-century ideal of the large and
vigorous family, in which the men devote themselves tirelessly to business
and their wives assume the task of "household management": running the
household, taking care of the family's possessions, raising and educating the
children.[39] Nor should one forget that whereas in more conservative authors, women's confinement to the home was explained on the basis of their
weak intellect and unstable character, in Bernardino's preaching the wife
performs the essential function of preserving the fortune patiently accumu-
lated by the husband: Bernardino's "possessions" are the "holy household
goods" of Alberti.[40] In Alberti's *Book of the Family,* in fact, orderly com-
mercial practice must be seconded by domestic order, so that the home does
not devour whatever is generated by outside activities. The wife's role thus
acquires a certain prominence (if one wants to call it that) in the mentality of
the merchant class, although in reality her function remains completely subordinate.

Insofar as Bernardino, in his popular preaching of what has been
termed an ethical-social character, sought to offer his public a comprehensive model of social comportment, he thus supplied society with its underpinnings, or at least played a part in a process of social restructuring. In this
way, the two apparently incongruous aspects of his moral preaching acquire
a logical and organic coherence. On the one hand, he incorporates fundamental elements of the outlook of the dominant class—that urban and mercantile bourgeoisie—within an explicitly Christian framework.[41] On the
other, in a procedure typical of homiletics (and even more, of what today is
called "moral theology"), within this presentation of hegemonic cultural
models he lays claim to one area as the traditional preserve of Christian doc-

trine. In effect, apart from proverbial pronouncements deriving from biblical and patristic sources (which by then had become proverbial on a popular level as well), this was restricted to the narrow field of specifically sexual
ethics: an outcome certainly favored by Bernardino's personal predilections
and doctrinal formation.

This narrowing of scope seems perfectly suited to the role of vernacular
preaching in fifteenth-century Italian society. In fact, if the aim of preaching
was to present models of religious comportment, doctrines to believe, and
pious practices to observe, the test of the reception and penetration of these
models—and here we touch on the difficult question of the efficacy of Bernardino's preaching—at this historical moment must not be sought in a
strict regulation of conduct of the sort that the Counter-Reformation later
aspired to impose, but rather in persuading people to accept a religious
model as the only valid one because it alone could lead to salvation. One can
thus understand why Bernardino's preaching on marriage and family nar-
rowed its focus to the private sphere: precisely because the only mechanism
of control, and the one that drove all of Bernardino's preaching, was sacramental confession. In substance, all of Bernardino's preaching on sex, marriage, and family was directed toward sacramental confession: "And
therefore I urge you to bring your girls tomorrow, since I think I can promise
that you'll never hear a more useful sermon. I'm not saying that your married girls should come: I'm saying both the married ones and those to be
married; and in my sermon I'll speak so decently that I won't dirty myself
one little bit. I'm terribly worried about you, because I fear that so very few
of those who are married will be saved. Out of every thousand holy matri-
monies, I believe that 999 are marriages of the devil."[42]

NOTES

Originally published in *Atti del Convegno storico bernardiniano in occasione del sesto centenario della nascita di S. Bernardino da Siena* (L'Aquila, 1982), pp. 97–110.

1. *Florence 1424*, 1:419. In this essay, I use the following abbreviations to refer
to the works of Bernardino of Siena:

a. for the Latin works: *Opera omnia*, 9 vols. (Quaracchi, 1950–65).
b. for the vernacular sermons:
Padua 1423 = *Opera omnia*, vol. 3 (Venice, 1745).
Florence 1424 = *Le prediche volgari: Quaresimale fiorentino 1424*, ed. Ciro
Cannarozzi, 2 vols. (Pistoia, 1934).

Florence 1425 = *Le prediche volgari: Quaresimale fiorentino 1425,* ed. Ciro Cannarozzi, 3 vols. (Florence, 1940).

Siena 1425 = *Le prediche volgari: Predicazione del 1425 in Siena,* ed. Ciro Cannarozzi, 2 vols. (Florence, 1958).

Siena 1427 = *Le prediche volgari dette nella piazza del Campo l'anno 1427,* ed. Luciano Banchi, 3 vols. (Siena, 1880–88); my references are to the reprint edited by Piero Bargellini (Milan, 1936). (These sermons are now available in a new edition: *Prediche volgari sul Campo di Siena, 1427,* ed. Carlo Delcorno, 2 vols. [Milan, 1989].)

2. *Siena 1427,* sermon 19, "Come il marito dié amare la donna, così la donna il suo marito," pp. 391–420; sermon 20, "Dell'ordinato amore che debba èssare infra la moglie e'l marito," pp. 420–47; sermon 21, "Come el matrimonio debba èssare considerato," pp. 447–62; sermon 22, "Come si debbano onorare le vedove," pp. 462–85.

3. *Florence 1424,* 1:381 and 382.

4. *Siena 1427,* sermon 39, pp. 893–919. Sodomy is not directly related to the subject of this essay, though it was a constant preoccupation of Bernardino. The autograph manuscript now in Budapest contains, at no. 213, a draft of "Against Sodomy" (Contra soddomiam), which has been published in *Opera omnia,* 9:427–30; see Cesare Cenci, "Un manoscritto autografo di San Bernardino a Budapest," *Studi francescani* 61 (1964): 371–72. Bernardino seems to have used it for sermon 31 of the Florentine Lenten cycle of 1424. Indeed, on that occasion he dedicated three successive sermons to the subject: sermon 30, "On the vice of the sodomites" (Del vizio dei sodomiti); sermon 31, "On sodomy" (Della sodomia); and sermon 32, "On the damnation of the sodomites" (Della dannazione dei sodomiti): *Florence 1424,* 2:30–71. He returned to this theme the following year during the Florentine Lenten cycle (sermon 36, "On the sin against nature" [Del peccato contro natura]), the Assisi series (sermon 10, "On sodomites" [De sodomitis]), and the Siena series (sermon 29, "This is the sermon on the vice of sodomy" [Questa è la predica dello vizio della sodomia]): see *Florence 1425,* 2:270–90; Dionisio Pacetti, "La predicazione di S. Bernardino da Siena a Perugia e ad Assisi nel 1425," *Collectanea Franciscana* 10 (1940): 16; and *Siena 1425,* 2:98–112. The definitive version of the text is sermon 15, "On the horrible sin against nature" (De horrendo peccato contra naturam), in the *De Evangelio aeterno,* in *Opera omnia,* 3:267–84; most of his sources here are canonical. Bernardino preached yet again on this subject in Padua in 1443 (sermon 25, "Against sodomy" [Ad sodomitas]): see Dionisio Pacetti, "Nuovo codice di prediche inedite di S. Bernardino da Siena," *Bullettino di studi bernardiniani* 1 (1935): 201.

5. Because of the approach taken in this essay, I will omit mention of the many studies of Bernardino's social teachings that take their inspiration from an ill-conceived notion of "Christian sociology," such as Battista Nardini, "La famiglia cristiana nel pensiero di S. Bernardino," *Bullettino di studi bernardiniani* 10 (1944–50): 22–54 (which summarizes the thesis Nardini presented at the Pontificio Ateneo Antoniano in Rome in 1945: "De christiana familia ex operibus S. Bernardini

Senensis"); Candido Mesini, "La sociologia di San Bernardino da Siena," in *S. Bernardino da Siena: Saggi e ricerche pubblicati nel quinto centenario della morte, 1444–1944* (Milan, 1945), pp. 341–77; and Fredegando [Callaey] d'Anversa, "S. Bernardino da Siena e la famiglia," *L'Italia francescana* 21 (1946): 69–83.

6. David Herlihy and Christiane Klapisch-Zuber, *Les Toscans et leurs familles: Une étude du catasto florentin de 1427* (Paris, 1978); for the abridged English edition, see *Tuscans and Their Families: A Study of the Florentine Catasto of 1427* (New Haven, 1985).

7. Herlihy and Klapisch-Zuber, *Les Toscans,* pp. 393–419.

8. See also Christiane Klapisch-Zuber, "Déclin démographique et structure du ménage: L'exemple de Prato, fin XIVe–fin XVe," in *Famille et parenté dans l'Occident médiéval* (Rome, 1977), pp. 259–61 ("Demographic Decline and Household Structure: The Example of Prato, Late Fourteenth to Late Fifteenth Centuries," in *Women, Family, and Ritual in Renaissance Italy,* trans. Lydia G. Cochrane [Chicago, 1985], pp. 23–35); David Herlihy, "Vieillir à Florence au Quattrocento," *Annales: Economies, sociétés, civilisations* 24 (1969): 1338–52. Klapisch emphasizes the discrepancy between the demographic data and the "representation" of the marriage age in family memoirs: on the latter, see also the remarks of Leonida Pandimiglio, "Giovanni di Pagolo Morelli e la ragion di famiglia," *Studi sul Medioevo cristiano offerti a Raffaello Morghen* (Rome, 1974), 2:574–76, based on the memoir written between 1393 and 1411 by Giovanni di Pagolo Morelli, *Ricordi,* ed. Vittore Branca (Florence, 1956).

9. See Charles M. De La Roncière, "Pauvres et pauvreté à Florence au XIVe siècle," in *Études sur l'histoire de la pauvreté, Moyen Age–XVIe siècle,* ed. Michel Mollat (Paris, 1974), pp. 661–85.

10. Herlihy and Klapisch-Zuber, *Les Toscans,* p. 414.

11. On widows and their role in late medieval family and society, see Paolo Cammarosano, "Aspetti delle strutture familiari nelle città dell'Italia comunale, secoli XII–XIV," *Studi medievali,* ser. 3, 16 (1975): 434–35; this essay has been published in French in *Famille et parenté,* pp. 181–94. In his discussion of widows, Bernardino seems to have been especially attuned to the sociological situation of the localities where he was preaching. Indeed, a draft of the sermon "For widows" (Pro viduis), found only in the *Itinerarium anni* (*Opera omnia,* 8:249, no. 116), was evidently prepared for preaching in Tuscany in the years 1424–27 (see sermon 28 in *Florence 1425,* 2:127–45; sermon 22 in *Siena 1427,* pp. 462–85). After that time, Bernardino apparently had no desire to return to this particular topic; in fact, the Latin *opus* contains no trace of a sermon on widows.

12. Klapisch-Zuber, "Demographic Decline and Household Structure," pp. 30–31; Manlio Bellomo, *Ricerche sui rapporti patrimoniali tra coniugi: Contributo alla storia della famiglia medievale* (Milan, 1961).

13. The various aspects of Bernardino's preaching on matrimonial ethics find their fullest and final expression in sermons 17, "On proper marital behavior" (De coniugii honestate); 18, "On marital modesty" (De pudicitia coniugali); and 48, "On good wives" (De domina honesta): *Opera omnia,* 1:204–26, and 2:100–108).

14. On the influence of Peter John Olivi, see Roberto Rusconi, "La tradizione manoscritta delle opere degli Spirituali nelle biblioteche dei predicatori e dei conventi dell'Osservanza," *Picenum Seraphicum* 12 (1975): 25–28 and 61–65. On one aspect of the connection between Olivi's writings and Bernardino's teachings, see Roberto Rusconi, "Apocalittica ed escatologia nella predicazione di Bernardino da Siena," *Studi medievali,* ser. 3, 22 (1981): 85–128.

15. Cenci, "Un manoscritto autografo," pp. 345–46, nos. 70–72; compare the texts published in Victorin Doucet, "De operibus manuscriptis Fr. Petri Ioannis Olivi in Bibliotheca Universitatis Patavinae asservatis," *Archivum Franciscanum Historicum* 28 (1935): 414 and 173–74. Bernardino rearranged the texts of Olivi's *quaestiones* in a draft sermon, which refers to another sermon outline "On God's judgment against the lustful" (Contra luxuriosos iudicia Dei) in the *Itinerarium anni,* and which he drew on to prepare the two sermons "On marriage" (De matrimonio) delivered in Perugia in 1425: see Cenci, "Un manoscritto autografo," p. 347, no. 78; *Opera omnia,* 8:258, no. 133; and Pacetti, "La predicazione," p. 179, sermons 18 and 19.

16. On the reactions to Olivi's teachings on marriage, see Anneliese Maier, "Per la storia del processo contro l'Olivi," *Rivista di storia della Chiesa in Italia* 5 (1951): 326–39. The sixth *quaestio* of Olivi's *De perfectione evangelica,* entitled "An virginitas sit simpliciter melior matrimonio," has been published by Aquilino Emmen, "Verginità e matrimonio nella valutazione dell'Olivi," *Studi francescani* 64 (1967), fasc. 4, pp. 11–57; the text is found on pp. 21–57. See also David Burr, "Olivi on Marriage," *Journal of Medieval and Renaissance Studies* 2 (1977): 183–204.

17. "De amore sanctificativo" (*Padua 1423,* pp. 202–6); the sources of this sermon include a draft sermon in the Budapest manuscript (Cenci, "Un manoscritto autografo," p. 349, no. 86). "Del debito del matrimonio" (*Florence 1424,* 1:381–404); the sources of this sermon include sermon 3 of the *Sermones imperfecti,* in *Opera omnia,* 8:17; for its dating, see p. 18 nn. 1 and 2, and Dionisio Pacetti, "I codici autografi di S. Bernardino da Siena della Vaticana e della Communale di Siena," *Archivum Franciscanum Historicum* 28 (1935): 516. For Perugia (De matrimonio), see Pacetti, "La predicazione," p. 179. "Dell'ordinato amore che debba èssare infra la moglie e'l marito" (*Siena 1427,* pp. 420–47). In sermon 17 of Bernardino's *De christiana religione,* in contrast to his usual practice, he draws up his points *sub titulo quaestionis,* evidently under the influence of Olivi's matrimonial *questiones* (which, moreover, is not noted in the *Opera omnia*). And in one of his last works, the *Tractatus de Spiritu Sancto et de inspirationibus,* Bernardino draws on Olivi's commentary *In Mattheum* for his discussion of the decency of conjugal relations (*Opera omnia,* 6:300).

18. The reference is in sermon 13 of the *Sermones imperfecti,* in *Opera omnia,* 8:59. For the manuscript in question, see the *Itinerarium anni,* in *Opera omnia,* 8:172; Dionisio Pacetti, *De Sancti Bernardini Senensis operibus: Ratio criticae editionis* (Quaracchi, 1947), p. 83.

19. *Opera omnia,* 8:186–87, no. 9. The passages from the *Arbor vitae* are found on fols. 84d–87a of the Venetian edition of 1485 and on fols. 141c–145 of the

Sienese autograph manuscript U.6.1: see Dionisio Pacetti, "I codici autografi di S. Bernardino da Siena della Vaticana e della Comunale di Siena," *Archivum Franciscanum Historicum* 29 (1936): 530. On Ubertino of Casale's influence on Bernardino, see Rusconi, "La tradizione manoscritta delle opere degli Spirituali," esp. pp. 84–86 and 98–123; on their eschatological doctrines, see Rusconi, "Apocalittica ed escatologia."

20. *Siena 1427,* pp. 391–420.

21. *Opera omnia,* 9:100–105.

22. "De matrimonio regulato, inordinato et separato": sermon 13 of the *Sermones imperfecti,* in *Opera omnia,* 8:57–67; on its dating, see p. 60 n. 6, and Pacetti, "I codici autografi," *Archivum Franciscanum Historicum* 28 (1935): 516.

23. In the rest of the sermon (pp. 62–67), Bernardino discusses clandestine marriage and adultery—treating even adultery in terms of the marriage debt. Material concerning clandestine marriage, in particular some *quaestiones* by Richard of Mediavilla, is included in two draft sermons in the Budapest manuscript: Cenci, "Un manoscritto autografo," pp. 367 (no. 185) and 365 (no. 166); published in *Opera omnia,* 9:421–24. The latter draft, based largely on canonistic sources, was used for sermon 37 in the Sienese series in 1427 (*Siena 1427,* pp. 835–60). There is also a reference to clandestine marriage in *De Evangelio aeterno,* in *Opera omnia,* 3:108.

24. For an overview of the "functioning" of the bourgeois family in the fourteenth and fifteenth centuries and of relations between the spouses, based on the literature of the merchant class, see Alberto Tenenti, "Famiglia borghese e ideologia nel Quattrocento," in his *Credenze, ideologie, libertinismi tra Medioevo ed età moderna* (Bologna, 1978), pp. 121–35, esp. pp. 128–29; this essay was originally published as "Famille bourgeoise et idéologie au Bas Moyen Age," in *Famille et parenté,* pp. 431–40.

25. Herlihy and Klapisch-Zuber, *Les Toscans,* pp. 394–400.

26. *Siena 1427,* pp. 399–400; Nardini, "La famiglia cristiana," p. 30. Note, however, that in his sermons Bernardino advises against a big gap in age between the spouses, whereas the tendency of the urban merchant class was to exploit an age difference equivalent to a full generation between husband and wife in order to further strategies of marriage alliance between lineages: Christiane Klapisch-Zuber, "'Parenti, amici, e vicini': Il territorio urbano d'una famiglia mercantile nel XV secolo," *Quaderni storici* 11 (1976): 968 ("Kin, Friends, and Neighbors: The Urban Territory of a Merchant Family in 1400," in *Women, Family, and Ritual,* pp. 86–87). Klapisch-Zuber's essay is based on the memoir written between 1379 and 1421 by the Florentine merchant Lapo di Giovanni Niccolini de' Sirigatti, *Il libro degli affari proprii di casa,* ed. Christian Bec (Paris, 1969).

27. Herlihy and Klapisch-Zuber, *Les Toscans,* pp. 586–88.

28. "De çelotipia coniugum" (Cenci, "Un manoscritto autografo," p. 349, no. 86; published in *Opera omnia,* 9:389–90). This draft draws on the preceding one, no. 85, which was reutilized for sermon 13 in the *Sermones imperfecti;* but above all

it refers to to the *quaestiones* by Olivi transcribed earlier in the manuscript. For the Florentine sermon "Del matrimonio," see *Florence 1425,* 2:173–89.

29. *Florence 1424,* 1:381. See also sermon 3 of the *Sermones imperfecti,* in *Opera omnia,* 8:17: "Nullam nempe carnalitatis et honestatis evidentius signum est quam aegre et moleste ferre vel congaudere cum contra abusiones matrimonii et carnis spurcitias praedicatur."

30. "De coniugii honestate" (*Opera omnia,* 1:204–7).

31. See Roberto Rusconi, "Il sacramento della penitenza nella predicazione di San Bernardino da Siena," *Aevum* 47 (1973): 235–86.

32. "De multitudine malorum quae ex vanitatibus subsequuntur" (*Opera omnia,* 2:82–83).

33. A polemical reference to matrimonial strategies and the related phenomenon of exorbitant dowries is found in sermon 19 of the Sienese series in 1427 (*Siena 1427,* pp. 395–96). However, Bernardino never developed a comprehensive analysis of this subject, since his tools of social analysis and ethical purpose were inadequate to this task. His Latin writings contain only sporadic mentions of the subject. In the context of the restitution of illicit profits, he discusses a usurer's daughter's restitution of her dowry, in sermon 35 of *De christiana religione,* in *Opera omnia,* 1:437–38. In sermon 42 of *De Evangelio aeterno,* in contrast, in the context of his treatment of contracts and usury, he devotes an entire chapter to the question "Quod homo licite pacisci potest pro interesse damni emergentis de praesenti, ubi ostenditur quare pignus dotis uxoris marito non computatur in sortem" (*Opera omnia,* 4:352–56). The sources for this chapter are in large part the *Decretum,* the *Decretals,* the *Digest,* and the canonists, but above all Peter John Olivi's treatise *De contractibus usurariis.* On Olivi's influence on Bernardino's "economic ethics," see Ovidio Capitani, "S. Bernardino e l'etica economica," in *Atti del Convegno storico bernardiniano,* pp. 47–68.

34. Herlihy and Klapisch-Zuber, *Les Toscans,* p. 441. It is equally important to recognize the influence that Bernardino's Latin sermons would have on the preaching by Observant friars over the following decades. A particularly telling bit of evidence concerning the impact of Bernardino's marital ethics is found in Cherubino da Siena (more correctly: da Spoleto), *Regole della vita matrimoniale,* ed. Francesco Zambrini and Carlo Negroni (Bologna, 1888), p. 79: "That new star, our father St. Bernardino, preached at great length on these subjects, moved by his desire to instruct souls." See also Paolo Sevesi, "Il beato Michele Carcano da Milano O.F.M.," *Archivum Franciscanum Historicum* 4 (1911): 472.

35. See Pandimiglio, "Giovanni di Pagolo Morelli," p. 557 n. 17, who draws a parallel between Morelli and Leon Battista Alberti: "This demonstrates that in the Florentine merchant class circulated a set of moral and practical teachings, that must have been carried by certain books."

36. See Roberto Rusconi, "Fonti e documenti su Manfredi da Vercelli O.P. ed il suo movimento penitenziale," *Archivum Fratrum Praedicatorum* 47 (1977): 51–107; Rusconi, "Note sulla predicazione di Manfredi da Vercelli O.P. e il movimento

penitenziale dei terziari manfredini," *Archivum Fratrum Praedicatorum* 48 (1978): 93–135; Rusconi, *L'attesa della fine: Crisi della società, profezia, e Apocalisse in Italia al tempo del Grande Scisma d'Occidente (1378–1417)* (Rome, 1979), pp. 236–46.

    37. *Florence 1425,* 1:227.

    38. Ibid., pp. 234–35.

    39. The expression comes from Franco Sacchetti, *Il Trecentonovelle,* ed. Emilio Faccioli (Turin, 1970), novella 123, p. 322: "Your job is to look after the household management." On this topic, see Cammarosano, "Aspetti delle strutture familiari," esp. p. 434; and Ruggiero Romano and Alberto Tenenti, "*I libri della famiglia* di Leon Battista Alberti," published originally as the introduction to Leon Battista Alberti, *I libri della famiglia* (Turin, 1969), and reprinted in Ruggiero Romano, *Tra due crisi: l'Italia del Rinascimento* (Turin, 1971), pp. 137–68, esp. pp. 142–48 and 162. Romano and Tenenti also refer the reader to Christian Bec, *Les marchands écrivains à Florence, 1375–1434* (Paris, 1967).

    40. Leon Battista Alberti, *I libri della famiglia,* book 3, in *Opere volgari,* ed. Cecil Grayson, vol. 1 (Bari, 1960), p. 163: "santa cosa la masserizia." See Bernardino's famous sermons on taking a wife. The first rudimentary outline is in the Budapest manuscript (Cenci, "Un manoscritto autografo," p. 367, no. 183; published in *Opera omnia,* 9:425–26). From this sprang sermon 46, "On taking a wife, and the dangers of remaining without one" (Del pigliar moglie e del pericolo di restare senza), of the Florentine Lenten cycle of 1425 (*Florence 1425,* 2:22–36); sermon 12, "On marital affection" (De amicitia coniugali), of the series in Perugia that same year (see Pacetti, "La predicazione," p. 176); and sermon 19, "How a husband should love his wife, and the wife her husband" (Come il marito dié amare la donna, così la donna il suo marito), of the Sienese series in 1427 (*Siena 1427,* pp. 391–420). To flesh out the functional image of women, marriage, and family, this group of sermons should be supplemented with the series on the "good wife," running from sermon 25 in the Florentine cycle in 1424 (*Florence 1424,* 2:405–24) right down to sermon 30 of the Sienese sequence in 1427 (*Siena 1427,* pp. 633–88). Bernardino's definitive statement on the subject is sermon 48, "On the good wife" (De domina honesta), in his *De christiana religione* (*Opera omnia,* 2:100–108), a very succinct exposition, based on the biblical wisdom literature and the *Decretum,* and preceded—not accidentally—by two polemical sermons denouncing female "vanity": sermons 46, "On the many evils that follow from vanity" (De multitudine malorum quae ex vanitatibus subsequuntur), and 47, "Against making oneself up and wearing wigs, and against the long trains on women's gowns (Contra se fardantes et capillos adulterinos portantes, atque contra feminas caudatas) (*Opera omnia,* 2:73–99).

    41. Zelina Zafarana, "Per la storia religiosa di Firenze nel Quattrocento: Una raccolta privata di prediche," *Studi medievali,* ser. 3, 9 (1968): 1017–32.

    42. *Siena 1427,* pp. 399–400.

10

St. Francesca and the Female Religious Communities of Fifteenth-Century Rome

Anna Esposito

The recent essays of Arnold Esch have notably improved our understanding of the social setting in which St. Francesca Bussa dei Ponziani lived, a setting that was more or less representative of her time. They have also shed light on the political resonances of her social position and on her strong ties with Rome, the city where she was born and where her personal and religious experience unfolded.[1] But these important studies are cast essentially in terms of social and political history, and touch only marginally on the world of female religiosity surrounding Francesca, from her closest fellow religious to the various devout women who appear to have been in contact with her. My essay, in contrast, is dedicated precisely to that world—formed of individuals, but even more of groups and communities—since by analyzing it we can better understand Francesca's experience. Using Esch's information, I will seek to place these women in relation to the urban sociopolitical environment from which they sprang. In particular, I will examine the oblates of Tor de' Specchi, a group founded by Francesca Ponziani, extending my analysis of its social composition over a period of roughly fifty years in order to trace its variations and changes.[2]

A careful reading of Francesca's *vita* and especially her canonization proceedings will allow us to delineate with some precision her social and spiritual environment and bring out the importance in her life of ties with other women.[3] These women included members of her own social class, the wealthy urban nobility, with whom she maintained normal social contacts, and others (such as her sister-in-law Vannozza, her oblates, and other "sisters of penitence") with whom she established "privileged" relationships. It

is no coincidence that two-thirds of the witnesses at her canonization proceedings were women: in the inquest of 1440 they were primarily women
who had grown up or grown old with Francesca, while in the later inquests,
in 1451 and 1453, women of this generation were joined by their daughters
and granddaughters.[4] Active, engaged, and alert, these women described
with precision Francesca's saintly habits, her praiseworthy charitable activities, and her miracle-working powers, which they had observed in the most
varied places and circumstances. It almost seems as if some woman was always at hand, ready to note and remember the details of even the most ordinary of events, whereas the men, who appear "primarily as beneficiaries of
miracles, as persons of little faith, or simply as people by now long deceased," were too involved in the tumult of everyday life to take much notice of Ceccolella (as Francesca was affectionately known), to whom they
typically resorted only in emergencies, and often at the urging of their wives,
mothers, and sisters.[5] It is no accident that about half of the male witnesses
were clerics, and that the few men who provided more significant evidence,
going beyond personal matters, were members of religious orders with
whom Francesca was in contact.[6] A typology of Francesca's miracles attests
once again to the traditional separation between male and female interests
and environments: the men's place was the outside world, the often conten-
tious and violent world of work and political life; women were found in the
home, with its whole penumbra of relationships (these, too, not always
peaceful) with mothers-in-law, sisters-in-law, and children. The differences
in their lives obviously gave rise to different problems, and thus Francesca
had to intervene mainly to heal "the terrible wounds of the men" (but also
to soothe their hatreds and pacify their souls) and the "horrible illnesses of
the women," caused largely by childbirth, nursing, abortions, sterility, and
other typically feminine ills.[7]

Apart from the oblates, the most frequent witnesses at the canonization
proceedings were ladies of the urban nobility to which Francesca also belonged, both by birth and through her marriage to Lorenzo Ponziani, one of
the richest raisers of livestock in Rome.[8] Arnold Esch has shown that they
and their kin (who appeared as witnesses and as beneficiaries of miracles)
came predominantly from very specific political and economic circles of the
city: either from families in the party of the pro-Colonna nobility, who
along with the Bussa and the Ponziani had shared in governing the last free
commune of Rome in 1395–98, or from families of the popular party, who
aligned more closely with the nobility after the unsuccessful attempt to cast
off papal rule in 1400.[9] Details fortuitously included in their depositions
and the testimony concerning Francesca's domestic life make it possible to
describe the way of life of Roman noblewomen in the fifteenth century, from

the management of a large household with many servants to the worldly duties that went with their status, from their love of jewels and expensive clothing to their punctilious attention to their persons and hence the use of cosmetics, wigs, and high-heeled shoes.[10] The attention to pomp and public display, which in the course of the century would become steadily more exaggerated as a way of marking social differences beyond any possibility of ambiguity, appears unexpectedly in their depositions, where it is highlighted by their very insistence on the poverty of Francesca's clothing. As one witness said (and her testimony was amply confirmed by the others), "she always saw Francesca wear tight clothing, made from common cheap cloth and worked simply and without ostentation, because of her humility."[11]

Francesca's more meaningful relationships, however, were with the women who shared more closely her spiritual experience. A true, profound, and intimate communion of aspirations and sentiments bound her to her sister-in-law Vannozza, "with whom the Lord had joined her not only by ties of blood but also by similarity of character and conduct."[12] Francesca's spiritual father and the author of her *vita*, Giovanni Mattiotti, encapsulated the relationship between the two women: "These two most beloved sisters-in-law spent almost thirty-eight years together in such harmony and with such marvelous affection that there was never any discord between them, neither major nor minor, but they remained one in heart and soul."[13] Indeed, as long as she lived, Vannozza shared all the experiences of her sister-in-law, partaking intimately in Francesca's decisions and initiatives, rather than merely copying her model. Both longed to go to "a desert place in order to serve God," but the "ties of marriage" prevented this.[14] Both conducted themselves with profound humility, begging for alms without their husbands' knowledge in places where they went unrecognized, "and sometimes suffered curses and insults as a reward for their begging."[15] They visited churches and sanctuaries to hear the mass and sermons and receive the sacraments: they were together when the parish priest of Santa Cecilia gave them an unconsecrated host and when, returning from a visit to the basilica of St. Peter, they fell into the Tiber while attempting to take a drink.[16] Both practiced charity toward the poor and the sick with such dedication that they occasionally provoked the anger of their relatives.[17] The sisters-in-law tended each other during their frequent illnesses: Vannozza cared for Francesca immediately after her marriage, when she fell so gravely ill "that she could neither take food nor move," and Vannozza was the first person Francesca told of her miraculous recovery; while Francesca in turn nursed Vannozza during her many infirmities and was at her side during the final illness that led to her death.[18]

This event was described by several witnesses and by Giovanni Mattiotti in his *vita* in terms that confirm yet again the way that Vannozza's life mirrored Francesca's, even to foreshadowing (albeit on a reduced scale) the circumstances of Francesca's death. A divine vision announced Vannozza's death to Francesca several days before it occurred in April 1431, just as one would announce her own: "and because Vannozza was most welcome in the eyes of God," added Francesca's priest-biographer, "along with other devout persons I remained with her until her death, which was almost certified by the said vision."[19] Francesca never left her sister-in-law's side; with her miraculous powers, she aided Vannozza in her struggle with the devil as she received the final sacraments—a struggle that she herself had so often had to face—and in the end saw her soul ascend to heaven.

At Vannozza's funeral, which took place in the church of Santa Maria in Aracoeli, "there was a great crowd of people. Every joint of the deceased's body felt to the touch like soft wax. And out of devotion the people carried off parts of Vannozza's clothing."[20] Mattiotti's account of this episode immediately calls to mind the similar scenes following Francesca's death, amply documented by testimony at her canonization proceedings. For Francesca, however, the "great crowd" swelled to "an innumerable throng," "a tremendous multitude of men"; after three days of exposure her body was not merely supple like wax but looked "as if it were alive," and "a delightful perfume emerged as if lilies and roses had been strewn in the casket and on her body"; the pious stripping of the deceased's clothes, to be kept as miraculous relics, became in Francesca's case a moment of such intensity that "in the crowds and crush of people the aforesaid witnesses and the others who were looking after the body could scarcely prevent all of her clothes from being carried away."[21]

And yet Vannozza, whose name crops up so often in Francesca's *vita* and canonization proceedings, remains a cipher to us. We know nothing of her last name, her family, or her origins, despite Lugano's arbitrary assertion that she belonged to the Santacroce family.[22] All we know is that she was a maternal aunt of the priest Giovanni Schiavo and that, since she had been accepted into the Ponziani family, she probably sprang from an equally prominent lineage.[23]

Fortunately, we are better informed about the women who formed the group of oblates of Tor de' Specchi, whom the documents describe as "chaste women living in the Campitelli district."[24] Except for their distinctive oblation in the order of the friars of Monte Oliveto in Santa Maria Nova, this group was similar in aims and organization to other communities of female penitents, especially those connected with the mendicant orders.

The names of the first thirteen are recorded in their act of oblation, which took place in 1433.[25] This document, too, confirms the very close ties between the families of the old and new civic nobility, which in 1395–98 left their mark on the last years of the free Roman commune. Indeed, five of the first oblates seem to have belonged to the family of Lello Petrucci, a typical member of the new class of cattle ranchers and agricultural merchants, who were linked with the noble party.[26] All five were (like Anastasia, the widow of Pietro di Giovanni Cenci) widows of men who came either from families directly involved in the political events of the end of the century or from families like the Beccaluva, the Vincenzi, or the Biondi, whose members had often held high office in the Roman commune.[27] This first group of oblates also included Brigida, the widow of Carlo dei Foschi de Berta (a member of one of the oldest and noblest families of Rome, which after 1398 probably aligned more closely with the popular party); Anastasia, the widow of Tommaso Clarelli; Iacoba, the daughter of Ludovico Capizucchi; and Paolina, the widow of Giuliano Porcari—all families of established noble standing and considerable economic resources.[28]

Testimony in the canonization proceedings makes frequent reference to the social standing of the oblates of Tor de' Specchi. The proceedings of 1451, in particular, contain sections dealing specifically with the "conversion of many women [to God]" due to Francesca's reputation for sanctity, the establishment of the congregation, and the growth and "sanctimony" of the group.[29] When the witnesses, both male and female, were questioned about these topics, they unanimously praised the devout and impeccable conduct of the women who adhered to Francesca's rule. They were equally consistent in affirming that "every day many noblewomen who are Roman citizens leave the world and join the group"; "many other noblewomen entered and continue to enter, living in a praiseworthy manner in the fear of God"; and "large numbers have come and continue to come to the aforesaid congregation because of the blessed Francesca."[30] The emphasis not only on the noble origins but also on the sheer number of women is entirely accurate, since the congregation of Tor de' Specchi was much larger than other such groups, which usually counted no more than five or six members.

An examination of the names of female oblates who entered the group after 1433 confirms that most were of aristocratic origin. But with the passage of time, members of the old leading families of the medieval commune were joined by representatives of the newer urban nobility, a nobility that was linked to commerce, prestigious intellectual activities, and the church, and that no longer made a distinction between its fortunes and those of the papal court, which had definitively installed itself in Rome.[31] The number of recruits from other classes and from localities outside of Rome remained low; nevertheless, even these few indicate the growing appeal of the community and the spread of its reputation outside the city limits.

In the period between her husband's death in 1444 and her own in 1454, Mabilia Papazurri, the wife of Francesca's son Battista Ponziani, belonged to the group of oblates. Her presence in the congregation, of which she even became the leader, has until now escaped notice.[32] But it is significant not only as evidence of the "salutiferous fruit" of Francesca's life and doctrine, which led Mabilia to adopt her ideals and follow her example (despite having been, early in her marriage, at odds with her mother-in-law over the management of the household), but also because it reveals the indifference of other members of the Ponziani family toward the sanctity of their relative.[33] Apart from Mabilia, none of them—not even Francesca's son Battista—testified in the canonization proceedings or seemed to realize the exceptional character of Francesca and the congregation she founded.[34] Thus, right after her mother's death, Vannozza, daughter of Mabilia and Battista Ponziani and hence the granddaughter of our saint (and yet another family member who never testified at the canonization proceedings), contested certain bequests to the oblates contained in her mother's will and thereby started what would be a protracted lawsuit against the women of Tor de' Specchi. The case eventually came before two of the most expert jurists in Rome: Lelio della Valle and Ludovico of Terni, lawyers at the papal consistory.[35]

A different Vannozza, one of the oblates, came from a family of "new men." The widow of Giacomo Santacroce of the Arenula district, head of a family that began to establish itself on the civic scene in the early decades of the fifteenth century, she was the mother of many sons, some of whom came to prominence in the second half of the century: Andrea, a lawyer at the papal consistory; Onofrio, bishop of Tricarico; and Paolo, Pietro, and Valeriano, all three of whom were wealthy merchants.[36] Vannozza joined Francesca's congregation after a fit of depression (*ex disperatione et insania*) led her to attempt suicide. Out of respect for her noble offspring, her name was suppressed until 1453, although her miraculous recovery from insanity and a self-inflicted sword wound had already been mentioned in the hearings of 1440. Vannozza herself, who had testified several times about some of Francesca's miraculous deeds, "did not wish to come forward to make a deposition in regard to this article" concerning her own story, although she did acknowledge privately to the bishop in charge that "what was contained in this article was true."[37] It was Agnes, daughter of Paolo di Lello Petrucci and governess of the oblates, who disclosed Vannozza's name and her oblation "according to the rule and congregation of the said women, promising to observe it until her death"—an event that had already transpired by the time this deposition was made in 1453.[38] And Vannozza was not the only member of the Santacroce family to be devoted to Francesca. Her daughter-in-law Andreozza, the wife of her son Pietro, made several depositions, some of which concerned miraculous cures she herself and her little son Bartolomeo had experienced; Andreozza's mother, Paolozza, widow of Carlo Zeusi dell'Isola, also testified about these cures.[39]

The entire "new" family of the Gezzo displayed profound devotion for Francesca, their neighbor in the Trastevere.[40] Giovanna, for instance, was miraculously cured of a terrible fever in 1440, and her brother Pietro, too, was the beneficiary of a similar cure. In 1444–45, in the deposition concerning Pietro's wondrous return to health, Giovanna was described as "one of the fellow sisters of the blessed Francesca."[41] Indeed, the miracle may have provided the impetus for her entry into Tor de' Specchi, as one certainly did for Angelozza, daughter of Antonio dello Chicco of the Campitelli district, who went on to become head of the congregation on various occasions.[42] Angelozza herself described the event: "When she became gravely ill from the plague, she entrusted herself to the blessed Francesca, whom she had not known during her lifetime; but when she saw her body in the church of Santa Maria Nova, she vowed that if Francesca delivered her from her illness, she would enter the blessed Francesca's congregation and live in accordance with its rule. As soon as the vow was made, the blessed Francesca appeared to the witness saying 'Daughter, you shall not die,' and immediately she began to improve and eventually was healed. And after she was healed she entered the blessed Francesca's congregation in the Campitelli district."[43] All of this happened in June of 1449. Nearly three years later, in May 1452, Angelozza was the beneficiary of another miracle, whereas the following September it was the turn of her sister-in-law Ieronima, wife of her brother Nicola.[44] It was Nicola (who in 1476 was the oblates' procurator) who gave concrete expression to his family's devotion by giving the congregation of St. Francesca a house located in the Campitelli district—a donation made in 1481, when the oblates were headed by his sister.[45] The notarial act explains that his donation was inspired "by reverence for the omnipotent God and his glorious mother the Virgin Mary; and by the said Nicola's professed devotion for the women of the congregation of the blessed Francesca, that they might pray to God for his soul; and by the brotherly and honest love and affection that he had and has for their president, his sister; and by the many favors and honest services the said Nicola acknowledged having received."[46]

With Angelozza we have arrived at a generation of women who had not known Francesca personally, but were drawn to her congregation by the fame of her sanctity and the prestige of the institution. Such was the case with Paolina di Giovanni Massaruzio, Mattuzia di Ambrosio, Benedetta di Antonio di Saba, Eufrosina di Antonello of Terni, and Anastasia di Petruccio Scarafone, whose oblations were recorded by the notary Gregorio di Nicola of Segni in a protocol dating from 1455.[47] It was also true of Benedetta Lucrezia di Antonio Ponziani, whom we find as an oblate in 1476 and as their president in 1502, and whose father, a soldier in the Marches and elsewhere, had testified in the proceedings of 1451 about Francesca's widespread reputation for sanctity in the places he had visited.[48] Other names turn up in various notarial documents concerning the oblates' management of their landed property and real estate. In 1482 Girolama di Tommaso Cosciari, Aventina di Stefano Giovenale, Lucrezia di Mattuzzo Ianzi, and Stefania di Mattia Margani appeared among the professed for the first time.[49] Ten years later, among the fifteen oblates present when a lease was drawn up (representing virtually all of the women in the congregation, as the document states), we find the first mention of Iacobella di Iacobo Micco, Maria Maddalena di Lorenzo Ricci, Paola di Mariano di Buzio dello Coccio, Gregoria di Buzio Cardelli, and Francesca di Francesco Mentabona."[50] In 1494, only two years after this lease, no fewer than twenty-six "women of the congregation and religious house of the blessed Francesca" gathered "on the portico of the home in which the said tertiaries resided" for the sale of a vineyard.[51] Among them a couple of names stand out: Marzia, daughter of Master Gaspare of Verona, the well-known biographer of Paul II and professor of rhetoric at the Studium Urbis; and Cristofora di Francesco Petrone, who may have been descended from another writer on Roman matters, Paolo di Lello Petrone.[52]

The full significance of the life that Francesca and her oblates chose can only be understood within the context of similar female communities in fifteenth-century Rome. This female quest for a more intense religious experience lived outside the framework of traditional monastic settings was a widespread phenomenon in late medieval Italy, especially in certain geographic areas.[53] Even for Rome, where research is still in its early stages, we know of various fifteenth-century communities of bizzoche and tertiaries and a number of recluses and anchoresses who were walled up, either in their own homes or in various churches, particularly the basilicas of St. Peter and of St. John in the Lateran.[54] I will concentrate here on those groups that were in contact with Francesca and her oblates, in order to emphasize their resemblance in inspiration and in practice. In my opinion, these affinities can be attributed to their frequent contacts, common problems, and similar ways of life, about which the canonization proceedings offer assorted evidence. For all these "devout women," "religious women," and "women of good and honest lives," Francesca undoubtedly represented a model on which to pattern their own existence as penitents, just as in establishing her group and its rule Francesca must surely have found inspiration in existing communities with which she was in contact.

Francesca had a special friendship with Margherita Martelluzzi, a woman who testified quite frequently in the canonization proceedings, though without ever being identified as a tertiary.[55] In fact, she was the leader of a group of *mantellate* who resided in one of her houses near the piazza of San Lorenzo in Lucina, in the Campomarzio district.[56] This group was linked with the Augustinian order, and until 1454 was under the spiritual direction of Fra Cesario Orsini of Rome, bachelor of sacred theology and rector of the confraternity of Santa Maria del Popolo, to whom in 1431 the prior general of the order had entrusted all of the Augustinian *mantellate* and female penitents in Rome.[57]

Along with Rita di Iacobo Coluzia, another *mantellata* from the same house, Margherita testified repeatedly on the life and miracles of the blessed Francesca, emphasizing the long friendship she enjoyed with the saint and her family, "since she even knew the mother of the blessed Francesca and was famous for this. For this witness had known the blessed Francesca herself for as long as thirty years before Francesca's death and had a special friendship with her."[58] Their relationship was so familiar that she could report on the daily habits of the saint, such as her practice of wearing woolen clothing even for sleeping, "since the witness was quite close to her, and was in the house of the sisters during the four years before her death."[59] She testified to the frequency of Francesca's ecstasies, some of which occurred while she was praying in the garden of Margherita's house in Campomarzio: "She often saw [this], in particular in Santa Maria in Aracoeli at the time of Vannozza's death; and on another occasion in her garden in Campomarzio the witness watched her kneel for two hours, rapt in ecstasy while reciting the office; and afterward, when she returned to herself, she continued the office, praising God."[60] She bore witness as well to the "holy and praiseworthy" works that Francesca performed, her "patience in adversity and charity toward God and her neighbors" during the thirty years she had known her, and her reputation for sanctity, such that her life was presented as a model by "intelligent and learned men" in public sermons that Margherita heard many times in Rome and her companion Rita di Iacobo Coluzia heard in Viterbo.[61]

Margherita's spiritual family of "sisters of penitence of the order of the Hermits of St. Augustine de Urbe" came from the same well-to-do and noble classes that typically were the social source of Francesca's oblates. Margherita was the daughter of Tommaso Martelluzzi, a notary in the

Campomarzio district who, together with Pietro Mattuzzi, was a leader of the popular party in 1398 and in the attempted coup against the pope two years later.[62] Another *mantellata* of the same house was the "noble and religious lady Iacobella, daughter of the late Blasio di Bartolomeo Tosti," and thus a member of one of the most prominent families of the Campomarzio district.[63] Her will, dated 17 March 1439, casts a revealing light on this female community, which seems to have been particularly devoted to the cult of St. Monica, whose body had recently been translated to the church of Sant'Agostino.[64] Iacobella must have been a widow: even though this long document makes no mention of her husband's name, certain bequests refer to an *anulus subarrationis*—a wedding ring—and a house received as a wedding gift.[65] The figure of another "sister" also surfaces in this document: Francesca, daughter of Fra Cesario, who after Margherita seems to have been the most important of these female penitents. Her father may even have been the Augustinian friar Cesario mentioned earlier, who must have married before taking his vows; his presumed wife, a certain "Madonna Antonia," also eventually became a tertiary, since her terse death notice described her as "Madonna Antonia, tertiary, the former wife of Fra Cesario."[66]

Rita di Iacobo Coluzia has already been mentioned as one of the witnesses at the canonization proceedings of 1451; her deposition on the miraculous effects of Francesca's presence and words, which "enflamed and inspired this witness to love God and to contemn the world," is of particular interest.[67] We also have the will she drew up in Viterbo on 9 July 1473, which informs us that on this date the residence of these Augustinian *mantellate* was "commonly called the house of the *mantellate* of the late lady Margherita Martelluzzi."[68] I have not managed to uncover any further information about the family to which Rita was born; from her will we learn only that her sister Agnes was abbess of the nearby monastery of Santa Maria in Campomarzio, while another sister, Maria, had been married to Nardo Cena, a member of an important merchant family.[69] Like Iacobella Tosti, Rita seems to have had a considerable personal fortune.

Another *pinzochera* who followed the penitential rule of St. Augustine—and apparently had considerable wealth at her disposal—is Pacifica Salvati, who is known to have belonged to Margherita's group from 1444 to 1450.[70] The names of other sisters who gathered around this spiritual mother appear in a notarial act of 1463, which indicates that in this year Margherita's group was composed of four other women, in addition to Rita and herself: Maria di Giovanni di Cola di Paolo, Bensivenuta di Cola di Paolo, Stefania di Giovanni of Albano, and Beatrice of Magliano.[71] This community thus remained small but still managed to make a place for itself in Roman religious life: over the second half of the century, the *"pinzochere* residing in the home of the late Tommaso Martelluzzi" would often be remembered in the wills of pious Romans.

A Franciscan tertiary *de observantia* mentioned in the canonization proceedings of 1440 and 1443, Margherita from the Trastevere neighborhood of Rome, founded a community later known as the "domus de Margherita alle scale," the house of Margherita by the stairs.[72] The canonization proceedings call Margherita a "woman devout in every way," and say that "she was in contact with Lady Francesca herself" and "had been very familiar with the blessed woman during her life."[73] She was one of the *honestis domnabus,* the good women who remained in the house at Trastevere to pray by Francesca's body on the night she died, despite a painful malady of her arm, which was cured by simply touching the infected limb to the saint's body.[74] Nor was this the only miracle Margherita experienced: having gone "with other good women" (probably the women of her group) to visit Francesca's tomb in the church of Santa Maria Nova despite "a serious illness concerning the flow of blood," "while praying there, she felt herself to be freed of the infirmity by divine grace."[75] On another occasion, her faith in Francesca's miraculous powers led to the cure of Geronima, wife of Antonio Romano: Margherita gave her "a cloth she had that Lady Francesca had worn during her lifetime," instructing her to "lay this cloth devoutly over the infirmity and God will give you grace."[76]

Another piece of clothing that Francesca had worn was owned by Angelella, whose sister, Caterina, was married to Iacobo di Romano of the Trastevere neighborhood of Rome. Angelella was a Franciscan tertiary who may well have belonged to Margherita's group, and she too was "quite well acquainted and on intimate terms with the said Lady Francesca" and fully alert to her mediating powers. The cloth she loaned her sister to cure her little nephew was given "out of devotion to Lady Francesca"; and it was this faith in her powers that made possible the miracle, which was witnessed by another member of the Third Order of St. Francis: Francesca, who perhaps was a companion of Angelella.[77]

Another Franciscan tertiary, Caterina of Perugia, "a woman of good and honest life," took part in the canonization proceedings of 1440. I believe her to be the same Caterina of Orte who was prioress of a group of female Franciscan tertiaries located in the Campomarzio district in a place called Monte Accettabile or Monte Citorio.[78] This identification is supported by certain correspondences between Caterina's deposition and a notarial document. Article 122 of the canonization proceedings states that Caterina was "persecuted" quite harshly "by a certain person who must remain nameless, a person superior to her in power and in name," and the resulting anxiety prevented her from "serving God and her order as she would have liked." Francesca, to whom Caterina had turned for advice, replied: "Do not doubt nor withdraw from the place in which you serve God, but be patient and trust in God, because the person who persecutes you will himself suffer the persecution of others and you will emerge triumphant."[79] A few days later her prophecy was fulfilled. On 6 August 1438, the protonotary of the Campidoglio, Antonio di Nicola Salomone, registered a "guarantee" made by the nobleman Lorenzo di Ludovico Rapilazio of the Colonna district, who promised (subject to a penalty of 500 lire *di provesini*) not to harm either the persons or property of various groups of female religious in the Campomarzio district, including that of Caterina of Orte.[80] How exactly Lorenzo had harassed them is not specified, but we do learn from this document that three other women lived with Caterina: Marta, Nicolosa, and Francesca.[81] Further information on this community of pious women, commonly called "the Perugians," is provided by two papal documents.[82] In 1423, a bull of Martin V authorized the sale of a house in Campagnano bequeathed "pro usu mulierum honestarum," for the use of good women, by Stefania Coitto of Campagnano, and the acquisition of another house for the same purpose in the Campomarzio district of Rome "in the place known as Monte Accettabile," near that of the Franciscan tertiaries Francesca and Margherita di Todi; this house would be used to lodge other Franciscan tertiaries—Margherita, Caterina, and Agnes—who lived in Rome but lacked a residence.[83] In 1451, Nicholas V repeated the obligation binding Caterina of Orte and the other sisters to observe the ancient rule of the Third Order under the guidance of a priest chosen by the women themselves, and at the same time prohibited the guardian and the friars of Santa Maria in Aracoeli "from summoning the said sisters to the chapter at any time or bothering them or presuming to interfere with any of them in any way." Blame for having deviated from the traditional manner of life was not leveled at Caterina, the leader of the group; indeed, she was lauded because she "had lived and continued to live under this rule for nearly sixty years . . . in a praiseworthy manner and without any stain of vice." Rather, it was the other sisters in the community who were accused of having been "led astray by levity or vanity."[84] Caterina, in fact, had once sought Francesca Ponziani's advice on the delicate question of receiving a new companion in her group, and her deposition in the canonization proceedings of 1440 records the saint's reply: "I do not recommend that you receive her; but she will be received and inducted by the others, and before the year is out she will cast off the robe she receives." And so it happened: though not accepted by Caterina, Francesca, the daughter of Ritozza di Antonio of Patrica, was inducted "by certain companions living communally in the house known as the one with a hundred windows, in the Ripe district near the river." But before a year had passed "she left both that house and the religious life, abandoning her habit or vestments."[85]

With Allegra, a Dominican tertiary cured of a serious disease of the breast by Francesca's miraculous intervention, we are back in the Trastevere. Allegra was probably a member of the community that had its seat "in the houses of the church of Santa Cecilia in Trastevere," in the palace of the titular cardinal of Santa Cecilia not far from the Ponziani family home.[86] The day after her marvelous recovery, which took place on 24 February 1440, Allegra visited two churches that she had long been unable to attend because of her illness: she heard mass at Santa Cecilia, which was evidently nearer to her, and then went to hear the word of God preached at Santa Maria sopra Minerva, the main Dominican church of Rome.[87] A notarial document of 11 May 1448 names the women who belonged to the small Dominican community of Santa Cecilia: Angelina Farfelli, Maddalena of Florence, Angelina, the mother of Fra Eusebio, Giovanna, Maddelena, and Allegra herself.[88]

The female communities mentioned here are merely those that the canonization proceedings show to have been in direct contact with Francesca. However, there must have been many more such groups. One sign of this (apart from the documented presence of other communities in Rome) is the very silence of contemporary chroniclers about the congregation of Tor de' Specchi and Francesca's reputation. In the eyes of Paolo di Lello Petrone, Paolo dello Mastro, and Stefano Infessura—all writers who lived in the Ponte and Trevi districts, far from Francesca's usual haunts—no particular significance was attached to a community that seemed no different from its numerous counterparts in Rome.[89] Even this tertiary's reputation for sanctity must not have struck them as particularly noteworthy in a city that probably witnessed many similar phenomena, such as the collective devotion that followed the death of Francesca's sister-in-law, Vannozza. In any case, it is no accident that the only chronicler to record Francesca's death and her reputation for sanctity was Stefano Caffaro, whose sister-in-law Angela, wife of Pietro Caffaro, testified about her sister's miraculous cure in the canonization proceedings of 1440.[90]

But the something special that set Francesca apart from other female penitents was not lost on people with more refined sensibilities and a deeper experience of religious life, such as the Franciscans Bernardino of Siena and Giovanni of Capistrano, or the masters general of the Augustinian, Dominican, and Franciscan orders. Some witnesses recalled having heard in Rome "intelligent and learned men state and publicly preach on various occasions that the blessed Francesca was a saint because of her saintly life and miracles." In particular, "Master Tommaso of the kingdom of Naples of the Dominican order, Master Matteo of the Order of St. Augustine, Fra Antonio of Monte Savello, and Fra Giovanni of Capistrano of the Franciscan order preached publicly to the people that she was a saint."[91] In Siena, "the life of the blessed Francesca was preached by St. Bernardino, who declared that she was blessed because of her saintly life, and similar sermons were preached by Fra Giovanni of Capistrano."[92]

Thanks to their preaching, the fame of Francesca's sanctity and that of her group reached communities of penitents in other cities, and even outside Italy. Thus the Franciscan tertiary Bartolomea, daughter of the late Stefano Duodena of Arezzo, came to Rome in 1438, drawn by devotion to visit the blessed Francesca, whose saintly life had been publicly preached in Arezzo; and while there she saw a small golden rod descend from heaven to the cell where Francesca was praying, giving tangible expression to her fervor. According to the testimony of various oblates in the canonization proceedings of 1451, Bartolomea returned to Rome several years later with the "sisters" of her community to visit Francesca, who, however, had died in the interim.[93] An example from a place very much farther from Rome is provided by Caterina "de Cardenas," from the city of Alcalá de Henares in the diocese of Toledo, who obtained from Julius II permission to build a chapel in her home and live there with other religious women, on the model of the oblates of Tor de' Specchi.[94]

The widespread practice of associating in groups of female *bizzoche* and tertiaries, so typical of the period when Francesca gave life to her congregation of oblates, like the frequent contacts between the various communities, did not die with Francesca. Just as the objects and clothing she had used survived, circulating as miraculous relics among the women who had been in touch with her, so too did the example of her life, authoritatively proposed as a model by mendicant preachers, and the association she founded, whose tradition has lasted to this day.

NOTES

Originally published in *Culto dei santi, istituzioni, e classi sociali in età preindustriale*, ed. Sofia Boesch Gajano and Lucia Sebastiani (L'Aquila and Rome, 1984), pp. 539–62.

1. Arnold Esch, "Die Zeugenaussagen im Heiligsprechungsverfahren für S. Francesca Romana als Quelle zur Sozialgeschichte Roms im frühen Quattrocento," *Quellen und Forschungen aus italienischen Archiven und Bibliotheken* 53

(1973): 93–151; Esch, "Tre sante ed il loro ambiente sociale a Roma: S. Francesca Romana, S. Brigida di Svezia, e S. Caterina da Siena," in *Atti del Simposio internazionale cateriniano-bernardiniano, Siena 17–20 aprile 1980,* ed. Domenico Maffei and Paolo Nardi (Siena, 1982), pp. 89–120.

2. This essay represents part of a larger investigation of female religiosity in fifteenth-century Rome. Here I have limited my citations to those sources that bear most directly on this specific topic.

3. For the *vita* written in Latin by Francesca's confessor Giovanni Mattiotti, see *Acta Sanctorum,* March, vol. 2 (Antwerp, 1668), pp. 93–178. A new critical edition has just appeared: Alessandra Bartolomei Romagnoli, *Santa Francesca Romana: Edizione critica dei trattati latini di Giovanni Mattiotti* (Vatican City, 1995). Only one edition of the vernacular version of 1469 is currently available: Mariano Armellini, *Vita di S. Francesca Romana scritta nell'idioma volgare di Roma del sec. XV* (Rome, 1882). The portion describing her visions was republished by Maria Pelaez, "Visioni di S. Francesca Romana: Testo romanesco del sec. XV," *Archivio della Società romana di storia patria* 14 (1891): 365–409. For a study of the sources concerning Francesca's life, see Gabriele Maria Brasò, "Identificazione delle fonti autografe della biografia di S. Francesca Romana," *Benedictina* 21 (1974): 165–87.

For her canonization, see *I processi per Francesca Bussa dei Ponziani (Santa Francesca Romana), 1440–1453,* ed. Placido T. Lugano (Vatican City, 1943). André Vauchez did not consider the case of Francesca because it fell outside the chronological boundaries of his study of medieval canonization proceedings, but the information he provides about female sanctity in a slightly earlier period, and especially its mystical aspects, is very helpful for our understanding of Francesca: André Vauchez, *La sainteté en Occident aux derniers siècles du Moyen Age d'après les procès de canonisation et les documents hagiographiques* (Rome, 1981). See also the remarks of Giulia Barone, "Processi di canonizzazione e modelli di santità nel basso Medioevo," *Quellen und Forschungen aus italienischen Archiven und Bibliotheken* 62 (1982): 343–49.

4. Esch, "Tre sante," p. 91.

5. Ibid., p. 92.

6. Esch, "Die Zeugenaussagen," p. 102.

7. Esch, "Tre sante," pp. 92 and 94. In his depictions of miraculous events from the saint's life, the painter of the frescoes of the Cappella Vecchia of Tor de' Specchi tended to emphasize those that involved highly conspicuous wounds, which would immediately strike the observer's attention. On this fresco cycle see Attilio Rossi, "Le opere d'arte del monastero di Tor de' Specchi in Roma," *Bollettino d'arte* 1 (1907): 4–22; and Vincenzo Golzio and Giuseppe Zander, *L'arte in Roma nel secolo XV* (Bologna, 1968), pp. 285–88.

8. On the Bussa family, see Esch, "Die Zeugenaussagen," p. 137; on the Ponziani, see pp. 120–22 and 138–40, and "Tre sante," pp. 101–2.

9. On the events of 1398, see Arnold Esch, *Bonifaz IX. und der Kirchenstaat* (Tübingen, 1969), pp. 240–76, and "La fine del libero comune di Roma nel giudizio dei mercanti fiorentini: Lettere romane degli anni 1395–98 nell'Archivio Datini,"

Bullettino dell'Istituto Storico Italiano per il Medioevo e Archivio muratoriano 86 (1976–77): 235–77.

10. Lugano, *Processi,* p. 239.

11. Ibid., p. 238: "semper vidit b. Franciscam propter humilitatem vestes strictas ex modico panno factas et viles deferre simpliciter factas sine pompa."

12. Ibid., p. 22: "quam sibi Dominus non solum sanguinis propinguitate sed etiam morum et honestatis similitudine copulaverat."

13. Armellini, *Vita,* p. 3: "le quali doi dilettissime cognate stettero insiemi quasi trenta et octo anni in tanta unione et con tanto mirabile amore che infra esse non fu mai discordia né grande né piccola, ma erano de uno core et de una anima."

14. Lugano, *Processi,* p. 176, Armellini, *Vita,* p. 3.

15. Lugano, *Processi,* p. 22: "et aliquando pro elemosinis obiurgationes et obpropria patiebantur."

16. Ibid., p. 83; Armellini, *Vita,* pp. 2–3.

17. As happened, for example, when they offered some poor invalids all of the wine in a small cask jealously treasured by their father-in-law (Lugano, *Processi,* p. 33; *Acta Sanctorum,* March, 2: 92).

18. Lugano, *Processi,* p. 10: "ut ne cibum posset capere nec se mutare de loco"; Armellini, *Vita,* p. 4.

19. Lugano, *Processi,* p. 254; Armellini, *Vita,* p. 22: "et perché la dicta Vannozza era acceptissima al cospecto divino io remansi con essa con più devote persone nanzi lo suo obito, quasi certificato per la sopradicta visione."

20. Armellini, *Vita,* p. 23: "ce fu grande concurso de puopolo. Era lo dicto cuorpo defoncto in tucte genture ad palmare come cera morbida. Et per devotione parte delli panni della decta Vannotia fuoro portati alli puopoli."

21. Lugano, *Processi,* p. 103–5, esp. p. 104: "vix ipsi prenominati testes et alii qui erant ad custodiam dicti corporis, propter ipsam multitudinem et concursum, potuerunt evitare quin omnes ipsi panni fuissent per predictos deportati. Sed tandem aliqui ex eis aliquam partem ex devotione portarunt; et quo toto tempore dictum corpus erat ita tractabile ac si fuisset cera vel si vivum fuisset et nullam labefactionem seu putrefactionem passum, ut solita sunt corpora humanarum personarum; ymo ibidem continue apparebat odor suavissimus ac si in dicta cassa et super ipso corpore fuissent apposita lilia ac rose." See also pp. 257–58: "Presens erat in ecclesia S. Marie Nove quando innumerabiles persone causa devotionis corpus beate Francisce visitabant, ac manus et pedes osculabantur et ipsius vestes per petias devotionis causa deportabant, dicentes ipsam sanctam et beatam propter miracula que fiebant."

22. Lugano, introduction to the *Processi,* p. vi.

23. Esch, "Die Zeugenaussagen," p. 140.

24. Placido T. Lugano, "L'istituzione delle Oblate di Tor de' Specchi in Roma secondo i documenti," *Rivista storica benedettina* 14 (1923): 272–308; see also the register of documents following the introduction to the *Processi,* pp. xxxv–xl.

25. Ibid., pp. xxxvi–xxxvii.

26. Esch, "Die Zeugenaussagen," p. 114.

27. Ibid., pp. 141–45.

28. Ibid., p. 116.

29. Lugano, *Processi* (year 1451), arts. 38–40.

30. Ibid., p. 251: "plures hodie concurrunt nobiles mulieres cives romane seculum relinquentes"; "plures alie nobiles intrarunt et continue intrant sub timore Domini laudabiliter viventes"; "plures numero ad dictam congregationem propter beatam Franciscam venerunt et continue veniunt."

31. Arnold Esch, "Dal Medioevo al Rinascimento: Uomini a Roma dal 1350 al 1450," *Archivio della Società romana di storia patria* 94 (1971): 1–10.

32. In a deed of 28 July 1454 drawn up by the notary Gregorio di Nicola of Segni in which Pietro Millini was named procurator of the "congregation of the blessed Francesca dei Ponziani," Mabilia "uxor quondam Baptiste de Pontianis" was mentioned as "olim presidens dicte congregationis," the former president of the said congregation (Rome, Archivio di Stato [henceforth ASR], *Collegio dei Notai Capitolini* [henceforth *Not. Cap.*] 1684, fol. 91r). See however the chronological list of presidents published in *La nobil casa delle Oblate di S. Francesca Romana in Tor de' Specchi nel V centenario della fondazione* (Vatican City, 1933), p. 167.

33. Mabilia's "conversion" took place while she was suffering very intense pain, which brought her to entrust herself "body and soul" to Francesca. In her deposition at the proceedings of 1453 (Lugano, *Processi,* pp. 184–85), Mabilia declared that, although she had often been urged by the priest Giovanni Mattiotti, her confessor and Francesca's, "to imitate her life and morals, she scorned this suggestion. . . . Then she submitted to the rule of the blessed Francesca and served her devoutly from then on" (Dixit se esse domnam Mabiliam de qua articulatur, et cum sepius monita fuisset per presbiterum Johannem romanum confessorum et patrem spiritualem b. Francisce ut illius vitam et mores imitaretur; ipsa hoc facere sprevit. . . . Deinde regule beate Francisce se submisit et illam devote sempre servavit [p. 185]). The reference to "salutifero fructu" appears on p. 249.

34. For example, all of the Ponziani continued to be buried in the family chapel in the church of Santa Cecilia, and not (as one might have expected) near Francesca's miracle-working body in Santa Maria Nova (Lugano, introduction to the *Processi,* p. viii n.).

35. Vannozza Ponziani's first husband was Mattia Muti and her second husband was Giovan Battista Forteguerri of Pistoia (ibid., pp. vii–viii). The act by which the dispute was entrusted to the two designated arbiters is found in ASR, *Not. Cap.* 1684, fol. 135v (16 June 1455); the loss of this notary's other protocols makes it impossible to trace their decision.

36. Anna Esposito Aliano, "Famiglia, mercanzia, e libri nel testamento di Andrea Santacroce (1471)," in *Aspetti della vita economica e culturale a Roma nel Quattrocento* (Rome, 1981), pp. 197–220.

37. Francesca's confessor Giovanni Mattiotti testified concerning this miracle: "Qui dixit se hoc scire, videlicet, quod contencta in dicto articulo vera esse, audivit dici a dicta domna matrona, quam pro honestate noluit nominare; et tempore quo dicta matrona predicta retulit fuit in presentia supranominati Reverendi Episcopi Commissarii, qui dominus Episcopus Commissarius retulit verum esse quod dicta

matrona, quam etiam nunc idem dominus Episcopus propter honestatem nominare non vult, recitavit ipsi domino Episcopo et ipsi presbitero Johanni, vera esse que continentur in dicto articulo, et quod noluit comparere ad deponendum super dicto articulo" (Lugano, *Processi,* p. 177).

38. Ibid., p. 178. Vannozza was not buried in the Santacroce family chapel in the church of Santa Maria "in Publicolis," but in Santa Maria Nova, the church where Francesca's tomb was located. See the book of the Necrologies of the Confraternity of the Consolation in ASR, *Ospedale di S. Maria della Consolazione,* reg. 1300, fol. 9.

39. Lugano, *Processi,* pp. 287 and 293.

40. They probably descended from "the merchant Gezo," who in 1407 was one of the men who acquired the right to collect customs duties at the port of Ripa (Luciano Palermo, *Il porto di Roma nel XIV e XV secolo* [Rome, 1979], p. 333). Between 1384 and 1405, he also leased houses belonging to the basilica of St. Peter.

41. Lugano, *Processi,* p. 297; the miraculous cure is recorded on p. 320.

42. In 1476 (*La nobil casa,* p. 52 n. 32); 1481 (ASR, *Not. Cap.* 1729, fol. 109v); 1482 (*Not. Cap.* 1729, fol. 143); 1492 (*Not. Cap.* 127, fol. 21); and 1494 (*Not. Cap.* 1181, fol. 463).

43. Lugano, *Processi,* p. 303: "Cum ex peste esset graviter infirma, se recommittendo beate Francisce, quam in vita non cognovit, sed dumtaxat in morte in ecclesia S. Marie Nove defunctam vidit, vovit, si ab illa liberaretur infirmitate, intrare domum b. Francesce congregationis et secundum regulam ipsarum vivere. Et facto voto, videbatur ipsi testi indidisse b. Francescam sibi dicentem 'Filie non morieris' et subito meliorare incepit et successive sanata est. Et postquam sanata fuit domum b. Francesce congregationis in regione Campitelli intravit."

44. Ibid., pp. 327 and 329. The second miracle for Angelozza came about by means of a book of hours Francesca had used during her lifetime, which was placed on Angelozza's chest.

45. *La nobil casa,* p. 52 n. 32.

46. "Ob reverentia Omnipotentis Dei et sue gloriose matris Virginis Marie et ob devotionem quam ipse Cola dixit habere in dictas dominas dicte congregationis b. Francesce ut orent Deum pro anima sua et ob fraternalem et honestum amorem et dilectionem quem et quam habuit et habet erga dominam presidentem eius germanam sororem et ob multa grata et honesta servitia que dictus Cola confexus est habuisse et recepisse" (ASR, *Not. Cap.* 1729, fol. 109v [3 October 1481]).

47. ASR, *Not. Cap.* 1684, fol. 152.

48. On her presence in the congregation in 1476, see *La nobil casa,* p. 52 n. 32; on her presidency, see ASR, *Not. Cap.* 126, fol. 240. For her father's testimony in 1451, see Lugano, *Processi,* p. 222.

49. ASR, *Not. Cap.* 1729, fol. 143.

50. ASR, *Not. Cap.* 127, fol. 21.

51. "Mulieres congregationis et religiose domus b. Francisce . . . in porticu domus residentie dictarum bizocharum" (ASR, *Not. Cap.* 1181, fol. 463).

52. On Gaspare's family, see Anna Modigliani, "Testamenti di Gaspare da

Verona," *Scrittura, biblioteche, e stampa a Roma nel Quattrocento,* ed. Massimo Miglio (Vatican City, 1983), pp. 611–27.

53. For an overview, see Romana Guarnieri, entry "Pinzochere," *Dizionario degli Istituti di Perfezione,* vol. 6 (Rome, 1980), col. 1721–49, which discusses the phenomenon in all of Italy and provides bibliographical references for various specific localities. See also Giovanna Casagrande, "Note su manifestazioni di vita comunitaria femminile nel movimento penitenziale in Umbria nei secoli XIII, XIV, XV," in *Prime manifestazioni di vita comunitaria maschile e femminile nel movimento francescano della penitenza, 1215–1447,* ed. Raffaele Pazzelli and Lino Temperini, Proceedings of the Conference of Franciscan Studies, 30 June–2 July 1982, Rome (*Analecta T.O.R.* 15, no. 135) (Rome, 1982), pp. 459–79; and Mario Sensi's essay "Anchoresses and Penitents in Thirteenth- and Fourteenth-Century Umbria," in this volume.

54. See Guarnieri, "Pinzochere," cols. 1731–33; Lino Temperini, "L'ordine della penitenza a Roma," in *Il movimento francescano della penitenza nella società medioevale,* ed. Mariano d'Alatri, Proceedings of the Third Conference of Franciscan Studies, Padua, 25–27 September 1979 (Rome, 1980), pp. 447–74; and Temperini, "Fenomeni di vita comunitaria tra i penitenti francescani a Roma e dintorni," in Pazzelli and Temperini, *Prime manifestazioni di vita comunitaria,* pp. 603–53.

55. See Esch, "Die Zeugenaussagen," pp. 145–46, who, however, does not note that she was a tertiary.

56. The residence of this community is indicated in the testament of Rita di Iacobo Coluzia (Rome, Archivio generale degli Agostiniani [henceforth AGA], fondo *S. Agostino,* C. 3, parchment 40).

57. AGA, *S. Agostino,* C. 10, fol. 87, and "Registri dei priori," Dd. 5, fols. 229 and 234. Further information on Fra Cesario can be found in Giovanni Michele Cavalieri, *La sacra cintura* (Milan, 1737), pp. 3–6; and Balbino Rano, "Nostra Signora de la Consolacion y su Archiconfredia," *Anima una* 1 (December 1957–January 1958): 80. In 1454 Fra Benedetto of Montefalco, prior of Santa Maria del Popolo, was named confessor "mantellatarum morantium Rome," "exortandum ipsum ut legeret eis aliquam regulam ipsarum et instrueret eas in cerimoniis ac dedimus licentiam eisdem mantellatis ut possent sibi eligere quemcumque nostri Ordinis ad predictum offium [sic] dominicum" (AGA, "Registri dei priori," Dd. 6, fol. 171). The registers of the priors general of the order record measures relating to a reform of the Roman *mantellate* in 1466, to which I plan to return in a future study of female religiosity in Rome.

58. Lugano, *Processi,* p. 222: "quia ipsam matrem b. Francisce cognovit et pro tali reputata fuit. Nam ipse testis eciam annis XXX ante obitum b. Francisce ipsam b. Franciscam cognovit et secum conversationem habuit specialem."

59. Ibid., p. 241: "quia ipsa testis sibi erat multum familiaris: in domo consororum per quatuor annos ante obitum ipsius."

60. Ibid., pp. 231–32: "sepius vidit . . . presertim in Araceli; tempore obitus Vannotzie et eciam quandam alia vice in orto ipsius testis in Campomartio vidit ipsam per duas horas, genibus flexis, offitium dicens contemplando in extasim constitutam; et postea in se reversa officium continuavit laudans Deum."

61. Ibid., pp. 260 (the sermons) and 253 (article 41): "De continuatione ipsius sanctitatis et fama laudabili et paciencia in adversis et caritate erga Deum et proximum."

62. Esch, "Tre sante," p. 99.

63. On this family see Domenico Jacovacci, *Repertori di famiglie romane,* in Biblioteca Apostolica Vaticana (henceforth BAV), *Ottob. lat.* 2553, part 4, pp. 317–27; see also Pasquale Adinolfi, *La torre de' Sanguigni e S. Apollinare* (Rome, 1863), pp. 94–96.

64. Martin V's bull of 1426 authorizing the translation is in *Bullarium Ordinis Eremitarum S. Augustini,* ed. Lorenzo Empoli (Rome, 1628), pp. 258–59.

65. AGA, *S. Agostino,* C. 3, parchment 9.

66. "Madonna Antonia vizoca moglie che fo' de frate Cesario" was buried in the church of San Trifone. See Pietro Egidi, "Libro di anniversari in volgare dell'Ospedale del Salvatore," *Archivio della Società romana di storia patria* 31 (1908): 192.

67. Lugano, *Processi,* p. 245: "ipsam testem ad amorem Dei et seculi contemptum inflammabant et inducebant."

68. "Vulgariter dicta domus clamidate olim domine Margherite de Martellutiis" (AGA, *S. Agostino,* C. 3, parchment 40).

69. Jacovacci, *Repertori di famiglie romane,* BAV, *Ottob. lat.* 2549, part 2, pp. 873–76.

70. AGA, *S. Agostino,* C. 6, parchment 58; C. 9, fol. 72v.

71. ASR, *Not. Cap.* 1105, fol. 34v. This group was also known as "le Martellucce" or "le Martellate," from the name of its founder: Ottorino Montenovesi, "Chiese e monasteri romani: S. Lucia in Selci," *Archivi* 10 (1943): 91–92.

72. Esch, "Die Zeugenaussagen," pp. 145–46; ASR, *Ospedale del S. Salvatore,* reg. 28, fol. 251.

73. Lugano, *Processi,* pp. 124, 125, and 147.

74. Ibid., p. 122.

75. Ibid., p. 147: "Quedam domna Margarita, de regione Transtiberim, et tertii Ordinis sancti Francisci de observantia, femina utique devota, cum aliquod temporis pateretur gravem infirmitatem fluxus sanguinis, cui non poterit mederi, recommendavit se devotissime huic benedicte ancille Christi. Et dum assotiata aliis honestis mulieribus, licet difficulter tamen devotione eam ducente, visitavit corpus istius humillime ancille Christi in ecclesia sancte Marie Nove, devote obsecrans ipsam pretiosissimam dominam ut deprecaretur dominum nostrum Iesum Christum. Existens vero ibidem in oratione se liberam ab illa infirmitate divina favente gratia sentiit, ac si nullum unquam pateretur dispendium."

76. Ibid., p. 125: "Ipsa Margarita ex devotione dicte domine Francisce, unum pannum quem habebat de pannis quos ipsa domina Francisca induebatur in sua vita, tradidit ipsi Jeronime et dixit: 'impone pannum istum cum devotione super dicta infirmitate, et Deus faciet tibi gratiam.'"

77. Ibid., pp. 128–29: "Sciens dicta Caterina dictam Angilellam fuisse satis domesticam et familiarem dicte domine Francisce, ipsam Angillelam sororem dicte testis, devotione ipsius domine Francisce compulsa rogavit, ut si apud eam Angilellam

esset aliquis pannus vel de aliquibus rebus ipsius quondam domine Francisce, quod amore caritatis sibi concederet, quoniam sperabat quod pro meritis dicte domine Francisce prefatus eius filius a dicta infirmitate liberaretur."

78. In the sixteenth century, this house was known as the monastery of Santa Croce or Montecitorio (Mariano Armellini, *Le chiese di Roma dal secolo IV al XIX,* ed. Carlo Cecchelli, vol. 1 [Rome, 1942], p. 379). Beatrice Cenci was educated in this institution (Ottorino Montenovesi, *Beàtrice Cenci davanti alla giustizia dei suoi tempi e della storia* [Rome, 1928], p. 30).

79. Lugano, *Processi,* p. 187: "Quaedam domna Caterina, de tertio Ordine sancti Francisci, mulier quidem bone vite et honeste, cum quandam gravissimam persecutionem pateretur a quandam persona, quam non licet nominari; que quidem persona ei erat superior in potentia et in nomine; ista vera domna Caterina angustiata et afflicta quia, ut sibi videbatur, non poterat Deo et suo ordini servire ut optabat, tandem devotione ducta ivit ad consilium istius Deo devotissime domine Francisce, et cum sibi narraret causam sue afflictionis, illa anima Deo acceptissima sibi respondit: 'Noli dubitare nec recedas a loco in quo Deo servis, sed habeas patientiam et spem in Deo, quia persone que te persequuntur aliunde persecutionem patientur et tu victoriose remanebis'; quod paucis post diebus factum est ad laudem Dei."

80. AGA, *S. Agostino,* C. 10, fol. 79.

81. Notarial documents are often silent on the reasons behind disputes and lawsuits. On notarial vagueness in recording information about place of origin in their protocols, see Clara Gennaro, "Mercanti e bovattieri nella Roma della seconda metà del Trecento," *Bulletino dell'Istituto Storico Italiano per il Medioevo e Archivio muratoriano* 78 (1967): 162–63.

82. Armellini, *Le chiese di Roma,* 1: 379.

83. *Archivum bullarum, privilegiorum, instrumentorum et decretorum fratrum et sororum tertii ordinis S. Francisci,* ed. Francesco Bordoni (Parma, 1658), no. 44, pp. 95–96.

84. "Ne dictas sorores ullo unquam tempore ad capitulum convocare aut illas molestare seu alias de eis . . . quomodolibet intromittere presumant"; "a sexaginta annis citra sub ipsa regula . . . sine cuiusvis reheprensionis macula ac alias laudabiliter vixisset et viveret"; "levitatis seu vanitatis cause seducte" (Archivio Segreto Vaticano [henceforth ASV], *Reg. lateran.* 474, fol. 140v). For the death notice of Caterina, who died in 1461, see *Necrologi e libri affini della Provincia romana,* ed. Pietro Egidi, Fonti per la storia d'Italia, 44 (Rome, 1908), 1: 425.

85. Lugano, *Processi,* p. 198.

86. *Bullarium Ordinis Fratrum Praedicatorum,* ed. Thomas Ripoll, vol. 3 (Rome, 1731), p. 150; ASV, *Reg. Vat.* 403, fol. 13, cited in Alberto Zucchi, *Roma domenicana,* vol. 1 (Florence, 1938), p. 59.

87. Lugano, *Processi,* p. 271.

88. ASR, *Not. Cap.* 1232, fol. 70.

89. Francesca seems to have kept to the Campitelli district, where the house of the oblates was located, and Trastevere, the location of her husband's house (Esch, "Die Zeugenaussagen," pp. 106–7).

218

ANNA ESPOSITO

90. Stefano Caffaro, "Diari," ed. Giuseppe Coletti, *Archivio della Società romana di storia patria* 8 (1885): 559.

91. Lugano, *Processi,* p. 260: "diversis vicibus ab intelligentibus viris et litteratis dici et predicari publice audivit b. Francescam fore sanctam propter ipsius sanctam vitam et miracula. Interrogata a quibus audivit, dixit quod audivit a magistro Thoma de Regno Ordinis Predicatorum, magistro Mattheo Ordinis S. Augustini, a frate Antonio de Monte Sabellis Ordinis S. Francisci, a frate Iohanne de Capistrano Ordinis S. Francisci publice coram populo predicari ipsam esse sanctam."

92. Ibid., p. 260: "dixit quod ipsa diversis vicibus Senis vitam beate Francisce a sancto Bernardino predicari audivit, qui ipsam beatam affirmavit propter ipsius sanctam vitam, et similiter audivit a frate Iohanne de Capistrano predicari." If we can trust a late biography of St. Francesca, St. Bernardino pronounced a panegyric on her in 1440 (Raoul Manselli, entry "Bernardino da Siena," in *Dizionario Biografico degli Italiani,* vol. 9 [Rome, 1967], p. 221).

93. Lugano, *Processi,* pp. 269–70: "devotione ducta ad visitandum beatam Francescam, eo quod a quibusdam servis Dei audiverat multa miracula de sanctitate ipsius; et cum venisset ad domum congregationis eiusdem beate Francisce; ipsa beata erat tunc in sua cellula orando: prefata vero Bartholomea existens in sala cum sororibus in Christo ipsius Dei famule, cum magna voce plangendo et singultiendo clamavit et dixit: numquid non videtis ea que ego video? Illius vero respondentibus nichil se videre nisi solita, ipsa adiecit dicens: Ego video virgulam auream de celo descendentem super illam cellulam cum liliis aureis circumfusam et ornatam; per quod denotabatur quanto fervore amoris et animi ipsa anima Deo devota orabat sponsum suum." One of her companions, Iacobella de Brunomonte, testified that she was present when Bartolomea came to Rome "causa visitandi b. Francisce, cuius vitam sanctam audiverat publice predicari in civitate aretina" (p. 270).

94. ASV, *Reg. lateran.* 1241, fol. 231v (year 1510).

II

Living Saints: A Typology of Female Sanctity in the Early Sixteenth Century

Gabriella Zarri

All of a sudden, without any preaching or persuasion, throngs of people in the city of Perugia were spontaneously roused to say: "Here's the saint. Here's the saint arriving. Let's go out to meet her." Crowds of men, women and children hastened to greet her and accompanied her into the city of Perugia with great rejoicing and celebration.

Bontempi, Legenda volgare di Colomba da Rieti

Recent essays have indicated the insights that might be gleaned from studying early modern saints as a significant presence in a world that accorded them a particular social role and assigned them a cultural value as models for imitation.[1] The saint was a familiar figure in the daily experience of early modern society, the expression of a potent sacral creativity, and the product of a cultural setting that recognized in the saint elements that made him or her the embodiment of the current religious ideology. Forged in the imitation of Christ and earlier saints to become, in their turn, a "mirror" for their contemporaries, these charismatic objects of veneration appear to us in an image doubly deformed, refracted through two lenses: the hagiographic stereotypes that presumably served as their inspiration, and the new models that they themselves created. The storehouse of religious images and the reality of spiritual experience combined to form a representation in which historical elements lost their distinctive shape, blurring into the standard pattern of hagiographic legends and making way for a new reality: the "saint in the eyes of others."[2] The unique way of life or particular charismatic gifts of these devout individuals attracted the attention of more or less numerous groups of followers, while their ability to work miracles won them popular fame. As a reference point for large segments of the populace, they assumed a prominent place in the political and social equilibrium of their communities, competing with other powers, such as medical and magical talents, which always yielded before their miracle-working capacities. The saint was no longer simply a model to be imitated, but a singularly effective "social operator."

With these premises in mind, I intend to analyze the relationship between certain "holy women" and their society, moving from the legends of their lives to the cultural setting that produced them and from whatever contemporary canonization proceedings survive to the social groups interested in promoting their cults. Finally, I will attempt to sketch the typology of early sixteenth-century holy women that is presented by the hagiographic legends.[3]

While various studies have considered medieval and Counter-Reformation saints from this perspective, I think it will be useful to examine here some early sixteenth-century figures who seem to epitomize the spiritual tensions, structural transformations, and social crisis of early modern Italy.[4] When the economic and demographic expansion of the late fifteenth century had been broken and in some cases shattered beyond repair by the Wars of Italy, which, with their train of famines and epidemics, awakened social tensions and helped deepen the rift between prospering cities and a countryside laboring under harsh taxation, popular piety sought protection and security in miracles while ecclesiastical institutions, torn between restoring the old ways and welcoming new models of religious life, remained locked in a long struggle with the Protestant Reformation. In an arc of time roughly corresponding to the Wars of Italy, laypersons and members of religious orders who evoked the pauperistic tradition, such as the preachers of penitence, roused throngs and inspired spontaneous cults, while charismatic figures endowed with extraordinary powers became the center of attention for entire cities, revealing a popular concept of austere sanctity that found its embodiment in the absolute poverty of hermits or the penitential practices and protracted fasts of female mystics.[5] Other models of religious life thus took their place alongside the ideal of monastic life, traditionally presented by the church as the highest form of perfection: the eremitic life was not only a popular image of sanctity, but the actual choice of spiritual aristocrats;[6] while the apostolic life and the example of the early church became the reference point for new lay religious movements that worked actively in the social arena and pursued perfection in this world by combining the active and contemplative lives.[7]

Even as these models of religious life resurfaced in the early sixteenth century in response to the difficult social and ecclesiastical situation, and martyrdom as the supreme sign of sanctity gained fresh currency as a consequence of the Wars of Religion and the acts of violence suffered by missionaries, the monastic model continued to play an important role in the church.[8] In fact, the reorganization of the religious orders resulting from the Observant movement and the reaction of the Tridentine church to the Protestant Reformation tended to reaffirm the status of monastic life as the highest state of perfection—so much so that all expressions of sanctity (apart from the saintly bishop, updated to fit the post-Tridentine model of the ideal prelate) were set in the framework of monastic institutions and religious orders.[9] But this development was the resolution of the tangled cross-currents of the early sixteenth century, in which the blossoming of spontaneous cults and cults promoted by princes and members of religious orders was further complicated by the theological debate on the saints provoked by the Reformation—a debate that eventually left its imprint on the post-Tridentine church's very conception of sanctity and on the reform of the canonization process.[10] In this essay, I do not intend to scrutinize the issues at stake in the theological debate or to explore the spirituality of the figures discussed.[11] Rather, limiting my analysis to those early-sixteenth-century "holy women" who became objects of devotion during their lifetimes or immediately after their deaths, I will attempt to answer some fundamental questions concerning the social significance of the public reverence accorded to certain devout women whom their contemporaries called "living saints."

"There arrived in Ferrara a nun who is a living saint," noted an anonymous local chronicler on 7 June 1500. "It is said that she received communion daily from an angel and this communion was her only sustenance."[12] Summoned to Ferrara by Ercole I d'Este, who had previously succeeded in wrenching from Viterbo the stigmatic Lucia of Narni, this "saint" joined the ranks of devout nuns in Ferrarese convents who passed their days praying for the prince and his city.[13] The Perugian chronicler Matarazzo also emphasized the intercessory function of charismatic women, when he indicated the reasons for the popular devotion for Colomba of Rieti.[14] But these female mystics possessed another attribute that increased their importance and explains the great interest they attracted: their gift of prophecy and power of insight. While images or relics could act as intercessors and purveyors of thaumaturgic powers, the prophecies and revelations of the "living saints" assured them an irreplaceable political and social role.[15] Thus Colomba of Rieti and many other emulators of Catherine of Siena became counselors to princes, while astute noblewomen were able to uncover political secrets by feigning saintliness.[16]

While prophecies and revelations were a characteristic feature of the cult of the living saints, they were not in this period an exclusive prerogative of women. I have already mentioned the cults that formed around hermits and preachers of penitence, in a historical setting in which many popular prophecies were even recited in town squares by wandering storytellers.[17] However, there is no question that the number of charismatic women known for their prophetic gifts swelled in the first half of the sixteenth century. On the one hand, this phenomenon suggests a broader understanding of women's roles in a society that was particularly receptive to their contribution in the social and ecclesiastical arenas; on the other, it indicates the particular attention accorded to certain powers that were held to be typically female.[18] Indeed, prophecy and mysticism have their place in wider debates concerning the status of women, though in this essay I can merely indicate some subjects as deserving further investigation.

The extraordinary number of women reputed to be saints in sixteenth-century Italy was pointed out at the end of the century by the Oratorian Tommaso Bozio, who marveled that there existed "so many women in a single time and province, adorned with such gifts of divine inspiration . . . as in this our Italy alone," adding that since the era of Constantine there had never been such a potent concentration of female sanctity in one time and place.[19] Bozio's intentions as an apologist might lead us to think he had exaggerated the extent of the phenomenon, which he interpreted in Counter-Reformation terms; but we can note instead that his catalog of blessed women is far from complete, given the number of devout women known for their sanctity in the early Cinquecento.

We still lack a complete list of the blessed men and women who were the object of local cults before the establishment of the Congregation of Rites, and evidence of popular cults that were opposed by ecclesiastical authorities comes to light only haphazardly. However, the quantitative information we do possess about people who, having died in odor of sanctity, received uninterrupted devotion and obtained institutional recognition allow us to point to this female presence as one of the most significant facts of the period between the last decade of the fifteenth century and the middle of the sixteenth.[20] What is more, various studies and documents show that other nuns, mystics, and visionaries had a reputation for sanctity at the time, even if their cults, transmitted through little-known hagiographic texts, were never approved by the church. This evidence allows us to add to the already lengthy list of devout women who were officially recognized as beatified, and also raises the question of why cults that formed around female "saints" who had enjoyed widespread fame during their lifetimes failed to spread and were even, in some cases, suppressed. Here I will consider their hagiographic legends as a further expression of interest, on the part of both ordinary people and religious and intellectual circles, in the "living saints" whose social and cultural role I intend to explore.

Among the female figures who were renowned for their sanctity in the early sixteenth century, I have selected for study those whose cults began during their lifetimes or immediately after their deaths and were promoted through the drafting and diffusion of a hagiographic "legend" or the instigation of initial canonization proceedings. These criteria are met by four-teen "blessed women," of whom five have never received institutional rec-ognition, while two have been proclaimed saints: Veronica of Binasco, Colomba of Rieti, Osanna of Mantua, Margherita of Russi, Chiara Bugni, Elena Duglioli dall'Olio, Arcangela Panigarola, Stefana Quinzani, Gentile of Ravenna, Angela Merici, Lucia of Narni, Caterina of Racconigi, Paola Antonia Negri, and Caterina de' Ricci. My sample excludes both eminent personalities such as Catherine of Genoa and Camilla Battista Varano, whose reputation for sanctity was linked primarily with their writings and their influence on spiritual doctrines, and minor figures whose cults were kept alive within convent walls, spreading only belatedly to an urban setting or remaining restricted to their religious order.[21] With these limits in mind, and in full awareness that an exhaustive survey of local cults could lengthen the list of cases examined here, I still believe that my sample is adequate to open a discussion that is sure to develop in unforeseen directions.

Shining Stars and Mirrors of Virtue

The ancient founders of our illustrious Christian religion were no less wise than [the ancient Romans], since they too erected superb statues and images and built magnificent temples to those captains and first founders of our unsullied faith, and also described their unique works so that those who came after them could and even should reflect on them, and by re-flecting on them would be inspired to follow in their footsteps, and by following them could reach the goal so greatly desired. With this in mind, noting that in our times had appeared that bright and shining star and re-markable image and mirror of virtues, the glorious virgin of Christ Sister Colomba of Rieti (who has enlightened mortals with her resplendent works), so that such a great light might be beneficial to people of all sorts—not only Umbrians, Tuscans, and learned men but all Italians, es-pecially those who are not skilled in Latin—I have erected and built this gleaming statue and lofty triumphal arch, not of white marble or other stone, nor of hard metal, but of everlasting words.[22]

So wrote Leandro Alberti in 1521 as he prepared to publish his transla-tion of the biography of Colomba of Rieti completed fifteen years earlier by his fellow Dominican Sebastiano Bontempi in the monastery of San Dom-enico in Perugia.[23] In his evocation of the ancient Romans and early Chris-tians who honored virtue by proclaiming it to posterity in imperishable monuments, Alberti seems to recognize the deep gulf separating a world in which the virtuous deeds of its heroes had to be recorded in marble from an age that could employ a new medium, no less worthy of being called artistic, which made it possible to build literary monuments that were permanent and reproducible. Thanks to printing, a saint's reputation for "virtue" could spread beyond strictly local or regional bounds to cover the entire peninsula, surpassing in a single stroke the channels of diffusion and mediation that had slowed the presentation or modified the narration of the deeds of Christian heroes. Printing became the favored medium for promoting a cult, casting it in the terms considered most suitable for canonization, or perhaps reinterpreting it in the light of changing ecclesiastical or religious developments. Printing was no less important as a means of transmitting models of spiritual life and devotional practices written in the vernacular for those who, as Alberti said, were "not skilled in Latin." Of course, despite all the translators' efforts at popularization and the impressive amount of literature in the vernacular, the written word inevitably continued to be directed at limited social groups and remained an elitist product that only rarely, as in the case of hagiographic legends, was influenced by elements of popular culture.[24]

As he prepared to publish his translation of the life of the blessed Colomba, then, Alberti displayed an awareness of the cultural and propagandistic significance of the printing press, an awareness shared by the many other monks and friars who cultivated the genre of hagiography. The Dominicans, above all, were active in rewriting traditional legends using what they claimed to be a critical methodology, in publicizing the old and newer saints of their order, and in promoting the cults of the "living saints," even writing the biographies of devout nuns like Veronica of Binasco who were not members of their order.[25] While the Dominicans were not alone in promoting the cults of devout female mystics, being joined in this work by illustrious laymen like Gianfrancesco Pico and by writers from other religious orders, it was nonetheless the Dominicans who compiled one of the first printed collections of saints *per annum,* which was to open the way for the many ponderous compilations of similar nature promoted by the Counter-Reformation; and they were the first to come to the defense of Catholic tradition in the debate on the saints provoked by Reformation tracts.[26]

Among the Franciscans, the most widely diffused hagiographic models, apart from the life of St. Clare, were the legends of two fifteenth-century mystics, Caterina Vigri of Bologna and Eustochia Calafato, whose influence was particularly strong within convent walls; while those women affiliated with the Third Order of St. Francis who acquired a reputation for sanctity were noted for their part in a general movement of religious renewal that involved commitment to social causes or issued in the Capuchin reform.[27]

Of the "living saints" studied here, only a single Franciscan nun, Chiara Bugni, became the subject of a biography that, while remaining within the ambit of the Franciscan spiritual tradition, resembled the legends of her female contemporaries in other religious orders.

Venerated by the people as wonder-working saints and upheld by their own followers as models for imitation, the "living saints" were publicized through preaching and through the drafting of their legends—many of which, however, never made it into print. After the publication of the deeds of Osanna Andreasi (in 1505–7) and Veronica of Binasco (1518), and the abridged translation of the life of Colomba of Rieti (1521), hagiographic production seemed to slow and change direction. The legends of "living saints" that had not been printed by that date continued to circulate in manuscript form in monasteries and among the devout, reaching a wider audience only at the end of the sixteenth century, when they were summarized and adapted to the new religious climate in the hagiographic compilations of the individual orders.[28]

To be sure, in 1524 there were two new editorial initiatives: Ambrogio Catarino's vernacular translation of Raymond of Capua's legend of St. Catherine of Siena, and Girolamo Scolari's new edition of the life of Osanna of Mantua, the *Libretto della vita et transito della beata Osanna*.[29] But the controversy stirred by the latter book, whose reprint in 1524 had to include a justificatory supplement confirming her extraordinary charismatic gifts, indicates the presence of internal resistance and objections—in short, signs of a change of climate.[30]

If the Reformation-inspired debate on the saints helped in the long run to promote a new efflorescence of hagiography, there can be no doubt that at first it effectively discouraged the publication of legends, whose distribution remained entrusted to the traditional channels, and brought greater prudence to the authorization of local cults by pointing out the need for more rigid controls and centralized standards in the canonization process.[31] An analysis of hagiographic writings concerning the "living saints" and the promotion of their cults will reveal this process in action.

Famous during her lifetime for her mystical and prophetic gifts and commonly known as "the second Catherine," Colomba of Rieti was the first in a whole parade of devout women who, inspired by Catherine of Siena's example, led religious lives affiliated with the Third Order of St. Dominic. Born in Rieti in 1467 into the family of a cloth retailer, Colomba arrived in Perugia in 1488. There she gathered a group of young women and widows, and founded a convent of Dominican tertiaries with civic support.[32] When she died in that convent in 1501, she immediately became the object of a popular cult because of her thaumaturgical powers and exemplary life. The story of her deeds and revelations, written in Latin shortly after her death by her confessor, Sebastiano Bontempi, and translated into Italian by the author himself, also contains a substantial list of miracles wrought by the "blessed woman" during her life and after her death—a clear sign that the legend was intended to support the immediate opening of the beatification process.[33] In spite of this, no proceedings were begun, and not even Alberti's edition of the *vita,* which contained evidence that the cult was not purely local, managed to obtain official recognition of Colomba's sanctity.[34] It was not until 1566 that Pope Pius V, in a concession *vivae vocis oraculo,* allowed her to be honored by "simple commemoration" in the convent she herself had founded.[35] In 1626, as a result of Urban VIII's decree forbidding the cults of those who had not been beatified or canonized by the Holy See, the first canonization proceedings were opened in Perugia. These were followed in 1629–30 by a second, conducted by the bishop; and the cult was approved definitively in 1713.[36]

Though she was always associated with Colomba in the minds of their contemporaries, the case of Osanna Andreasi of Mantua was quite different. Born in Mantua in 1449, she lived in her own home as a Dominican tertiary, dedicating herself to charitable works and following attentively the political vicissitudes of the Gonzaga court until her death in 1505.[37] Her legend was composed in two distinct versions by the Dominican Francesco Silvestri and the Olivetan Girolamo Scolari, and both versions were published immediately and reprinted several times.[38] The promotion of her cult was immediate. Thanks to the involvement of the duke and duchess of Mantua, Gianfrancesco Gonzaga and Isabella d'Este, the local cult swiftly won papal approval, granted by Leo X's decree of 8 January 1515, and the preliminary phase of the canonization proceedings opened in May and June of the same year.[39]

The cult of the Augustinian nun Veronica of Binasco also achieved rapid approval. Born in 1445 in Binasco, near Milan, of "mediocri parenti" (her father was a peasant and small-scale merchant), Veronica Negroni entered the Augustinian convent of Santa Marta in Milan at the age of twenty-two.[40] After her death in 1497, she was venerated by her fellow nuns, who had collected her revelations. When these were reworked by the Dominican Isidoro Isolani in 1517 and published the following year, her visions and *vita* reached a wider audience than the small devout circle headed by Arcangela Panigarola and Bishop Denis Briçonnet.[41] It was Briçonnet's intervention in the name of Francis I of France that impelled Leo X to authorize the cult within the convent on 15 December 1517.[42]

Arcangela Panigarola was both Veronica's disciple and the architect of her reputation. Born in Milan in 1468 to Gotardo, chancellor to Duke

Giangaleazzo Sforza, she entered the Augustinian convent of Santa Marta in 1483. There she held office as novice-mistress, vicaress, and finally prioress for many years. Arcangela's revelations nourished a spiritual community that advocated an ecclesiastical renewal based on the prophecies of the blessed Amadeo Menezes da Silva and the impending coming of the Angelic Pope, whom they identified in Denis Briçonnet.[43] Venerated by Gian Antonio Bellotti, the commendator of Grenoble, who collected her revelations, and by the Franciscan theologian Giorgio Benigno Salviati, who wrote her *vita*, Panigarola was revered above all by the French people, such as Denis Briçonnet and his brother, who frequented her convent.[44] When the king of France lost Milan, the spiritual community around this visionary nun dissolved and her reputation faded. After her death in 1525, her fame was revived by Federico Borromeo and again at the end of the seventeenth century by Ottavio Inviziati; but her cult, which was restricted to a social and cultural elite and only feebly rooted in its civic environment, was never institutionally recognized.[45]

Chiara Bugni earned her reputation some years earlier. Born in Venice to a noble family in 1471, at the age of eighteen she entered the Ospedale del Santo Sepolcro, a hospice run by a group of female Franciscan tertiaries that lodged pilgrims on their way to the Holy Land. In 1499 the hospice became a cloistered convent; Chiara was named prioress in 1504 and continued to hold that office for seven years.[46] Her fasts, ecstasies, and miracles prompted the pope to commission Cardinal Domenico Grimani, the protector of the Franciscan order, to visit her convent in 1507.[47] Venerated by the Kabbalist theologian Francesco Zorzi, who collected her revelations and wrote a first draft of her legend, Bugni probably aroused suspicion because of the prodigious deeds ascribed to her.[48] In 1511 she was deposed from the office of prioress and threatened with expulsion from the order. She lingered in obscurity until her death in 1514, but her reputation for sanctity survived in pious Venetian circles, and early in the seventeenth century Bartolomeo Cimarelli circulated her biography.[49] However, her cult never acquired a civic dimension; and unlike the Benedictine Eufemia Giustiniani, who was invoked during the plague in the sixteenth century, Bugni did not enjoy a postmortem reputation as a miracle worker.[50]

In the first decade of the sixteenth century, the "living saint" par excellence was Lucia Broccadelli of Narni, who bore visibly on her body the stigmata of Christ.[51] Born in 1476 to a noble family of Narni, Lucia married and entered the Third Order of St. Dominic in Viterbo. Her stigmata aroused veneration in Viterbo and attracted the attention of Duke Ercole I d'Este of Ferrara, who brought her to his city to head a convent of tertiaries and publicized her reputation throughout Europe. Lucia's fame was inextricably linked to her stigmata, and their mysterious disappearance cast a pall of suspicion over her sanctity; she was stripped of her priorship and confined to her convent, where she lived in obscurity for another forty years. Lucia's death in 1544 did not spark an immediate revival of her civic cult. But the memory of the popular devotion she had inspired remained alive within the convent walls, and the Dominican Arcangelo of Viadana collected depositions concerning her cult, which were summarized by Razzi in 1577 and published by Marcianese in 1616.[52] During the first half of the seventeenth century, Lucia's civic cult was thus rekindled, to win definitive approval from the Congregation of Rites in 1710.[53]

Widely known and venerated during her lifetime for the ecstasies in which she relived the Passion of Christ, Stefana Quinzani replaced Osanna Andreasi in the role of adviser to the Gonzaga, but she did not have the same fortune after her death.[54] Born in 1457 to a poor family in Orzinuovi, near Brescia, she resided in Crema from 1473 to 1500; it was there that she began to suffer the pains of the Passion every Friday, as two formal documents signed by authoritative witnesses attest. She died in Soncino on 2 January 1530, in the convent of Dominican tertiaries she founded, leaving to her confessors the record of her visions and revelations. They drafted a Latin legend of her life, which was the basis of two vernacular versions that circulated in manuscript form within the order; but Stefana's reputation depended essentially on Serafino Razzi's 1577 compendium of the manuscript legends.[55] Stefana was certainly venerated even outside the Dominican order, since the Oratorian Tommaso Bozio numbered her among those who enjoyed particular gifts from God, but her cult was recognized only in 1740.[56]

Caterina Mattei of Racconigi met with a similar fate. Born in 1486 to an artisan family of modest economic means, Caterina was a silk weaver who became a Dominican tertiary in 1513, living first in her own house and then with two other tertiaries, Sister Osanna and Sister Colomba. On the death of Claudio, lord of Racconigi, in 1523, she was exiled to Caramagna, where she died in 1547.[57] Venerated for her gifts as a mystic and prophet, she left a record of herself in the *vitae* written by her confessors and revised by Gianfrancesco Pico while she was still alive.[58] But unlike Stefana Quinzani, Caterina of Racconigi was immediately proposed as the object of a public cult, and the documentation necessary for official approval began to be gathered only three years after her death.[59] The cause won the support of the dukes of Savoy and the bishop of Saluzzo, Bartolomeo Ancina, who worked to obtain her beatification at the end of the sixteenth century. But unexpected events or conflicts of interest kept the dukes of Savoy from following through with their plans, and Caterina was not honored with papal approval until 1807.[60]

While the humble female tertiaries whose entire lives had been a continuation of the teachings of Catherine of Siena were dying off one by one, a young Dominican nun was making a name for herself for ecstasies, visions, and mystical phenomena that made her every bit the equal of the holy tertiaries of the older generation. Caterina de' Ricci, born in 1522 to a noble family and equipped with a better education than the average person, initially attracted notice for the miraculous healing she obtained through Savonarola's intercession in 1540, but soon after that she began having mystical experiences and received the stigmata.[61] Immediately surrounded by the veneration of gentlewomen and confessors who began to publicize her raptures and revelations in 1542, Caterina became a focus of attention within her order, which rediscovered in her many of the traits that had characterized the living saints of the early Cinquecento. Caterina de' Ricci, who died in 1590 after serving as prioress of the convent of San Vincenzo in Prato for forty-four years, was thus a transitional figure between the hagiographic model of the early decades of the sixteenth century, patterned on St. Catherine of Siena, and the ideal nun of the Tridentine reform.[62] For this reason, I shall consider here only the early legends of her life, written between 1542 and 1555.[63]

The legend of Elena Duglioli, born in 1472, claims that she was the daughter of the Turkish emperor Mahomet; destined to convert Constantinople, she was carried off to Bologna by angels. After her marriage in 1487 to the Bolognese nobleman Benedetto dall'Olio, Elena supposedly lived as a virgin, dedicating herself to charitable works.[64] So renowned in her lifetime that she was cited as an example of chastity and so venerated after her death in 1520 that she attracted the attention of Pietro Aretino, Elena Duglioli dall' Olio owed the fostering of her cult to the canon regular Pietro of Lucca.[65] It was he who summarized her life story in a vernacular legend (later expanded by an unknown author) and addressed a letter to Pope Leo X setting forth her marvelous deeds and requesting that canonization proceedings be opened.[66] However, some of the miraculous deeds for which she was extolled were controversial, and the cause of her beatification was championed by neither the city nor a religious order.[67] As a result, the cult of Elena Duglioli, who was listed among the "blessed" in sixteenth-century catalogs of Bolognese saints, did not win official recognition until three centuries after her death.[68]

Margherita Molli, who was born in Russi in 1442 and died in Ravenna in 1505, was noted for her life of prayer and penitence. Blind from childhood, she spent her life in Russi and Ravenna in the homes of family and friends until one of her followers, Lorenzo Orioli, acquired a house for her. She founded a confraternity whose rule is attributed to her. Gentile Giusti was born in Ravenna in 1471; around 1496 she married a shoemaker from the Veneto, to whom she bore two children. She knew Margherita, whom she claimed as her spiritual mother, and after the death of her husband and her younger child (the other son, Leone, became a priest), she sponsored in her own house a spiritual circle that brought together priests and laity. Gentile welcomed the priest Girolamo Maluselli into her home and through him became the inspiration for a congregation of regular priests, which received canonical approval a few years after her death in 1530. Neither Margherita of Russi nor Gentile of Ravenna has yet been honored with the approbation of the Holy See, but their cases were the subject of preliminary beatification hearings in 1537. Their reputation for sanctity is primarily due to the propagandistic efforts of the canon regular Serafino of Fermo, and to the pressure exerted by Federico Gonzaga, duke of Mantua, to initiate beatification proceedings, which were opened during the pontificate of Paul III.[69] These proceedings reveal the papacy's growing caution about confirming local cults. While in the cases of Osanna and Veronica a papal brief acknowledging their cults preceded the opening of the inquest into the sanctity of their lives, in the case of Margherita and Gentile the investigation of their lives, virtues, and miracles was made a prerequisite for considering their beatification, and the investigation did not provide sufficient justification for a papal brief approving the cult.[70] With the failure of this attempt to obtain official recognition of the sanctity of the two devout women from Ravenna, their fame remained dependent on the spiritual writings of Serafino of Fermo and the institutional memory of the congregation of secular clergy they had inspired.[71]

The legends of Margherita and Gentile presented an example of lay religious life notably different from that of the "blessed women" mentioned previously, and this attempt to win public recognition and direct the attention of the faithful toward a new type of sanctity proved abortive. However, other women who followed a spiritual direction similar to theirs did manage to attract the attention of much larger circles of devout people.

Angela Merici was close to Osanna Andreasi and Stefana Quinzani and probably knew of Chiara Bugni's reputation for sanctity, but she distrusted flamboyant forms of mysticism. Her cult and her saintly reputation were linked instead to her charitable activities and the manner in which she institutionalized them.[72] Many cities invited her to organize their hospital services, and in so doing she devised a new form of female religious life. On her death in 1540, she left a large number of followers who continued the work she had begun, and some critics who questioned the suitability of such a religious organization for women.[73] But the cult promoted by her disciples met with a broad consensus, and the preliminary information hearings concerning her beatification opened in 1568, providing the essential data for her first *vita*.[74]

The "divine mother" Paola Antonia Negri was one of the most controversial female figures with a cult in the first half of the sixteenth century. Born in Castellanza (Gallarate) in 1508, Virginia Negri associated herself in 1530 with Countess Ludovica Torelli and professed vows in the congregation of the Angelic Sisters of St. Paul with the name of Paola Antonia. In 1536 she became novice-mistress, and later she was sent to Vicenza and Padua to reform the convents there. A faithful interpreter of the teachings of Battista of Crema, she enjoyed great repute in her congregation, and from 1539 she was venerated for her prophetic gifts and religious teachings by a large group of devout persons with close ties to the Barnabites, including Serafino of Fermo.[75] She settled in Venice in 1548, but three years later the civil authorities of Venice censured her conduct and banned her from their territories.[76] Within her own congregation, too, Negri was the object of attacks: after an apostolic visit in 1552, she was compelled to enter a cloistered convent of Poor Clares, and she did not emerge from this forced isolation until a few months before her death in 1555. Her cult, however, did not die out, and even many years after her death her teachings were being circulated and her legend was reprinted with the approval of a long list of authorities.[77] Although at the beginning of the seventeenth century Negri was considered blessed by the same Venetian circles that had rejected her during her lifetime, the continuation of her cult was decisively compromised by the opposition she had aroused within her own congregation, and the divine mother's reputation for sanctity never had the civic and popular quality that might later have justified the opening of canonization proceedings on the basis of a cult "from time immemorial."[78]

While the debate over the saints provoked by the Protestant Reformation certainly led the Catholic Church to exercise greater caution in approving local cults and reopened the discussions about canonization procedures that would find their definitive solution in the creation of the Congregation of Rites and the dispositions of Urban VIII, even the most rigid Roman discipline is not enough to explain the lack of success of many of the most popular "living saints." Rather, it seems that a combination of various factors was responsible for impeding the full expression of their cults.

From the cases cited above, we can conclude that a prince's intervention was decisive for opening and furthering canonization proceedings. The Gonzaga dukes of Mantua, the king of France, and the house of Savoy managed to achieve their aims, while "blessed women" who lacked this kind of support, perhaps because they lived in peripheral areas like Orzinuovi or in cities that were not directly subject to a princely authority, could not find in their local communities adequate pressure groups. Since saints, with their miracle-working powers and their exemplary values, normally represent an element of equilibrium in society, they can become a means by which the existing authorities create consensus, by displaying their devotion for the saints. This is true for any civic community, but it is all the more true for princes, who tend to reinforce their power by investing it with sacral legitimization. It is no coincidence, as we shall see in greater detail, that the typical blessed women of the first decades of the Cinquecento were court prophets, who were quick to establish a direct connection between political and thaumaturgic power. Obviously, a change in the political regime would lead to the abandonment of any cult too closely linked to it: the collapse of French rule in Milan plunged Arcangela Panigarola into silence; and the consolidation of papal rule in Bologna brought on the eclipse of Elena Duglioli, whose fame had flourished in strict connection with the dominance of the papal legate, while giving new life to the cult of the older civic saint, Caterina Vigri, who was linked to the rule of the Bentivoglio family.[79]

If political power was a decisive element in the diffusion of a saint's cult and in the canonization process, it worked in tandem with the larger circle of witnesses who could testify to the life and thaumaturgic virtues of the charismatic object of veneration. Among these, the authors of the hagiographic legends had a role of particular importance. In the cases we are considering, they either knew the "blessed woman" personally or enjoyed access to revelations recorded by her fellow nuns or confessors.[80] They wrote with the intention of promoting her cult, carefully registering miracles performed during her lifetime and after her death. Except for Gianfrancesco Pico della Mirandola and Giovan Battista Fontana, all were members of religious orders and authoritative figures by virtue of their learning and the offices they held within their orders. They were often joined in their devotion to the "saint" and in the diffusion of her cult by powerful prelates, like Cardinal Ippolito d'Este, Bishop Denis Briçonnet, Cardinal Francesco Alidosi, Bishop Antonio Pucci, and Cardinals Sigismondo and Ercole Gonzaga; and they were always supported by a substantial number of nobles who were ready to testify to the extraordinary virtues of the charismatic women.[81] It is no surprise that the most numerous witnesses to the sanctity of these women were the monks and friars to whom they usually confided their revelations, followed by their fellow nuns and family members.[82] Then came the people they had miraculously cured: persons of more humble origin, but still from respectable social milieux like the artisan class—as was to be expected, given the essentially civic nature of the cults and the procedure followed by the canonization process.[83] Where the common people appeared en masse and made their pressure felt was in the streets, when they prevented a "blessed woman" from leaving their city, or at her tomb, where contact with her holy body gave them access to the kind of thaumaturgic power they were quick to recognize with humble wax votive offerings.[84]

If the existence of a popular cult was a necessary prerequisite for canonization, the fostering of the process remained in the hands of a small pressure group, usually consisting of political authorities and a particular religious order. The failure of some of these beatification processes thus suggests a lack of support not only on the part of civic political institutions, but also within the religious orders that had "constructed" and publicized these "living saints." After their exhilarating initial public recognition, the Dominican tertiaries slipped into obscurity, to be replaced before long by other figures, like Caterina de' Ricci, who brought more prestige to the order and better suited the new religious climate. The death in 1522 of Pietro of Lucca, the principal promoter of the sanctity of Elena Duglioli, marked a sudden break in the fortunes of that devout woman, unique both in the virtues ascribed to her and her lack of institutional support. The cults of Chiara Bugni and Paola Antonia Negri were brusquely truncated by their own religious congregations, which reduced them to silence through enforced claustration. Articulating a spirituality that was to nourish future generations and that already inspired many Christians of his own day, and with the support of a newly formed religious congregation, in 1537 Serafino of Fermo proposed two obscure women as candidates for beatification, even though they lacked the mystical attributes that continued to bring glory to various other nuns. That his enterprise met with some success and won the support of the duke of Mantua and Cardinal Gonzaga (who had been more closely linked with the Dominican tertiary Stefana Quinzani) can be taken as signs of a changed religious climate. It was not just the increased rigor of Rome or the lack of political backing that impeded immediate public recognition of the cults of Colomba of Rieti, Lucia of Narni, Stefana Quinzani, Caterina of Racconigi, and Elena Duglioli. Lukewarm support or even outright opposition on the part of the orders that had promoted their causes also played its part, as did a change in the model of sanctity that the ecclesiastical authorities wished to propose as a mirror and example to the Christian people.

Holy Women and Renaissance Culture

Of modest social extraction, in most cases, and perhaps illiterate, but always accompanied by confessors and secretaries who interpreted and transcribed their revelations and sent their letters and messages, the "living saints" emerged from anonymity and attracted the attention of princes, nobles, ecclesiastical officials, and intellectuals thanks to their mystical and charismatic gifts.[85] Persuaded of the supernatural powers of the "blessed women," their biographers depicted them as endowed with divine wisdom: Veronica was taught by an angel, Osanna by the Virgin Mary, and Stefana by St. Paul, who guided her to a spiritual profundity surpassing that of any theologian.[86] Sometimes they attained such expertise that, like Elena Duglioli, they were able to write Chaldean and Hebrew, and "this seemed miraculous in a simple woman, who never went to school to learn her letters."[87] Neither Angela Merici nor Paola Antonia Negri had an education based on books or acquired at school, yet they were consulted by preachers and theologians and expounded the Scriptures.[88] However, their biographers' insistence that the wisdom of these "blessed women" was a supernatural gift did not manage to forestall the criticism and opposition of those who insisted that teaching was an exclusively masculine role. Some even expressed doubts concerning the prophecies of canonized saints like Catherine of Siena and Birgitta of Sweden, in order to underscore their distrust of charismatic women whose virtues had yet to be proven or to silence definitively these women who, as Caterina of Racconigi's biographer was anxious to emphasize, were "destined to save mankind through their salutiferous counsels and examples, and not to preach from a pulpit nor interpret the law from a lectern."[89]

Although some looked on them with distrust simply because they were female, and therefore more predisposed to revelations but also more susceptible to illness and diabolical illusions, these charismatic women were nevertheless surrounded by followers who believed in their supernatural powers and availed themselves of their aid and counsel.[90] They thus assumed the roles of teacher and mother, effectively reversing traditional female subordination, which was reconstituted only in part through their submission to their spiritual fathers.[91] Indeed, strong ties bound these devout women to their confessors, who were not only the repositories and guardians of their revelations, but also judges of their inspiration, charged with discriminating between divine gifts and diabolical illusions. The success of the blessed women hung by the slender thread of the "discernment of spirits," and their biographers concentrated their attention on this subject in order to reassure their readers about the supernatural source of the marvels they recounted and so prove the sanctity of the protagonists of their narratives.

The legends of the female mystics discussed here conform to an age-old hagiographic stereotype that would remain substantially unchanged for centuries to come. Born of Christian parents, from childhood on the future saint feels a calling, which is expressed by her renunciation of the world and intention to serve God alone. She exercises her virtues and combats the devil, and is rewarded by God with supernatural gifts. She suffers persecution, which she bears patiently, to be universally recognized as a saint at the moment of a death crowned by miracles. Within this stereotype, certain traditional elements, such as the mystical marriage and the exchange of hearts, received particular emphasis, while others, such as ecstasies, prophecies, stigmata, and struggles with the devil, assumed a distinctive character in keeping with the spirituality and the sociocultural setting of each saint.[92]

The model of Catherine of Siena was a constant reference point for the lives and activities of many of the "living saints" considered here: for the Dominican tertiaries, of course, but in certain aspects also for women who belonged to other religious orders, like Veronica of Binasco and Arcangela Panigarola.[93] The *vita* of Elena Duglioli, in contrast, was structured around punctilious parallels with the life of the Virgin Mary, while those of other blessed women lacked allusions to a specific saintly model.[94] The evocation of the example of Catherine of Siena, with her prophetic fervor and yearning for ecclesiastical renewal, was one element in a more general movement of reform whose spokesmen included Aldus Manutius; but at the same time it helped to define in social and ecclesiastical terms these female figures of the early decades of the Cinquecento.[95]

The modest social origin of many of the "living saints" explains in part their failure to enter nunneries and their preference for affiliation with the Third Orders of penitence.[96] But there were also more strictly spiritual reasons for their refusal to enter convents: a preference for the mixed life, held to be superior to the cloistered life if not to the contemplative one; their sense of having a social and ecclesiastical mission. When Osanna "could not devote herself to outstanding works and contemplation as she desired, because of the crowds of people," Christ responded that "such works of charity are dearer and more pleasing to him than any contemplation" and declared that he had "chosen her to do this for the salvation of souls, and for this reason he never wanted her to enter a convent . . . so that she might be a mediator for the salvation of souls," and he urged her to pray for Italy, which was "menaced by a great calamity."[97] Stefana Quinzani, who had long led an exclusively contemplative life, received an equally peremptory command from God: "My daughter, I would rather that you exert yourself and lead an active life, because the life that incorporates both activity and contemplation is more perfect." From then on Stefana began to "visit the sick and the suffering and devote herself to the active life, which she did until her death."[98] Christ showed Caterina of Racconigi a multitude of people who needed to be led back to the faith, saying: "My daughter, behold the many sinners, both male and female, you are destined to restore to me; if I had allowed you to enter some convent as you wished, I would have lost them and you would not have won such glory in heaven."[99] Elena Duglioli and Gentile of Ravenna shared this same model of the mixed life: both were equally famous for their intense lives of prayer and for their charitable works, in harmony with the spirituality of the Oratories of Divine Love and similar confraternities that sprang up in various Italian cities in the early decades of the sixteenth century; and the spirit that animated Angela Merici was no different. The serious political and social crisis then rocking Italy, the wars tearing it apart, bringing in their wake famines and epidemics, created ample opportunities for individual initiative: Stefana gave shelter to orphans, while Elena, whose social origins sensitized her to the problems of fallen nobles, worked to found the confraternity of the Shamefaced Poor and raised dowries for poor girls, and Gentile assisted the plague-stricken.[100] And it is important to note the markedly lay character of this spiritual orientation—in what may be a polemic for the perennially invoked reform of the church, Stefana Quinzani's biographer has St. Paul exclaim, "Oh how many laypeople surpass the religious in perfection!"—which allowed even married women to be proposed as models of sanctity.[101] It is true that preachers sang Elena Duglioli's praises for remaining a virgin in marriage, making her universally known for this and offering her as a sort of symbolic counterpoise to the new venereal disease that had invaded Italy with King Charles VIII of France.[102] But it is equally true that Gentile of Ravenna was juxtaposed with Margherita of Russi as a model for married women, making her one of the last aspirants to sanctity who was neither a virgin nor a nun.[103]

Dedicated to maintaining an active presence in society as providers of aid to the poor and needy, but even more as teachers, these devout women nevertheless owed their reputations for sanctity to the mystical gifts that singled them out. Sparing in their eating, diligent in prayer, and severe in discipline, they lived in perfect abstinence and raptures of ecstasy, repeating in their own bodies Christ's Passion.

Total abstinence from food, "a unique gift, one that truly surpassed the ordinary limits of human nature," was considered to be a sign of sanctity and was sometimes concealed out of humility.[104] Going beyond the traditional ascetic norm, their inedia acquired a special meaning linked directly with the mystery of the eucharist, for spurning all bodily food, these women lived on the eucharist alone.[105] At a time when frequent communion was not only unusual but often actually prohibited, the *vitae* analyzed here made a signal contribution to this practice, publicizing it long before the regular clerics thought to promote it in their sermons.[106] Except for Margherita, Gentile, and Angela Merici, all of the female mystics discussed here were said to have received communion miraculously from God or angels.[107] Moreover, it is certain that the practice of frequent communion was something that the authors of the legends especially hoped to encourage in their readers. The images in the printed editions of the *vitae* of Veronica of Binasco (published in 1518) and Colomba of Rieti (1521) confirm this: both books contain engravings showing angels bringing the miraculous communion to a woman kneeling before the altar. These are eucharistic miracles that place exclusive emphasis on the suitability of frequent communion, in keeping with a general spiritual trend that found particularly vigorous expression in a brief work by Elena Duglioli.[108] Aside from brief mentions in the *vitae* of Colomba of Rieti and Chiara Bugni, apologetic efforts in defense of the real presence of Christ in the eucharist appeared only in the *vita* of Stefana of Orzinuovi, written later than the other two and probably affected by the polemics with the Protestant reformers.[109]

If abstaining from food was considered a sure sign of sanctity, the other mystical gifts that marked these women—ecstasies and stigmata—were no less probative. In 1500, certifying with all the weight of his personal authority the presence of visible stigmata on the blessed Lucia of Narni, Ercole I d'Este mentioned other "deeds worthy of admiration" that confirm the notoriety of the "living saints" discussed here. "In that part of Lombardy under the rule of the most serene republic of Venice, Sister Stefana Quinzani of the Third Order of St. Dominic was held to be a most devout virgin: many things were revealed to her by the Holy Spirit, and rapt in ecstasy she saw many more." Stefana also relived the agonies of the Passion, as was attested by a document whose authoritative witnesses Ercole cited.[110] But the prince's testimony did not stop there:

> Furthermore, in the city of Perugia we heard of the venerable sister Colomba residing there; for several years she had received the eucharistic sacrament not in both species but in the single form of bread, and eating no other food she has miraculously lived now for four years and still lives. . . . There also lives in the city of Mantua the venerable Sister Osanna, of distinguished reputation and considered to be a saint, and in our city of Ferrara several other nuns of the same order who are often rapt by the divine spirit and redolent of sanctity. Moreover, in many other places in Italy we heard of many women who, inspired with heavenly divinity, bear witness to us that our Catholic faith is the true faith and the holy Roman church is the mother of the faith."[111]

Colomba, Stefana, and Osanna are here enrolled in a larger cohort of ecstatic women. Even if their identities have now been lost, these women represented a particular form of communication with the divine that was
exceptionally widespread around 1500.

While it is true that ecstatic experience has been present throughout the
history of Christian spirituality, it is equally true that its expression has been
encouraged or discouraged for a variety of reasons. Under the influence of
Neoplatonism, which favors mysticism and ecstasies, and in a cultural climate strongly marked by astrological studies, magical beliefs, and prophetic tensions, ecstatic experiences took on special importance and
became the object of philosophical and theological analysis. Distinctions
were made between *abstractio naturalis* and *praeter naturam,* and between
ecstasies and raptures.[112] Raptures were asserted to be superior to prophecies; and since it seemed clear that raptures could be caused by illness and
the devil, as well as by God, great care was dedicated to defining the divine
nature of raptures and their effects in order to be able to distinguish them
from diabolical illusions.[113] While the "living saints" were rapt in ecstasy
during prayer and received visions and revelations that confirmed the Catholic faith, women deceived by the devil could only make impious pronouncements against heavenly dogmas.[114] Divine revelations filled our women with
joy and happiness, but left the others depressed and miserable.[115] But ecstasies could also be faked. "A certain woman, in order to win a reputation for
sanctity, feigned rapture from her senses in public." When Osanna exposed
her, first by "a certain interior light" and then by a "heavenly discourse,"
and rebuked her sharply, she repented and promised "never again to commit such wicked deeds."[116]

Supernatural gifts, diabolical illusions, and fakery intertwined in a climate of intense mysticism where ecstasies were considered the fullest form
of communication with the divine. Their surprising effects were described
in terms that displayed the supernatural gifts of the visionary or emphasized
the sweetness of her vision. Often the ecstatic experience showed on her
face, which became beautiful, glowing, and rosy-cheeked like that of a
young girl; but no mystic matched the ardor of Elena Duglioli, whose heart
was "so fired and inflamed with Divine Love that sometimes it had to be
cooled with strips of linen soaked in water."[117] Moreover, heavenly visions
were always accompanied by angelic music, according to a common image
that found its highest expression in Raphael's St. Cecilia, inspired by Elena
Duglioli.[118]

Ecstatic visions were closely linked with pictorial representations of the
divine and the heavenly world. Not only did certain *vitae* contain descriptions of Christ and the devil derived from the most common forms of ico-

nography, but sometimes the blessed women themselves made explicit reference to paintings, as when Stefana Quinzani, at a loss to describe the Christ she had seen, said: "However beautifully he is depicted in the chapel of the prefect of Brescia, the one I saw was far more beautiful."[119] More interesting still, the visions of some of the "living saints" received visual interpretation in the images and pictorial cycles of famous artists like Bernardino Luini and Marco d'Oggiono, who drew on the revelations of Arcangela Panigarola.[120]

If mystical experiences revealed a world of light and were expressed in the sweet language of divine love, they were nevertheless accompanied by constant reminders of the Passion. Their tenacious imitation of Christ led these women to flagellate their bodies and clothe them in horrifying hairshirts; but their fidelity to their Spouse was rewarded with participation in the agonies of his Passion.[121] Just as Catherine of Siena received invisible stigmata, her more modern imitators suffered intensely in unity with their Lord. If Lucia of Narni received bleeding stigmata, Stefana periodically relived the Crucifixion in her own body: "Rapt from her senses, stretched out on the ground, holding a crucifix in her hands, her limbs now contracted, now splayed out, her whole body was shaken as if she were suffering terrible blows."[122] Osanna felt the pains of the crown of thorns and the wounds in the side and feet.[123] Caterina of Racconigi managed "through much prayer to have the wounds concealed," but she could not hide her crown, which Gianfrancesco Pico described in minute detail: "From the top of her head to the nape of her neck there was a perfectly round circle so deeply marked in the bone that the little finger of a child could fit in it, and all along it were raised points flecked with coagulated blood."[124] Every Friday, Caterina de' Ricci relived the suffering of the Passion.[125]

For some these were real and painful stigmata, even if (like Catherine of Siena's controversial stigmata) they were invisible; for others they were simple illusions if not downright frauds.[126] Whatever the case, the bloody wounds of the Lord were a constant lodestar for the spirituality of these holy women, who aspired, like Osanna, to keep the crucified Christ always present, to see "everywhere . . . her Savior reddened by his previous blood, . . . to be wounded with his wounds for his love." Rivers of blood intoxicated Osanna, who wanted to "stay hidden in Christ's holy side" and "place her mouth to his most blessed side."[127] If the *vitae* of the Dominican "living saints," shaped by the model of Catherine of Siena, tended to conceive the imitation of Christ primarily as sharing the extraordinary gift of stigmatization, the blessed Chiara Bugni was in no way their inferior. Like St. Francis, she had in her side an open wound that spurted blood: her biographer Francesco Zorzi saw "this hole as large as a red chick-pea," which he described in detail.[128] Arcangela Panigarola, like the Dominican holy women, suffered the pains of the Crucifixion every Friday, while Veronica of Binasco and Elena Duglioli displayed their devotion to Christ's Passion in other ways: Veronica in the periodic recurrence of her visions, and Elena in "intense chest pains . . . which she, desiring to model herself after her cherished leader Jesus Christ, earnestly requested so that she might secretly share some of the pain of his bitter suffering."[129] None of this, however, is found in Margherita and Gentile, whose emulation of Jesus took the form of patient endurance of debilitating illnesses.[130]

Mystical gifts and ecstatic raptures were only one aspect of the sanctity of these devout women, who from their intimacy with God acquired insight into the supernatural mysteries that they voiced through their prophetic powers. At a time when the desire to know the course of future events fed an interest in predictive astrology, and the expected dawning of the new age favored the spread of apocalyptic prophecies, curiosity about all forms of prophetic insight was heightened. On the one hand, people explored the possibility that divination might have natural causes; on the other, they recognized that revelations could spring from three sources: natural, demonic, and divine.[131] The biographers of the "living saints," convinced of the supernatural origins of their prophecies, sought to demonstrate their authenticity in the face of skeptics and critics and asserted the superiority of divine revelations over astrology. At the same time, they assigned the prophetesses an important political role as advisers to princes. As Francesco Silvestri stated,

> Those who predict future events have always been held in the highest esteem in all nations, because nothing is more pleasing to men than reliable information about future events. . . . Avid for this firm anchor, princes surround themselves with physiognomists, astronomers, and geomancers, who foretell events that they themselves could not accurately judge through their own ingenuity and diligence. Princes put such faith in these men that, even though they know it is impossible to foresee the true outcome of human actions and indeed are often deluded and disappointed, nevertheless because they do sometimes accurately predict future events and discern some signs of future probity and malice, they heed and revere them. No human being can speak with more certainty about hidden and future events than those who gaze upon them in clear and certain divine truth. . . . Whoever manifests future events as revealed by divine light surely cannot err.[132]

For this reason, Osanna became "the heavenly oracle" of the marquises of Mantua; Colomba was consulted by the Baglioni and the Borgia; Lucia of

Narni was carried off to Ferrara on the orders of Ercole I d'Este; Arcangela was heeded and venerated by Lautrec, the governor of Milan; Caterina of Racconigi was an intimate of Claudio of Savoy and the spiritual mother of the king of France; Elena was a guest at the court of Monferrato; Stefana corresponded regularly with Ercole I d'Este and the Gonzaga; and Caterina de' Ricci was visited by the mother of the duke of Florence.[133]

More powerful than the astrologers and able to unmask superstitious fortune-telling, the "true prophetesses" became a reference point for princes, to whom they revealed state secrets and foretold future events concerning their persons.[134] But it was above all in periods of tension or calamity that they assumed political roles of special prominence: after enjoining the powerful to penitence, justice, and peace, the prophetesses offered their powerful intercessory prayers on behalf of the people. Some people mended their ways when reproached by Colomba of Rieti, while others perished unrepentant; but the saint's protection of her people never failed, even when her prophecies, unheeded, could not avert a fratricidal struggle.[135] And if their prophecies indicated that natural calamities like plagues or the horrors of war were caused by sin and should be remedied by conversion, these women's powers of intercession could still shield the people from divine wrath. After repeatedly announcing the scourges that threatened Italy and calling for peace, their prayers succeeded in warding off or attenuating the impending punishment of their cities.[136] The intercession of Colomba and Osanna was responsible for curbing the plague in Perugia and Mantua; the same thing happened in Racconigi.[137] Thanks to Osanna's prayers, the wrath of God was slow to show itself: she loved her city so much that "she asked God to be merciful and inflict all of the sufferings and torment on her own body instead, since she would be happy even to be chopped into pieces and roasted for the well-being of the city of Mantua."[138] Because of the sacrifice of Caterina of Racconigi, who desired to "interpose herself between God's wrath and the afflicted people and for this reason lost her life," a truce was declared in the wars of Piedmont.[139] Stefana, too, was always mindful of the welfare of her city, for which her praises were sung: "Pay heed to whoever says / that this woman is the root / of Lombardy's health. / It is right that we bestow / praise on she who merits it. / She it is who restrains / the wrath of the enraged."[140]

Able to predict the future and furnish princes with useful advice, capable of shouldering responsibility for the defense of a people who sought their help and considered them "heavenly treasures," the imitators of St. Catherine became the potent expression of a religiosity located within the walls of the cities on which their protection was concentrated, making them inseparable from the Renaissance courts in which they operated. In

Perugia, "both the magistrates of the city and the people insistently called on the blessed Colomba's aid" during the plague, "and if any fell ill they came to see her."[141] A similar interest in the welfare of her city is evident in the *vita* of Chiara Bugni, which portrays this virgin as the powerful protectress of the doge and the Venetian dominion.[142] The legend of Arcangela Panigarola, in contrast, focused on the renewal and salvation of the church, even if collecting and diffusing prophecies of a political nature was certainly not foreign to the spiritual ambience of her convent of Santa Marta.[143]

Although they were addressed particularly to the princes as providers of justice and peace, the prophecies of the blessed women did not neglect the church, denouncing its corruption and hoping for its reform. "Oh dearest child," declared Osanna, "how God deplores the state of the church. Alas, how monstrous and horrible it is to see the presence and breathe the stench of so many sins . . . oh how many evils loom, especially against the church, for the age-old and deeply rooted habit of sinning."[144] But the devout women, not content with hurling prophetic invectives from afar, approached the pope directly. Veronica of Binasco went to Rome "on God's orders" to meet with Alexander VI, to whom she "conveyed Christ's message as secretly as possible" and from whom she received public recognition of her sanctity; while Colomba of Rieti sent the same pope one of her visions, which began "to reproach and admonish with such authority" that those present were terrified, "and soon thereafter rebellion against the pope erupted and other misfortunes occurred."[145] But these direct addresses to the head of the church were not enough to bring about reform. A black-robed Christ appeared to Caterina of Racconigi and denounced clerical behavior in Erasmian tones: "My servants are scorned; my churches are despoiled while their palaces are richly adorned; my revenues are not distributed to my poor and to true ministers, but are given to villains and ruffians, whores and concubines; their mules, dogs, and sparrow-hawks are preferred to my honor, my Church, and my faithful servants." Christ had suffered greatly so that the church "could be his unblemished Bride," but his sons have been unfaithful to him and to the church, "which they have trampled underfoot, being impious, partisan, and cruel, hungry for vengeance and human blood."[146] The visions of Arcangela Panigarola denounced clerical corruption in very much the same terms and, lamenting the prelates' indifference toward the people, foretold the coming of an Angelic Pope.[147]

But Christ's warnings, transmitted by these female servants of God, remained unheeded: new visions showed Arcangela "the papal throne turned upside-down"; and Caterina of Racconigi beheld the sword of the Lord, which demands justice, and a "bloody dagger," which displays "great wrath and fury toward the ungrateful and obstinate."[148] Caterina prayed that God "would sent the people rulers and pastors who will be mindful of God's honor and the salvation of souls, so that finally the former light might be restored and spiritual beauty return to the church of Christ, and peace be established everywhere." However, "the ship of Holy Church" was already on the shoals, and the scourge of God at hand: "the Turks will come to Italy, and having devastated it, they will fall out among themselves"; but in the end the little boat would arrive safely in port, perhaps leading to the conversion of all the peoples of the earth.[149]

The looming menace of the Turks, so prominent in popular prophecy, is here presented as a divine chastisement; but more often it was associated with the theme of conversion, as in the legend of Elena Duglioli, the vision of Arcangela Panigarola, and the prayer of Stefana Quinzani for "her Turkish children."[150] However, an incidental declaration in one of Stefana's visions that "even among the infidels many would be saved by her" is not enough to prove that she was particularly interested in the conversion of the "New World," a topic that engaged the attention of two of her biographers.[151]

The theme of reform, so vividly present in Arcangela Panigarola and the Dominican tertiaries, was not foreign to the other devout women discussed here, though it was conceived in different terms. Absent were the prophetic invectives against ecclesiastical corruption, which as late as 1524 inspired Catarino's withering blast at the city of God and the Roman court.[152] Instead, reform was presented as a renewal of one's own life through the practice of charity and prayer, in fidelity to the pope and without the ringing denunciations that the Protestant reformers had made their own—denunciations that must have made the sack of Rome seem like God's just scourge.[153] This event, in contrast, led Gentile of Ravenna to distance herself from all prophetic behavior. As Serafino of Fermo wrote:

> She could not bear talk denigrating the reputation of prelates or priests. Her great compassion was demonstrated during the sack of Rome, whose ruin seemed to make many people rejoice, whereas she wept as she prayed day and night in the sight of God, considering, with her soul consumed with charity, both the sufferings of the victims and captives and the horrendous sins of the victors, the outrages perpetrated on the pope and prelates, the profanation of churches and holy places. Knowing that these things entailed harm for the whole republic of Jesus Christ, she lamented them more than her own losses, just as she loved Jesus Christ more than herself.[154]

Similarly, Angela Merici worked to renew religious life while renouncing all forms of prophetic intervention, and Paola Antonia Negri addressed the spiritual letters revealing her visions to the fathers assembled at the Council of Trent.[155]

If their attitude toward prophecy and church reform distinguished the Dominican holy women from those linked with the canons regular and the new religious congregations, another distinctive feature defined the peculiar character of the followers of Catherine of Siena and the cultural interests of their biographers. In their *vitae*, the traditional theme of spiritual combat and the struggle with the demonic tempter acquired exceptional promi- nence, in evident connection with the growing concern with magic and the inquisitors' commitment to define in theory and combat in practice the complex phenomenon of witchcraft.[156] And there can be no doubt that some of the monks and friars (not to mention Gianfrancesco Pico) who were in contact with these female mystics also had a special interest, whether practical or theoretical, in the world of magic and witches.[157] The half-forgotten Mantuan inquisitor Friar Domenico of Gargnano, who in 1508 led a fierce attack on "the witches, who continually increase in num- ber and do great harm," was in contact with "living saints" like Lucia of Narni and Stefana Quinzani and had a hand in promoting the cult of Osanna Andreasi.[158] Silvestro Prierio, who had direct ties with the ecstatic Elena Duglioli and even became her spiritual director, was also a famous author of demonological tracts.[159] Having stated his thoughts on divina- tion and written the dialogue *Strix*, Gianfrancesco Pico sensed the theo- retical necessity of analyzing mystical phenomena and, after observing Caterina of Racconigi scientifically, wrote her biography.[160] Similarly, Leandro Alberti, inquisitor of Bologna and translator of Pico's dialogue *La strega*, took the trouble of translating the life of Colomba of Rieti.[161] None of the writings of the Dominicans Francesco Silvestri and Isidoro Isolani in- dicates any special interest in the problem of witchcraft, but their *vitae* of the blessed Osanna Andreasi and Veronica of Binasco did not depart from the schema common to the other biographies, in which the difference be- tween devilish illusions and mystical effects was defined theoretically, the criteria for differentiating between diabolical and divine actions were indi- cated, and the blessed woman was portrayed as the antithesis of the witch or the antidote to witchcraft.[162]

The authors of these *vitae* were treading dangerous ground when they set about narrating the wondrous deeds of female mystics endowed with supernatural gifts, since their culture accepted the possibility that similar effects could be produced by opposing powers—by God or by the devil. They thus hastened to mention, in order to refute them, accusations that their heroines were victims of diabolical illusion or practitioners of magic. While Colomba, Osanna, Stefana, and both Caterina of Racconigi and

Caterina de' Ricci were merely considered suspect, Gentile was actually denounced as a sorceress and Paola Antonia Negri was accused of being a magician.[163] Faced with the problem of discernment of spirits, the authors all addressed it in the same way, resolving the question by proposing practical criteria. Sanctity could be recognized by its fruits: the saints' virtues, especially humility, were proof of divine action; and their fidelity to the church, expressed in their proselytism and obedience to their confessors, was the surest way of recognizing the presence of the Holy Spirit.[164] But there were also those, like Gianfrancesco Pico, who sought a theoretical solution to the complex problem of the discernment of spirits and found it in the presence of the divine light by which Caterina of Racconigi distinguished true visions from diabolical illusions.[165]

However, identifying the divine light as the touchstone that guaranteed a vision's authenticity did not completely satisfy Pico's theoretical curiosity. He went on to discuss the nature of this light, reaching cognitive certainty only with the decisive aid of Caterina's practical knowledge of the matter:

> Once when I was talking with her about various subjects, we happened to speak about the essence of that light; and I told her about a great theologian who had been illuminated by this light and who, in recounting his experience, told me that he was not certain whether it was an enhanced form of the light of faith or a new and different light. . . . She assured me that it was not the light of faith, but rather a new light to which the light of faith contributed; and they augmented one another, since the new light was of greater intensity and strength while the other was of greater breadth, and together they created a very great splendor in the intellect. To tell the truth, these things were explained with such subtlety by this uneducated virgin that no learned theologian could have listened to her without being astonished.[166]

Although they insisted on the divine nature of these mystics' marvelous powers, the authors of their *vitae* recounted prodigies that certainly did not help dissipate the suspicions of diabolical illusions that surrounded these unusual saints. These women were transported through the air; they passed in and out through closed doors; they were carried to Jerusalem in spirit or in the flesh.[167] Nor can the presence of these motifs in the legends be explained by scriptural references to the ability of spirits to transport bodies— though these precedents do exist and were duly cited as authorities by the biographers. Rather, the context in which they were raised clearly indicates that the cultural frame of reference was the belief in the witches' sabbath.[168] So renowned were the miraculous flights of Caterina of Racconigi that she was called "the *masca* of God," according to Pico, who explained: "People who live in Piedmont use the word *masca* instead of 'witch.' In giving her this name, they meant simply that she was borne by the good angels in the same way that the demons carry witches."[169]

Indeed, Caterina was transported from place to place just like a witch, not only in spirit but in the flesh. There is no doubt, added Pico, that angels are endowed with the same power that demons are generally conceded to have: "And certainly we cannot deny to certain virgins guided by the Holy Spirit a power that in antiquity was attributed to Pythagoras, Abaris, and other worshipers of demons, and in later times ascribed to witches."[170] What witches could do through demonic agency was possible for holy women through the ministry of angels, but the goals of their amazing flights were diametrically opposed: while witches gathered at their sabbath to worship the devil and trample on the Christian faith, the holy women traveled to Jerusalem to venerate the cross and were transported invisibly to various places to convert sinners or perform acts of charity.[171] The "*masca* of God" thus constituted a new sort of being, designed to offset the witch. She was added to a world already crowded with spirits, with belief in witches increasing steadily and cases of possession multiplying. But while the theories of philosophers and theologians helped feed the growing obsession with the devil that the inquisitors hastened to extirpate (after codifying its nature and modes of expression), the authors of the legends—who certainly fit within this logical frame—intended above all to present their holy women as a remedy for the raging manifestation of Evil.

The devil was an immediate reality for these devout female mystics as well. If he occasionally attempted to corrupt them by appearing as an "angel of light" or a flattering tempter, he revealed himself more often in the well-known likeness of a Moor, an Ethiopian, or a repellent animal, and showed his brute force as he joined in violent and no-holds-barred battle with the brides of Christ.[172] Pico was quick to assure his readers that these were not some hagiographical commonplace, but rather real battles that took place tangibly, leaving behind scars, bruises, and "foul and disgusting fumes" and occurring so often that they surpassed in number and intensity all those "which have been written about in the past thousand years (because not all have been described in writing) . . . whether involving the monks who lived in the deserts of Egypt or religious hermits."[173] Though the devil was more aggressive than ever before in history, these holy women were ready for battle: greasing themselves like wrestlers—and, one might add, like witches—they fought heroically and always emerged victorious.[174] They not only won their personal battles, but also acquired such mastery over the forces of evil that they could break spells, liberate the possessed, and cast out demons; even when exorcism proved ineffective, the power of the holy women could not fail.[175]

Victorious over the devil, the "living saints" also worked to counteract the baneful influence of witches. If their thaumaturgical powers usually competed with medical knowledge and the efficacy of medicine, their intervention was particularly helpful during childbirth and in calming the fury of the elements: in these junctures when witches were most feared, the holy women's prayers were most effective.[176] The authors of the *vitae* thus pressed their campaign to demonstrate the superiority of divine power over that of demons or magic, while adding another tile to the mosaic depicting the brides of Christ as the antithesis of witches. True, the holy women resembled witches in their bodily insensibility during rapture, and the test of the needle-prick to which some "living saints" were subjected calls to mind the practice of hunting for the witch's mark. But the pains they felt on emerging from ecstasy served to indicate the divine nature of their ecstatic phenomena, and the gift of tears with which many holy women were honored can be interpreted as a foil to the witch's inability to cry.[177] However, the contrast between witches and holy women is sharpest and most significant in their biographers' insistent references to the perfect chastity of the protagonists of their narratives. Just as witches were symbols of lust, engaging in sexual intercourse with the devil and aiding illicit love-affairs with their own magical arts, the holy women represented and promoted purity, offering freedom from carnal temptations and ensuring perpetual chastity. Elena Duglioli not only renounced her perfectly licit conjugal relations—living for twenty-nine years with her husband "without either of them ever feeling any carnal desire, though both were in good health and fine physical condition, with all of their body parts perfectly formed"—but after (like St. Thomas) receiving the belt of chastity, she conveyed this capacity to others.[178] Like Elena, Caterina of Racconigi and Stefana also received belts of chastity and were freed from temptation, while Gentile and Paola Antonia Negri obtained this divine gift for monks who requested their intercession.[179]

These holy women were not simply the antithesis of witches, whose harmful actions they sought to neutralize: they were also presented as their competitors. Their biographers described the invisible journeys of the devout women, their "obstetrical" powers and their mastery over the elements—all powers that were ascribed to witches—and some did not shrink from including in their accounts objects with strong magical connotations, such as the rings that the brides of Christ received from him in token of their mystical marriage, making them instruments of miracles. Indeed, the rings of Arcangela Panigarola and Caterina de' Ricci were famed for their thaumaturgic powers, while Caterina of Racconigi's ring, invisible to all save its owner, appeared miraculously to two priests and Stefana Quinzani's appeared to one of her fellow nuns.[180]

The ability to make itself visible was not, however, the principal property of Stefana's ring, which consisted rather in the power to drive away demons: "Take it away, take away that ring," cried a devil who did not want to leave the body of a possessed woman; and another complained, "Stefana wishes to cast me out."[181] Moreover, Stefana possessed another ring, given to her by St. Paul, which had these powers and more. With this ring on her finger, she "had no fear of the devil, nor of anyone in the world" and could withstand without collapsing both the mystical joys of visions and the terrible agonies of the Passion.[182] The miraculous effects of this ring fascinated her biographer, who nevertheless did not hide the ambiguity inherent in the object itself, and affirmed that many "marveled that this woman, a bride of Christ, wore this ring, and some murmured about it."[183] Here again, magical and miraculous elements were interwoven in the legends of the "living saints," presumably in order to draw magical beliefs into the sphere of the sacred, but in reality helping to further blur the already thin line separating magic from religion in the culture of early modern Europe.

The Passing of the Living Saints

Enormously popular during the first three decades of the sixteenth century, the "living saints" who followed in the footsteps of Catherine of Siena saw their fortunes fade abruptly after 1530. They had been defined by their political and social role in urban settings and by their contributions to the longed-for reform of the church, and these functions lost their importance when political and ecclesiastical conditions changed. Mystics, prophetesses, and miracle workers, the new Catherines had acquired particular importance in the most difficult junctures of the Wars of Italy, in the years when continuous political upheavals destabilized regimes, sharpened civic strife, and encouraged princes to resort to the prophetic counsel of charismatic women who promised to be powerful protectors of their cities. The year of "universal peace," which brought a reestablishment of order in the Italian states, marked the beginning of the end for the political role of the living saints. The story of Stefana Quinzani's death is emblematic of this change: she died on 2 January 1530, after hearing "the news that universal peace had been declared among the rulers" and singing the *Nunc dimittis*, recognizing the completion of her earthly mission.[184] Only Caterina of Racconigi, who lived and worked in a corner of Italy that remained troubled by wars until the middle of the sixteenth century, retained her role as court prophetess and counselor of princes, a role still evident in the supplements Morelli added to Pico's *vita* between 1533 and 1550. But in general, by 1530 the function of political prophecy was radically transformed, and even popular prophecy had gone into a steep decline. The ecclesiastical authorities themselves, with their numerous and repeated condemnations, helped to stem a movement that demonstrated unexpected vitality and popularity.

In the ecclesiastical sphere, too, the situation had changed radically. In the first two decades of the century, the Catherinian movement had catalyzed diverse efforts to promote the renewal of the religious orders and the reform of the church, as the interests of monks and friars from various cultural and spiritual backgrounds crystallized around these charismatic female mystics. But the advent of the Protestant Reformation led ecclesiastical figures to rally to the defense of their institutions, deflected the attention of many members of religious orders from promoting the cults of the "living saints" to the doctrinal controversy, and inspired increased caution in preaching and in publicizing visions and spiritual doctrines that would soon come to seem suspect.

In fact, the promoters of the cults of the Dominican tertiaries and of Veronica of Binasco (including Sebastiano Bontempi, Francesco Silvestri, and Isidoro Isolani) were Dominican friars of Savonarolan stamp from the reformed convents of the Tuscan-Roman and Lombard congregations, or ardent lay Savonarolans like Gianfrancesco Pico.[185] But members of other religious orders as well, such as the Olivetan Girolamo Scolari and the Franciscan Giorgio Benigno Salviati, were equally avid admirers of Savonarola.[186] The memory of the prophet of Florence remained alive in the Bolognese friary of San Domenico, where Leandro Alberti (whose cultural role and relations with intellectual circles in early-sixteenth-century Bologna deserve greater attention) was active.[187] It is possible that the more obscure authors of the legends of Lucia of Narni and Stefana Quinzani were also followers of Savonarola, but there is no doubt whatsoever that the friars who compiled the legends of Caterina de' Ricci, including Nicolò Alessi and Serafino Razzi, were indefatigable supporters of Savonarola.[188] Although Razzi identified Caterina de' Ricci as the most fully realized of the "new Catherines," he collected and retold the *vitae* of many other early-sixteenth-century women who had replicated in their own persons the exemplary life and deeds of Catherine of Siena.[189] Moreover, the efforts of the reformed Dominican congregations in Tuscany and Lombardy to export their own methods and models of religious life gave an impulse to the internal reform movement of the Dominican order as a whole. For instance, we know that the reform attempted in the Spanish province of Castile in 1509–11 was closely linked with elements of the Lombard congregation and centered on the figure of the visionary Maria of Piedrahita, a follower of Savonarola and Lucia of Narni and a protégé of the duke of Alba, who, imitating Ercole I d'Este, established a great convent for Maria and her numerous followers.[190]

Though undeniably motivated by broader yearnings for ecclesiastical reform, the "Catherinian movement" promoted by the followers of Savonarola came to be configured as the continuation of the work he had begun and the apologetic confirmation of the truths he had preached. However controversial the prophetic figure of the friar of San Marco may have been, one could hardly contest the authenticity of the prophecies of Catherine of Siena, whose sanctity had been canonically approved; and so Savonarola's prophetic tension indirectly charged the "living saints" and flickered from city to city through the voices of these devotees of the friar and imitators of St. Catherine. In this way, Savonarola's followers managed to keep his memory alive and create multipliers of his prophetic pronouncements; but they could not keep the "living saints" from suffering from the growing disenchantment with prophecy that ripened around 1530, nor could they themselves steer clear of the increasingly violent criticism launched at Savonarola.[191] The success of the "new Catherines" had evidently run its course: after the universal peace, the cults of the blessed female civic guardians lost some of their vigor, while prophecies concerning church reform became entangled with the attacks and criticism of the Protestant reformers and with the persistent belief in the approach of the end of time, which inspired theologians and spiritual figures to adopt different attitudes toward prophecy.

But these reasons alone do not explain why the cults of Chiara Bugni and Elena Duglioli failed to find widespread acceptance. Their *vitae* were never published, perhaps because of suspicions on spiritual and doctrinal grounds. Apart from their enthusiasm for the devotion to the milk of the Virgin—a devotion that was ridiculed by Erasmus just a few years later—doctrinal concerns must have prompted prudence in publicizing *vitae* written by authors whose orthodoxy was not entirely certain.[192] The canon regular Pietro of Lucca, the chief promotor of Elena Duglioli's cult, was investigated in 1511 for having preached erroneous notions regarding the Incarnation; but he was known chiefly for his spiritual writings, including the *Regule de la vita spirituale et secreta theologia,* which promised that "by a certain brief form of prayer, a man can by himself, without papal authority, obtain the true jubilee and plenary indulgence."[193] A similar interest in universal salvation underlay some of Chiara Bugni's visions, in which she sought to make public the miracle of Christ's blood, which she had received and collected in a phial for the remission of the sins of all people; and other visions asserted that "faith alone was enough" to obtain salvation.[194] Such statements acquired dangerous resonances after the appearance of Martin Luther; but even apart from that, the legend of Chiara Bugni must have seemed peculiar for its mixture of vaguely symbolic, Kabbalistic, and magical motifs. Still, even if Chiara was silenced as early as 1511, perhaps for reasons that had more to do with the discipline of her order than suspicions about her orthodoxy, the author of her *vita,* the Franciscan Francesco Zorzi, continued to be widely known as a cultivated and devout friar and enjoyed the friendship of leading proponents of Catholic reform such as Gasparo Contarini, Gregorio Cortese, and Federico Fregoso. It was only after the publication in 1536 of one of his major works, the *In sacram scripturam problemata,* that the elderly Kabbalist theologian was censured by the Master of the Sacred Palace, Tommaso Badia.[195] By then, the visionary Chiara Bugni, hailed by Zorzi as the unveiler of esoteric doctrines and bearer of a message of universal conversion and salvation, was long forgotten, though Zorzi's teachings and the fascination of the Kabbala perhaps lingered on, to attract the attention of people active in Venice some twenty years later.[196]

Imitators of Catherine of Siena or "enlightened" repositories of arcane doctrines, the living saints who had been active in the early decades of the Cinquecento thus seemed to have exhausted their purpose. The new type of holy woman that Serafino of Fermo proposed in 1535 as a model for imitation differed from her predecessors: less weight was given to her powers of prophecy and mysticism, and greater importance attached to her virtues.

The Protestant Reformation, the division of Christendom, and the appearance of "visionaries" who claimed to be prophets were interpreted by the canon regular Serafino of Fermo as signs of the end of time: since the time had come to "prepare the throne of the Antichrist," it was necessary to be wary of revelations that could be the devil's doing and to remain on guard against mystical manifestations, "ecstasies, raptures, prophecies, miracles, and other marvels" achieved with suspicious ease and without the constant exercise of virtue.[197] The virtues, especially humility and charity, were the foundation of sanctity. Starting from this conviction, Serafino of Fermo sketched a portrait of Margherita and Gentile of Ravenna that retained some of the features of earlier living saints, but sought to emphasize above all their lives of prayer and charity, pursued in simplicity and fidelity to the church and without flamboyant fervor or miracles.[198] Serafino declared bluntly that "the principal indication of sanctity is obeying God's teachings and conquering all sins," denounced as a "foolish opinion of the vulgar herd" the belief that sanctity consisted of "extreme acts," and argued that "the middle way" was the only path to saintliness.[199] Though he valued virtue more highly than prophetic and charismatic gifts, Serafino was still far from the concept of "heroic virtue" that was to characterize Counter-Reformation saints. His "discretion" or "middle way" pointed toward a form of sanctity that, though inspired by the urgent need to distinguish "God's devout" from the "devotees of the devil," could include a broad range of people, from virgins like Margherita to married women like Gentile and laypeople who lived their faith without belonging to any ecclesiastical institution.[200] Margherita and Gentile, two commoners especially known for their lives of asceticism and prayer, but with numerous followers who considered them spiritual teachers and mothers, were thus offered as models for imitation in a sort of transitional stage between the conception of sanctity prevalent in the early sixteenth century and that of the Counter-Reformation. Angela Merici had a similar place, whereas the Angelic Paola Antonia Negri, whose life of piety was well known to Serafino of Fermo, continued to display the signs of the "visionary" sanctity that was becoming increasingly worrisome to church leaders.[201] The kind of holy woman exalted by Serafino in his *vitae* of Margherita and Gentile seems to reflect the ideal type of sanctity then being elaborated in circles close to the nascent congregations of regular clerics—such as, to cite one noteworthy example, Bonsignore Cacciaguerra's biography of Felice of Barbarano, written to celebrate a virgin dedicated entirely to prayer and eucharistic piety.[202]

To be sure, when Serafino of Fermo proposed his model of sanctity, expressions of ecstatic and visionary piety had hardly disappeared, and could involve both individual women and entire convents.[203] But it is also true that the church leadership was increasingly sensitive to the dangers of the phenomenon and tended to discourage its spread. Catarino now utterly rejected the Catherinian ideal that he had earlier done so much to disseminate: emphasizing the possibility of diabolical snares (to which "stupid little nuns and silly women" were particularly vulnerable) and warning against the recrudescence of mystical phenomena such as visions and stigmatizations, he blamed Savonarola's followers for continuing to cultivate an extremely dangerous kind of spirituality and became a fierce opponent of all forms of visionary piety.[204] The Savonarolans themselves were well aware of the persecution of the Spanish *Alumbrados* and so did their best to distinguish the divine nature of the mystical phenomena experienced by Caterina de' Ricci from the false visions of a nun of Cordova.[205] With Spanish "Illuminism" now openly persecuted, the Italian groups that gathered around female mystics and visionaries would soon come under stricter control as well. Not even the Angelic Paola Antonia Negri, the principal exponent of the doctrine of Battista of Crema (who had himself been accused of being a beghard), could avoid suspicion and persecution. But the groups drawn to these devout women by the charisma of their spiritual motherhood were not thoroughly dismantled until the 1550s. It was precisely in this period that incidents deeply troubling to church authorities multiplied, and many of them involved women: in Venice, Guillaume Postel's esoteric mysticism seemed to bring Chiara Bugni back to life in the person of the humble "Mother Jeanne," while the messianic preaching of Albrisio found an audience in a convent of Poor Clares in Reggio Emilia.[206] At the same time, other prophetic phenomena, linked to Giorgio Siculo and the sects advocating radical reform, were spreading through the Este duchy and the Po valley, intensifying antiheretical repression and sharpening mistrust of spiritual groups with mystical or visionary tendencies.[207]

Once considered beacons of church reform and leaders of spiritual groups that were clearly orthodox, though not yet rigidly structured along the lines of the old religious orders, the "living saints" were progressively held suspect and reduced to silence. The strict cloister that had occasionally been imposed on certain holy women like Chiara Bugni and Paola Antonia Negri soon turned into universal enclosure in convents, preventing the nuns from engaging in any form of social activity and radically limiting their contact with the outside world. The figure of the new Catherine had definitively faded, and even the model of sanctity formulated by Serafino would soon be outdated.

If in the early years of the sixteenth century the ideal of the primitive church had inspired new forms of religious life such as that promoted by Angela Merici, the monastic tradition and the authority of the established orders tended to suffocate this "rule," claiming that it was unsound and full of perils for those who followed it.[208] After the Council of Trent, those convents of women that pursued a religious life characterized by charitable activity, like the Angelics, were forced back into the channel of traditional cloistered monasticism.[209] Indeed, the attack on Paola Antonia Negri in 1552 can only partially be ascribed to doctrinal concerns and suspicions of "Illuminism." Its main impulse came instead from the division within the congregation between those who, along with Negri, wished to remain faithful to the original spirit of the religious institution and those who, adapting themselves to the new era, wanted to introduce substantial modifications requiring that "profession and vows be made, as in other religious and cloistered orders," and that the lay members of the congregation adopt their own habit and rule.[210] In this context, it is obvious that Negri's influence on the congregation had to be reduced: it seemed intolerable that a woman should "give orders to priests," travel from city to city in the company of other women "visiting hospitals and female penitents, who were commended to her care," and have herself called Mother Mistress.[211] Giovanni Pietro Besozzi, superior of the congregation for many years and the principal architect of its institutional transformation, took it upon himself to dismantle the devotion to Negri, alleging the traditional ecclesiastical concerns: doubts about her chastity, suspicions of pride and diabolical illusion.[212] But the case of the Angelic Paola Antonia clearly marks the final phase of a process in which women had figured as protagonists. After the fleeting season in which conditions of political instability and social crisis, in a lively and open cultural and religious setting, had allowed women to play a distinctive role in the political, literary, and religious arenas, doctrinal and social imperatives plunged them back into silence and stillness. For a few decades, women were presented as spiritual teachers because of their mystical capacities; and an attempt was made to delineate a positive female image, offering holy women as an antidote to the witches who beset a world obsessed with the devil. But the order now being restored to civic and religious society demanded a return to traditional female roles and a repristination of female enclosure, leading women back into their homes or enclosing them in convents. In this regard, one argument advanced by Negri's detractors is particularly revealing: they did not deny the value of her charitable and spiritual activities, but concluded that "these things, however good they may be in themselves, nevertheless are not the business of women, who should remain in their houses and leave such matters to men."[213] In the face of such assertions, the invocation of the examples of St. Birgitta and St. Catherine of Siena by Negri's biographer seems anachronistic. In the new age then dawning, the only activity open to nuns was contemplation, which long continued to be pursued in a precarious equilibrium between mystical illumination and diabolical possession.

NOTES

Originally published in Gabriella Zarri, "Le sante vive: Per una tipologia della santità femminile nel primo Cinquecento, *Annali dell'Istituto storico italo-germanico in Trento* 6 (1980): 371–445. Now in Zarri, *Le sante vive: Profezie di corte e devozione femminile tra '400 e '500* (Turin, 1990), pp. 87–163.

1. Gabriele De Rosa, "Pertinenze ecclesiastiche e santità nella storia sociale e religiosa della Basilicata dal XVIII al XIX secolo," in *Chiesa e religione popolare nel mezzogiorno* (Bari, 1978), esp. pp. 80–81; Jean-Michel Sallmann, "Il santo e le rap-

presentazioni della santità: Problemi di metodo," *Quaderni storici* 14 (1979): 584–602.

2. Pierre Delooz, "Towards a Sociological Study of Canonized Sainthood in the Catholic Church," in *Saints and Their Cults: Studies in Religious Sociology, Folklore, and History,* ed. Stephen Wilson (Cambridge, 1983), pp. 189–216; see also Delooz, "Rapport entre saint réel et saint construit: La sainteté comme construction sociale," in *S. Antonio da Padova fra storia e pietà: Colloquio interdisciplinare su "Il fenomeno antoniano"* (Padua, 1977), pp. 421–26.

3. One might well ask whether it is possible to construct a typology of sanctity. Since sanctity is connected to principles based on the Bible and ecclesiastical tradition, it has not changed significantly in theological doctrine and many of its modes of expression have remained constant. Nevertheless, it seems important to analyze historically any variations in these modes of expression, since they indicate changes in the relationship between the social, cultural, and religious contexts and representations of sanctity. On the history of sanctity as "the history of the Christian discourse of sanctity," see Claudio Leonardi, "Dalla santità 'monastica' alla santità 'politica',", *Concilium* 15, no. 9 (1979): 84–97; translated as "From 'Monastic' Holiness to 'Political' Holiness," in *Models of Holiness,* ed. Christian Duquoc and Casiano Floristán, Concilium 129 (New York, 1979), pp. 46–53. On the evolution of a model of sanctity in relation to cultural changes, see Bernard Plongeron, "Sulla madre Agnese di Gesù: Tema e variazioni agiografiche, 1665–1963," *Concilium* 15, no. 9 (1979): 57–71; translated as "Concerning Mother Agnes of Jesus: Theme and Variations in Hagiography, 1665–1963," in Duquoc and Floristán, *Models of Holiness,* pp. 15–35.

4. For the Middle Ages, see especially *Agiografia altomedioevale,* ed. Sofia Boesch Gajano (Bologna, 1976); André Vauchez, *La sainteté en Occident aux derniers siècles du Moyen Age d'après les procès de canonisation et les documents hagiographiques* (Rome, 1981); and the essays in *Temi e problemi nella mistica femminile trecentesca,* Convegni del Centro di studi sulla spiritualità medievale, 20 (Todi, 1983), and *Atti del Simposio internazionale cateriniano-bernardiniano, Siena, 17–20 aprile 1980,* ed. Domenico Maffei and Paolo Nardi (Siena, 1982). For the early modern period, see Romeo De Maio, "L'ideale eroico nei processi di canonizzazione della Controriforma," *Ricerche di storia sociale e religiosa* 2 (1972): 139–60, reprinted in his *Riforme e miti nella chiesa del Cinquecento* (Naples, 1973), pp. 257–78; Gabriele De Rosa, "Sainteté, clergé, et peuple dans le Mezzogiorno italien au milieu du XVIIIème siècle," *Revue d'histoire de la spiritualité: Revue d'ascétique et mystique* 52 (1976): 245–64; Jean-Michel Sallmann, "Image et fonction du saint dans la région de Naples à la fin du XVIIe et au début du XVIIIe siècle," Mélanges de l'Ecole française de Rome, Moyen Age–temps modernes (henceforth *MEFRM*) 91 (1979): 827–74.

5. In addition to the sources and bibliography cited by Giovanni Miccoli, "La storia religiosa," *Storia d'Italia,* vol. 2, *Dalla caduta dell'impero romano al secolo XVIII* (Turin, 1974), pp. 966–75, see Adriano Prosperi, "Gian Battista da Bascio e la predicazione dei romiti alla metà del '500," *Bollettino della Società di studi valdesi*

138 (1975): 69–79; and Sanuto's report of a Servite friar who came to Venice in 1507 and "prophesized many things from the pulpit, menacing Venice with plagues and wars with the Turks and saying he was a prophet, so that he began to attract great crowds of people" (Marino Sanuto, *I diarii,* vol. 7, ed. Rinaldo Fulin [Venice, 1882], col. 40).

When the Dominican tertiary Fra Giorgio Alemanno died in Rome in 1502, "maximus fuit ad eum populi concursus et maxima pressura gentium: multi fratres stabant iuxta eum super et iuxta altare defendentes pressuram ne unus alium supprimeret." The friar was credited with "miracula facta de claudis et aliis infirmis sanitati restitutis" (*Jòhannis Burchardi liber Notarum ab anno 1483 usque ad annum 1506,* ed. Enrico Celani, in *Rerum Italicarum Scriptores* 32, part 1, vol. 2 (Città di Castello, 1911), p. 331. An equally large crowd gathered around the body of Matteo of Bascio, who died in Venice in 1552: "and if the religious canons had not hastened to remove the blessed body, it would have been stripped practically naked by the people who snatched at his miserable robe" (Prosperi, "Gian Battista da Bascio," p. 71).

The chronicler Matarazzo considered Colomba of Rieti's abstinence to be one of the reasons for the popular devotion she inspired: "and she followed the path and the footprints of St. Catherine of Siena and never ate or drank except for, on rare occasions, some jujubes" ("Cronache e storie inedite della città di Perugia dal MCL al MDLXIII," *Archivio storico italiano* 16, part 2 [1851]: 5).

6. I am referring to the well-known case of the Venetian nobles Paolo Giustiniani and Pietro Querini, on whom see Hubert Jedin, "Contarini und Camaldoli," *Archivio italiano per la storia della pietà* 2 (1953): 51–117, and Giuseppe Alberigo, "Vita attiva e vita contemplativa in un'esperienza cristiana del XVI secolo," *Studi veneziani* 16 (1974): 177–225.

7. Paolo Prodi, "Vita religiosa e crisi sociale nei tempi di Angela Merici," *Humanitas,* new ser., 19 (1974): 307–18.

8. At the end of the sixteenth century, the Oratorian Tommaso Bozio gave great prominence to martyrdom, naming hundreds of priests, monks, friars, and laypeople killed or imprisoned during the wars of religion or in the course of missionary activities (Tommaso Bozio, *De signis ecclesiae Dei libri XXIIII* [Rome: Ex bibliotheca Jacobi Tornerii, 1591], pp. 553–64). On Bozio, see Piero Craveri, entry "Bozio Tommaso," in *Dizionario Biografico degli Italiani (henceforth DBI),* vol. 13 (Rome, 1971), pp. 568–71; Vinicio Abbundo, "Note su Tommaso Bozio eugubino," in *Filosofia e cultura in Umbria tra Medioevo e Rinascimento,* Proceedings of the Fourth Conference of Umbrian Studies, May 1966 (Perugia, 1967), pp. 567–91.

9. See Pierre Delooz, *Sociologie et canonisations* (Liège, 1969); and Delooz, "The Social Function of the Canonization of Saints," in Duquoc and Floristán, *Models of Holiness,* pp. 14–24, which discusses the relationship between lay and clerical saints. On the Observant movement, see Mario Fois, "L' 'Osservanza' come espressione della 'Ecclesia semper renovanda,'" in *Problemi di storia della Chiesa nei secoli XV/XVII* (Naples, 1979), pp. 13–107.

10. On the historical evolution of canonization and beatification procedures

and the establishment of the concept of heroic virtue as a measure of sanctity, see the classic work of Prospero Lambertini (Pope Benedict XIV), *De servorum Dei beatificatione et beatorum canonizatione,* 5 vols. (Bologna, 1734–38; reprinted Prato, 1938–42).

11. On the spirituality of some of the women discussed here, see Massimo Petrocchi, *Storia della spiritualità italiana* (Rome, 1978), esp. "L'estasi delle mistiche italiane della riforma cattolica" (1: 155–81), "I grandi spirituali del Cinquecento" (2: 7–49), and "Dottrine e orientamenti spirituali della scuola lombarda del Cinquecento" (2: 61–109).

12. *Diario ferrarese dall'anno 1409 sino al 1502 di autori incerti,* ed. Giuseppe Pardi, in *Rerum Italicarum Scriptores* 24, part 7, vol. 1 (Bologna, 1928–33), p. 256.

13. On Ercole d'Este's negotiations with Viterbo concerning Lucia's move to Ferrara, see Luigi Alberto Gandini, *Sulla venuta in Ferrara della b. suor Lucia da Narni del Terz'Ordine di San Domenico, sue lettere ed altri documenti inediti 1497–98–99* (Modena, 1901); and Gandini, "Lucrezia Borgia nell'imminenza delle sue nozze con Alfonso d'Este," *Atti e memorie della R. Deputazione di storia patria per le provincie di Romagna,* 3d ser., 20 (1902): 285–340.

14. After listing Colomba's charismatic gifts of complete abstinence, ecstasy, and prophecy, Matarazzo concludes: "and because of the innumerable intercessory prayers that she made in Christ's ears and the conflicts that she resolved through prayer, the people called her a saint" ("Cronache e storie inedite," p. 5).

15. In the very years that Colomba of Rieti was living in Perugia, for example, a Madonna painted on a wall began to work miracles, attracting many people, "not only citizens and local peasants, but even from all the nearby towns." Perugia also possessed a precious relic taken from Siena not long before: the Virgin Mary's ring (ibid., pp. 8–9, 369, and 644).

16. Of Colomba as adviser to the Baglioni, Matarazzo says that "Signor Guido and Ridolfo often spoke with her, and she exhorted them to look to the good behavior of the city, lest they be threatened with great ruin" (ibid., p. 5). On the roles of Osanna of Mantua and Lucia of Narni, see Gabriella Zarri, "Pietà e profezia alle corti padane: Le pie consigliere dei principi," in *Il Rinascimento nelle corti padane: Società e cultura* (Bari, 1977), pp. 201–37.

In 1542 Camilla Pallavicini, who "made a career of being a saint," was exiled from Venice for espionage: "Lady Camilla Pallavicina, known as the Saint, was banned from Venice because she meddled in affairs of state and under cover of sanctity was overly familiar with the French ambassador" (Benedetto Nicolini, *Lettere di negozi del pieno Cinquecento* [Bologna, 1971], pp. 33–35 and 177).

17. Ottavia Niccoli, "Profezie in piazza: Note sul profetismo popolare nell'Italia del primo Cinquecento," *Quaderni storici* 14 (1979): 500–539; some versified prophecies from 1495–1510 even included Colomba of Rieti and Osanna of Mantua among the modern prophets (see pp. 512–13).

18. Women's contributions to the charitable institutions organized by the Oratories of Divine Love and other lay confraternities, which have been seen primarily in terms of the "Catholic Reformation," deserve attention as part of a broader and

more complex development. The same can be said of women's roles in diffusing Reformation ideas in evangelical circles and in propagating the principles of the Council of Trent through the Companies of the Most Holy Sacrament and the Schools of Christian Doctrine. The female contribution to Protestantism in other European countries has been the object of numerous studies: see Roland H. Bainton, *Women of the Reformation in Germany and Italy* (Minneapolis, 1971); Miriam Usher Chrisman, "Women and the Reformation in Strasbourg (1490–1530)," *Archiv für Reformationsgeschichte* 63 (1972): 143–67; Nancy L. Roelker, "The Role of Noblewomen in the French Reformation," *Archiv für Reformationsgeschichte* 63 (1972): 168–95; and Natalie Zemon Davis, "City Women and Religious Change," in her *Society and Culture in Early Modern France* (London, 1975), pp. 65–95.

19. "Tot uno saeculo ex una provincia foeminas, tot ac tantis divinitatem spirantibus donis ornatas . . . ut hoc nostro ex Italia sola" (Bozio, *De signis ecclesiae Dei*, p. 570). Bozio listed thirteen Italian women who enjoyed a reputation for sanctity in the sixteenth century (pp. 566–69), drawing his information largely from Serafino Razzi and the published hagiographical legends, and noting in particular the women who, like Maria Bagnesi and Felice of Barbarano, were closest to the Oratorians. He also mentioned the names of various nuns who were known for their devout lives.

20. Delooz's data show that forty-four Italians who died during the time of the Wars of Italy (1494–1559) have been beatified; twenty-one of them were women, to whom should be added two female saints (Delooz, *Sociologie et canonisations*, pp. 458–61).

21. Catherine of Genoa's *Book of Life* and Varano's autobiographical letters should be studied as spiritual treatises and can hardly be compared to the hagiographic legends discussed here. For bibliographical guidance, see Petrocchi, *Storia della spiritualità*, 1: 164–70 and 175–81. On Catherine of Genoa, see Sosio Pezzella, entry "Caterina Fieschi Adorno," in *DBI*, vol. 22 (Rome, 1979), pp. 343–45.

Restricted or belated recognition characterized the cults of many women who appear in the menologies of their orders and in compilations of local saints and blessed persons. For instance, Paola Montaldi, a Poor Clare in Mantua (d. 1514), and Paola Gambara Costa, a Franciscan tertiary in Binasco (d. 1515), were not beatified until the nineteenth century; their cults coincided notably with those of the Dominican Osanna of Mantua and the Augustinian Veronica of Binasco, suggesting a sort of sacred competition: see the entries on Paola Montaldi and Paola Gambara in the *Bibliotheca Sanctorum*. Note that I have also excluded another group of women: those for whom popular cults developed immediately after their deaths, but about whom no contemporary legends have survived. For example, a biography of the Dominican tertiary Maddalena Panetieri of Trino (d. 1503) was supposedly written around 1534, but the only surviving copies are late and full of discrepancies: see the entry "Panetieri" in *Bibliotheca Sanctorum*, vol. 10, cols. 77–78.

22. *La vita della Beata Colomba de Rieto del terzo habito della penitentia del glorioso Padre San Domenego, per il ven. Patre F. Leandro delli Alberti Bolognese de*

l'ordine de' predicatori in volgare composta (Bologna: Girolamo de' Benedetti, 15 April 1521), dedication to Sister Girolama Teppola.

23. Famous for his historical and geographical writings, Alberti (d. 1541) lived in Bologna for many years, though he occasionally left that city to fill important offices in the Dominican order (Abele L. Redigonda, entry "Alberti Leandro," in *DBI*, vol. 1 [Rome, 1960], pp. 669–702). Sebastiano Bontempi (d. 1521) was a prominent figure in Perugia, where he was librarian and prior of the convent of San Domenico and prior of the province of Rome. He studied mathematics and astrology and taught moral philosophy at the University of Perugia, and held the title of Magister (Master). Confessor of the blessed Colomba starting in 1494, he was relieved of this duty three years later following accusations of being a magician and suggesting to Colomba the prophecies that made her famous (Vittor Ivo Comparato, entry "Bontempi Sebastiano da Perugia," in *DBI*, vol. 12 [Rome, 1970], pp. 437–38).

24. See Jacques Le Goff, "Clerical Culture and Folklore Traditions in Merovingian Civilization" and "Ecclesiastical Culture and Folklore in the Middle Ages: Saint Marcellus of Paris and the Dragon," in *Time, Work, and Culture in the Middle Ages,* trans. Arthur Goldhammer (Chicago, 1980), pp. 153–88; Jean-Claude Schmitt, "La parola addomesticata: San Domenico, il gatto, e le donne di Fanjeaux," *Quaderni storici* 14 (1979): 416–39; Maurizio Bertolotti, "Le ossa e la pelle dei buoi: Un mito popolare tra agiografia e stregoneria," *Quaderni storici* 14 (1979): 470–99 (translated as "The Ox's Bones and the Ox's Hide: A Popular Myth, Part Hagiography and Part Witchcraft," in *Microhistory and the Lost Peoples of Europe,* ed. Edward Muir and Guido Ruggiero [Baltimore, 1991], pp. 42–70).

25. In presenting his translation of the life of Mary Magdalene, Silvestro Prierio distinguished his work from that of an earlier devout translator: "First and foremost, because I intend to write new histories; secondly, because that person wrote his own reflections rather than the life of these saints, whereas I intend to write only what is absolutely certain, claiming as fact nothing that is uncertain" (*Vita di Sancta Maria Maddalena* [Bologna: Giovanni Antonio de' Benedetti, 14 September 1500]). Prierio also prepared a new edition of the life of Agnes of Montepulciano, in connection with a revival of her cult: the recognition of her body performed in 1510 was accompanied by a miracle described in Serafino Razzi, *Vita de i Santi e beati del sacro ordine de' Frati Predicatori così huomini come donne: Con aggiunta di molte vite che nella prima impressione non erano* (Florence: Bartolomeo Sermantelli, 1588), part 2, p. 37. Prierio's prefatory letter addressed to the Elders of Montepulciano clearly stated his desire to reach a wider audience: "I resolved . . . to publish this sacred legend in such a form that not only those skilled in the Latin language but even common people could harvest some spiritual fruit from it" (*La sacra historia di Sancta Agnese de Montepoliciano,* trans. Andrea Pisano [Bologna: Hieronimo di Pelati, 1514]). Prierio also set about publicizing the life of a saintly Dominican friar who had recently died: Fra Ambrosio da Soncino, *Vita e conversatione sancta del beato Iacobo converso de l'ordine de predicatori: Nuovamente morto a Bologna,* revised and abridged by Silvestro Prierio (Bologna: Giovanni Antonio de Benedetti, 1501).

26. *Catologus sanctorum et gestorum eorum diversis voluminibus collectus:*

Editus a Rev.mo in Christo Patre domino Petro de Natalibus de Venetiis dei gratia episcopo Equilino multis novis additionibus decoratus, revised and corrected by Alberto Castellano O.P. (Venice: Nicolaum de Franckfordia, 1516); Friedrich Lauchert, *Die italienischen literarischen Gegner Luthers* (Freiburg im Breisgau, 1912).

27. Caterina's *vita* was published in 1502 by Sabadino degli Arienti and Eustochia's in 1505 by C. Lanza, on the basis of legends written by two nuns and companions of the "blessed women," Illuminata Bembo and Jacopa Pollicino, which did not appear in print until centuries later (1787; 1903 and 1942): see Serena Spanò, entry "Caterina Vigri," in *DBI,* vol. 21 (Rome, 1979), pp. 381–83, and Enrico Pispisa, entry "Calafato Eustochia," in *DBI,* vol. 16 (Rome, 1973), pp. 402–3. The influence of these nuns within the convents of Poor Clares is evident from the devotion to them displayed by two nuns who were themselves known as "blessed": the Milanese Giulia Tornielli, who wrote down the revelations that Caterina Vigri dictated, and Cecilia Coppoli of Foligno, to whom Jacopa Pollicino wrote a letter about the death of the blessed Eustochia. See Agostino Saba, *Federico Borromeo e i mistici del suo tempo con la vita e la corrispondenza inedita di Caterina Vannini da Siena* (Florence, 1933), pp. 24–25; Antonio Fantozzi, "Documenti intorno alla beata Cecilia Coppoli clarissa (1426–1500)," *Archivum Franciscanum Historicum* 19 (1926): 194–225 and 334–84; and Fantozzi, "La riforma osservante dei monasteri delle Clarisse nell'Italia centrale," *Archivum Franciscanum Historicum* 23 (1930): 361–82 and 488–550. On Eustochia, see also Francesco Terrizzi, *Il "Libro della Passione" scritto dalla b. Eustochia Calafato clarissa messinese, 1434–1485* (Messina, 1975).

Catherine of Genoa, Angela Merici, and Maria Lorenza Longo were all associated with the Third Order of St. Francis. On Longo, founder of the Capuchin nuns in Naples, see Francesco Saverio Da Brusciano, "Maria Lorenza Longo e l'opera del Divino Amore a Napoli," *Collectanea Franciscana* 23 (1953): 166–228; and Agostino Falanga, *La ven. Maria Lorenza Longo fondatrice dell'ospedale "Incurabili" e delle monache cappuccine in Napoli, 1463–1524* (Naples, 1973). Her first *vita* was composed by Mattia Bellentani of Salò, and her beatification is still in process: see Matthias a Salò, "Historia Capucina," ed. Melchior a Pobladura, in *Monumenta Historica Ordinis Fratrum Minorum Capuccinorum,* vol. 6 (Rome, 1950), pp. 255–72; Silvino da Nadro, *Acta et decreta causarum beatificationis et canonizationis OFM cap. ex regestis manuscriptis SS. rituum congregationis ab anno 1592 ad annum 1964* (Rome and Milan, 1964), pp. 1119–30.

28. Serafino Razzi's compendium of Dominican saints and blesseds (first ed., Florence: Bartolomeo Sermantelli, 1577) has already been mentioned. The *vitae* of the blessed Franciscans were compiled by Marco da Lisbona, *Croniche degli Ordini instituiti dal P. S. Francesco,* trans. Orazio Diola of Bologna (Parma: Erasmo Viotti, 1581–82). These works were soon followed by similar compilations offered by the other religious orders.

29. *Vita miracolosa della Seraphyca sancta Catherina da Siena* (Siena: Michelangelo di Bart. F. for Giovanni di Alixandro, 10 May 1524). This was not the first Italian translation of Catherine's *vita:* see Marie-Hyacinthe Laurent, "Essais de bib-

liographie catherinienne: Les premières éditions italiennes (1474 [75]–1500)," *Archivum Fratrum Praedicatorum* 20 (1950): 348–68. However, the *Vita miracolosa* enjoyed great popularity in the sixteenth and early seventeenth centuries. Without pretending to make an exhaustive survey, I counted eight editions between 1562 and 1612, while finding none between the first printing of 1524 and the 1560s. If further research does not turn up other editions dating from Catarino's lifetime, we might conclude that he had refused to nourish Catherine's cult any further. In fact, Catarino's later rift with the Savonarolans and harsh criticism of the Florentine prophet are well known; this translation, however, dates from his Savonarolan period, and defends prophecy and the "renewal of the church" in a long chapter entitled "Digression of the translater on the truths prophesized by our saint, with twelve arguments against the opinion of her opponents" (1524 ed., book 3, chap. 5, fols. 71–76). The editions of the second half of the sixteenth century contain some additions to the "Digression," which will be discussed below (see note 89).

30. Zarri, "Pietà e profezia," pp. 233–34.

31. Manuscript copies of the legends circulated widely, and not only inside monasteries. On 15 January 1517, Camillo Falcone was cured of a wound while "reading the deeds of Veronica"; but the first Latin edition of the work did not appear until 1518 (see below, note 41; the passage cited comes from the vernacular translation of 1581, p. 255). Sometimes the legends were publicized in sermons or read in small groups: in 1549 a possessed women was freed of her demon as soon as a Dominican began to read "the wonderful deeds" of Caterina of Racconigi (p. 191 of the *Compendio*, cited in note 58).

32. On Colomba's life, see Ettore Ricci, *Storia della beata Colomba da Rieti* (Perugia, 1901), and Baleoneus Astur, *Colomba da Rieti: "La seconda Caterina da Siena," 1464–1501* (Rome, 1967). On the political affairs of Perugia and the Baglioni regime, see Baleoneus Astur, *I Baglioni* (Florence, 1964).

33. Sebastiano Bontempi, *Legenda latina,* in *Acta Sanctorum,* May, vol. 5 (Paris and Rome, 1866) pp. 150*–223*; Bontempi's *Legenda volgare di Colomba da Rieti* is in the Biblioteca Augusta, Perugia, MS D62.

34. To Sebastiano Bontempi's list of Colomba's miracles, Alberti added one that took place in Bologna by virtue of some of her relics and published ten epitaphs in her honor, most of which were composed by nuns in northern Italian cities. There is also a sixteenth-century manuscript poem celebrating Colomba: the "Columbeidos," by the Dominican Niccolò Alessi of Perugia, who also wrote a *vita* of Caterina de' Ricci. A new *vita,* which drew on the depositions at Colomba's first canonization proceedings, was published in the seventeenth century: Giuseppe Balestra, *Vita della b. Colomba da Rieti fondatrice del nobilissimo monastero delle Colombe di Perugia* (Perugia: Stampa Camerale, Sebastiano Zecchini, 1652).

35. Archivio Generale dell'Ordine dei Predicatori (henceforth AGOP), sec. 10, no. 875: *Memoriale de Beata Columba super Elevatione Ritus seu extensionis aut concessionis officii et missae,* p. 2.

36. Ibid. See also Astur, *Colomba da Rieti,* p. 319, which gives a different date for the concession of Pius V.

37. The best biography of Osanna is still that of Giuseppe Bagolini and Lodovico Ferretti, *La beata Osanna Andreasi da Mantova terziaria domenicana, 1449–1505* (Florence, 1905).

38. Francesco Silvestri, *Beatae Osannae Mantuanae de tertio habitu Ordinis Fratrum Praedicatorum vita* (Milan: Alessandro Minuziano, 1505); translated as *La vita e stupendi miraculi della gloriosa vergine Osanna Mantovana del terzo ordine de' Frati predicatori* (Milan: Alessandro Minuziano, 1507). Silvestri's Latin *vita* was reprinted in *Acta Sanctorum,* June, vol. 4 (Paris and Rome, 1867), pp. 558–601. Hieronymus (Scolari) Monteolivetanus, *Libretto de la vita et transito de la beata Osanna da Mantua* (Mantua: Leonardo Bruschi, 1507), translated into Latin and published in *Acta Sanctorum,* June, vol. 4 (Paris and Rome, 1867), pp. 601–64, and reprinted with a *Confirmatio et additio* under the title *Libretto de la vita et transito della beata Osanna da Mantova nuovamente corretto et con una nova aggionta* (Bologna: Heirs of Benedetto di Ettore Faelli, 1524). A new Italian edition of Silvestri's work was published in 1577 in Vicenza by Giorgio Angelieri, and Francesco Osanna reprinted it twice in Mantua, in 1590 and 1610. On Silvestri, Scolari, and the promotion of Osanna's cult in the sixteenth century, see Zarri, "Pietà e profezia," pp. 223–37.

39. There is an incomplete manuscript copy of the 1515 proceedings in AGOP, sec. 10, no. 2490, fols. 17–34. The depositions of some of the witnesses questioned in 1515 were published in *Mantuana Canonizationis B. Osannae de Andreasiis Tertii Ordinis Sancti Dominici Summarium* (AGOP, sec. 10, no. 2492 B, pp. 1–21). In 1693 the beatification proceedings were resumed, on the basis of a cult "from time immemorial."

40. For a brief biography and bibliography, see the entry under her name by Renata Orazi Ausenda, *Enciclopedia cattolica,* vol. 8, col. 1735.

41. Isidoro Isolani, *Inexplicabilis mysterii gesta Beatae Veronicae Virginis praeclarissimi Monasterii Sanctae Marthae urbis Mediolani: Sub observatione Regulae Divi Augustini* (Milan: Gotardus Ponticus, 1518); reprinted in *Acta Sanctorum,* January, vol. 2 (Brussels, 1864), pp. 169–211 (which is the source of my citations). According to a chronicle written around 1650 by Francesco Bonardo, agent of the convent, Isolani based his *vita* on an earlier text by Sister Benedetta of Vimercate: "In the year 1516 a certain friar of Santa Maria delle Grazie in Milan came many times to our convent for a certain reason, and speaking with our Reverend Mother Arcangela he offered to correct it and render it into Latin, which he did, and it was printed" (Biblioteca Ambrosiana, Milan, Ms L 56: *Origine e progressi del Ven. monastero di S. Marta di Milano con la vita e morte di alcune monache del medemo,* p. 61). Isolani's work was not translated and printed in Italian until 1581 for lack of money, as the nuns stated in the prefatory letter: *La santissima e miraculosa vita della Beata Veronica monaca del Ven. Monasterio di Santa Marta di Milano, con parti delle sue mirabili et celesti visioni, raccolte dal R.P.F. Isidoro degli Isolani* (Brescia: Vincenzo Stabbio, 1581). The nuns also cited the high cost of printing as the reason for not listing the many miracles that Veronica had worked since 1518: "because there were a great number of miracles, printing them would have doubled the cost" (*La san-*

tissima e miraculosa vita della Beata Veronica, p. 256). Sebastiano Canazzi made a new translation of the work: *La santissima et prodigiosa vita della beata Vergine Veronica da Binasco* (Pavia: Giovan Battista Rossi, 1624).

42. The brief was printed in the Latin edition of Isolani's legend. The Milanese Isidoro Isolani, a Dominican master of theology, belonged to the Lombard Congregation and was prior of various friaries, including those of Cremona and Pavia. He wrote many pamphlets and treatises on the burning issues of his day, from denunciations of magic and witchcraft to discussions of the immortality of the soul and the immaculate conception. He also wrote a short tract against Luther that won him the epithets of "indoctissimus" and "homo simplex et idiota." In one of his best-known treatises, *De imperio militantis ecclesiae,* written in 1515 but not published until 1517, he affirmed the superiority of the council over the papacy and identified Denis Briçonnet, the bishop of Toulon, as the "pastor angelicus" whose coming was awaited and predicted by various prophetic movements. A supporter of the French, Isolani received a pension from the senate of Milan on the recommendation of Francis I. On Isolani's life and writings, see the article by Filippo Argelati in the *Bibliotheca Scriptorum Mediolanensium,* vol. 20, col. 244–247; Lauchert, *Die italienischen literarischen Gegner Luthers,* pp. 200–15; Nansen Defendi, "La 'Revocatio M. Lutherii ad Sanctam Sedem' nella polemica antiluterana in Italia," *Archivio storico lombardo,* ser. 8, 4 (1953): 66–132; Adriano Prosperi, "America e Apocalisse. Note sulla 'conquista spirituale' del Nuovo Mondo," *Critica storica* 13 (1976): 1–61; Abele Redigonda, "La Summa de donis sancti Joseph di Isidoro Isolani," *Cahiers de Joséphologie* 25 (1977): 203–21. Among the ever-growing number of works on prophecy in early modern Europe, see especially Marjorie Reeves, *The Influence of Prophecy in the Later Middle Ages: A Study in Joachimism* (Oxford, 1969), and her more recent synthesis on the subject, *Joachim of Fiore and the Prophetic Future* (London, 1976).

43. The connection between the spiritual community of Santa Marta and the origins of the Society of Eternal Wisdom, which gave rise to the Barnabites, was first noted by Orazio Premoli, *Storia dei Barnabiti nel Cinquecento* (Rome, 1913), pp. 400–13; but see especially Carlo Marcora, "Il Cardinale Ippolito I d'Este, Arcivescovo di Milano (1497–1519)," *Memorie storiche della diocesi di Milano* 5 (1958): 429–48. More recent studies have emphasized the influence of the "Apocalypsis Nova" on the spiritual formation of the Milanese group and demonstrated the links between the followers of Amadeo and of Savonarola: Eugenio Giommi, "La monaca Arcangela Panigarola, madre spirituale di Denis Briçonnet: L'attesa del 'pastore angelico' annunciato dall'Apocalypsis nova' del Beato Amadeo fra il 1514 e il 1520" (thesis, University of Florence, 1967–1968, directed by Prof. Giuseppe Alberigo); Cesare Vasoli, *Profezia e ragione: Studi sulla cultura del Cinquecento e del Seicento* (Naples, 1974), pp. 123–26; and Maria Teresa Binaghi, "L'immagine sacra in Luini e il circolo di Santa Marta," in *Sacro e profano nella pittura di Bernardino Luini* (Milan, 1975), pp. 49–76, which draws extensively on the historical data in Giommi's thesis. One should note, however, Isolani's reservations concerning the

group's faith in Amadeo's prophecies, which were reworked by Giorgio Benigno Salviati, Arcangela's biographer: "Vidi ego codicem quendam mira iam iamque ventura predicentem cuius auctor quisquis ille est divinae Apocalipsis librum ad sua vota trahit" (*De Imperio militantis ecclesiae libri quattuor* [Milan: Gotardo Pontico, 1517], fol. 131). The text of the prophecies has been published by Anna Morisi, *"Apocalypsis nova": Ricerche sull'origine e la formazione del testo dello pseudo Amadeo* (Rome, 1970).

44. Arcangela maintained an interesting correspondence with the Briçonnet brothers, who declared themselves her spiritual sons. In a papal brief of 30 December 1514, Leo X authorized Bellotti to gather Panigarola's revelations "ne juxta dictum Apostoli huiusmodi spiritus extinguatur," and reserved the right to review and approve the resulting book (Premoli, *Storia dei Barnabiti*, pp. 414–15). Benigno's *vita* is preserved in the Biblioteca Ambrosiana, Milan (Ms O 165 sup.): Giorgio Benigno Salviati, *Legenda dela Veneranda Vergine suor Archangela Panigarola*. A member of Cardinal Bessarion's household, Benigno entered the service of Federico of Montefeltro as tutor to his son, before moving to Florence and associating himself with the court of Lorenzo de' Medici and the Salviati family. Exiled from Florence after the expulsion of the Medici, he wrote his pro-Savonarolan *Profeticae solutiones,* perhaps hoping thereby to win permission to return to the city. Ever ambitious and intent on furthering his own ecclesiastical career, he was constantly involved in prophetic movements with a strong political coloring, and with his writings helped feed hopes for church reform and the coming of the Angelic Pope. On Benigno's life and writings, see Cesare Vasoli, "Notizie su Giorgio Benigno Salviati (Juraj Dragišić)," in *Profezia e ragione*, pp. 17–120.

45. Federico Borromeo, *Philagios sive de amore virtutis libri duodecim* (Milan, 1623), book 3, fols. 99–126; and Ottavio Inviziati, *Vita virtù e rivelazioni della venerabile madre Arcangela Panigarola priora dell'insigne nobilissimo monistero di S. Marta in Milano dell'Ordine di S. Agostino tratta dagli antichi manuscritti di esso monistero* (Milan: Heirs of Ghisolfi, 1677). Although based on the manuscript legend, Inviziati's *vita* downplays its numerous visions and prophecies, focusing instead on Arcangela's virtues and exemplary behavior.

46. Giovanni Musolino, Antonio Niero, and Silvio Tramontin, *Santi e beati veneziani: Quaranta profili,* Biblioteca agiografica veneziana, 1 (Venice, 1963), pp. 255–59.

47. On this episode and on Bugni's reputation for sanctity, Sanuto reports: "The abbess, named Sister Chiara Bugni, who is thirty-five years old and is presently the abbess, works many miracles; it is said that she has not eaten for forty days, and goes into ecstasies on Fridays; in short, she performs remarkable miracles. It is said that on Good Friday we will know everything—that is, she will die, etc. And Brother Francesco Zorzi, guardian of San Francesco della Vigna, who is her director, entered the convent but does not want to say anything, saying only that it is a great thing; you will know more later. Cardinal Grimani, who was commissioned by the pope to inspect the convent, said upon his return: 'This is an amazing thing' " (Sanuto, *I diarii,* vol. 7, col. 40).

48. Zorzi's Latin draft of the *vita* of Chiara Bugni has been lost; but a translation by the Florentine friar Andrea Pilolini, who officiated in the convent of Santo Sepolcro beginning in 1541, has survived. Although this manuscript was not completed until 1583, the translation seems faithful to Zorzi's draft, even noting the spaces Zorzi left blank in order to insert notes or miracles; it also mentions several drawings intended to illustrate the visions. After a short preface on Bugni's birth and her decision to enter the convent of Santo Sepolcro, the legend lists her mystical and charismatic gifts and describes her visions, which date primarily from 1503 to 1508; for the period 1506–7 it almost becomes a sort of chronicle. The *vita* gives particular prominence to the miracle of Christ's blood and the Virgin's milk, which were given to Chiara and kept in two phials for the remission of sins and nourishment of spiritual life. Because of the loss of the original and the long interval between the first draft of the *vita* and the translation, we cannot rule out the possibility that the translator made changes in Zorzi's text. However, the accuracy of the transcription and the preservation of certain visions that contain doctrines considered highly suspect— such as the vision concerning the incarnation of Christ, discussed in the following note—lead us to conclude that Pilolini's translation is substantially faithful to Zorzi's text. In any case, Zorzi was an esteemed theologian, who only late in life was considered not entirely orthodox. On Zorzi and his writings, see Cesare Vasoli, "Intorno a Francesco Giorgio Veneto e all''armonia del mondo,'" in *Profezia e ragione,* pp. 131–403. His *vita* of Chiara is conserved in the archive of the convent of San Francesco della Vigna in Venice in a paper codex of 150 folios, numbered up to fol. 87, entitled *Origine del Monastero delle Monache del Santo Sepolcro presso alla Pietà di Venetia;* on fol. 6v begins the "Vitta di una Santa Monacha del Monastero del santo Sepolcro di Venetia nominata la Beata Chiara, descritta dal Rev. Padre Fra Francesco Giorgi dell'ordine d'osservanza dei Fratti di San Francesco," cited here as Zorzi, "Vitta."

49. The *vita* explains the harsh measures taken against Bugni as a disciplinary action by the superiors of her order, who thought she attracted too many people to the convent with her mystical displays and violated the convent's rules by remaining prioress for seven years (Zorzi, "Vitta," fol. 90). The hypothesis that Bugni was subjected to a doctrinal censure, based on a possible link between Zorzi and the sect of Gabriele Biondo, needs further investigation: see Carlo Dionisotti, "Resoconto di una ricerca interotta," *Annali della Scuola Normale Superiore di Pisa: Lettere, storia, filosofia,* ser. 2, 37 (1968): 259–69; Aldo Stella, *Anabattismo e antitrinitarismo in Italia nel XVI secolo* (Padua, 1969), pp. 4 and 110–14; and Vasoli, *Profezia e ragione,* pp. 121–23 and 160–68. A central theme of the legend is universal salvation, granted by God to those who have faith and not mediated through the church. Indeed, according to Chiara's visions, many people would be saved by the blood of Christ she received; those who see it "with true faith would obtain indulgence and plenary remission of all of their sins" (Zorzi, "Vitta," fol. 59v; see also fols. 63 and 68v). Another of her unusual "doctrines," linked with the gift of the Virgin's milk, concerned the Incarnation: Christ "was formed with the most pure blood of the Blessed Virgin, collected from the purest places here and there all over

her body, in supreme purity" (fol. 78v; see also fols. 80 and 82). Both of these themes unavoidably call to mind the Lateran canon Pietro of Lucca, who also in 1511 was investigated for having preached that Christ was conceived from the Holy Spirit through three drops of blood that penetrated Mary's heart: see Delio Cantimori, "Le idee religiose del Cinquecento: La storiografia," in *Storia della letteratura italiana,* ed. Emilio Cecchi and Natalino Sapegno (Milan, 1964), pp. 38–43. It may be sheer coincidence that the inquisitorial trial of Pietro of Lucca and the disciplinary actions against Chiara Bugni took place at the same time; to my knowledge, no direct links between the preacher and the mystic have been proven. However, Chiara's visions certainly contained elements that could easily be labeled as heterodox and deemed capable of attracting a popular following, a possibility that the superiors of her order abruptly foreclosed by forbidding her to speak. On Chiara's later reputation, see Silvio Tramontin, "Cataloghi dei 'santi veneziani,'" in Musolino, Niero, and Tramontin, *Santi e beati veneziani,* pp. 34–35; and Marco da Lisbona, *Croniche degli ordini instituiti dal P. S. Francesco,* part 4, vol. 3, collected principally by Bartolomeo Cimarelli (Naples: Novello de Bonis, 1680; first ed., Venice, 1621), pp. 751–909. Cimarelli transcribed the legend faithfully in 1612, modifying only the spelling and the arrangement of the chapters. There is a short summary of Chiara's legend in Luke Wadding, *Annales minorum seu trium ordinum a S. Francisco institutorum,* vol. 15, *1492–1515* (Quaracchi, 1933), pp. 541–48.

50. Musolino, Niero, and Tramontin, *Santi e beati veneziani,* pp. 236–42, and *Venezia e la peste, 1348–1797: Catalogo della mostra* (Venice, 1979), p. 258.

51. Adriano Prosperi, entry "Broccadelli Lucia," in *DBI,* vol. 14 (Rome, 1972), pp. 381–83; Zarri, "Pietà e profezia," pp. 208–20.

52. Arcangelo Marcheselli of Viadana, an assiduous promoter of the legends of the Dominican "holy women" who transcribed the two different legends of Caterina of Racconigi, apparently composed a *vita* of Lucia of Narni that has since been lost: Jacques Quétif and Jacques Échard, *Scriptores Ordinis Praedicatorum,* vol. 2 (Paris, 1721), p. 209. For his first brief printed biography of Lucia, Razzi drew on an oral tradition that went back to Marcheselli; and in the *vita* published by Marcianese there are references to "manuscript books" and to information taken from Arcangelo of Viadana: Razzi, *Vite de i santi* (1588 ed.), part 2, p. 83; Giacomo Marcianese, *Narratione della nascita, vita e morte della beata Lucia di Narni dell'ordine di San Domenico: Fondatrice del monastero di Santa Caterina da Siena di Ferrara* (Ferrara: Vittorio Baldini, 1616).

53. Ferrara, Archivio Arcivescovile, *Residui ecclesiastici, S. Caterina da Siena,* 3/26: material concerning the cult of Lucia of Narni and her beatification proceedings.

54. Giuseppe Brunati, *Vita o gesta di santi bresciani,* vol. 2 (Brescia, 1856), pp. 43–65; Antonio Cistellini, *Figure della riforma pretridentina* (Brescia, 1948), pp. 38–46 and 175–97; Vittorio Tolasi, *Stefana Quinzani. Donna, suora, e beata (1457–1530): Inediti dell'epistolario Gonzaga e sintesi del processo di beatificazione* (Brescia, 1972). Stefana carried on a correspondence with princes and nobles in various courts, not only the Gonzaga.

55. AGOP, sec. 10, no. 2857, fasc. 13: *Excerpta ex scriptis f. Baptistae de Salodio per fr. Dominicum de Calvisano*, a summary of the Latin legend of Stefana. The two vernacular translations of the Latin legend are preserved in various manuscripts: the translation of Fra Pietro, dedicated to the Mother Superiors Prisca de' Rizzoli of Soncino and Bianca de' Sessi, is found in AGOP, sec. 10, no. 2864, and the parish archive of Soncino; while that by Pietro of Durno, preserved in MS Vaticano urbinate no. 1755, has been published by Paolo Guerrini, "La prima 'Legenda volgare' de la beata Stefana Quinzani d'Orzinuovi secondo il codice Vaticano-Urbinate latino 1775," *Memorie storiche della diocesi di Brescia*, ser. 1, 1 (1930): 67–186. The abridged version in Razzi, *Vite de i Santi* (1577 ed.), part 2, pp. 136–149, based on the Vatican manuscript, constituted the main source for the *vita* of Stefana that Domenico Codagli included in *L'historia orceana* (Brescia: Giovan Battista Borella, 1592). The first seventeenth-century biography relied on the vernacular legend: Francesco Seghizzi, *Vita della beata Stefana Quinzani da gli Orzinovi vero ritratto di Christo Crocifisso monaca dell'ordine di S. Domenico: Fondatrice del monastero di S. Paola di Soncino* (Brescia, 1632).

56. Tommaso Bozio, *De signis ecclesiae Dei*, p. 568.

57. Renzo Amedeo, *Operai nella vigna del Signore: Santi, vescovi, e religiosi garessini* (Carrù, 1962), pp. 35–88.

58. Caterina's first *vita* was the account of her revelations, written by her confessors Gabriele Dolce of Savigliano (d. 1525) and Domenico of Bra. Two mutilated manuscripts of this legend, which recounts Caterina's life and visions until 1525, have survived: one in the parish archive of Borgo di Garessio, and the other in AGOP, sec. 10, no. 661; these manuscripts are described in Amedeo, *Operai,* pp. 73–80. Caterina's second legend was written in Latin by Gianfrancesco Pico della Mirandola, who drew on the earlier *vita,* adding new material about events until 1532 and rearranging the legend to form something like a treatise: each book is prefaced by a statement of its philosophical premises and a refutation of doubts concerning the authenticity of the phenomena described. But like the other, Pico's legend is incomplete, since he died before Caterina. The Dominican Pietro Martire Morelli took it upon himself to complete Pico's work, adding accounts of the events in Caterina's life between 1533 and 1547 and the miracles that occurred until 1554. Morelli's additions were integrated into Pico's text, but distinguished by marginal notations indicating the author of each part. The most complete *vita* of Caterina is thus the one known as the Pico-Morelli version. We have a sixteenth-century Latin copy of this legend in the Biblioteca Nazionale of Turin and an Italian translation in the AGOP, and at least five sixteenth-century manuscripts of Pico's legend in Italian translation. An Italian translation of the Pico-Morelli version was published around 1680 with the title *Compendio delle cose mirabili della venerabil serva di Dio Catterina da Raconisio Vergine integerrima del Sacro Ordine della Penitenza di S. Domenico, distinto in Dieci libri e composto dall'Ill.mo Sig. Giovanni Francesco Pico . . . et ultimato dall'umile servo di Giesù Christo Fr. Pietro Martire Morelli da Garressio dell'ordine de' Predicatori* (no place or date of publication). A comparison of this printed text with the manuscripts reveals no significant differences; my citations are

generally to the printed edition. A list of the manuscripts containing Pico's *vita* of Caterina (to which one should add the copy in the Biblioteca Universitaria of Bologna) can be found in Charles B. Schmitt, *Giovan Francesco Pico della Mirandola, 1496–1533, and His Critique of Aristotle* (The Hague, 1967); on Morelli, see Amedeo, *Operai*, pp. 221–25.

59. AGOP, sec. 10, no. 660: first informational hearings "super moribus, gestis et vita ac miraculis" of Caterina, held by the podestà of Garessio on 7 June 1550 and recorded by the notary Bartolomeo of Garessio. Five witnesses were questioned: two of Caterina's fellow nuns, one friar, and two beneficiaries of miracles.

60. Amedeo, *Operai,* pp. 67–69, blames the wars for interrupting the proceedings seeking Caterina's beatification that had begun at the end of the sixteenth century; but we must not forget that at this time the Savoy family was engaged in promoting the cult of Margherita, one of their ancestors who had lived in Casale Monferrato in the first half of the fifteenth century: see Angelico Ferrua, entry "Margherita di Savoia," in *Bibliotheca Sanctorum*, vol. 8, col. 793–96.

61. The first accounts of Caterina's life date from this period and include a brief report by Fra Timoteo Ricci on her miraculous cure, the diary of Fra Modesto Masi (1542), and the *Apologia* by an anonymous Dominican, which narrates Caterina's wondrous deeds between 1542 and 1549 and contains in a nutshell all of the characteristic elements of her legend: see Guglielmo Di Agresti, *Santa Caterina de' Ricci: Testimonianze sull'età giovanile*, Collana Ricciana, Fonti 1 (Florence, 1963). For the vast bibliography on Caterina de' Ricci, see Guglielmo Di Agresti, "Bibliografia ricciana-savonaroliana," *Memorie domenicane*, new ser., 3 (1972): 229–301, and the volumes of the Collana Ricciana edited by Di Agresti. On the influence of the Savonarolan movement on the reform of Tuscan convents, with particular attention to Caterina de' Ricci and her monastery of San Vincenzo of Prato, see Guglielmo Di Agresti, *Sviluppi della riforma monastica savonaroliana* (Florence, 1980).

62. The legend responsible for Caterina de' Ricci's reputation was written and published after her death by Serafino Razzi, *Vita di S. Caterina de' Ricci con documenti inediti antecedenti l'edizione,* ed. Guglielmo Di Agresti, Collana Ricciana, Fonti 3 (Florence, 1965). Caterina's mystical gifts were comparable to those of the other Dominican holy women, both ancient and modern: in fact—Razzi affirms, comparing Ricci with Catherine of Siena, Clare of Montefalco, Birgitta of Sweden, Helena of Hungary, and Lucia of Narni—her raptures were almost always superior in length if not in intensity (pp. 301–6). But Caterina de' Ricci's sanctity was linked above all with her promotion of a strict monastic life in keeping with the Council of Trent (p. 192), and lacks the prophetic tension characteristic of the Dominican tertiaries of the early Cinquecento.

63. I will use the anonymous *Apologia* cited in note 61 and Alessi's Latin *vita,* written between 1550 and 1555 but left unpublished. It is now available in Di Agresti's edition, *Santa Caterina de' Ricci: Libellus de gestis di fr. Niccolò Alessi,* Collana Ricciana, Fonti 2 (Florence, 1964) (cited as Alessi, *Libellus*).

64. The best historical treatment of her life is still Giovanni Battista Melloni, *Atti o memorie degli uomini illustri in santità nati o morti in Bologna,* class 2, vol. 3

(Bologna, 1780), pp. 300–386. Elena's reputation for virginity was already widespread in Italy in the first decade of the Cinquecento, when Battista Fregoso cited her as an example of abstinence and continence: "in urbe Bononie duo ferantur esse nobili genere orti quibus abunde opes suppetunt matrimonio in adolescentiae flore coniuncti qui iam decimum et octavum annum in eodem thalamo eodemque lecto virginitatem illesam custodiunt" (Battista Fregoso, *De Dictis factisque memorabilibus collectanea a Camillo Gilino latina facta* [Paris: in Aedibus Golliotu de Pre, 1518], book 4, chap. 3, fol. 116). Many miracles took place at her tomb, as Pietro Aretino attests, albeit ironically: "in one year were hung more votive candles, more shirts and shifts, and more little paintings than there are around the tomb of blessed saint Elena dall'Olio in Bologna" (Pietro Aretino, *Sei giornate,* ed. Guido Davico Bonino [Turin, 1975], p. 93, with another reference to "Saint Elena" on p. 215).

65. The Lateran canon Pietro Ritta of Lucca (d. 1522) lived in Bologna for many years and wrote numerous devotional and ascetic works that were very popular in the sixteenth century. On his influence in Lucca, see Marino Berengo, *Nobili e mercanti nella Lucca del Cinquecento* (Turin, 1965), pp. 368–69; on his life and works, see Cesare Lucchesini, *Della storia letteraria del ducato lucchese,* vol. 1 (Lucca, 1825), pp. 219–20. A few of his works, such as the *Dottrina del ben morire* and the *Regule de la vita spirituale et secreta theologia,* have attracted scholarly attention: see Alberto Tenenti, *Il senso della morte e l'amore della vita nel Rinascimento: Francia e Italia* (Turin, 1977), pp. 310–15; and Delio Cantimori, "Le idee religiose," pp. 38–42. However, his entire literary production deserves study as examples of the minor vernacular works that circulated widely in devout circles during the first three decades of the Cinquecento. Ritta was a famous preacher, and many of his writings represent syntheses of his sermon cycles, as their dedicatory letters state: the *Arte nova del ben pensare e contemplare la passione dil nostro Signor Giesù Christo benedetto* (Bologna: Hyeronimo Benedetti, 1523) was the fruit of roughly two hundred sermons he gave in Venice, and the *Arte del ben morire* (Bologna: Hyeronimo Benedetti, 1518) also derived from a sermon delivered in Venice. Through his preaching, Ritta also spread word of Elena Duglioli's marvelous deeds, carrying her fame to many cities. In Cesena, where he preached in November 1515, Ritta "said many things about the Turks and the Moors and the holy Turkish woman who was a Christian in Constantinople and would be a canonized saint" (manuscript chronicle by Giuliano Fantaguzzi, cited from the transcription by Claudio Riva, "La vita di Cesena agli inizi del '500: Dal 'Caos' di Giuliano Fantaguzzi" [thesis, University of Bologna, 1969–70, directed by Prof. Paolo Prodi], p. 119). In Venice, Pietro of Lucca put the Augustinian hermit Girolamo Regino in contact with Elena Duglioli, as Regino stated in his prefatory letter to the 1518 edition of the *Arte del ben morire* (which he says he acquired because Duglioli had predicted that his death was imminent): "in this year of 1515 through the letters of a blessed virgin who remained intact throughout many years of holy matrimony thanks to the very great grace of her sweet and loving spouse Jesus Christ." The evidence of Pietro of Lucca's frequent stays in Venice and the similarities between some of his teachings and the *vita* of Chi-

ara Bugni, as well as Chiara and Elena's shared devotion to the Virgin's milk, suggest contacts between the followers of the two "blessed women." But the fact remains that Chiara Bugni was silenced in 1511, while Elena continued to enjoy great fame for another decade.

66. Biblioteca Comunale dell'Archiginnasio, Bologna, MS Gozzadini no. 292: Pietro Ruta (Ritta) da Lucca, *Narrativa della vita e morte della beata Elena Duglioli dall'Oglio che seguì li XXIII settembre 1520*, and *D. Petri Lucensis Can. Reg. Lat. Prioris S. Johannis in Monte Bonon. De progressu et exitu vitae d. Helene exemplar compendii epistolae ad Leonem Decimum Pont. Max* (cited as Pietro da Lucca, *Narrativa* or *Epistola*). Among the manuscripts currently being inventoried in the Archiginnasio library is a quarto volume of 190 leaves, containing an anonymous legend of the blessed Elena written by a contemporary of hers. Thanks to Dr. Mario Fanti, I was able to see the manuscript after this essay had already been drafted; I was thus able to take the anonymous legend into account only indirectly, through the accurate citations in Melloni, *Atti o memorie*. The Gozzadini MS 292 also contains texts concerning the "heart [that was] physically removed" from the virgin Elena and her miraculous milk. The first printed *vita* of Elena was that of Carlo Bentivoglio, *Compendio della vita della B. Elena dall'Olio, vergine, maritata e vedova* (Bologna: Heirs of Antonio Pisarri, 1693).

67. According to her legend, even though she was a virgin—indeed, as a token of her virginity—Elena received the miraculous gift of milk; this milk nourished her spiritual children (MS Gozzadini 292, *Del cuore*, fols. 14–15). On the basis of one of Elena's prophecies, Ritta maintained that her body would remain uncorrupted and the milk would continue to flow even after her death, as proof of her sanctity (Pietro da Lucca, *Narrativa*, fol. 2). But not everyone believed what her followers publicized and preached from the pulpits; this caused such sharp divisions within the city that the vice-legate of Bologna decided to hold an inspection of her body, which took place on 6 November 1520, in the presence of officials, surgeons, and prominent doctors. But even the incision of her breast did not settle the controversy. According to Alberti, "this body was found to be rotten and stinking and the breast full of rot, even if these canons said that the rot was milk" (Biblioteca Universitaria, Bologna, MS italiano 97: Leandro Alberti, *Historie di Bologna divise in 5 deche*, vol. 4, fol. 156r). According to the anonymous legend, the doctors themselves disagreed; Elena's followers won the support of Fiorenzuola, Pomponazzi, Girolamo of Carpi, and Niccolò of Genoa, against Ludovico Leoni and Angelo of Parma. To resolve this difference of opinion, on 30 December there was another inspection, which concluded that the body was uncorrupted; a favorable report was then sent to the Roman curia (Melloni, *Atti o memorie*, pp. 378–79).

68. Elena is listed among the beatified of Bologna by Gabriele Paleotti, *Archiepiscopale Bononiense sive de Bononiensis Ecclesiae administratione* (Rome, 1594), p. 595, and in a sixteenth-century manuscript that belonged to the Poor Clares of the convent of Corpus Domini: "The blessed dall'Olio . . . lived always in a most holy manner . . . she worked many miracles in life and after her death . . . and is buried in a most splendid sepulchre in San Giovanni in Monte, in the chapel of Santa Cecilia"

(Biblioteca Comunale dell'Archiginnasio, Bologna, MS B 1398: *Vite de' santi bolognesi*, fol. 10). Lambertini confirms the continuity of Elena's cult, but, since beatification proceedings were never opened in her case, includes hers among the "casus excepti" (Lambertini, *De servorum Dei beatificatione*, book 2, chap. 18, nos. 9–10, pp. 116–17). When beatification proceedings were subsequently begun, her public cult was recognized in 1828: see *Sacra Rituum Congregatione Bononien. Super confirmatione cultus ab immemorabili tempore praestiti B. Helenae ab Oleo seu super casu excepto a Decretis Sa.Me. Urbani Papae VIII* (Rome, 1828).

   69. Born in Fermo in 1496, Serafino Aceti de' Porti studied in Ravenna and then in Padua, where he probably met Antonio Maria Zaccaria, future founder of the Barnabites and Angelics. He became a Lateran canon and won fame as a preacher and author of spiritual works. He may have had ties with his fellow canon Pietro of Lucca, whom he mentioned as the confessor of Gentile of Ravenna and called "a man of exceptional learning and sanctity" (*Vita di due beatissime donne*, fol. 362). However, he was closer in spirit to the early Barnabites; he was strongly influenced by Battista of Crema, whose works he defended and diffused, and he was among the earliest admirers of the Angelic Paola Antonia Negri. Worried by the spread of heresy and quick to denounce suspect books like *Il sommario della dottrina cristiana*, then circulating in Modena, Serafino of Fermo framed the problem of "false" doctrines in apocalyptic terms, convinced that the events he was witnessing signaled the end of time: see Gabriele Feyles, *Serafino da Fermo, canonico regolare lateranense, 1496–1540: La vita, le opere, la dottrina spirituale* (Turin, 1942). On the ties between Serafino and the Barnabites, see especially Premoli, *Storia dei Barnabiti;* and on his Joachimite influences, see Prosperi, "America e Apocalisse," pp. 38–45. Serafino was too young to have met Margherita, but he certainly knew Gentile of Ravenna, whose spiritual son he professed to be; and he credited Margherita and Gentile with inspiring some of his teachings. He wrote their biographies in a short work entitled *Vita di due beatissime donne, Margherita e Gentile, brevemente per don Serafino da Fermo raccolta*, first published in Mantua shortly after 1535 and reprinted many times in various languages along with Serafino's other works; my citations are to *Opere del R.P.D. Serafino da Fermo Canonico regulare con aggiunte rispetto alle altre impressioni* (Venice: Al Segno de la Speranza, 1556), fols. 345–64. He expounded the teachings he received from Gentile in the short treatise *Del discernimento de i spiriti*, first published in 1535 and reprinted in *Opere del R.P.D. Serafino da Fermo*, fols. 371–406. A Latin translation of Serafino's *vitae* of the two blessed women is in *Acta Sanctorum*, January, vol. 3 (Brussels, 1863), pp. 161–64 and 525–29. Another sixteenth-century *vita* of Margherita and Gentile, drawn from the records of the first informational hearings for their beatification, was written by Hieronymus Rubeus, a historian from Ravenna; see *Acta Sanctorum*, January, 3: 166–67 and 529–30. The records of the informational hearings on the lives, virtues, and miracles of the two women, held in May 1537 before the governor of Ravenna and surviving in two manuscript copies, have recently been published: Walter Ferretti, *Le beate Margherita e Gentile di Russi e il loro Processo di Santità, con note e appendici* (Faenza, 1978).

70. In a letter of 26 August 1537 addressed to Ercole Gonzaga, the cardinal of Mantua, Cardinal Simonetta, who had the task of "expediting the beatification proceedings of the two women of Ravenna," informed him that the pope "has decided that since this is a matter of great importance, it must be treated and decided in consistory." Cardinal Simonetta made a similar declaration to Federico Gonzaga, the duke of Mantua, in a letter sent that same day: "His Holiness has decided that since the present times are very turbulent and calamitous, and since the matter is serious and of great importance, it can only be handled in consistory." The pope promised to decide the matter in the consistory that was to be held in November; but no recognition of the cult came from that session, if the case was even discussed: see Ferretti, *Le beate Margherita e Gentile,* pp. 87–89 (which, however, attributes the letter to the cardinal of Sermoneta, Nicolò Caietani; the reading "Simonetta" is confirmed by Serafino da Fermo, *Vita di due beatissime donne,* fol. 364v). Thus, because of the "turbulent and calamitous" times, Duke Federico Gonzaga could not manage to obtain the papal brief of recognition that twenty years earlier his predecessor Gianfrancesco had been able to procure for the recognition of the cult of the blessed Osanna.

71. Thanks to the circulation of the writings of Serafino of Fermo, the fame of the two blessed women spread widely, and their lives of prayer were offered as models for many generations of the devout by Luigi di Granata, *Trattato dell' orazione et devotione* (Venice: Gabriel Giolito de Ferrari, 1578), pp. 183–84, collected with his other writings in *Tutte le opere* (Venice: Gabriel Giolito de Ferrari, 1577–79), vol. 2; he draws the examples of Margherita of Russi, Elena Duglioli, and Osanna of Mantua from Serafino da Fermo, "Della oratione interiore," in his *Opere,* fol. 54. Tommaso Bozio, too, mentions the blessed Margherita, basing his remarks on Rubeus' biography (*De signis ecclesiae Dei,* pp. 214 and 509).

The Congregation of the Chierici regolari del Buon Gesù, founded in 1526 by Girolamo Maluselli, a follower of Gentile of Ravenna, was canonically approved by Paul III in 1538 and confirmed by Julius III in 1551. Almost exclusively local in nature, it was suppressed by Innocent X in 1651 because it had only ten members. The congregation arose from an earlier Compagnia del Buon Gesù, involving both priests and laity, whose inspiration and rule were provided by the two blessed women of Ravenna. In 1617 one of the fathers of the congregation reprinted Serafino's works on the two women, together with a biography of Maluselli: Simone Marini da Ravenna, *Vite gloriose delle due beate Margherita e Gentile et del P. d. Girolamo Fundatori della Religione de' Padri del Buon Giesù di Ravenna* (Venice: Ambrosio Dei, 1617). The rules of the Compagnia del Buon Gesù were recently edited by Innocenzo Colosio, "Serafino da Fermo (†1540), le BB. Ravennati Margherita e Gentile e le Regole della Compagnia del Buon Gesù," *La nuova rivista di ascetica e mistica* 2 (1977): 246–58.

72. For basic biographical and bibliographical information, see Nicola Raponi, entry "Angela Merici," in *DBI,* vol. 3 (Rome, 1961), pp. 187–89. Among the many recent studies, see especially Teresa Ledóchowska, *Angèle Merici et la Compagnie de S.te Ursula à la lumière des documents* (Milan and Rome, 1967), translated as *Angela Merici and the Company of St. Ursula According to the Historical Documents*

by Mary Teresa Neylan (Milan, 1968); and the writings of Angela Merici, *Regola, ricordi, legati: Testo antico e testo moderno,* ed. Luciana Mariani and Elisa Tarolli (Brescia, 1976). See also Charmarie J. Blaisdell, "Angela Merici and the Ursulines," in *Religious Orders of the Catholic Reformation: In Honor of John C. Olin on his Seventy-fifth Birthday,* ed. Richard L. DeMolen (New York, 1994), pp. 99–136.

73. Gabriele Cozzano, *Risposta contro quelli persuadono la clausura alle vergini di S. Orsola,* written around 1544–46 and published in Ledóchowska, *Angèle Merici,* 2: 332–59; Prodi, "Vita religiosa e crisi sociale," pp. 313–16.

74. *Le Justificationi della vita della Reverenda Madre Suor Angela Terzabita,* depositions of witnesses at the informational hearings of June–October 1568, recorded by the notary Giovan Battista Nazari and hence known as the "Processo Nazari"; cited here from Ledóchowska, *Angèle Merici,* 1: 313–24. Nazari also wrote a report on the "life and death of the blessed Sister Angela Merici," which essentially follows the depositions of the four witnesses at the hearings; it is published in Giuditta Bertolotti, *Storia di S. Angela Merici, 1474–1540* (Brescia, 1926), pp. 215–24. The Capuchin friar Mattia Bellintani of Salò also wrote, but did not publish, a *vita* of Merici: Matthias a Salò, "Historia Capuccina," ed. Melchior a Pobladura, in *Monumenta Historica Ordinis Fratrum Minorum Capuccinorum,* vol. 6 (Rome, 1950), pp. 77–112. The first printed legend of the saint appeared anonymously in Brescia in 1600; written by the Florentine Ottavio Gondi on the basis of the Processo Nazari, it met with great success and was reprinted many times. My citations are to the 1616 edition, which also contains Merici's testament: *Vita della b. Angela bresciana prima fondatrice della Compagnia di S. Orsola, composta dal M.R.P. Ottavio Fiorentino* (Brescia: Comincini, 1616). For an interpretation of Mattia of Salò's biography of Angela Merici in the light of his other writings and Capuchin spirituality, see Costanzo Cargnoni, "Vita della B. Angela da Desenzano nell' 'Historia Capuccina' di Mattia da Salò: Agiografia e letteratura spirituale della riforma tridentina," *L'Italia francescana* 52 (1977): 187–218.

75. Premoli, *Storia dei Barnabiti;* Massimo Petrocchi, "Dottrine e orientamenti spirituali della scuola lombarda del Cinquecento," in his *Storia della spiritualità,* 2: 61–109; Adriano Prosperi, entry "Besozzi Giovanni Pietro," in *DBI,* vol. 9 (Rome, 1967), pp. 680–84. See also Richard L. DeMolen, "The First Centenary of the Barnabites, 1533–1633," in DeMolen, *Religious Orders of the Catholic Reformation,* pp. 59–96.

76. In February 1551, the Council of Ten expelled Negri and the Barnabites from Venice, perhaps for political reasons, believing her to be a spy in the service of the governor of Milan, as Besozzi stated many years later: Premoli, *Storia dei Barnabiti,* p. 95. This motive does not seem improbable in the light of a similar episode that had taken place ten years earlier (see note 16), although the Ten recorded only a vague expression of displeasure at "their way of acting and the ladies' gatherings they held" (Pio Paschini, *Venezia e l'inquisizione romana da Giulio III a Pio IV* [Padua, 1959], pp. 68–70). In reality, even if this was the official justification offered by the Venetian authorities, we should note that the Ten had received a series of denunciations that questioned the orthodoxy of Negri's congregation and aroused sus-

picions of "Illuminism" on her part: "We have recently been informed that they gave too much authority to their Mother Mistress, a Milanese woman of thirty-six or thirty-seven years of age whom the men and women of this congregation and the priests call 'divine,' and they say that she is imbued with the Holy Spirit and consider her sanctified and incapable of sin; that in her private assemblies, which included both men and women, not only daily events but also words and thoughts were subjected to detailed scrutiny; that the priests knelt before this Mother Mistress, who granted or denied them permission to celebrate mass and taught and interpreted the Scriptures" (letter of 17 February 1551 in response to the papal nuncio, in which the part beginning with "call divine" was crossed out; my citation comes from Stella, *Anabattismo e antitrinitarismo,* p. 126; the official letter sent to the nuncio, without the passage quoted above, is in Premoli, *Storia dei Barnabiti,* p. 100). If political motivations had a certain bearing in the expulsion of the Barnabites from Venice, there can be no doubt that accusations like those received by the Ten prompted her congregation to change its course and later served to justify the actions it took against Negri.

77. *Lettere spirituali della devota religiosa Angelica Paola Antonia de' Negri milanese: Vita della medesima raccolta da Giovan Battista Fontana de' Conti* (Rome: In Aedibus Populi Romani, 1576) (cited as Fontana, *Vita*). This legend, written hastily to accompany the second edition of Negri's letters, resembles in many ways the hagiographic legends of the holy women of the early sixteenth century. This printing, which is dedicated to Monsignor Angelo Cesi, bishop of Todi, opens with a list of dozens of bishops, priests, monks, friars, and nobles who are invoked as witnesses to Negri's sanctity. On the contested attribution of Negri's letters and on Besozzi's response to Fontana's *Vita,* see Premoli, *Storia dei Barnabiti,* pp. 195–97 and 266–67, and Petrocchi, *Storia della spiritualità,* 2: 72, who accepts the attribution of the letters to Negri as demonstrated by Giovanna Maria Caldiroli, "L'ambiente e la personalità dell'Angelica Paola Antonia Negri, 1508–1555," (thesis, University of Perugia, 1968–69).

78. Negri is listed as "blessed" in Tiepolo's seventeenth-century catalog of Venetian saints: Silvio Tramontin and Giorgio Fedalto, *Santi e beati vissuti a Venezia,* Biblioteca agiografica veneziana, 5 (Venice, 1971), p. 20.

79. Perhaps hoping to improve relations with Emperor Charles V, and certainly seeking to explain away a pro-French prophecy made by Panigarola that had proven false, Giorgio Benigno Salviati wrote: "Although some things appear to have taken place differently from the way she predicted, this is no reason to be amazed, since sometimes God grants a prophecy but not understanding, and often one thing is mistaken for another, as happened once to this virgin, who saw the election of the present emperor and thought it was the king of France because she had seen the election and heard the cry 'Long live the King.' When she told me these things in the presence of the reverend sister Bonaventura, I asked her whether a king other than the king of France might be meant, especially since she told me she had seen a beautiful banner with a red cross; and I told her: 'Mother, this is the king of Spain, because his sign is a red cross.' I have no idea why God allowed this to happen, but I do know that she was terribly humiliated as a result" (*Legenda,* fol. 15).

Francesco Alidosi, papal legate in Bologna from 1508 to 1511 and a harsh foe of the Bentivoglio faction (whose regime had collapsed in 1506), was noted for his devotion to Elena Duglioli. As the contemporary chronicler Girolamo Bolognini related, "On 4 January 1510, the legate of Bologna . . . before his departure went several times early in the morning to the house of a certain little saint in the Miola neighborhood, the wife of a certain Ser Benedetto dall'Olio, named Lady Elena; and he entreated her to make special prayers for him and celebrated mass there in her house, giving her the eucharist with his own hand; and later he gave her 600 ducats in several installments, which she could spend for God, as she saw fit." The chronicler Fileno delle Tuate, known as Seccadenari, mentioned Elena's relations with Popes Julius II and Leo X, whom she had probably met when they were papal legates in Bologna: On 24 September 1520 died Elena Duglioli, "who was considered a very saintly woman. Pope Julius did not disdain her friendship, nor did Pope Leo, who spoke with her on many occasions. Many cardinals had dealings with her, as did other great prelates" (Melloni, *Atti o memorie,* pp. 329–30).

Caterina Vigri's first biographer, Sabadino degli Arienti, mentioned Ginevra Sforza Bentivoglio's devotion for the saint: Sabadino de li Arienti, *Gynevera de le clare donne,* Scelta di curiosità letterarie inedite o rare dal secolo XIII al XIX, Dispensa 223 (Bologna, 1969), p. 204. This devotion is confirmed by the presence of many women of the Bentivoglio family in Caterina's convent of Corpus Domini. This convent of Poor Clares does not seem to have served as a gathering place for the Bentivoglio faction following the collapse of their regime, though perhaps this should be explored. There is no doubt, however, that Elena's cult arose as a support for the legate and the pope, and that the followers of this "living saint" sought to concentrate civic attention on her, creating a cult that would offset and outweigh those linked to the Bentivoglio family. This, I believe, is the reason behind the construction of the chapel of Santa Cecilia in the church of San Giovanni in Monte, promoted by Elena and her powerful protectors, Antonio and Lorenzo Pucci, and Raphael's painting of St. Cecilia: this project was intended to eclipse the Bentivoglio oratory in the Augustinian monastery of San Giacomo, with its series of frescoes of St. Cecilia recently completed by Francia, Costa, Aspertini, and others. For interpretations of Raphael's painting as an expression of Neoplatonic culture and religious thought, see Stanislaw Mossakowski, "Raphael's 'St. Cecilia': An Iconographical Study," *Zeitschrift für Kunstgeschichte* 31 (1968): 1–24, and Daniel Arasse, "Extases et visions béatifiques à l'apogée de la Renaissance: Quatre images de Raphaël," *MEFRM* 84 (1972): 403–92; on the oratory of Santa Cecilia, see Maurizio Calvesi, *Gli affreschi di Santa Cecilia in Bologna* (Bologna, 1960), and Daniela Scaglietti, "La Cappella di Santa Cecilia," in *Il tempio di San Giacomo Maggiore in Bologna: Studi sulla storia e le opere d'arte, regesto documentario* (Bologna, 1967), pp. 133–46. If Elena's cult, despite its popularity, did not manage to supplant the well-established devotion for the civic "saint" Caterina, which in 1524 received its first formal recognition with the grant of a proper office and mass, the reason is not only that it lacked the institutional support of a religious order, but also that it had lost its political function. During her lifetime, Elena had been valuable for her prophetic and charismatic powers, which added luster to the papal government, and for her readiness to side with the pope against the partisans of the Council of Pisa (which included the Bentivoglio faction): when asked to pray for a cardinal who had joined this French-backed council, Elena replied that "she would not pray for those who went against the church and the supreme pope and rebuked him sharply, declaring that he and all his accomplices were deluded and that all such assemblies were the work of the devil" ("Leggenda anonima," in Melloni, *Atti o memorie,* p. 354). But as a "relic" Elena could not compete with the more famous Caterina. In any case, by 1524 the papal government had put down firm roots in Bologna, soothing its leading citizens by granting them new senatorial seats and adopting as its own the civic cult of Caterina Vigri. On Elena Duglioli, see now "L'altra Cecilia: Elena Duglioli Dall'Olio, 1472–1520," in Zarri, *Le sante vive,* pp. 165–96.

80. The legends (except for the latest, that of Angela Merici) all mention notes taken during the lives of the blessed women; but their principal sources remained the informational hearings that recorded the testimony of those who had known the "living saint." Fontana's statement that he wrote the *vita* of Paola Antonia Negri on the basis of earlier drafts by Morigia and Zaccaria is dismissed by Premoli, *Storia dei Barnabiti,* p. 77.

81. In 1500 Ippolito d'Este attested to the authenticity of Lucia of Narni's stigmata; the document is published in Domenico Ponsi, *Vita della beata Lucia vergine di Narni* (Rome, 1711), p. 205. While still protonotary, Sigismondo Gonzaga witnessed and signed the notarial act describing Stefana Quinzani's ecstasies of the Passion in 1500 (Brunati, *Vita o gesta,* 2: 62–64). Ercole Gonzaga supported the beatification of Margherita and Gentile (see note 70).

The documents describing Stefana's ecstasies in 1497 were redacted in the presence of two priests, three monks, four doctors of law, one medical doctor, one knight, a ducal referendary, and eight other people, including Verdello, the gentleman from Crema in whose house Stefana was lodged. Those present at the next ecstasy, in 1500, included the Gonzaga marquises and the protonotary Sigismondo with their secretaries and other courtiers, Osanna of Mantua, members of religious orders, and citizens of Mantua (ibid., pp. 55–64). The Lateran canon Antonio of Venice's statement at Gentile's informational hearings is also noteworthy. Speaking of the spread of her cult, he said that "the holy devotion of the blessed Margherita and Gentile" converted 400 people: "gentlemen and gentlewomen, members of religious orders, counts, knights, doctors, prelates, lords, and citizens, with every other manner and mode of human status and condition" (Ferretti, *Le beate Margherita e Gentile,* p. 60).

82. Only five people—two priests and three friars—testified at the preliminary hearings for Osanna of Mantua in 1515, at least according to the portion of the document that has survived (AGOP, sec. 10, no. 2490: mutilated manuscript copy of the proceedings, fols. 17–34), which should be integrated with the three depositions printed in AGOP, sec. 10, no. 2492 B: *Mantuana Canonizationis B. Osanna de Andreasiis tertii Ordinis Sancti Dominici Summarium,* pp. 1–21. Of the seven witnesses who testified about the life and virtues of Gentile of Ravenna, three were Lateran

canons, another three were priests, and the other a suffragan bishop. However, of the nine witnesses who testified concerning Margherita of Russi, who died thirty-two years before the proceedings, only one was a priest (Ferretti, *Le beate Margherita e Gentile,* pp. 27–81). At the 1550 hearings on behalf of Caterina of Racconigi, held before the podestà of Garessio, five witnesses testified, including a Dominican tertiary who had known her for thirty years and had lived with her for five years (AGOP, sec. 10, no. 660). On the other hand, only four lay witnesses testified for Angela Merici in the Processo Nazari in 1568. They were joined in 1591 by a canon regular from Brescia, who confirmed Angela's virtues and miracles and added the story of another miracle that he had heard from a Capuchin friar (Ledóchowska, *Angèle Merici,* 1: 313–25).

In the informational hearings mentioned above, the main witnesses were the family or friends with whom the holy woman had lived for many years: the Molli and Orioli for Margherita; Maluselli for Gentile; Capello (especially her fellow nun, Osanna Capello) for Caterina of Racconigi; Antonio Romano and Agostino Gallo for Angela Merici. If we examine the miracles mentioned in the legends, we note that a good number of nuns, monks, and friars were the object of miraculous healings or conversions by virtue of the blessed women. Obviously, the beneficiaries of miracles varied according to the situations in which the charismatic women lived: miracles involving nuns are prevalent in the legends concerning women who lived in religious communities, while conversions of priests or prelates are especially common in legends that depict the "living saint" as a force for ecclesiastical reform.

83. A few days after Osanna's death in 1505, nine beneficiaries of her miracles made depositions: except for one physician, all were artisans or merchants (AGOP, sec. 10, no. 2490, fols. 3–16v). In the beatification hearings concerning Margherita of Russi, witnesses mentioned many miracles that she had wrought on behalf of people close to her, inhabitants of Russi, Ravenna, and the surrounding area, in all probability including peasants; but the beneficiaries of the miracles were not called to testify. The hearings were supposed to be conducted by questioning trustworthy people, and the governing council of Ravenna believed that taking the depositions of prominent citizens was the way to comply with the request from Rome for information about the two women's reputation for sanctity: "Although we could have responded ourselves, we wanted to collect the judgments and opinions of other distinguished and noble people of this city, especially their contemporaries" (Ferretti, *Le beate Margherita e Gentile,* p. 24).

84. The efforts of the people of Viterbo to keep Lucia of Narni in their city are documented even in nonhagiographical sources: see Zarri, "Pietà e profezia," p. 209. Sebastiano Bontempi noted the desire of the citizens of Narni to retain Colomba of Rieti: "When they approached the city of Narni a great crowd of people stood on the walls to see her. Throngs of men and women received her with great rejoicing, like a jubilee." Shortly thereafter, the people of Rieti sent ambassadors to Perugia, to get the "saint" to return to her native city: "But when this reached the ears of the common people, they placed guards around her and sent the messengers back empty-handed" (Bontempi, *Legenda volgare,* fols. 19v and 28). Similarly, Margherita of

Russi was welcomed in Rimini with popular veneration: "When she went to Rimini, all the people and clergy came to see her, and everyone acclaimed her and revered her as a saint" (Serafino da Fermo, *Vita di due beatissime donne,* fol. 347v).

Pandolfo Nassino of Brescia noted the death of Angela Merici and described her funeral in the church of Sant'Afra: "On January 28 she was borne to Sant'Afra . . . with as much ceremony and as great a crowd as if she were a lord, because this Sister Angela so preached the faith of God Almighty to everyone that she was beloved by all . . . and she stayed like this in the church of Sant'Afra for a good many days without any part of her body putrefying in the least, and she was then placed in a tomb in that church where she was buried with the greatest honor." Indeed, one witness at Angela's beatification hearings said that her body remained unburied for a period of thirty days (Ledóchowska, *Angèle Merici,* 1: 326 and 324). Elena Duglioli's body was also buried with great pomp and honor, as the chroniclers unanimously attest (Melloni, *Atti o memorie,* pp. 350–51). Sebastiano Bontempi, after describing the solemn procession that accompanied Colomba of Rieti's body to the church, states that the burial had to be delayed for four days "instante maximo concursu virorum ac mulierum civitatis et comitatus ac circumstantium urbium, osculari volentium manus et pedes ipsius beatae virginis Columbae"; although priests guarded the body, "nihilominus non poterant custodiri vestes illius a raptu instantibus perinde turbis cum signetis, panniculis et Pater-nostris pro contactu venerandi corporis" (*Legenda latina,* p. 217*).

85. Osanna Andreasi, Chiara Bugni, Arcangela Panigarola, Elena Duglioli, Caterina de' Ricci, and Paola Antonia Negri came from noble or wealthy families; these women were certainly literate, and some left letters or other writings. Various letters from Andreasi are found in the Gonzaga archives; but her contemporaries doubted the authenticity of the spiritual letters printed as an appendix to the legend by Scolari, who sought to authenticate them by showing them to two witnesses, the secretary of the Gonzaga and the vicar of Santa Maria di Gradaro (Scolari, *Libretto de la vita* [1524 ed.], fol. 115). In addition to their correspondence, Ricci and Panigarola left spiritual tracts: for Ricci, see Collana Ricciana; for Panigarola, see Biblioteca Ambrosiana, Milan, MSS E 56 and O 248 sup. (*Epistolario di Arcangela*), and MS H 258 inf. (*Giardino Spirituale*). According to her legend, Bugni wrote letters and dictated the *Discorsi spirituali* that, after her death, were transcribed and published by Cimarelli. Elena Duglioli supposedly wrote a short treatise entitled "Breve e signoril modo del spiritual vivere e di facilmente pervenire alla Christiana perfezione" and addressed to Anna, marchioness of Monferrato; this work is published in Melloni, *Atti o memorie,* pp. 436–42, who cites two sixteenth-century editions of the pamphlet on pp. 322 and 343. I have already mentioned the problem of the authenticity of the *Lettere spirituali* attributed to Paola Antonia Negri (see note 77). Lucia of Narni, too, wrote letters, some of which have been published in Gandini, *Sulla venuta,* pp. 67 and 97–101. Margherita of Ravenna and Angela Merici at least inspired the rules of the congregations they founded. The rest of these "living saints" probably did not know how to write. "If I knew how to write or had the clerk ready at hand, I would make more copies of my letters to your Lordship," declared Stefana

Quinzani to the marquis Gonzaga; Stefana's voluminous correspondence was executed by various scribes hired for the occasion (Tolasi, *Stefana Quinzani,* p. 16).

Sebastiano Bontempi noted the importance of the confessor in interpreting revelations: when her order subjected Colomba to an inexperienced confessor, "Multa tamen signa per idem tempus sopita, et plures revelationes neglectae fuerant, vel melius ut dixerim suffocatae" (*Legenda latina,* p. 204*). Veronica of Binasco's revelations were collected in three volumes by her fellow nuns (Isolani, *Inexplicabilis,* p. 170). Caterina of Racconigi asked the Dominican provincial of Lombardy to assign her a reliable confessor "to whom she could confide her secrets and who could answer the letters she receives from princes and great scholars (Pico-Morelli, *Compendio,* p. 67).

86. The angel taught Veronica to recite the Roman office and even dictated a book to her: "Composuit Veronica opus praeclarissimum Angelo dictante, quod divina ira ab mortalium oculis creditur ablatum, Virgine adhuc vivente. Futurum vero affirmavit, ut coenobio Divae Martae volumen ipsum providentissimo Dei munere aliquando restitueretur" (Isolani, *Inexplicabilis,* p. 182). Note that these statements date from the period in which the *Apocalypsis nova* was circulating in her convent. On Osanna, see Silvestri, *La vita e stupendi miraculi,* book 3, chap. 1. Regarding Stefana, it was said that "St. Paul conversed regularly with her in human likeness and taught her many things and gave her to understand many things that are to come." Stefana's wisdom was such that the author of her legend did not hesitate to say "she had theology more clearly in her mind than any master of theology on earth" (Guerrini, "La prima 'Legenda volgare,'" pp. 116 and 150).

87. Pietro da Lucca, *Narrativa,* p. 7. Although uneducated people's knowledge of languages could be (as in these cases) presented as a divine gift, it might also be considered the work of the devil; indeed, in the early sixteenth century, knowledge of esoteric languages on the part of the "unlettered" constituted a sign of witchcraft, and was the subject of philosophical discussions in Bologna: see Paola Zambelli, "Aut diabolus aut Achillinus: Fisionomia, astrologia, e demonologia nel metodo di un aristotelico," *Rinascimento,* ser. 2, 18 (1978): 77.

88. "I also thought it remarkable," declared the knight Chizzola at the preliminary hearings for the beatification of Angela Merici, "that she knew how to use Latin so well, never having studied Latin letters; and also that without having studied the Holy Scriptures, she could create such beautiful, learned, and spiritual sermons, which sometimes lasted an hour" (Ledóchowska, *Angèle Merici,* 1: 319; see also Ottavio Gondi, *Vita della beata Angela,* p. 19). It was said that Paola Antonia Negri "did not know how to read or write any better than other women usually do, but if anything rather less well, since she made mistakes in reading and wrote slowly"; and yet she knew the letters of St. Paul "wonderfully well" and "expounded the psalms and all of Holy Scriptures so theologically" that she was visited by many bishops and famous preachers like Serafino of Fermo (Fontana, *Vita,* pp. 56–57).

89. St. Paul declared (1 Timothy 2:12): "I permit no woman to teach or have authority over men; she is to keep silent." In keeping with this precept, the Dominican philosopher and theologian Bartolomeo Sibilla, author of a treatise that was very

popular at the end of the fifteenth century and throughout the sixteenth, asserted that one was not obliged to believe the prophecies of St. Catherine and St. Birgitta, since such prophecies could result from "phantasia nimis fatigata" or "ex industria humana exercitata," and since these female saints might themselves have been deluded, "eo quid forte non sine culpa presumpserunt illa facere quae ad eas non pertinuerunt." Sibilla went on to say that prophecies were not necessary for salvation, since Christians already had the Scriptures and the Church fathers. Perhaps God might send some women "tamquam doctrices et prophetas" to make up for the negligence of the clergy and cause them embarrassment, as he did with the prophets of both sexes sent to the Jewish people. But this could cause confusion: there were female saints greater than Catherine and Birgitta, such as Elisabeth, who did not prophesy "sed solum studuisse profectioni virtutum; nihil se intromittens de impertibentibus earum statibus" (Bartholomaeus Sibylla, *Speculum peregrinarum quaestionum* [Rome: Eucharium Silber alias Franck natione Alamanum, 1493], dec. 1, chap. 8, quest. 1, quaestiuncula 6, fols. 146v–147). Sibilla was not alone in expressing such thoughts: he echoed the opinions of many other theologians, who always looked askance on women. What is important to note here is that an open confutation of this passage appeared in various sixteenth-century editions of the *Vita miracolosa* of St. Catherine of Siena translated by Catarino (see note 29). The confutation, which asserted that women too can have prophetic charisma, constituted much of point 9 in a twelve-point *Digression* devoted to upholding the validity of prophecy and the "truth of the future renewal of the church." But this confutation did not appear in the first edition of the work, published in 1524; it was thus a later addition to rebut a text whose author already numbered among the "classic" writers of philosophical-theological literature: Sibilla was not named explicitly in the confutation, but was indicated simply as a "modern master" who wrote of "who knows what wandering questions (for such is the title of his book)." Since I have not been able to find a second edition of the *Vita miracolosa* published during Catarino's lifetime, I could not determine whether the confutation of Sibilla's work should be attributed to Catarino himself or to the editors of the later reprintings; it is ascribed to Catarino by Quétif and Echard, *Scriptores Ordinis Praedicatorum*, 1: 872, which lists twelve editions of Sibilla's work between 1493 and 1609. But apart from the *Vita miracolosa*'s direct reference to the *Speculum peregrinarum quaestionum*, Sibilla's work is noteworthy for its discussions of divination, ecstasy, raptures, and the prophecies of sibyls, sorceresses, and seers—all topics that must have been very much on the minds of the authors of the legends of the "living saints," and that certainly were hotly debated at the end of the fifteenth century and remained of topical interest long thereafter.

Sebastiano Bontempi summarized the doubts of philosophers, physicians, and theologians concerning Colomba of Rieti, listing their objections in points that closely corresponded to Sibilla's theses. The philosophers discussed Colomba's ecstasies and wondered "an fuerit arreptitia, vel laboraret humore terrestri, vel usu rationis privata pythonizaret quasi energumenta. . . . Fabulabantur insuper de Circe, de mulieribus stabulariis, ac de Mercurio, qui solvissent hominum mentes, eosque mutassent in bestiarum formas, abdicassentque nonnullos duris curis." The doctors discussed her prolonged abstinence: "Tentabant medici consequenter, ob veritatem suae abstinentiae, de unguibus et capillis: scrutabantur de sudore aut odore aliquo, non minus de passione muliebri et secessu: observabant loquentis dentes, colorem facei et acies oculorum" (*Legenda latina*, p. 187*; and see Sibylla, *Speculum*, dec. 1, chap. 8, quest. 1, quaestiuncula 2, fol. 144). Similar doubts were expressed, albeit less subtly, by those who did not believe in the ecstasies of Osanna of Mantua: "They said she was a ditzy broad, and that her rapture from her senses was either faked or provoked by some wicked demon—or, as most people thought, caused by her feeble-mindedness" (Silvestri, *La vita e stupendi miraculi*, book 1, chap. 13). However, Pico-Morelli, *Compendio*, p. 143, reminds "certain Wise Men of our era" that God often wanted the people to be instructed by women, "whom he chose to send as teachers to humble their pride."

90. Sibilla synthesized the reasons for women's greater receptiveness to revelations under three headings: their physiology, their lack of reason, and their abundance of emotions (*Speculum*, dec. 1, chap. 8, quest. 1, quaestiuncula 5, fol. 146r–v). The same explanations were offered by Prierio: "quia propter complexionis fluxibilitatem facilius impressiones patiuntur, consequenter autem ad revelationes spiritibus separatis imprimentibus habiliores sunt." Women's greater susceptibility to diabolical illusions is a commonplace in demonological literature that Prierio—to cite an author who was equally involved in hagiography and demonology—explained as follows: Women are "in omnia facinora proniores et ad quadam etiam aptiores, ut ad ea quae obstetricum ministerio patrantur"; they are more credulous; their physiological make-up renders them more receptive to impressions; they are more talkative than men (Silvestro Mazzolini Prierio, *De strigimagarum daemonumque Mirandis libri tres* [Rome, 1575], book 2, chap. 5, pp. 157–58). See in general Marcello Craveri, *Sante e streghe: Biografie e documenti dal XIV al XVI secolo* (Milan, 1980).

91. Paola Antonia Negri was addressed as "divine Mother," a title that aroused the ire of her opponents. The biographers of the "living saints" unanimously recognized their gift of teaching. Serafino of Fermo even claimed that large crowds rushed to hear Margherita of Ravenna, "so that sometimes more than three hundred people hung on her teachings and on her account followed the way of the Gospel, and they publicly addressed her by the title of Teacher" (Serafino da Fermo, *Vita di due beatissime donne*, fol. 347).

92. The gifts of mystical marriage and the exchange of heart, present in the life of Catherine of Siena, were repeated in the legends of the Dominican "living saints" in exaggerated form, as if to demonstrate their greater perfection. Thus Caterina of Racconigi married Christ not once, but three times. This triple marriage, which already figured in the legend composed by Ludovico Dolce and Domenico of Braida, was explained by Pico as "an increase in the grace and heavenly gifts granted her through perceptible signs" (Pico-Morelli, *Compendio*, pp. 6–10 and 24). The same is said of the triple exchange of hearts. Among the blessed women who were not Dominicans, the gift of the mystical marriage recurs in Negri's legend (Fontana, *Vita*,

pp. 80–81) and the exchange of hearts in that of Elena Duglioli (Pietro da Lucca, *Narrativa*, p. 2).

93. Colomba of Rieti's biographer cited the legend of St. Catherine: "si in Legenda S. Catharinae Senensis, mutato vocabulo ponatur Soror Colomba, de ipsa essentialia morum et facta cuncta verificantur omnio" (Bontempi, *Legenda Iatina*, p. 184*). The reference to Catherine in Isolani's legend of Veronica of Binasco is equally explicit: "Quisquis es qui isthaec demiraris, legito Divae Catharinae Senensis praeclarissima gesta, quibus facili ingenio Veronicae Virginis electae ex millibus ad sanctitudinem venerandam incitaberis" (Isolani, *Inexplicabilis*, p. 182). The legends of the blessed women often mention apparitions of St. Catherine or reading about her: Colomba listened to a reading of Catherine's *vita* (Bontempi, *Legenda latina*, p. 155*), while Osanna read her *vita* and dialogue (Silvestri, *La vita e stupendi miraculi*, book 1, chap. 18; and Scolari, *Libretto de la vita* [1524 ed.], fol. 96r–v).

94. Ritta listed Elena Duglioli's various "conformities" with the Virgin Mary, beginning with the miracle of virginity in marriage: like St. Anne, Elena's mother had three husbands; like Joseph, ser Benedetto, Elena's forty-year-old husband, married a fifteen-year-old girl; Elena lived in chastity with her husband for twenty-nine or thirty years, as Mary and Joseph are believed to have done; like the Mother of God, Elena lived in the three conditions of virgin, married woman, and widow; and finally, "the ninth conformity was in her tall physical stature and very similiar good looks (Pietro da Lucca, *Narrativa*, pp. 7–8).

95. Aldus was mindful of the grave crisis in the church when, presenting his printed edition of Catherine of Siena's *Epistole* to Cardinal Francesco Piccolomini, he expressed the hope that these letters "would spread throughout the world like solemn preachers" and contribute to the reform of individuals and the church. Furthermore, the letters Catherine had written to fourteenth-century popes were of such topical interest, given the present situation in which "the infidels are equipped with a stupendous army and arrayed on sea and land with the intention of destroying the faith of Christ," that it almost seemed "that they were addressed to the popes of our era rather than those of hers" (Catherine of Siena, *Epistole* [Venice: Aldo Manuzio, 1500]).

96. It is well known that entering a convent involved payment of such a substantial dowry that the convents were in effect reserved to the nobility or the well-to-do bourgeoisie. Girls from poorer families could sometimes find a place among the lay sisters. For an analysis of Florentine convents in social terms, see Richard C. Trexler, "Le célibat à la fin du Moyen Age: Les religieuses de Florence," *Annales: Economies, sociétés, civilisations* 27 (1972): 1329–50.

97. Silvestri, *La vita e stupendi miraculi*, book 2, chap. 2; Scolari, *Libretto de la vita* (1524 ed.), fols. 33 and 44r–v.

98. Guerrini, "La prima 'Legenda volgare,' " p. 154.

99. Pico-Morelli, *Compendio*, p. 97.

100. After taking in female orphans and young girls in order to educate them, Stefana decided to establish a convent of tertiaries; her project was approved in 1512, and by 1529 it housed thirty professed women (Cistellini, *Figure della riforma*,

p. 45; and Guerrini, "La prima 'Legenda volgare,'" p. 176). On Elena, see Melloni, *Atti o memorie*, pp. 367–68. On the origins of the pious foundation for the Shamefaced Poor in Bologna, see Pio Paschini, *La beneficenza in Italia e le "Compagnie del Divino Amore" nei primi decenni del Cinquecento: Note storiche* (Rome, 1925), pp. 93–95, which contains the letters establishing it; and Giovanni Ricci, "Povertà, vergogna, e povertà vergognosa," *Società e storia* 5 (1979): 305–37. On Gentile, see Serafino da Fermo, *Vita di due beatissime donne*, fol. 353v.

101. Guerrini, "La prima 'Legenda volgare,'" p. 149.

102. Battista Fregoso, who cited Elena Duglioli as an example of abstinence and continence, spoke of the appearance of syphilis as a prodigious sign and marveled at the means by which it was transmitted: "Id quod in ea maxime mirum fuit, erat quod contagionis vires in coitu solo exercebat, a genitalibusque membris primordia sumebat" (*De Dictis factisque memorabilibus*, book 1, chap. 4, fol. 25v).

103. Serafino da Fermo, *Vita di due beatissime donne*, fol. 353v.

104. Guerrini, "La prima 'Legenda volgare,'" p. 109. Total abstinence from food was widely held to be an irrefutable sign of sanctity. One woman suggested that an invalid be brought to see Colomba of Rieti because "est apud S. Dominicum una Soror, quae non comedit cibum et plura facit signa sanctitatis" (Bontempi, *Legenda latina*, p. 175*). Stefana confessed to having forced herself to eat to avoid falling victim to the wiles of the devil, "who often tempts me by saying that I am a saint because I do not eat" (Guerrini, "La prima 'Legenda volgare,'" p. 109. "To conceal her abstinence," Caterina of Racconigi pretended to eat meat, but later rose from the table and threw it away (Pico-Morelli, *Compendio*, pp. 140–41). Chiara Bugni's confessor urged her to eat so that she would not be able to brag "that she fasted more than Moses, Elijah, or the Son of God himself" (Zorzi, "Vitta," fol. 49). Excessive abstinence, moreover, could be a diabolical temptation if it was not accompanied by humility: Pico recalled a conversation with Caterina of Racconigi in which "we happened to speak about a widow who practiced more abstinence than was suitable, and we suspected that it was some snare of the devil" (Pico-Morelli, *Compendio*, p. 177).

105. Veronica of Binasco donated to the poor bread that she had pretended to eat in the refectory: "Angelici panis caelestis edulii et pasci meruit et nutriri" (Isolani, *Inexplicabilis*, p. 181); Chiara Bugni stated that she could not eat anything else after communion (Zorzi, "Vitta," fol. 20); Stefana went "for many days without material food, nourished only by the food of the sacrament" (Guerrini, "La prima 'Legenda volgare,'" p. 103).

106. Colomba was denounced to the master general of the Dominican order "de quotidiano usu Eucharistiae et sedula Confessione, ac de tanta veneratione secularium, quasi fuisset virgo Maria" (Bontempi, *Legenda latina*, p. 180*); Chiara Bugni received communion every Friday, "but when she saw that this unusual practice might disturb the nuns, she abstained from it" and communicated only in spirit (Zorzi, "Vitta," fol. 21v); Elena Duglioli was driven from two churches in a row for receiving the eucharist too often (Melloni, *Atti o memorie*, pp. 324–25); Caterina of Racconigi abstained from communion "so as not to cause her parish priest to marvel at her," and when she joined the Third Order, "her superiors did not allow her to

receive communion as often as she would have liked" (Pico-Morelli, *Compendio,* p. 36); Angela Merici became a tertiary in order to receive communion more frequently (Ledóchowska, *Angèle Merici,* 1: 320).

107. See Isolani, *Inexplicabilis,* book 7, chaps. 2–6, pp. 206–8; Bontempi, *Legenda latina,* p. 162*; Scolari, *Libretto de la vita,* fols. 91–92; Zorzi, "Vitta," fol. 22; Salviati, *Legenda,* fol. 15v; Pico-Morelli, *Compendio,* pp. 35–38; Pietro da Lucca, *Narrativa,* p. 5; Guerrini, "La prima 'Legenda volgare,'" pp. 129–31; Fontana, *Vita,* pp. 81–82.

108. The Lateran canon Paolo Maffei contributed significantly to the revival of eucharistic piety in the fifteenth century (Petrocchi, *Storia della spiritualità,* 1: 129–31). The Dominicans, too, warmly supported frequent communion, though they did not go so far as to advocate receiving it daily. Bontempi, however, took a different line, maintaining the suitability of daily communion (*Legenda latina,* p. 187*). In her "Brieve et signoril modo del spiritual vivere," Elena Duglioli identified prayer, meditation, and daily mass as the ways to join with God. Recognizing that laypeople could not receive the eucharist every day, she recommended instead a daily spiritual communion, assigning this a value equal to sacramental communion: "In this way, every time the soul wishes to be united with its divine love, it receives spiritual communion and earns the same merit that it would have in sacramental communion. Thus St. Augustine said *Crede et manducasti*—that is, if you believe with perfected faith, which is nothing other than desiring with all your heart to be united with your Lord in faith, you have received communion." Elena regretted not being able to receive the eucharist daily and clearly resented the condition of unjustified subordination this imposed on the laity. "In this way," she continued, "the true servants of God receive communion every day, sometimes more happily than those priests, in so much as they are, or feel themselves to be, more pure, more worthy, and more eager for this blessing" (Melloni, *Atti o memorie,* p. 349). Even if her intent was to exalt the value of communion, Elena's words take on particular resonance when we realize that this pamphlet must have been printed around 1520. In devout circles, as evidenced by Elena's words, spiritual communion and mystical union with God had become supreme values at the very moment when Protestant reformers were calling into question the mass and the eucharist. Different paths led "spirituals" and reformers to the same conclusion: a devaluation of the sacrament in the name of "perfected faith" and as a consequence of a custom that had hitherto discouraged sacramental communion. On the practice of frequent communion, see Joseph Duhr, entry "Communion fréquente," in *Dictionnaire de spiritualité ascétique et mistique,* vol. 2 (Paris, 1953), col. 1234–92. The miraculous communion and eucharist did not become common themes in religious art until the seventeenth century: see Emile Mâle, *L'art religieux de la fin du XVIe siècle et du XVIIe siècle et du XVIIIe siècle: Etude sur l'iconographie après le Concile de Trente* (Paris, 1951), pp. 72–76.

109. Bontempi, *Legenda latina,* p. 162*; and Zorzi, "Vitta," fol. 21. The devil caused Stefana to doubt that Christ's body could be present "in such a tiny morsel" of bread, but the Lord confirmed her faith by making "a lovely little child" appear to her in the host (Guerrini, "La prima 'Legenda volgare,'" p. 138).

110. Ercole claimed to have seen the notarial document that described Stefana Quinzani's ecstasies of 1497, signed "manu plurium praestantium virorum et sigillis eorum munitam." The document is edited in Brunati, *Vita o gesta,* 2: 55–61.

111. "In partibus Lombardie, sub iurisdictione Serenissimi venetorum dominii soror Steffana de Quinzano, tercii ordinis Sancti Dominici reperitur virgo quippe devotissima: et cui per revelationem divini Spiritus multa ostensa sunt et in extasi rapta plurima vidit. . . . Audivimus praeterea in civitate Perusii venerabilem sorerem Columbam ibi adesse; que iam pluribus annis non sub duplici specie sed sub una specie tantum panis in eucharistie sacramento communicatur et nullo alio sumpto cibo miraculose iam quartum annum vixit et vivit. . . . Extat etiam in civitate Mantue venerabilis soror Susanna fama et opinione sanctitatis preclara et in hac nostra civitate Ferrarie alie plures moniales eiusdem ordinis que sepe spiritu divino rapiuntur et sanctitate redolent; nec non et aliis multis Italie locis plures audivimus que celesti numine afflate nobis testimonium reddunt et fidem hanc catholicam nostram veram esse et sanctam Romanam ecclesiam esse fidei matrem" (*Spiritualium personarum feminei sexus facta admiratione digna* [Nuremberg, 1501]). This unnumbered six-page pamphlet was published by Ercole I d'Este to honor Lucia and the other female mystics who brought fame to Italy and confirmed the truth of the Catholic faith; the British Museum in London contains copies of this pamphlet in both Latin and German.

112. The debate about ecstasies and raptures was mentioned more or less explicitly in many of the *vitae* of the "living saints" and summarized by Sibilla in a few *quaestiunculae.* After providing a philosophical response to the question "unde causatur in animabus extasis sive raptus," Sibilla set forth the four degrees of contemplation, or "extatice conversationis in Deum," and wondered whether Plato and Aristotle could have gained as much theological knowledge through natural means as Adam and Paul did in their ecstasies; his answer was no (*Speculum,* dec. 1, chap. 8, quest. 1, quaestiunculae 2–4, fols. 143v–146). Isolani admitted that *abstractio mentis* could be natural, if it followed the natural order, or *praeter naturam;* in the latter case *abstractio* was termed *raptus* and could be caused by illness, evil spirits, or God. Even certain ancient philosophers, like Socrates, Plato, Xenocrates, Plotinus, and others, could reach a state of rapture, but the raptures of the saints were considered superior (*Inexplicabilis,* p. 183). Bontempi defined ecstasy as "excessum mentis a se ipso simpliciter secundum quem scilicet qui extra suam ordinationem ponitur. Raptus vero supra hoc connotat quamdam violentiam" (*Legenda latina,* p. 189*).

113. Gianfrancesco Pico declared that rapture was superior to prophecy, since the ancients or infidels might sometimes obtain "an understanding of hidden things contained under the sublunary sphere," but they could never arrive at knowledge of "the second, immortal life." On the other hand, the raptures God granted to the saints enabled them to know "things sublime, humble, and ordinary" (Pico-Morelli, *Compendio,* pp. 94–95). Of course, Pico did not dwell on this point in his *vita* of Caterina of Racconigi, since he had already treated it at length in his *De rerum praenotione.* Francesco Silvestri shared Isolani and Pico's conviction that rapture could have several causes, a conviction which by then was thoroughly embedded in theo-

logical doctrine: "The most learned men affirm that there are three causes by which man can be robbed of the use of his senses: either through bodily infirmity, which sometimes prevents the vital spirits from reaching the organs; or through diabolical cunning, which fills men's minds with fantastic illusions; or truly through divine power, which raises our souls to the knowledge of things that are above human intelligence" (*La vita e stupendi miraculi*, book 2, preface).

114. Since Osanna's raptures always happened while she was praying, her parents, who had thought her to be ill, became convinced that she was subject to "divine ecstasies" (ibid., chap. 1). Veronica of Binasco also went into ecstasy during prayer, especially during mass and after communion (Isolani, *Inexplicabilis*, p. 183). The same was true of Chiara Bugni (Zorzi, "Vitta," fol. 19r–v). When they returned to their senses after their ecstasies, these women were enflamed with divine love; this could not be the devil's work (Silvestri, *La vita e stupendi miraculi*, book 2, preface). In fact, "Sathan Christi Maximi saevissimus hostis creditur, adversum cujus caelestia dogmata impia semper molitur" (Isolani, *Inexplicabilis*, p. 183).

115. Chiara Bugni remained in ecstasy from Friday until the following Saturday, "and then returned to her senses with great joy in her heart and on her face, so that it seemed evident from her joy that she had come from heaven" (Zorzi, "Vitta," fol. 11v). Although Osanna suffered the agonies of the Passion in her ecstasies, when she came to her senses she "seemed full of joy and no longer in pain" (Scolari, *Libretto de la vita* [1524 ed.], fol. 164v). In general, theological doctrine considered joyfulness a key test in the discernment of spirits, as the Spanish Dominican Antonio de la Peña stated firmly in the trial of the visionary nun Maria, an emulator of Lucia of Narni, which was held in Valladolid in 1509–11: "Est enim doctrina sanctorum quod visiones diabolicae communiter finiuntur in tristitia et miseria; revelationes vero divinae in gaudio et hilaritate animae et corporum" (Vicente Beltrán de Heredia, *Historia de la reforma de la provincia de España, 1450–1550* [Rome, 1939], p. 116).

116. Silvestri, *La vita e stupendi miraculi*, book 5, chap. 6. Gentile exposed an ecstatic woman who instead was deceived by the devil (Serafino da Fermo, *Vita di due beatissime donne*, fol. 358v).

117. The faces of Margherita and Paola Antonia Negri became glowing (Serafino da Fermo, *Vita di due beatissime donne*, fol. 349v, and Fontana, *Vita*, p. 77); Caterina of Racconigi's face alternated between "milky brightness and rosy radiance" (Pico-Morelli, *Compendio*, p. 184); Stefana's face seemed "rosy and youthful," and after her death, the face of this seventy-year-old woman became "beautiful, shiny, and smooth like that of a fifteen-year-old girl" (Guerrini, "La prima 'Legenda volgare,'" pp. 114 and 180). The way in which Elena's face was transformed into that of a sixteen-year-old during communion was famous (Pietro da Lucca, *Epistola*). Ecstasies were often accompanied by intense odors, like that which emanated from Chiara Bugni after communion (Zorzi, "Vitta," fol. 20). On Elena's burning heart, see Pietro da Lucca, *Narrativa*, p. 6.

118. "Interea Angelicus concentus personuit Veronicae auribus" (Isolani, *Inexplicabilis*, p. 178); Osanna, Stefana, Elena, and Chiara heard angelic melodies or

sang with the angels (Scolari, *Libretto de la vita,* fol. 5v; Guerrini, "La prima 'Legenda volgare,'" p. 120; Pietro da Lucca, *Narrativa,* p. 5; Zorzi, "Vitta," fol. 25v). The association of ecstasies with angelic music, a traditional theme in Christian spirituality, gained strength in the fifteenth century and spread along with the representation of St. Cecilia holding a portable organ. The arrangement of the angels playing their instruments in Raphael's St. Cecilia reflects a mathematical principle of harmony and demonstrates the artist's understanding of Ficino's Neoplatonic philosophy (Mossakowski, "Raphael's 'St. Cecilia,'" pp. 6–12). To express Cecilia's beatific vision, Raphael melded Neoplatonic ideas with the Christian spirituality of the Oratories of Divine Love (Arasse, "Extases et visions béatifiques," pp. 420–23).

119. "Ita pulcher sicut est depictus in capella prefecti Brixie, sed iste est valde pulchrior" (AGOP, sec. 10, no. 2857, fasc. 13: *Excerpta ex scriptis F. Baptistae de Salodio*). Osanna saw the baby Jesus with "his curly hair like gleaming gold" and the devil "in human form, very ugly and red, with red eyes that seemed to blaze with fire" (Scolari, *Libretto de la vita,* fols. 7 and 90).

120. Luini painted for the convent of Santa Marta a Madonna (commissioned by Denis Briçonnet) and an altarpiece depicting the Annunciation; Marco d'Oggiono painted an altarpiece of the three archangels that reflects the imagery of the *Apocalypsis nova* (Binaghi, "L'immagine sacra in Luini," pp. 64–67). A follower of Leonardo de Vinci, Marco d'Oggiono was also responsible for the miniatures in MS O 165 sup. of the Biblioteca Ambrosiana, Milan, which contains the *vita* of Arcangela Panigarola (Carlo Marcora, *Marco d'Oggiono* [Oggiono-Lecco, 1976]).

121. Bontempi, *Legenda latina,* pp. 160* and 182*; Guerrini, "La prima 'Legenda volgare,'" p. 97; Fontana, *Vita,* p. 7.

122. Notarial document recording Stefana Quinzani's ecstasies of the Passion in 1500, in Brunati, *Vita o gesta,* 2: 62.

123. Scolari, *Libretto de la vita,* fols. 23v, 26, and 78v; Silvestri, *La vita e stupendi miraculi,* book 3, preface.

124. Pico-Morelli, *Compendio,* p. 20.

125. "Apologia di un domenicano," in Di Agresti, *S. Caterina de' Ricci: Testimonianze,* pp. 28–31; Alessi, *Libellus,* pp. 417–19 and 459.

126. Isolani connects the appearance of stigmata in so many Dominican women with Sixtus IV's decree prohibiting the depiction of Catherine of Siena with bleeding stigmata, and underscores the importance of the recent beatification of Osanna of Mantua, who (like Catherine) had received invisible stigmata (*De Imperio militantis ecclesiae,* book 2, tit. 7, question 2, 8). The stigmatization of these holy women of the early Cinquecento thus has a specific historical meaning, linking them with the long chain of Catherine's defenders stretching from Caffarini in the fifteenth century to Lombardelli at the end of the sixteenth: Thomas Antonii de Senis "Caffarini," *Libellus de supplemento legende prolixe virginis beate Catherine de Senis,* ed. Giuliana Cavallini and Imelda Foralosso (Rome, 1974), part 2, treatise 7, pp. 121–211; and Gregorio Lombardelli, *Sommario della disputa a difesa delle Sacre Stigmate di S. Caterina da Siena* (Siena, 1601). But it was also a phenomenon that often provoked skepticism: many doubted the miraculous nature of Lucia of Narni's

stigmata, on which Colomba of Rieti's opinion was solicited (Bontempi, *Legenda latina*, pp. 194*–95*); and Osanna's stigmata were disputed (Scolari, *Libretto de la vita* [1524 ed.], p. 155). Even the stigmata of St. Francis of Assisi stirred much controversy (André Vauchez, "Les stigmates de Saint François et leurs détracteurs dans les derniers siècles du Moyen Age," *MEFRM* 80 [1968]: 595–625). Of course, stigmatization is a recurrent theme in Christian spirituality, occurring in many periods: see Johannes M. Höcht, *Von Franziskus zu Pater Pio und Therese Neumann: Eine Geschichte der Stigmatisierten* (Stein am Rhein, 1974).

127. Letters of Osanna Andreasi, in Bagolini and Ferretti, *La beata Osanna Andreasi,* appendix, pp. vii and liii.

128. Zorzi, "Vitta," fol. 35v; but the description of the "wound" occupies fols. 34–36. On the anniversary of the stigmatization of St. Francis, blood gushed from Chiara's side (Zorzi, "Vitta," fol. 47).

129. Benigno Salviati, *Legenda,* fol. 17; Isolani, *Inexplicabilis,* p. 195; Pietro da Lucca, *Narrativa,* item 12, p. 6.

130. Serafino da Fermo, *Vita di due beatissime donne,* fol. 355.

131. See Sibylla, *Speculum,* dec. 1, chap. 8, quest. 1, quaestiuncula 1: "si divinationes in animabus raptis insint eis a natura" (1493 ed., fols. cxli v–cxliii v); and, in greater detail, Pico, *De rerum praenotione,* pp. 418–23. All of the *vitae* recognized that effects that appeared to be divine could be produced either by nature or by the devil, who transformed himself into an "angel of light" and led people astray under a semblance of good. A primary task of the theologian was thus to distinguish divine gifts from illusions. The most thorough theoretical discussion of divination is in Pico's *De rerum praenotione,* which established the fulfillment of prophecies as the criterion for recognizing divine revelation. After arguing that divine revelation could be either relative or absolute, Pico claimed that the prophets of God always spoke the truth, while the prophecies of those deceived by the devil were not fulfilled (p. 431). Pico then indicated other criteria for the discernment of spirits, deriving them from actual cases as well as the Bible and theological literature (pp. 682–96).

132. Silvestri, *La vita e stupendi miraculi,* book 5, preface. The superiority of prophets over astrologers was also emphasized by Bontempi, who distinguished between their capacities: astrologers could foresee some events, but not contingent details nor things subject to the will; they could not predict God's vengeance, nor what crimes would anger God or cause him to send scourges, nor what penitence would placate him. Prophets could know all this, since they recognize sin and its evil effects (Bontempi, *Legenda latina,* p. 202*). Moreover, prophets are given knowledge of the soul's condition, life eternal, and what happens in the heavenly orbs and underground (Pico-Morelli, *Compendio,* pp. 94–95).

133. Silvestri, *La vita e stupendi miraculi,* book 1, chap. 33 and book 4, chaps. 7 and 12; Bontempi, *Legenda latina,* pp. 198*–199*; Razzi, *Vita de i Santi* (1588 ed.), part 2, pp. 179–83, and Gandini, *Sulla venuta in Ferrara della Beata suor Lucia da Narni;* Pico-Morelli, *Compendio,* pp. 139, 181, and 53–54; Melloni, *Atti o memorie,* pp. 341–44; and "Apologia di un domenicano," p. 67. Lautrec, uncle of Gaston de Foix, had this famous captain buried in the convent of Santa Marta and

made his confessions to Bellotti (Biblioteca Ambrosiana, Milan, MS L 56: "Memorie della morte e sepolcro di Gastone di Foix, 9 febbraio 1516," pp. 260–68; Binaghi, "L'immagine sacra in Luini," p. 59). Part of Stefana's correspondence with the Gonzaga was published by Cistellini and part by Tolasi; her *vita* also mentions Stefana's close relations with the Este and the Gonzaga (Guerrini, "La prima 'Legenda volgare,'" p. 125).

134. Caterina of Racconigi unmasked two people who had "a demonic familiar as adviser" (Pico-Morelli, *Compendio*, p. 68). Osanna is labeled a "true prophetess" in Scolari, *Libretto de la vita*, fol. 160. Political prophecies were ascribed to Colomba (Bontempi, *Legenda latina*, pp. 184*–85* and 195*–96*), Osanna (Scolari, *Libretto de la vita*, fols. 76v and 98–99), Caterina of Racconigi (Pico-Morelli, *Compendio*, pp. 86–87, 88, and 90–91), and Margherita of Ravenna (Serafino da Fermo, *Vita di due beatissime donne*, fol. 351). Moreover, "living saints" such as Elena Duglioli and Caterina of Racconigi predicted the deaths of various people, including political figures and popes, and foretold the births of princes' children.

135. Bontempi, *Legenda latina*, p. 209*.

136. Scolari, *Libretto de la vita*, fols. 50v and 95–96; Benigno Salviati, *Legenda*, fol. 146; Pico-Morelli, *Compendio*, pp. 49–55.

137. Bontempi, *Legenda latina*, p. 178*; Silvestri, *La vita e stupendi miraculi*, book 4, chap. 4; Pico-Morelli, *Compendio*, pp. 83–84.

138. Scolari, *Libretto de la vita*, fol. 95v; see also Silvestri, *La vita e stupendi miraculi*, book 4, chap. 4.

139. Pico-Morelli, *Compendio*, p. 128.

140. Guerrini, "La prima 'Legenda volgare,'" p. 134.

141. Bontempi, *Legenda volgare*, fol. 31v; Colomba is called a "heavenly treasure" on fol. 31r.

142. Zorzi, "Vitta," fol. 15. Zorzi also reports the vision of a French hermit, "who had predicted many things to King Charles of France about Louis his successor, all of which came true down to the most minute detail." This vision revealed that there existed in the world only three people "whose prayers placated God and gained his favor . . . one was in Germany, the second in France and the third in the city of Venice." "And perhaps," Zorzi continued, Chiara Bugni "is that soul who is so pleasing to God" (fol. 55).

143. A codex from the convent of Santa Marta contains the legend of Sister Andrea, a Benedictine nun from San Salvatore in Pavia, including a letter she sent to Emperor Charles V enjoining him, on the basis of a prophetic vision, to make peace in Lombardy. The letter echoes some of the themes discussed above: only this nun's prayers could placate the Lord; God wished to send peace but the princes did not want it, for "as if blinded by love of their own renown, each has grown callous toward the rest and they persecute each other like Turks and infidels, caring nothing for my honor, nor for the salvation of souls, nor for the restoration of the holy mother church which they have reduced to ruins"; among all the Christian princes, only the emperor could bring peace. (Biblioteca Ambrosiana, Milan, MS 0 248 sup., fols. 13v–14).

144. Scolari, *Libretto de la vita,* fol. 52; see also Silvestri, *La vita e stupendi miraculi,* book 2, chap. 6.

145. Isolani, *Inexplicabilis,* p. 176; Alberti, *La vita della Beata Colomba de Rieto,* chap. 33; Bontempi, *Legenda latina,* p. 196*.

146. Pico-Morelli, *Compendio,* p. 48.

147. Benigno Salviati, *Legenda,* fols. 181v–183 and 249–50; the latter have been published in Marcora, "Il cardinale Ippolito I d'Este," pp. 438–39.

148. Benigno Salviati, *Legenda,* fol. 110; Pico-Morelli, *Compendio,* p. 121.

149. Pico-Morelli, *Compendio,* pp. 121 and 91.

150. Elena's *vita* presented her as the daughter of Mahomet, sultan of the Turks, destined to convert Constantinople (Pietro da Lucca, *Epistola* and *Narrativa*). Angela predicted the death of the Great Sultan, which she said had already happened in spirit: "The Great Sultan was called Bo because he had not been baptized" (Benigno Salviati, *Legenda,* fol. 15).

151. For Stefana's prayer and vision, see Guerrini, "La prima 'Legenda volgare,'" p. 143. Interest in the "New World" figures prominently in Isolani's *De Imperio militantis ecclesiae* and Serafino da Fermo's *Breve dichiaratione sopra l'apocalipse de Gioanni, dove si prova esser venuto il precursor di Antichristo et avvicinarsi la percossa da lui predetta nel sesto sigillo.* On these two texts, see Prosperi, "America e Apocalisse," pp. 9–12 and 40–45.

152. Catarino placed his invective in an apocalyptic context, convinced by external signs "that now is the time of the coming of the Lord." "Do not Christian eyes now see the true nature of this miserable world: political upheavals, kingdoms toppling, rebellious peoples, tyrannous oppression; here Turks, there heretics, everywhere the wicked and half-hearted . . . and what is worse, within the City of God, infinite pride and ambition, immense greed, intolerable pomp and splendor, profound gluttony, unspeakable lust, horrible plundering and injustice and duplicity." He went on to assert the need for ecclesiastical reform in clearly Savonarolan terms: "but I declare that there are excellent reasons to believe that the sack is now filled and God is coming boldly with his sword. And therefore to all those who say that now is not the time to rebuild the house of God, I answer with the words of the prophet Haggai. . . . It is enough to say that God's judgment usually comes when it is least expected and awaited: and when the sack of vices is full, as is manifestly the case in our most wretched day" (*Vita miracolosa della Seraphyca sancta Catherina,* book 3, chap. 5, "Digressione del traductore," point 8, fol. 73r–v).

153. I have already mentioned Elena's loyalty to the pope and in particular her condemnation of the Council of Pisa (see note 79). Even Arcangela Panigarola, despite her sharp criticisms of the clergy and religious orders and her personal involvement with the French promoters of the Pisan council, wanted nothing to do with this enterprise; and she repeatedly refused to have mass celebrated in her convent during the period of the interdict: see Benigno Salviati, *Legenda,* fol. 21, and, more amply, Biblioteca Ambrosiana, Milan, MS I 165 sup., fol. 21, cited in Marcora, "Il cardinale Ippolito I d'Este," pp. 446–47.

154. Serafino da Fermo, *Vita di due beatissime donne,* fol. 361r–v.

155. Angela Merici's distrust of visions was cited as evidence of her humility by Agostino Gallo during the informational hearings on her beatification, and was repeated in all of her biographies: see Ledóchowska, *Angèle Merici,* 1: 323; "Vita Nazari," in Bertolotti, *Storia di S. Angela Merici,* pp. 215–16; Gondi, *Vita della beata Angela,* p. 18. The first edition of Negri's *Lettere spirituali* dates from 1564; on their contested attribution, see note 77.

156. The definition of witchcraft developed over centuries, and the prosecution of witches began in the fourteenth century; but even if witchcraft was already a widespread practice and established cultural category well before the end of the fifteenth century, there is no doubt that it became a more urgent concern as a result of the repressive measures announced in the bull *Summis desiderantes affectibus* of Innocent VIII (1484) and the appearance of the first printed demonological treatise, the *Malleus maleficarum* (1486). From then on, the debate over witchcraft became increasingly animated, to the point of involving entire regions in the interplay between theoretical reflection and inquisitorial practice. For bibliographical guidance on this large and complex probleem, see Franco Cardini, *Magia, stregoneria, superstizioni nell'Occidente medievale* (Florence, 1979), and *La stregoneria in Europa,* ed. Marina Romanello (Bolognia, 1978). The most important demonological tracts of the fifteenth and sixteenth centuries are analyzed in *The Damned Art: Essays in the Literature of Witchcraft,* ed. Sydney Anglo (London, 1977).

157. The revival of witch trials in Emilia around 1500 was accompanied by a debate over witchcraft, starting around 1520, which involved inquisitors and intellectuals of various backgrounds, from the jurist Ponzinibio to the philosopher Pomponazzi, and produced several treatises, from the *Quaestio de strigibus* of Bartolomeo Spina, vicar of the inquisitor of Modena from 1518 to 1520, to the treatises of Prierio and Pico. On this debate, see Bertolotti, "Le ossa e la pelle dei buoi," pp. 470–75; and Peter Burke, "Witchcraft and Magic in Renaissance Italy: Gianfrancesco Pico and His Strix," in Anglo, *The Damned Art,* pp. 32–52. On the activities of the Modenese inquisition during the first half of the sixteenth century, see Albano Biondi, "Streghe ed eretici nei domini estensi all'epoca dell'Ariosto," in *Il Rinascimento nelle corti padane,* pp. 165–69.

158. Mentioned by Alberti as a philosopher and famous orator, Friar Domenico of Gargnano was a well-known preacher who taught theology at the Studio of Bologna. As inquisitor of Mantua, he pressed charges against Pietro of Lucca (see note 193) and urged more vigorous prosecution of witches: Leandro Alberti, *Descrittione di tutta Italia* (Venice: Pietro de i Nicolini da Stabbio, 1551), p. 324; and Giuseppe Brunati, *Dizionario degli uomini illustri della riviera di Salò* (Milan, 1887), p. 63. The quotation in the text comes from a letter of Domenico of Gargnano to the marquis Gianfrancesco Gonzaga, dated 7 April 1508, in which the inquisitor asked the marquis to proceed more rigorously against witches and buttressed his request with a recent papal brief "which commanded that this sect of witches be exterminated." He also reported on the trial of a witch, who "confessed without torture or threats" to having done everything described in the inquisitorial manuals: she went on flights; trampled the cross; denied her faith, the Virgin Mary, baptism, and the

heavenly court; renounced Christ and accepted the devil as God; worshiped the devil and served him for twenty-seven years; brought him the consecrated host and profaned it; denied believing in the real presence of Christ in the host, "and indeed, when the priest said mass, she, on orders of the Mistress of the Game, said 'You lie through your teeth, you lie through your teeth'; and finally, she performed many harmful spells. However, continued Friar Domenico, after her confession the witch showed remorse, and so she was condemned to abjure her beliefs and be "placed on an ass and other minor things" (Mantua, Archivio di Stato, *Archivio Gonzaga,* envelope 2472, c. 670). Domenico of Gargnano also signed the first certification of Lucia of Narni's stigmata (Ponsi, *Vita della beata Lucia,* p. 197, doc. 1); witnessed the ecstasies of Stefana Quinzani in 1497 and 1500 (Brunati, *Vita o gesta,* 2: 61–62); read Scolari's *vita* of Osanna at the author's request (Scolari, *Libretto de la vita* [1542 ed.], fol. 162v); and urged the marquis of Mantua to honor her with a costly chapel (in the letter cited here).

159. Prierio wrote his treatise *De Strigimagarum daemonumque mirandis* in 1521, citing cases of witchcraft that had occurred near Bologna and contributing to the theoretical debate on witchcraft that aroused such interest in Emilia. But the Dominican theologian had long been an attentive observer of phenomena connected with the devil's presence in people. As early as 1502 he published his *Tractatulus quid a diabolo sciscitari et qualiter malignos spiritus possit quisque expellere de obsessis* (Bologna: Caligola Bacilieri, 1502; new edition with additions and corrections, Bologna: Giovanni Rossi, 1573), a manual for exorcists based on theory and Prierio's personal experience ("que lectione et experientia didici") and divided into three sections: rules for the priest to observe regarding his own person and that of the possessed; instructions for recognizing the devil's wiles; and a list of "catholic and reliable exorcisms" against the many "blasphemies" in circulation. Silvestro Mazzolini Prierio was Elena's spiritual director, according to her anonymous legend, which added that she raised in her house one of his nephews, who later became a Dominican by the name of Fra Aurelio. Melloni identifies this child as Fra Aurelio Mazzolini, who made his profession in Bologna in 1507 and distinguished himself through his philosophical and theological studies (*Atti o memorie,* pp. 326–27). The chronicle of San Domenico does record the profession of a Fra Aurelio Mazzolini in 1507, but without indicating his kinship with Prierio; however, in 1509 another novice made his profession, assuming the name of Fra Silvestro, and of him it is noted that he was "nepos Magistri Silvestri dignissimi de Prierio" (Bologna, Archivio del convento di San Domenico, *Cronaca di Ludovico da Prelormo,* fol. 252).

160. Pico stated that he was led to write the nine books of the *De rerum praenotione* because he had "learned through experience that sometimes revelations presented as true turned out to be false." When Caterina of Racconigi's revelations were recognized as authentic, after wishing to "investigate first with diligence and proper consideration the movements of her soul, before lending credence to her," and corresponding with her for eight years, Pico wanted to meet her personally in order to question her about her predictions (Pico-Morelli, *Compendio,* pp. 60–61). Pico's *Dialogus in tres libros divisus titulus est Strix sive de Ludificatione daemonum* (Bolo-

gna, 1523) clearly fit with his other cultural interests. But it was equally a part of the debates over witchcraft then in progress in Emilia, and drew its inspiration from the polemics over the harsh punishment of some witches in the area of Mirandola, who were sentenced to be burned at the stake by the Dominican inquisitor Girolamo Armelini of Faenza. On Armelini, who had been one of Pietro of Lucca's accusers in 1511 and in 1523 denounced the Aristotelian philosophy of Tiberio Russiliano, see Paola Zambelli, "Una disputa filosofica ereticale proposta nelle Università padane nel 1519," in *Il Rinascimento nelle corti padane,* pp. 511–13.

161. Alberti prepared the first edition of Pico's *Strix* for publication in 1523, dedicating it to the vice-legate of Bologna, Altobello Averoldi; and in 1524 he translated it into Italian. Toward the middle of the century, Turino Turini made a new translation of it, which was reprinted in the nineteenth century as *La Strega ovvero degli inganni de' demoni: Dialogo di Giovan Francesco Pico della Mirandola tradotto in lingua toscana da Turino Turini* (Milan, 1864).

162. Isolani did enter the debate over magic and divination with his *Libellus adversus magos, divinatores, maleficos eosve qui ad religionem subeundam maleficis artibus quempiam cogi posse asservant* (Milan: J. A. Scinzenzeler, 1506).

163. Bontempi, *Legenda latina,* p. 180*; Scolari, *Libretto de la vita* (1524 ed.), fol. 161v; AGOP, sec. 10, no. 2857, fasc. 13 (*Excerpta ex scriptis f. Baptistae de Salodio*); Pico-Morelli, *Compendio,* p. 54; "Apologia di un domenicano," pp. 19–23; Serafino da Fermo, *Vita di due beatissime donne,* fol. 354; Fontana, *Vita,* p. 103.

164. Bontempi, *Legenda latina,* p. 186*; Scolari, *Libretto de la vita* (1524 ed.), fols. 161v and 172; Pico-Morelli, *Compendio,* pp. 63 and 111; Guerrini, "La prima 'Legenda volgare,'" p. 124.

165. "But above all I wanted to understand the nature of that light by which, it was said, she knew what was hidden in human hearts and what would happen in the future. For this reason I sought to discover the 'touchstone' by which she distinguished between true and false, as we seek to do in our discernment of spirits, and I tried to learn from her whether she had ever been mistaken" (Pico-Morelli, *Compendio,* p. 61).

166. Ibid., p. 63.

167. Flying: Bontempi, *Legenda latina,* p. 169*; Silvestri, *La vita e stupendi miraculi,* book 3, chap. 21; Isolani, *Inexplicabilis,* p. 207; Pico-Morelli, *Compendio,* pp. 28, 55–56; Pietro da Lucca, *Epistola;* Zorzi, "Vitta," fol. 19v. Passing through closed doors: Bontempi, *Legenda latina,* pp. 168*, 169*, and 171*; Silvestri, *La vita e stupendi miraculi,* book 4, chap. 5. Jerusalem: Bontempi, *Legenda latina,* p. 163*; Silvestri, *La vita e stupendi miraculi,* book 2, chap. 18; Scolari, *Libretto de la vita,* fols. 107–9; Pico-Morelli, *Compendio,* p. 56.

168. In the preface to book 2 of his *vita* of Caterina of Racconigi, which discusses her familiarity with angels, Pico sought to justify what he was about to relate, addressing himself both to "crude thinkers, inexperienced and ignorant," and to "the learned." To the former he explained that all "the schools of philosophy," except for one or two, recognized "the foresight of superior minds, and divine visions, and foreknowledge, and predictions of future events"; he reminded the latter that

"the books of the Pythagoreans and the Platonists" and ancient "histories" attested to contacts between humans and demons and "wrote and affirmed that the bodies of philosophers were borne by demons for great distances," as happened to Pythagoras, Abaris, and Empedocles. What happened to philosophers in antiquity, continued Pico, "nowadays happens to witches, who are carried to the game of Diana or Herodias, as we have discussed at length in our dialogue entitled *Strega, or the Stratagems of the Devils.*" What demons can do, concluded Pico, can surely be done by angels: the readers of Caterina's *vita* should not be surprised, then, "when they read that Caterina's body was carried for long distances by her guardian angels so that she could perform great deeds." Having placed Caterina's mystical gift of angelic transportation in the context of the night flights of witches, Pico offered further proof of the veracity of his claims, citing the many other holy women who were believed to have this unusual gift: "But those who deny that the bodies of holy women can be carried through the air, and that without leaving home they can perform distant deeds and wander abroad in spirit, and that while their bodies remain immobile their likenesses can appear to others, will certainly not accept what has been written of Osanna of Mantua in our day: that she traveled through the air and was twice carried through the air by heavenly spirits. Many other such things that are commonly preached of her and other holy virgins will leave them shaking their heads" (Pico-Morelli, *Compendio,* p. 28).

169. Ibid., p. 52.

170. Ibid., p. 56. Pico discusses whether angels transport people in spirit or in the body—a problem debated in similar terms in demonological literature—on pp. 54–56.

171. Colomba and Osanna were carried to Jerusalem to visit the holy places and follow the stages of Christ's Passion; there they saw the sites and were seen by other people, as if they were physically present (see note 167). Note that while Bontempi's Latin *vita* simply states, "De peregrinagio autem et singulis quibuslibet ita distincte exposuit, quemadmodum est, et velut ii qui corporaliter circuierunt pariter affirmant," Alberti's translation expands on this theme and even mentions the distance Colomba traveled in spirit, evidently to make it seem even more marvelous (Alberti, *La vita della Beata Colomba de Rieto,* chap. 16). Caterina of Racconigi was rapt in spirit to Jerusalem, and returned to her senses bearing some relics of the cross (Pico-Morelli, *Compendio,* p. 56). Of course, even if their hagiographical context inclines one to interpret these trips to Jerusalem in terms of the contrast between witches and holy women, one should not forget that pilgrimages to Jerusalem were a fairly common devotional practice. Angela Merici, for example, made a normal journey to Jerusalem, but her trip, too, was marked by a miracle: a temporary blindness kept her from seeing the sites of the Passion with her own eyes (Ledóchowska, *Angèle Merici,* 1: 315). Caterina of Racconigi appeared to a man about to commit a mortal sin and converted him; she was transported "in her body on an invisible journey of 160 miles" to convince a prince to make peace; and she was carried to the king of France several times (Pico-Morelli, *Compendio,* pp. 53–55). Osanna of Mantua was transported by angels to the sickbeds of those who needed her (Silvestri, *La vita e stupendi miraculi,* book 3, chap. 21).

172. The biblical expression "angel of light," explained Pico, indicates diabolical deception "under the semblance of good" (Pico-Morelli, *Compendio*, p. 174). This was the most frequent temptation for mystics, and to recognize it spiritual directors suggested spitting on the vision: a devilish trick would be revealed, while saints would not be struck by the spit (Ledóchowska, *Angèle Merici*, 1: 323; and Di Agresti, *Santa Caterina de' Ricci: Testimonianze*, p. 32). The devil appeared to Osanna in the form of a Moor or Ethiopian (Silvestri, *La vita e stupendi miraculi*, book 3, chap. 13); to Caterina of Racconigi in human form or "in the likeness of various beasts, sometimes birds or serpents or quadrupeds, and sometimes monstrous combinations of them" (Pico-Morelli, *Compendio*, p. 146); to Veronica in the form of a fire-breathing ox (Isolani, *Inexplicabilis*, p. 186).

173. Pico-Morelli, *Compendio*, pp. 145 and 161. On the holy women's battles with the devil and the signs they left on their bodies, see also Bontempi, *Legenda latina*, p. 158*; Zorzi, "Vitta," fol. 76; Guerrini, "La prima 'Legenda volgare,'" pp. 152–53; Isolani, *Inexplicabilis*, p. 178.

174. Bontempi, *Legenda latina*, p. 159*; Silvestri, *La vita e stupendi miraculi*, book 3, chap. 13; Scolari, *Libretto de la vita*, fols. 90v and 105; Isolani, *Inexplicabilis*, pp. 177–78; Pico-Morelli, *Compendio*, pp. 145–61 (Caterina greases herself on p. 146); Guerrini, "La prima 'Legenda volgare,'" pp. 152–53. Victory over the devil is a prominent theme in Stefana Quinzani's *vitae*, and one of the manuscripts containing her biography is adorned with a drawing of her trampling the devil in the form of a fire-breathing animal (AGOP, sec. 10, no. 2864).

175. In this case as well, what is distinctive about these holy women is not so much that they cast out demons (which, being a biblical miracle, almost always appears in saints' lives), but rather the frequency with which this miracle recurs in comparison with others, the emphasis on the holy women's power to undo spells, and the transmission of this power to their relics. Moreover, this miracle is described in ways that reflect the advances of demonological "science." For example, when Colomba of Rieti encountered a possessed woman, she recognized that the woman was the victim of a spell "quod sub brachio quaedam maleficia daemonumve nomina haberet ligata," and, after forcing her to the ground, "vi incantationes illas et praestigia excerpsit statimque combussit" (Bontempi, *Legenda latina*, p. 165*). Pico even availed himself of a possessed woman to authenticate a relic of the cross that Caterina of Racconigi had given him; the demon cursed Caterina, "calling down fire upon her and wishing that she be killed by dogs" (Pico-Morelli, *Compendio*, p. 41; on pp. 19 and 190–91, Pico emphasizes Caterina's power to liberate possessed women). Osanna, Stefana, and Elena had similar powers: see Scolari, *Libretto de la vita* (1524 ed.), fol. 65v; Guerrini, "La prima 'Legenda volgare,'" pp. 169 and 184–85; and Pietro da Lucca, *Narrativa*, which says that Elena "has liberated many possessed people and freed a woman from an incubus, and demons in Genoa, Vercelli, Cremona, Gubbio, Venice, Bologna, and many other places have acknowledged her marvelous powers." The power of the "living saints" against demons was not an exclusive prerogative of the Dominican women, since it also appears in the *vitae* of Elena, Chiara Bugni (Zorzi, "Vitta," fol. 87), and Paola Antonia Negri (Fontana,

Vita, pp. 55–56); but it is clear that the Dominican biographers laid particular emphasis on this characteristic role of early-sixteenth-century mystics. Indeed, the list of holy Dominican women who vanquished demons could be lengthened by adding the names of some figures recorded by Razzi but not analyzed here: the blessed Benvenuta of Friuli, famous for her battles with the devil, and Margaret Fontana, at whose name alone the demons "writhed, despaired, and suffered great torment" (Razzi, *Vita de i Santi* [1588 ed.], part 2, pp. 23–31 and 64). Of course, in the sixteenth century Friuli and Modena were areas in which witchcraft was unusually widespread and inquisitors were especially active.

176. Witnesses at the canonization proceedings of Margherita, Gentile of Ravenna, and Osanna of Mantua emphasized that doctors had been unable to cure illnesses that were then miraculously vanquished through these women's intercession. Fontana also related miraculous recoveries that took place after the patient had been "abandoned by the doctors," including one in which Paola Antonia Negri cured a woman who was under the care of "four doctors, two physicians and two surgeons" (Fontana, *Vita,* pp. 48–53).

It was said of Colomba: "Quod infirmi, quod in adversis perplexi, quot mulieres periclitantes in partu, invocatis suffragiis B. Columbae convaluerunt, communis plebs est testis, et publica vox et fama" (Bontempi, *Legenda latina,* p. 221*). Veronica also aided women in labor (Isolani, *La santissima e miraculosa vita,* pp. 255–56), as did Gentile (Ferretti, *Le beate Margherita e Gentile,* p. 67), and Stefana (Guerrini, "La prima 'Legenda volgare,'" pp. 169 and 186), while Elena "obtained the desired children for the most sterile of women, as was attested in Piacenza and Alessandria" (Pietro da Lucca, *Narrativa,* p. 10). But no legend stressed this more than the *vita* of Caterina of Racconigi: not only did she aid women in labor and induce fertility, but she also prevented abortions (Pico-Morelli, *Compendio,* pp. 203–5). Pico apparently intended Caterina's powers to offset the evil influence of "obstetric" witches, who were known to cause sterility and abortions. The same can be said of the holy women's power over the elements: if some of them, like Osanna and Stefana, vanquished fire, Caterina worked miracles "in air, water, and fire" (p. 209). Through her miraculous intervention, the hail that was about to fall on Racconigi was scattered and the city "was preserved from the storms and hail that struck neighboring towns." In fact, "while still a child, she learned from a supernatural voice that hail would come and devastate the crops, but that she should not prevent it, because in her lifetime there would never again be such damage from a storm. This was probably a sign that from her youngest days she was destined to ward off storms generated in the air," perhaps by witches (p. 211).

177. Paola Antonia Negri was pricked in various parts of her body by her sister, who did not understand the nature of her "abstractions" (Fontana, *Vita,* p. 73), and a fellow nun tried to bring Arcangela Panigarola to her senses by pricking her foot with a needle (Inviziati, *Vita virtù e rivelazioni,* p. 171); in both cases, once their ecstasies had ended, the holy women felt acute pain. On the gift of tears, see Isolani, *Inexplicabilis,* p. 174; Zorzi, "Vitta," fols. 17v and 19v; Alessi, *Libellus,* p. 213; Ferretti, *Le beate Margherita e Gentile,* pp. 65, 69, and 77; and Fontana, *Vita,* p. 76.

178. Pietro da Lucca, *Narrativa,* pp. 4 and 6; Pietro da Lucca, *Epistola.*

179. Pico-Morelli, *Compendio,* p. 22; Guerrini, "La prima 'Legenda volgare,' "
p. 98; Serafino da Fermo, *Vita di due beatissime donne,* fol. 357, and Ferretti, *Le
beate Margherita e Gentile,* pp. 56, 57, 62, 68, and 79; and Fontana, *Vita,* pp. 37–39
and 42–43.

180. Arcangela's ring had the power to cure illnesses of the eyes and stomach.
Unlike the other holy women, Arcangela did not receive her ring from God as a token
of their mystical marriage, but through another miraculous event (Inviziati, *Vita
virtù e rivelazioni,* pp. 217–27). This precious object was kept in the convent as a
relic, and its thaumaturgic powers were even recognized by Cardinal Federico Borromeo, *De christianae mentis incunditate libri tres* (Milan, 1632), p. 32. Caterina de'
Ricci's ring was a token of her marriage with Christ and served to defend her from
diabolical stratagems ("Apologia di un anonimo," p. 33); it was invisible and had the
power to extinguish a fire, convert people, and cure various ailments (Alessi, *Libellus*). For Caterina of Racconigi's ring, see Pico-Morelli, *Compendio,* p. 182; for
Stefana Quinzani's, see Guerrini, "La prima 'Legenda volgare,' " p. 126.

181. Guerrini, "La prima 'Legenda volgare,' " pp. 184–85.

182. Ibid., pp. 162–63. The bronze ring with an image of the Virgin and Child
that St. Paul gave to Stefana also had the power to "command evil spirits."

183. Ibid., p. 163.

184. Ibid., p. 178.

185. Savonarola's influence on Bontempi is obvious in the *vita* of Colomba
of Rieti, beginning with the prologue built around the theme of the Flood and
the Ark; moreover, accusations that Bontempi was a follower of Savonarola and, like
him, disobedient to the pope, came from Rome itself: "quasi consimiliter Pontifici
maximo habuissent contumacem." His explanations did not manage to dispel the
suspicions that surrounded him and Colomba, herself accused of being "ream, ignis
veluti Fratrem Hieronymum" (Bontempi, *Legenda latina,* pp. 201* and 209*). Bontempi was forbidden any further contact with Colomba, and she was assigned a new
confessor, Andrea of Perugia (AGOP, *Reg. litt. et act. J. Turriani,* IV, 12, fol. 48r, 29
December 1498).

A master of theology, Silvestri wrote two commentaries on works of Aristotle
and an anti-Lutheran pamphlet. He held important offices in the Dominican order,
becoming master general (1525–28). Savonarola's influence is apparent in the readings he ascribed to Osanna of Mantua: she read books about saints to draw "spiritual flowers" from them, but "above all, the books called *The Triumph of the
Cross, The Life of St. Catherine of Siena,* and her *Dialogue*" (Silvestri, *La vita e stupendi miraculi,* book 1, chap. 18). On Silvestri, see Daniel Antonin Mortier, *Histoire
des maîtres généraux de l'Ordre des Frères Prêcheurs,* vol. 5 (Paris, 1911), pp. 260–
84, and S. P. Wolfs, "Bericht über die Visitation des Klosters von Lille durch den Or-
densgeneral Franciscus Sylvestri von Ferrara OP, 10–22 Juni 1528," *Archivum
Fratrum Praedicatorum* 32 (1962): 327–38.

Isolani's close ties with the convent of Santa Marta and Arcangela Panigarola
are enough to indicate his Savonarolan orientation. He openly supported a church

reform based on the advent of an Angelic Pope, identified as Denis Briçonnet, and assigned the king of France a special role in ecclesiastical affairs. Arcangela's respect for Savonarola is evident in a vision in which she saw him in heaven in saintly glory (Benigno Salviati, *Legenda,* fol. 175; published in Marcora, "Il cardinale Ippolito I d'Este," pp. 442–43).

186. A monk renowned above all for his sanctity, Scolari was for many years prior of the monastery of Santa Maria di Gradaro in Mantua; it was there that he met Osanna Andreasi and wrote her *vita.* Although Savonarola is not mentioned explicitly, his influence clearly shaped the accounts of her visions and of the scourges that threatened both rulers and the church. Moreover, after composing the *vita,* Scolari asked Gianfrancesco Pico to edit it; Pico probably accentuated the prophetic elements of the legend (Zarri, "Pietà e profezia," pp. 223 and 231).

187. Ludovico of Prelormo's chronicle of San Domenico in Bologna (preserved in the archive of that convent) records the profession of Fra Girolamo Savonarola of Ferrara under the date of 26 April 1474, identifying him as "Beatus" (fol. 219); it also notes that he was burned at the stake in Florence "cum maxima ignominia" for the order, and that the rules of his congregation of San Marco were "much more strict and observant" than those of the Lombard congregation (fol. 69). Ludovico came to Bologna in 1528 and remained there for forty-four years as custodian of the tomb of St. Dominic (fol. 253); it was during this period that he composed his chronicle.

In addition to editing and later translating Pico's dialogue *Strix,* Alberti was associated with Luca Bettini, who published some of Savonarola's sermons in Bologna in 1515 and, together with Alberti, published in 1523 Gianfrancesco Pico's *Digressio* on the immortality of the soul (Cesare Vasoli, entry "Bettini Luca," in *DBI,* vol. 9 [Rome, 1967], pp. 752–54). In 1515 Alberti prepared a Latin and Italian edition of the *Vaticinia circa apostolicos viros* attributed to Joachim of Fiore, prefacing this pamphlet with a defense of the Calabrian abbot and dedicating it to Giuliano de' Medici, papal legate to Bologna. Alberti thus aligned himself with prophetic movements calling for church reform and blasting its hierarchy for corruption. Moreover, he was in contact with Achille Bocchi's Erasmian circle and voiced paternal affection for Marco Antonio Flaminio: Leandro Alberti, *De viris et foeminis illustribus Ordinis Praedicatorum libri sex* (Bologna: In aedibus Hieronimi Platonis, 1517), fol. 153r; Antonia Rotondò, "Per la storia dell'eresia a Bologna nel secolo XVI," *Rinascimento,* ser. 2, 2 (1962): 126. On the *Vaticinia,* see Marjorie Reeves, "Some Popular Prophecies from the Fourteenth to the Seventeenth Centuries," in *Popular Belief and Practice* (Cambridge, 1972), pp. 107–34.

188. Alessi was born in Perugia and spent much of his life in the Dominican friary there, a bastion of Savonarolan devotion that cherished the memory of Colomba of Rieti. On his life, see Alessi, *Libellus,* 1: xix–l.

189. The most complete biography of Razzi is found in the preface to Di Agresti's edition of the *vita* of Caterina de' Ricci; but see also Serafino Razzi, *Diario di viaggio di un ricercatore (1572),* ed. Guglielmo Di Agresti, *Memorie domenicane,* n.s., 2 (1971), a short work that provides information about the cults of holy women

in the early sixteenth century, gathered by Razzi in the course of his travels to various Dominican convents.

190. Beltrán de Heredia, *Historia de la reforma,* pp. 126–32. The Dominican tertiary Maria di Santo Domingo used her mystical and prophetic gifts to promote a more rigorous reform of the Dominican order. Her devotion to Savonarola was expressed in a vision that placed him among the saints. She was also a great admirer of Lucia of Narni, and the profile that emerges from the canonization proceedings held on Maria's behalf in 1509–11 resembles that of Lucia and clearly derives from Italian models. In particular, the cult of this Dominican tertiary was linked with that of Catherine of Siena: in 1511–12 Catherine's *vita* and letters were translated into Castilian by Fra Antonio de la Peña, a supporter of the sanctity of the blessed Maria (Beltrán de Heredia, *Historia de la reforma,* p. 132). The ties between the Castilian Dominicans and the Lombard congregation are documented in Vicente Beltrán de Heredia, *Las corrientes de espiritualidad entre los Dominicos de Castilla durante la primera mitad del siglo XVI* (Salamanca, 1941), pp. 8–9.

191. This process started with the expulsion of the friars from San Marco in Florence in 1545 and the publication of Catarino's *Discorso contra la dottrina et le profetie di Fra Girolamo Savonarola* (Venice: Gabriel Giolito, 1548), and reached its climax in 1558 with the proceedings against Savonarola's works instituted under Paul IV, where the Jesuit Laynez led the prosecution and the most prominent Tuscan and Roman followers of Savonarola made statements in his defense. On this trial, see Paolo Simoncelli, "Momenti e figure del savonarolismo romano," *Critica storica,* n.s., 11 (1974): 47–82.

192. As we said, Chiara Bugni had received and conserved in a phial the milk of the Virgin; she appeared in a vision to the blessed Simeone, who gathered the milk and ordered the people to form a procession (Zorzi, "Vitta," fol. 72). Devotion to the milk of the Virgin clearly influenced the legend of Elena Duglioli, who was endowed with miraculous milk as proof of her virginity. Erasmus mocked this devotion in his dialogue on pilgrimages: see *The Colloquies of Erasmus,* trans. Craig R. Thompson (Chicago, 1965), p. 295.

193. Pietro of Lucca had preached that Christ was not conceived in the uterus, but "in the breast of the blessed Virgin Mary, next to her heart, by three drops of blood," repeating an opinion that had struck him as pious. Accused of heresy by the inquisitor of Mantua, Domenico of Gargnano, he was summoned to defend himself before the apostolic delegates, Cardinals Domenico Grimani and Antonio del Monte. Pietro admitted to preaching that Christ left the place where he had been said to have been conceived and that "he came forth from the uterus in a natural birth and a miraculous birth"; but claimed that he had not preached this "as a fact," but as a "good and catholic" opinion. Having heard his response, the two cardinals decided to convene a commission of theologians to discuss the problem, and in the meantime ordered Pietro of Lucca to refrain from circulating this doctrine "since this matter is seen to be dangerous and disruptive" and prohibited Domenico of Gargnano "and his associates" from defaming Pietro "as a heretic." The commission of theologians met in Rome to reconsider the case, presented this time by the inquisitor Girolamo

Armelini of Faenza, and arrived at a sentence that, while absolving Pietro "since he had not held as a fact that Christ was conceived outside the natural place and setting," condemned the doctrine as heretical, reaffirming that it must be believed that Christ was conceived in the uterus of the Virgin Mary and that "one should not understand 'uterus' to mean 'breast' or any other part of the body." The Biblioteca Corsiniana contains a copy of the *Sententia contra don Petrum de Luca qui novam Mantue predicavit heresim*, pronounced 22 July 1511, drawn up by the notary "Iacobus Sketa Trebanus clericus Aquileiensis diocesis" and printed in Rome. Pietro da Lucca's *Regule* was first published in 1504; but as Cantimori noted, its promise that one could attain salvation without suffering the pains of purgatory also appeared in later editions, when it would have smacked of Lutheranism (Cantimori, "Le idee religiose," p. 39).

194. St. Francis of Assisi appeared to Chiara in a vision, singing the *Pange lingua*; when he reached the line "Ad firmandum cor sincerum sola fides sufficit," he repeated it sweetly three times. On another occasion she heard angels sing this hymn, repeating this same verse many times (Zorzi, "Vitta," fols. 58r–v and 60v).

195. Vasoli, "Intorno a Francesco Giorgio Veneto," pp. 224–25.

196. I refer in particular to Guillaume Postel, on whom (in addition to the studies of François Secret) see William J. Bouwsma, *Concordia Mundi: The Career and Thought of Guillaume Postel, 1510–1582* (Cambridge, 1957); Aldo Stella, "Il processo veneziano di Guglielmo Postel," *Rivista di storia della Chiesa in Italia,* 22 (1968): 425–66; and Stella, *Anabattismo e antitrinitarismo,* pp. 115–31.

197. Serafino da Fermo, *Del discernimento de i spiriti* (first published 1535), in *Opere* (1556 ed.), fols. 371 and 374v. He discussed the coming of the Antichrist at greater length in his *Breve dichiaratione sopra l'Apocalisse,* on which see Prosperi, "America e Apocalisse." Serafino attributed to Margherita of Russi a "document" urging that revelations not be valued too highly, even though she herself "abounded in divine revelations." Indeed, Margherita supposedly instructed her disciple Gentile "not to believe anything except what the holy church has determined, a precept that alone makes all diabolical illusions vanish." Serafino of Fermo's caution in accepting revelations was motivated by his conviction that the age of the Antichrist had dawned and reflected the division of Christendom and the preaching of different doctrines. This is why he was the first to declare so explicitly that fidelity to the church was the decisive criterion for the discernment of spirits (Serafino da Fermo, *Vita di due beatissime donne,* fol. 348v).

198. Like earlier saints, Margherita and Gentile were presented as "teachers" with a substantial number of followers, and both made prophecies. Indeed, Margherita purportedly predicted the sack of Ravenna, "the renovation of the church, and the destruction of the Mohammedan religion," and moreover, "God revealed to her that she would found an association dedicated to the Buon Gesù" (ibid., fol. 351). Gentile, too, supposedly foretold the sack of Ravenna and saw "in spirit distant things" (fols. 359v–360). Although he asserted that Gentile had the power to work miracles, Serafino emphasized her refusal to use it. He claimed that it was "Pietro of Lucca, a man of exceptional learning and sanctity," who advised her

against performing them (fol. 362). This is puzzling, given what Pietro preached about Elena Duglioli; perhaps Serafino was attempting to downplay the miraculous deeds attributed to Elena. In any event, the momentous changes shaking the Christian world certainly made it advisable to exercise greater prudence in accepting miracles and propagating prophecies. In Serafino's words, Gentile "was very discrete, did nothing unusual, and did not burst forth in excessive fervors or furors" (*Del discernimento*, fol. 395). Furthermore, miracles should especially be avoided in the period in which he was writing: "Since the arrival of the Antichrist is upon us, saints should not go about working miracles because this is how the Antichrist will draw great crowds" (fol. 394).

199. Serafino da Fermo, *Vita di due beatissime donne*, fol. 362; *Trattato della discretione*, fol. 177. This whole work was aimed at exalting "royal discretion, lover of moderation"—a concept repeated in the *vitae* of the two saints of Ravenna (fol. 361).

200. In the prologue to his treatise on discretion, Serafino declared that "he desired most to inspire those who judge it impossible to attain sanctity," and thus addressed himself to *all* Christians. We have already noted how unusual it is to find a model of lay sanctity like that represented by the two holy women of Ravenna. Although Gentile was later recognized for having inspired a congregation of regular clerics, her life unfolded like that of so many women of her day: marriage, children, widowhood. It was during this final phase of her life that Gentile filled her time with prayers and pious activities—which she performed not in her parish church or some convent, but in her own home. And like Elena Duglioli, Gentile had a small domestic chapel where she was allowed by papal privilege to celebrate the eucharist (Serafino da Fermo, *Del discernimento*, fols. 371 and 381; Melloni, *Atti o memorie*, p. 331).

201. Feyles, *Serafino da Fermo*, pp. 31–34.

202. Felice of Barbarano (1527–53) was born in a town near Rome. Inspired by St. Francis, she "went around poorly dressed and barefoot, eating rough and coarse food and keeping vigil for most of the night." Her *vita* was reprinted several times in the late sixteenth century: Bonsignore Cacciaguerra, *Dialogo spirituale molto utile, con la vita d'una devota vergine sua figliuola spirituale, et una lettera sopra la frequentia della Santissima Communione* (Venice: Giacomo Simbeni, 1568). A proponent of frequent communion, Cacciaguerra was close to the Barnabites and Oratorians and was also known to Serafino of Fermo: see Roberto Zapperi, entry "Cacciaguerra Bonsignore," in *DBI*, vol. 15 (Rome, 1972), pp. 786–88; Feyles, *Serafino da Fermo*, p. 46.

203. Serafino lamented that in his time many people "became not inspired, but insane." He cited the example of a Venetian woman whom he distrusted: "during mass, she panted and sighed so much that she seemed about to faint; and when she was admonished for this, she said that she could not contain herself." The nuns in a convent in the Romagna behaved similarly, "drawing a large crowd with their strange shrieking; although they seemed to be fired with charity by the words, it was eventually discovered to be a spirit from hell, of the sort that always wants to do something new" (*Del discernimento*, fol. 395r–v).

204. Catarino advised Savonarola's followers not to place too much faith in women, reminding them of Savonarola's own words: "Women, being ignorant and by nature weak in judgment and inconstant and quite frail and much inclined to vanity, are easily deceived by the devil's ingenuity." He also expressed concern over the renewed popularity of mystical phenomena, which had been seen in a different light just a few decades earlier: "We have heard reports of a certain nun and new stigmata." This must surely be a reference to Caterina de' Ricci, given both the date when this treatise was written and the explicit allusion to the relics and images of Savonarola, which Catarino wanted removed from circulation. But the phenomenon does not seem to have been limited to Caterina de' Ricci, since "from all sides I hear about the visions of nuns and non-nuns and stigmata and mysteries of the Passion which I find very suspicious, and I hope to God that some day they do not give birth to some great scandal" (*Discorso del Rev. P. Frate Ambrosio Catharino Polito, vescovo di Minori, contra la dottrina et le profezie di Fra Girolamo Savonarola* [Venice: Gabriel Giolito, 1548], fols. 21v–22). Serafino of Fermo had voiced the same distrust of stigmata a few years earlier, alluding clearly to the case of Lucia of Narni as an example of illusion: "There are innumerable people who share the stigmata and sorrows of Jesus Christ, and they are almost always deceived. Not long ago a person apparently had stigmata, and she was revered by the whole world and succeeded in persuading not only ignorant people and men of the world, but also a vast multitude of learned men and masters of theology. It all turned out to have been an illusion, and she lives to this day without so many miracles; however, it had many good results" (*Del discernimento,* fol. 398). It is worth noting that Serafino's opinion of the holy woman was not entirely negative: the disappearance of her stigmata had abruptly broken up a cult of European dimensions and created a barrier of distrust around the woman, but she could still act in a saintly manner, as Serafino understood sanctity.

205. Di Agresti, *Santa Caterina de' Ricci: Testimonianze,* p. 25. The *Apologia* of the anonymous Dominican, written in defense of Caterina around 1549, mentions the diabolical deception of a nun of Cordova, Maddalena of the Cross. Perhaps Alessi was alluding to this woman when he spoke of a nun who in Caterina's day was famous for her sanctity, but in reality had made a pact with a devilish "incubus" (*Libellus,* 1: 31–32). Spanish Illuminism was a complex and multifaceted phenomenon, which often took its start from the visions or revelations of a "blessed woman." It especially involved the Franciscan order, though it first surfaced in the appeal for reform made by the visionary Maria of Pietrahita, the Dominican tertiary whose ties with Italian followers of Savonarola have already been mentioned. The first persecutions of the *alumbrados* in Spain were carried out against the *dejados* after the edict of Inquisitor General Marrique in Toledo in 1525 and the subsequent trial in 1529. See Marcel Bataillon, *Erasmo y Espana: Estudios sobre la historia espiritual del siglo XVI* (Mexico and Buenos Aires, 1950), 1: 72–82 and 195–216; José C. Nieto, *Juan de Valdes and the Origins of the Spanish and Italian Reformation* (Geneva, 1970), pp. 56–97; and Nieto, "The Heretical Alumbrados Dexados: Isabel de la Cruz and Pedro Ruiz de Alcazar," *Revue de littérature comparée* 52 (1978): 293–313.

206. Giovanna, the "Virgin of Venice," called "Mater mundi" and a new Eve

by Postel, was expected to bring about the regeneration of humankind through her mystical marriage with Christ. This visionary also predicted the reform of the church and the conversion of the Turks; her ecstasies lasted from Friday until Sunday, and when she received the eucharist her sixty-year-old face became as youthful as that of a fifteen-year-old. On Mother Giovanna, in addition to the works cited in note 196, see Enea Balmas, " 'Le prime nove dell'altro mondo' di Guglielmo Postel," *Studi urbinati di storia, filosofia, e letteratura* 29 (1955): 334–77. On Albrisio, see "Il processo al medico Basilio Albrisio: Reggio 1559," ed. Albano Biondi and Adriano Prosperi, *Contributi* 2, no. 4 (1978).

207. Carlo Ginzburg, "Due note sul profetismo cinquecentesco," *Rivista storica italiana* 78 (1966): 184–227.

208. See Gabriele Cozzano, *Risposta contro quelli persuadono la clausura alle vergini di S. Orsola*, in Ledóchowska, *Angèle Merici*, 2: 332–59; and Prodi, "Vita religiosa e crisi sociale."

209. As is well known, the Tridentine decree *De regularibus ac monialibus*, in session 25, reinstated cloister for all female monasteries and compelled convents of tertiaries living in community to pronounce solemn vows, including cloister: see Raimondo Creytens, "La riforma dei monasteri femminili dopo i decreti tridentini," in *Il Concilio di Trento e la riforma tridentina* (Rome, 1965), 1: 45–83. The Angelics, as well, were compelled to accept enclosure and adapt their constitutions to the dispositions of the Council of Trent; as a consequence, the nature of their religious community was profoundly altered, losing some of the most distinctive features of the original congregation. These changes were summarized by the Angelic Paola Antonia Sfondrati: "In short, many important things changed: the election of superiors and the way it was done; and admitting girls to the order, who from then on had to come provided with dowries and income, as various popes decreed for many reasons. This had always been avoided in order to shun property; indeed, except for a very small number of sisters, nearly all of the rest had entered without even a minimal amount of possessions. And they put an end to the customary lengthy period of probation before profession and taking the veil, and other customs; with a time limit set for doing all this" (Rome, Archivio Generalizio San Carlo ai Catinari, MS L c 7: *Istoria dell'Angelica Paola Antonia Sfondrati circa l'Angeliche del monastero di S. Paolo di Milano, fondato dalla contessa di Guastalla*, fol. 99).

210. Fontana, *Vita*, p. 99; Prosperi, "Besozzi Giovanni Pietro," p. 682.

211. Fontana, *Vita*, pp. 103–5.

212. Prosperi, "Besozzi Giovanni Pietro," p. 683. Besozzi gathered the accusations of Negri's denigrators in his *Apologia*, written in response to the publication in 1576 of Fontana's *vita* of Negri.

213. Fontana, *Vita*, p. 104.

Women Religious in Late Medieval Italy: New Sources and Directions

Roberto Rusconi

When we first thought of gathering in one volume the most important essays by some young Italian scholars, scholars whose work had fundamentally transformed historical research on the religious life of late medieval Italy, we thought it would be useful to select texts that best illustrated their contributions to one rapidly developing field of study: the religious history of women.

In the decade between the initial conception of the volume and its appearance, first in an Italian version and now in this English edition, the study of women and religion has flourished as never before and changed in significant ways. For one thing, the study of women's history in general has continued its vigorous growth, while shifting fruitfully from the feminist approaches of its early days to the current methods of gender history. Studies on the religious and ecclesiastical history of late medieval Italy have also progressed considerably, and not only in areas concerned primarily with the history of female religious life. With these developments in mind, this afterword has been added to take account of the latest Italian contributions and to suggest, on their basis, some promising directions for future research. My focus will be not so much the devotional or spiritual life of women, as the women themselves who adopted some recognizable form of religious life, whether or not it was institutionalized, and the documents produced by and for them.

ROBERTO RUSCONI

A "Written" Church

Thirty-five years ago, in some of his early essays, Robert Brentano re-vealingly juxtaposed two thirteenth-century churches. In his judgment, the measure of the difference between the English and Italian churches in that period was furnished principally by the distinctive characteristics of the documentation generated, in both countries, by their institutions: eccle-siastical institutions, above all, but also all those other institutions that in some fashion entered into contact with the church.[1]

Since that date, however, the study of ecclesiastical history and of reli-gious life in Italy has been fundamentally transformed by a sort of "revolution"—to use an expression employed by Brentano himself a de-cade ago.[2] This "new ecclesiastical history" was defined by a particularly shrewd deployment of documentary sources as the basis for a reconstruc-tion of the past. Not that many years ago, this approach might have been deemed peculiar to a few research centers, chief among them the University of Padua in the Veneto and, in Umbria, the University of Perugia; but by now it has come to constitute a standard component of Italian medieval studies, as pursued throughout northern and central Italy.

One major focus of research on late medieval Italy has been the women who, in growing numbers, came to enter monastic institutions or to adopt other forms of religious life (even if, in point of fact, the number of female religious remained far less than that of male religious until at least the end of the eighteenth century).[3] As a consequence, an imposing mass of documen-tation was generated—documentation, moreover, whose characteristic fea-tures distinguish it from the corresponding documentation produced by male institutions of the same type. This array of materials runs the gamut from dry administrative records to fervid ascetic and mystical literature.

Monastic Archives and Civic Magistracies

The need to protect a convent's rights amid the complex tangle of civil and ecclesiastical jurisdictions so typical of the Middle Ages obliged the nuns who belonged to recognized institutions to carefully preserve the relevant documentation. The originals of papal letters and other documents issued by the papal or an episcopal curia were commonly stowed in a simple chest, or even in an ordinary cupboard. So too were more or less voluminous car-tularies, often redacted in authenticated copies by a public notary, with the primary purpose of having readily available these juridical records of a private nature. The specific method of conservation—an expression, so to speak, of the written self-awareness of an institution—has so far received scant attention, even when the documents pertaining to an individual convent have been preserved in that convent over the centuries, right down to our own times.[4] More often, as a consequence of the repeated suppressions of female religious institutions at the hands of the various Italian states, starting in the middle of the eighteenth century and continuing throughout the nineteenth, the bulk of the documentation concerning these institutions has flowed into the collections of the state archives in the individual Italian provinces.[5]

Inevitably, documentary sources of this type refer overwhelmingly, if not exclusively, to the institutional framework and economic and administrative aspects of female religious life, especially as lived within convents. Such sources generally do not reveal the specific context in which new forms of religious life first emerged, in association with movements of spiritual renewal or moments of ecclesiastical reform. In practice, the undeniable fluidity of female religious life is usually caught, at least on the documentary level, in the instant of its "regularization": that is, as it is being institutionally framed by the definitive imposition (and subsequent acceptance) of an approved monastic rule, with the attendant subordination to papal or episcopal jurisdiction or to a male religious order.[6]

In fact, from the outset the myriad forms assumed by female religious life—far more idiosyncratic than the corresponding male experiences— were subjected to a constant pressure toward increased regularization on the part of the ecclesiastical hierarchy. This process began in 1215 with the thirteenth constitution of the Fourth Lateran Council, *Ne nimia religionum diversitas,* and reached its point of closure (in every sense of the term) with the *Decretum de regularibus et monialium,* approved in the course of the twenty-fifth session of the Council of Trent, on 3–4 December 1563.[7]

The letters addressed to individual convents were regularly recorded in the papal registers in Rome, while the registers of episcopal chancelleries (when they existed, and when their records have survived) often first note the existence of the variegated communities of *religiosae mulieres,* from informal little clusters of female penitents to juridically recognized convents, when they became involved in a controversy: that is, when their rights were called into question by another ecclesiastical institution.[8] "Suits were a monastic pastime," as Robert Brentano observed ironically, though he may have underestimated the extent to which these legal squabbles—for male and female religious alike—arose from a very real need to defend juridically their sources of subsistence and hence, perhaps, their very existence.[9]

If the initial gestation of regular monastic institutions often eluded written notice, this is all the more true of those groups and individuals who adopted forms of the eremitical life (in the case of women, this generally meant voluntary reclusion) or created religious microcommunities. In such cases, one must turn to another kind of documentation: in particular, for northern and central Italy in the later Middle Ages, the laws that guided the functioning of civic magistracies (the statutes) and the decisions they issued (decrees and *riformanze*)—which also, one should note, often impinged on the various phases of the founding of regular monastic institutions. The governing councils of nearly every Italian city made a practice of distributing charitable donations to numerous "religious" persons, including those not institutionally recognized, on the occasion of civic and ecclesiastical holidays, thereby allowing us to plot a detailed map of the locations of individual *mulieres religiosae* and groups of female penitents who may not even appear in the documentation generated by ecclesiastical institutions. This has had particularly significant consequences for our knowledge of female voluntary reclusion, which in this civic documentation assumes far greater dimensions than one would have guessed from the hagiographical sources concerning the few anchoresses who acquired a reputation for sanctity.[10]

The use of civic sources has also shed new light on the phenomenon of women (and men) who gave themselves as oblates in the service, not of a monastery, but of a hospital: an expression of religious choice whose social consequences were immediately tangible.[11] A similar blending of social and religious concerns is evident in the documents concerning the practice of work by the Humiliate—women belonging to a pauperistic movement of evangelical inspiration, widespread in the Po valley, who gave concrete expression to their choice of religious life by electing to work with their own hands.[12]

Some very interesting information on the social composition of convents can be gleaned from the entire complex of documentation concerning them, and in particular from their necrologies, wherever they exist for the late Middle Ages.[13] For this period, however, the biographical data remain too sketchy to sustain grand interpretations that are particularly convincing—and the information on noninstitutionalized communities of religious women is even more scarce. Accordingly, a more fruitful approach might be the use of existing records to reconstruct the entire panoply of forms of female religious life, whether governed by a rule or not, extant in a given geographical area, in order to define the characteristic features of a sort of "territorial monastic system." Such a study could be directed at "the array of female monastic institutions, associated both with the mendicant orders and with the various branches of the Benedictine order; the chronology of the individual foundations; their geographical placement and even-tual changes of location, especially in connection with the shifting fortunes of urban centers; the size of each institution, along with the related question of restriction of access; other potential ways of organizing female religious life, such as the (more or less regular) communities of tertiaries and the communities of *religiosae mulieres* licensed directly by bishops"—and this list certainly does not exhaust the possibilities of studies framed in regional terms.[14]

Only by reconstructing this broader context, which is at once religious and social, can one craft a convincing study of the full range of forms of female religious life, which could not (and cannot) be forced entirely into the framework of regular monastic institutions.[15] Thus, this would also be a useful corrective to the tendency—evident in official documents and hagiographical literature—to project into the past the moving inspiration behind certain phenomena, reading them in the light of later developments.[16]

One last category of ecclesiastical institution in northern and central Italy was the confraternity, or religious association of devout laity; and between the thirteenth century and the Renaissance or early modern period, these particular institutions rather grudgingly began to grant women an active (if limited) role.[17] Confraternal statutes and administrative documents register a gradual shift from passive participation in the "spiritual merits" acquired by a woman's father or husband (with some limited involvement in confraternal worship and devotional activities) to full membership or even the creation of separate confraternities of devout women, especially in connection with the spread of Marian devotions, as in the confraternities of the Rosary founded in the last quarter of the fifteenth century.[18] As the fifteenth century progressed, finally, the authors of *sacre rappresentazioni*, which were normally performed by confraternities, came to include at least one woman: Antonia Pulci, who published no fewer than five of these religious dramas.[19]

"Nolens Intestatus Decedere": Notarial Protocols

The omnipresence of the public notary in the civic and ecclesiastical institutions of the Italian peninsula has historically made the notary a central figure in the production of documents, especially from the closing centuries of the Middle Ages. The practical juridical, economic, and above all patrimonial importance of the records jealously guarded in the archives of the corporate bodies for which they were prepared, together with the continued existence, right down to our own day, of the notarial profession, ensured that these documents would be preserved with great care, both by their con-

temporaries and by posterity. As a result, notarial records have survived
time's ravages more successfully than other forms of written documentation
and have come to constitute, for the late Middle Ages, a distinct section of
the state archives.[20]

The principal reason that the various forms and institutions of female
religious life appear in notarial protocols—that is, the original record kept
by a notary from which he certified copies of the documents he redacted—
was the practice of making wills.[21] "Nolens intestatus decedere," not wishing to die intestate, ran a standard legal formula, one that accurately reflected the outlook of individual testators.[22] Within each testament, a
special section was dedicated to bequests *devotionis causa*. In practice,
pious bequests were directed to religious institutions for which the testator
wished to display a devotional preference or with which she or he had established particular personal or familial ties. The form of those connections
naturally varied considerably, depending on whether the testator was an
aristocrat or a member of the middle classes. But beyond any differences,
the fact remains that many testaments seem to be dominated by a desire to
remember and reward the greatest possible number of ecclesiastical institutions and religious associations.[23] Analyzing the data furnished by such bequests even allows us to trace the focal points of religious piety within a
given area, generally (but not exclusively) urban.[24]

The distinctive character of female monastic institutions—and of their
patrimonies, in particular—is reflected also in the fact that they, unlike the
corresponding male religious orders, usually did not directly receive "goods
of their own, but only through bequests made to nuns in that convent or to
women whose later monastic profession can be documented or presumed.
The recipients are always linked by ties of kinship with the testators."[25] The
thoroughly personal character of such a relationship at least partly explains
the impressive number of bequests by women in favor of anchoresses and
female microgroups. Some testaments, however, clearly suggest that the testator wished instead to benefit the greatest possible number of religious
communities, both male and female, institutionally recognized and purely
voluntary.

In any case, there was a specifically female approach to testamentary
practice. Above all, many women emerge from the shadows of anonymity
only because of their appearance, whether as donor or recipient, in testaments. Their wills reflected not only their devotional preferences, but often
a personal involvement as well, for "it was women in particular who displayed a special interest in the forms of penitential life, institutional and private, communal and individual. . . . Bequests of this sort often lead one to
suppose that the testatrix herself participated in the penitential life."[26]

Legends, Miracles, and Canonization Proceedings:
From Anonymity to Sanctity

In late medieval and early modern Italy, a significant number of women came to enjoy an impressive reputation for sanctity, sometimes even within their own lifetimes—as did Lucia of Narni, the most famous "living saint of a nun" of that period.[27] This fame, however, could also result from a feigned sanctity, which was held to be something of a female specialty.[28]

The hagiographical literature concerning holy women in late medieval Italy has received considerable scholarly attention in recent years, in studies conducted with far more rigorous methods than in the past. Behind this literature often lay earlier sets of documents—in particular, canonization proceedings and miracle collections—which were subsequently reworked to form hagiographical *legendae*.[29] As in the case of testaments, these documents were produced with the assistance of public notaries: thanks in part to the increased insistence on formal certification imposed by canonical procedure, but also as a result of the growing social prestige of the "notarial style."[30] In those cases in which it has been possible to draw on a variety of sources, the information furnished by canonization proceedings, hagiographical *legendae,* and notarial protocols truly brings to life a complex web of social relations and devotional impulses.

As happens with testaments, the mass of documentation connected with a belief in the sanctity of some individual (whether male or female) allows many women to emerge from the absolute anonymity that otherwise marked their historical and social condition. Significant numbers of women, in fact, appear in the depositions of canonization proceedings and in miracle collections, not only to describe the prodigies of which they were beneficiaries or simply witnesses, but above all to attest to their close ties to other *mulieres religiosae.* An attentive reading of this documentation allows us to delineate with precision the social and religious setting in which they moved. Nor is there any reason to be surprised if the number of women who appeared to testify to the sanctity of another woman far surpassed the number of men.[31]

Indeed, in these records men appear "primarily as beneficiaries of miracles, as persons of little faith, or simply as people by now long deceased."[32] The only significant exception to this rule is represented, predictably, by members of the various religious orders, who appeared by virtue of the offices that brought them into contact with a devout woman: as her chaplain, director of conscience, confessor, and so on—and hence, not uncommonly, as author of the first hagiographical *legenda* drafted to promote the cult of a new "blessed woman." Even the typology of miracles reflects a gendered distinction in the context in which the miracles occurred: miracles involving men took place in the world outside the household, a hostile world characterized by tense and often violent relations, while those involving women unfolded in a domestic setting or within the web of social relations that centered on the family.[33]

In conclusion, despite often massive losses and scattering of records, once again it was the convent archive that represented the privileged place for preserving over time documents concerning the sanctity of a religious woman—though usually, in this case, one who belonged to an institutionalized female community.

"Scriptoria": Nuns' Writings

One area of enormous interest whose surface has barely been scratched by scholars is the general level of women's religious culture and monastic spirituality in the late Middle Ages. Part of the reason is that historians have seemed almost hypnotized by the scanty fragments of information regarding the intellectual achievements of a few outstanding figures, generally presented by their hagiographical biographers as uneducated women who became "learned" purely as a result of the supernatural intervention of divine grace.[34]

On the contrary, it is not at all necessary to wait for the fifteenth century or the beginning of the sixteenth to discover that many convents were filled with young women sprung from the nobility or the merchant bourgeoisie who were perfectly capable of reading both the vernacular and Latin, and perhaps even writing them as well.[35] In this connection, the significant recent advances in our knowledge of the history of female literacy also caution us against mechanically repeating that women's religious communication and devotional expression tended to be exclusively oral.[36] In fact, devotional literature produced for the laity included edifying texts directed specifically at women, starting with collections of the lives of holy women— not to mention the letters exchanged between devout women and their spiritual guides.[37]

At various points in the canonization proceedings opened immediately after the death of Francesca Bussa dei Ponziani in 1440, mention is made of her readings, even noting that after a certain point in her life she had to use eyeglasses.[38] And in Francesca's case, it was precisely her reading of ascetic and devotional works that constituted the cultural wellspring from which her visionary experiences flowed.[39]

What is more, life in regular monastic institutions entailed the performance of liturgical functions and collective worship that required at least a basic ability to read Latin. As for devotional and edifying works, while it is true that the Italian vernacular was closer to biblical and liturgical Latin than were the Germanic languages and other Romance tongues, this did not prevent the gradual creation in Italian, too, of a specific vernacular literature intended for use by nuns and female religious. The recorded text of the Lenten sermons delivered in Florence by the Dominican friar Giordano of Pisa early in the fourteenth century was copied for the use of the women in the convent of San Gaggio, near Florence, in the second half of the century;[40] but at the end of the following century, in 1492, it was an attentive woman who personally recorded for her own use and that of her fellow religious the sermons preached to the Franciscan nuns of Vicenza by the Observant Franciscan friar Bernardino of Feltre.[41]

The possibility of actual preaching by nuns and religious women was another question. Aside from episodes like that of the young tertiary Rose of Viterbo (†1252), who preached publicly in her city against the emperor Frederick II (at least according to hagiographical tradition), one can find abbesses preaching within the walls of their own convents, in keeping with a practice documented earlier in the Middle Ages and continued, for instance, in the sermons of the Vallombrosan nun, Umiltà of Faenza (1226–1310).[42] In the middle of the fifteenth century, the abbess of the convent of Santa Chiara in Florence preached to her nuns on the Nativity of Jesus.[43] And early in the next century, we encounter the striking figure of Domenica da Paradiso, charismatic founder of the Florentine convent of the Crocetta, whose audience also included groups of men and women who were devoted to her. The manuscripts of the sermons that she delivered starting in 1515, like those of her other works, form part of that broad stream of texts produced by scribes and secretaries in the service of female visionaries and religious women, amply documented in Italy from the turn of the fourteenth century: beginning with the Franciscan tertiary Angela of Foligno, reaching a high point with the towering figure of the Dominican tertiary Catherine of Siena, and continuing at least to the very end of the sixteenth century.[44] As for Domenica da Paradiso in particular, her personal career as a "living saint of a nun" evidently struck a resonant chord in a setting that still vibrated with the religious reform promoted a few years earlier by the Dominican friar Girolamo Savonarola.[45]

Numerous manuscripts of monastic origin intended for nuns' use contain vernacular translations of the normative texts of their orders, which often swelled into bulky compilations of ascetic writings; and even in the first half of the fifteenth century the rule of the Humiliate nuns, for instance, "included an exhortation to dedicate part of every day, especially during

Lent, to reading 'sacred and divine' books."⁴⁶ Beginning in the closing decades of the fifteenth century, the definitive spread of printing with movable
type multiplied dizzyingly the amount of devotional literature in circulation, first by reproducing older texts that had formerly circulated in manuscript and then by printing works written specifically for publication, in
Latin but above all in the vernacular. From the outset, a portion of these
writings was directed at female religious and monastic circles, in which they
often found their inspiration or even their origins.⁴⁷ Indeed, one should not
forget that one of the first printing shops in Florence, and one that was extremely active in publishing vernacular works of religious literature, was
operated by the Dominican nuns of San Jacopo a Ripoli, near Florence.⁴⁸

In fact, "whoever considers female religious life in the fifteenth and sixteenth centuries cannot help but be struck by the devotion and learning of
the Franciscan nuns. Significantly, it was the female branch that supplied the
order with that devout vernacular literature which the male branch produced in minimal quantities," since the Franciscan friars concerned themselves above all with works of immediate utility to their own pastoral
activities, in particular, preaching to the laity in the vernacular and hearing
the confessions of the faithful.⁴⁹

In any case, further information on the intellectual and cultural formation of these nuns and their religious communities can be derived from a
direct examination of the products of their "editorial" activities. These involved, in the first place, texts by female authors, running (in the fifteenth
century) from the visions "dictated" to Sister Illuminata Bembo by Caterina
Vigri of Bologna to the lost autograph of Battista Varano's *Vita spirituale*.
There is thus no reason to be surprised that, when the nuns of Corpus Domini announced Caterina of Bologna's death in 1463 to other convents of
Poor Clares, they invited their sisters to read and copy her "little book."⁵⁰

Insight into their cultural formation can also be gathered from the
handwriting typical of these nuns, which seems to have been strikingly old-
fashioned, at least by fifteenth-century standards. "One would be justified
in thinking that these nuns had learned to read and write in limited fashion,
as is shown by the products of their 'editorial' activities: those codices written in gothic characters, by then archaic with respect to the humanist script
that dominated book production."⁵¹ The contradictory indications on this
subject furnished by hagiographical accounts could thus be tested against
the surviving manuscripts copied by nuns, to find (perhaps) that they derived their writing models from other volumes in their own libraries.⁵²

We still lack, for the most part, adequate studies of the library collections in convents affiliated with the various religious orders. Such libraries
undoubtedly existed, albeit on different scales—and certainly not at all

comparable to some of the great monastic libraries of the male orders.[53] For example, the convent of Poor Clares of Santa Maria di Monteluce near Perugia—the leading center from which the Observant reform movement spread beginning in the middle of the fifteenth century—housed a genuine *scriptorium*, whose manuscript production provided the main nucleus of their library.[54] The social and cultural backgrounds of these women accustomed them to writing: "Characteristically, this group of nuns brought with them when they entered convent walls the memorializing habits of the ruling urban elites of late medieval Italy, which took the form of writing private memoirs (the *libri di famiglia*) and public ones (the civic chronicles)—both of which find their parallel in the redaction of convent chronicles."[55] This particular phenomenon touched virtually all of the convents involved in the Observant reform of the Poor Clares in central Italy, at the end of the fifteenth century and beginning of the sixteenth.[56]

A library also existed at the convent of Poor Clares of Corpus Domini in Bologna, where Sister Caterina Vigri's reputation for exceptional sanctity ensured that the manuscripts she copied with her own hand would be jealously preserved, right down to the present.[57] Like these writings, the *legendae* concerning the revered founders of female monastic institutions were treated with special respect. Normally—and obviously enough—convents kept copies of hagiographic texts regarding their founders, usually composed by clerics, often their confessors: the archive of the convent of Tor de' Specchi in Rome, for instance, contains the biography of Francesca Bussa dei Ponziani by her confessor.[58] However, when Sister Eustochia of Messina, founder of the Franciscan convent of Montevergine, died in 1486, her hagiographical biography was immediately written in the vernacular by the sisters themselves.[59] Nuns could thus be not only copyists of codices, but authors of texts, like that Sister Angelica who, as early as the thirteenth century, collected the miracles of St. Dominic of Caleruega narrated by Sister Cecilia of Rome.[60] But above all, they offered a different image of female sanctity, as emerges with great clarity from a comparison of the two *legendae* of Sister Margherita Colonna, the first written by her brother, the Roman senator Giovanni Colonna, and the second by another Clarissan nun, Sister Stefania.[61] However, the hagiographical *legendae* written by nuns only reached a wider audience thanks to the intervention of male intermediaries. The hagiographical biography of Caterina of Bologna, written by Sister Illuminata Bembo, and that of Eustochia of Messina, written by Jacopa Pollicino, were printed in 1502 and 1505, but in the Latin version of a friar; and the same thing happened later to the hagiographical biography of Veronica of Binasco composed by Sister Benedetta of Vimercate.[62]

Images of Women, Images for Women

Observations along much the same lines as those concerning nuns as writers and the composition of hagiographical *legendae* could also be offered in connection with images, in the entire gamut of representations running from miniatures in manuscripts to the great fresco cycles on church walls—and the walls of chapter halls and refectories as well. This form of historical documentation of female religious life remains largely unexplored, but its possibilities are readily apparent from the few pioneering studies in this area. One can begin at the most basic level with the influence of religious images on devout women—an influence that is magnified by the presumption that most women were barely literate, if not entirely illiterate—and illustrate this in striking fashion with the experience of female mystics and visionaries.[63] At the other extreme, there was the influence of women on images, for some works, or at least some of the subjects depicted in them, were aimed specifically at women: for example, certain miracles depicted in narrative panel paintings of the life of St. Francis presuppose a largely female audience for the scene represented.[64] The intermediate situation—and the one most obviously suited to further study—involves women commissioning images, from manuscript illuminations to paintings, a practice that is amply documented, and not only on the part of nuns and female religious. To tell the truth, studies in this area must explore a complex dialectic between image and representation, whose varied interactions are presently just beginning to be surveyed.[65]

Conclusion

At an earlier moment, one might have been content to bask pleasurably in the generous praise lavished on an emerging Italian historiography by a scholar of the stature of Robert Brentano—who recognized, moreover, that many of these younger scholars had been trained or influenced by medievalists as illustrious as Paolo Sambin, Cinzio Violante, Giovanni Tabacco, Giovanni Miccoli, Giorgio Cracco, Claudio Leonardi, Arsenio Frugoni, and Ovidio Capitani (and also, one should note, by historians of early modern Italy like Delio Cantimori and Paolo Prodi). Since these scholars have generally not been especially interested in "the Renaissance," which sometimes seems to be the only period of any note in the long history of Italy, it is entirely possible that even their names remain little known in the English-speaking world, outside of a tiny circle of specialists.

Now, however, it seems equally important to ensure—and this is one of the purposes of this collection—a genuine familiarity with a body of scholarship on late medieval Italy that has by now become quite substantial.[66] Not all that long ago, one could legitimately lament: "Italicum est, non legitur."[67] At the moment, fortunately, signs of a change for the better are not lacking.[68]

NOTES

An earlier version of this text was presented at the twenty-eighth International Congress on Medieval Studies, Kalamazoo, Michigan, 6–9 May 1993, in the session "Sources for Ecclesiastical History in Italy and England during the Late Middle Ages," organized by Laura Gaffuri (University of Padua) and Simon Forde (University of Leeds); the other participants were Daniel Bornstein (Texas A & M University), Robert N. Swanson (University of Birmingham), and Norman P. Tanner (Oxford University). In addition to those who took part in the discussion on that occasion, I would like to thank Anna Benvenuti (University of Florence) and Anna Esposito (University of Rome "La Sapienza") for their many helpful suggestions. Naturally, my bibliographical indications have been chosen to illustrate key points and do not pretend to be exhaustive. Further guidance on these and other topics can be found in the recent survey by Maria Giuseppina Muzzarelli, "Tematiche della storiografia italiana recente dedicata alla donna medievale," *Studi medievali,* ser. 3, 30 (1989): 883–908.

1. Robert Brentano, "The Bishops' Books of Città di Castello," *Traditio* 16 (1960): 241–54; "The Archiepiscopal Archives at Amalfi," *Manuscripta* 4 (1960): 98–105; "Sealed Documents of the Mediaeval Archbishops of Amalfi," *Mediaeval Studies* 23 (1961): 21–46; *Two Churches: England and Italy in the Thirteenth Century* (Princeton, 1968; 2d ed., Berkeley and Los Angeles, 1988).

2. Robert Brentano, "Italian Ecclesiastical History: The Sambin Revolution," *Medievalia et Humanistica,* n.s., 14 (1986): 189–97.

3. For a thorough treatment, see the collection of studies by Anna Benvenuti Papi, "*In castro poenitentiae*": *Santità e società femminile nell'Italia medievale,* Italia Sacra, 45 (Rome, 1990), and Enrico Menestò and Roberto Rusconi, *Umbria: La strada delle sante medievali* (Turin, 1991) (originally published in 1989 with the title *Umbria sacra e civile*).

4. Among the many possible examples, see in particular Giovanna Casagrande, "Inventario dell'archivio del monastero della Beata Colomba," *Bollettino della Deputazione di storia patria per l'Umbria* 73 (1976): 251–66, and Mario Sensi, "Il patrimonio monastico di S. Maria di Vallegloria a Spello," *Bollettino della Deputazione di storia patria per l'Umbria* 81 (1984): 77–149.

5. See, for example, the documentation used by Giovanna Casagrande and Paola Monacchia, "Il monastero di Santa Giuliana a Perugia nel secolo XIII," *Benedictina* 27 (1980): 509–68; Peter Höhler, "Il monastero delle clarisse di Monteluce di

Perugia, 1218–1400," in *Il movimento religioso femminile in Umbria nei secoli XIII–XIV,* ed. Roberto Rusconi (Florence, 1984), pp. 159–82; and Höhler, "Frauenklöster in einer italienischen Stadt: Zur wirtschafts- und sozialgeschichte der Klarissen von Monteluce und der Zisterzienserinnen von Perugia (13.–Mitte 15. Jh.)," *Quellen und Forschungen aus italienischen Archiven und Bibliotheken* 67 (1987): 1–107 and 68 (1988): 167–270.

On southern Italy, see the recent studies by Gerardo Ruggiero, "Il monastero di Sant'Anna di Nocera: Dalla fondazione al Concilio di Trento," *Memorie Domenicane,* n.s., 20 (1989): 5–166, and Anna Maria Facchiano, *Monasteri femminili e nobiltà a Napoli tra Medioevo ed età moderna: Il necrologio di S. Patrizia, sec. XII–XVI)* (Salerno, 1992).

6. A striking example of resistance to "normalization" is Clare of Assisi, who, despite the existence of many other rules drafted for nuns inspired by and affiliated with the Franciscan movement, managed to win approval for her own rule, though not until just before her death: see Maria Pia Alberzoni, *Chiara e il papato* (Milan, 1995), pp. 96–108 (with references to earlier works on the subject). It is interesting to note that Clare's rule, which in effect was not followed by any convent after her death in 1253 (apart from the notable exception of the convent of San Francesco in Prague, governed by Agnes of Bohemia), was put back into practice only in the course of the fifteenth century, by the Clarissan movement of Observant reform, which assured it a diffusion in manuscript that it had never had before. See Werner Maleczeck, *Das "Privilegium paupertatis" Innozenz' III. und das Testament der Klara von Assisi: Überlegungen zur Frage ihrer Echtheit* (Rome, 1995).

7. *Decrees of the Ecumenical Councils,* original texts ed. Giuseppe Alberigo et al., English translation ed. Norman P. Tanner (London and Washington, 1990), pp. 242 and 776–84.

8. See the observations of Giovanna Casagrande in the introduction to *Gli archivi ecclesiastici di Città di Castello,* Archivi dell'Umbria: Inventari e ricerche, 14 (Perugia, 1989), p. lxix.

9. Brentano, *Two Churches,* p. 246.

10. See the study by Mario Sensi, "Incarcerate e recluse in Umbria nei secoli XIII e XIV: Un bizzoccagio centro-italiano," in Rusconi, *Il movimento religioso femminile in Umbria,* pp. 85–121 (translated in this volume as "Anchoresses and Penitents in Thirteenth- and Fourteenth-Century Umbria"), and the bibliographical information on more recent studies provided by Giovanna Casagrande, "Il fenomeno della reclusione volontaria nei secoli del Basso Medioevo," *Benedictina* 35 (1988): 475–507.

11. Among the many studies included in *Uomini e donne in comunità,* ed. Giuseppina De Sandre Gasparini, Grado G. Merlo and Antonio Rigon, Quaderni di storia religiosa, 1 (Verona, 1994), see in particular Marina Gazzini, "Uomini e donne nella realtà ospedaliera monzese dei secoli XII–XIV" (pp. 127–44); Maria Grazia Cesana, "Uomini e donne nelle comunità ospedaliere di Como nel Duecento" (pp. 145–60); and Gian Maria Varanini, "Uomini e donne in ospedali e monasteri del territorio trentino, secoli XII–XIV" (pp. 259–300).

12. See Lorenzo Paolini, "Le umiliate al lavoro: Appunti fra storiografia e storia," *Bullettino dell'Istituto Storico Italiano per il Medio Evo* 97 (1991): 229–65, and Giuseppina De Sandre Gasparini, "In margine a un recente studio sugli umiliati: Qualche nota di storia comparata," *Rivista di storia e letteratura religiosa* 30 (1994): 85–102. For some essays of more general nature, see *Donne e lavoro nell'Italia medievale,* ed. Maria Giuseppina Muzzarelli et al. (Turin, 1991).

13. See, for instance, Facchiano, *Monasteri femminili e nobiltà a Napoli.*

14. Roberto Rusconi, "L'espansione del francescanesimo femminile nel secolo XIII," in *Movimento religioso femminile e francescanesimo nel secolo XIII,* Proceedings of the Seventh International Conference of Franciscan Studies, Assisi, 11–13 October 1979 (Assisi, 1980), pp. 311–12. Similar conclusions have also been reached by Anna Benvenuti, "La fortuna del movimento damianita in Italia, sec. XIII: Propositi per un censimento da fare," in *Chiara di Assisi,* Proceedings of the Twentieth International Conference of Franciscan Studies, Assisi, 15–17 October 1992 (Spoleto, 1993), pp. 102–6. One might add in passing that not only their geographical distribution but also their placement within a given territory distinguished the houses of the male orders from female convents, which tended, for instance, to be arranged in a belt just within the city walls: see Luigi Pellegrini, "Conventi mendicanti e spazio urbano nell'Italia dei secoli XIII–XIV," in *Chiesa e città,* ed. Cosimo Damiano Fonseca and Cinzio Violante (Galatina, 1990), p. 53.

15. See Attilio Bartoli Langeli, preface to *Archivi della Valnerina,* ed. Vittorio Giorgetti, Archivi dell'Umbria: Inventari e ricerche, 5 (Perugia, 1983), p. x, and Lucio Riccetti, "Primi insediamenti degli ordini mendicanti a Orvieto: Note per una introduzione alla documentazione esistente," in *Archivi di Orvieto,* ed. Marilena Rossi Caponeri and Lucio Riccetti, Archivi dell'Umbria: Inventari e ricerche, 9 (Perugia, 1987), p. xxix.

16. See, for example, Gian Maria Varanini, "Per la storia dei Minori a Verona nel Duecento," in *Minoritismo e centri veneti nel Duecento,* ed. Giorgio Cracco, Civis: Studi e testi, 7 (Trent, 1983), pp. 93–101, who documents the existence of certain *sorores minores* whose initial spiritual inspiration was not necessarily Franciscan.

17. On confraternal records, see Anna Esposito, "La documentazione degli archivi di ospedali e confraternite come fonte per la storia sociale di Roma," in *Sources of Social History: Private Acts in the Late Middle Ages,* ed. Paolo Brezzi and Egmont Lee (Toronto, 1984), pp. 69–79. Helpful information on current developments in this area of study can be found in *Confraternitas: The Newsletter of the Society for Confraternity Studies,* which began publication in 1990.

18. For bibliographical guidance, see Luciano Orioli, "Per una rassegna bibliografica sulle confraternite medievali," *Ricerche di storia sociale e religiosa* 9 (1980): 98; Giuseppina De Sandre Gasparini, "Confraternite e 'cura animarum' nei primi decenni del Quattrocento: I disciplinati e la parrocchia di S.Vitale in Verona," in *Pievi, parrocchie, e clero nel Veneto dal X al XV secolo,* ed. Paolo Sambin (Venice, 1987), p. 322; and the review essay by Giovanna Casagrande, "Women in Confraternities between the Middle Ages and the Modern Age: Research in Umbria," *Con-*

fraternitas: The Newsletter of the Society for Confraternity Studies 5, no. 2 (Fall 1994): 3–13. On the early sixteenth century, see also Nicholas Terpstra, "Women in the Brotherhood: Gender, Class, and Politics in Renaissance Bolognese Confraternities," *Renaissance and Reformation/Renaissance et Réforme,* n.s., 14 (1990): 193–212.

19. Her plays were reprinted several times in the late fifteenth century: see Anne Jacobson Schutte, *Printed Italian Vernacular Religious Books, 1465–1550: A Finding List* (Geneva, 1983), pp. 307–8, and Nerida Newbigin, "Plays, Printing, and Publishing, 1485–1500: Florentine 'sacre rappresentazioni'," *La Bibliofilia* 90 (1988): 269–96.

20. On the importance of notarial sources for the study of medieval Italy, see Martin Bertram, "Mittelalterliche Testamente: Zur Entdeckung einer Quellengattung in Italien," *Quellen und Forschungen aus italienischen Archiven und Bibliotheken* 68 (1988): 509–45, whose ample bibliography and interesting historiographical observations bring out clearly how Italian research differs from the French approach to notarial sources. See also Antonio Rigon, "I testamenti come atti di religiosità pauperistica," in *La conversione alla povertà nell'Italia dei secoli XII–XIV,* Proceedings of the Twenty-seventh Conference of the Centro di studi sulla spiritualità medievale, n.s., 4 (Spoleto, 1991), pp. 391–414.

21. This topic received prominent attention in *Archivi e cultura* 25–26 (1992–93), dedicated to "Donne a Roma tra Medioevo e età moderna"; see especially the contribution by Maria Luisa Lombardo and Mirella Vitali Morelli, "Donne e testamenti a Roma nel Quattrocento," pp. 23–130.

22. See *"Nolens intestatus decedere": Il testamento come fonte della storia religiosa e sociale,* ed. Attilio Bartoli Langeli, Archivi dell'Umbria: Inventari e ricerche, 7 (Perugia, 1985).

23. See, for instance, Tiziana Biganti, Maria Grazia Bistoni, Costanza M. Del Giudice, and Paola Monacchia, "I testamenti negli archivi degli enti religiosi di Perugia," in Bartoli Langeli, *"Nolens intestatus decedere,"* esp. p. 69.

24. See the information provided by Antonio Rigon, "Orientamenti religiosi e pratica testamentaria a Padova nei secoli XII–XIV (prime ricerche)," in Bartoli Langeli, *"Nolens intestatus decedere,"* pp. 41–63, esp. pp. 49–53; see also Robert Brentano, "Considerazioni di un lettore di testamenti," ibid., p. 4. For examples of the use of notarial sources to study rural areas, see Charles M. De La Roncière, "La place des confréries dans l'encadrement religieux du contado florentin: L'exemple de la Val d'Elsa," *Mélanges de l'École française de Rome, Moyen Age–temps modernes* 85 (1973): 31–77 and 633–71, and "L'influence des Franciscains dans la campagne florentine au XIVe siècle, 1280–1360," *Mélanges de l'École française de Rome, Moyen Age–temps modernes* 87 (1975): 27–103.

25. At least according to Biganti et al., "I testamenti negli archivi degli enti religiosi di Perugia," pp. 66–68.

26. According to Maria Immacolata Bossa, "I testamenti in tre registri notarili di Perugia, seconda metà del Trecento," in Bartoli Langeli, *"Nolens intestatus decedere,"* p. 92. See also the study by Claudio Bonanno, Metello Bonanno, and

Luciana Pellegrini, "I legati 'pro anima' ed il problema della salvezza nei testamenti fiorentini della seconda metà del Trecento," *Ricerche storiche* 15 (1985): 183–220, esp. pp. 194–95 and 206–7.

27. The obvious source on the "living saints" is Gabriella Zarri, "Le sante vive: Per una tipologia della santità femminile nel primo Cinquecento, *Annali dell'Istituto storico italo-germanico in Trento* 6 (1980): 371–445; now in Zarri, *Le sante vive: Profezie di corte e devozione femminile tra '400 e '500* (Turin, 1990), pp. 87–163 (translated in this volume as "Living Saints: A Typology of Female Sanctity in the Early Sixteenth Century"). The description of Lucia of Narni as a "suora sancta viva" is found in Zarri, *Le sante vive,* p. 89.

28. On this subject, see the essays in *Finzione e santità tra mediovo ed età moderna,* ed. Gabriella Zarri (Turin, 1991); unfortunately, the volume touches only glancingly on the medieval period.

29. For an excellent edition of a canonization proceeding, see *Il processo di canonizzazione di Chiara da Montefalco,* ed. Enrico Menestò (Florence and Perugia, 1984). For studies of miracle collections, see Jacques Dalarun, "Jeanne de Signa, ermite toscane du XIVe siècle, ou la saintetè ordinaire," *Mélanges de l'École française de Rome, Moyen Age–temps modernes* 98 (1986): 161–99, and Dalarun, *La sainte et la cité: Micheline de Pesaro (†1356), tertiaire franciscaine,* Collection de l'École française de Rome, 164 (Rome, 1992). On the production of hagiographical *legendae,* see *Le "Legendae" di Margherita da Città di Castello,* ed. Maria Cristiana Lungarotti with an introduction by Emore Paoli (Spoleto, 1994).

30. See Dalarun, "Jeanne de Signa," and Andrea Tilatti, " 'Per man di notaro': La beata Elena Valentinis da Udine tra documenti notarili e leggende agiografiche," *Cristianesimo nella storia* 8 (1987): 501–20.

31. For data concerning one specific case, see Anna Esposito, "S. Francesca e le comunità religiose femminili a Roma nel secolo XV," in *Culto dei santi, istituzioni, e classi sociali in età preindustriale,* ed. Sofia Boesch Gajano and Lucia Sebastiani (L'Aquila and Rome, 1984), pp. 539–62, esp. pp. 539–40 (translated in this volume as "St. Francesca and the Female Religious Communities of Fifteenth-Century Rome").

32. If one can generalize from the cases studied by Arnold Esch, "Tre sante ed il loro ambiente sociale a Roma: S. Francesca Romana, S. Brigida di Svezia, e S. Caterina da Siena," in *Atti del Simposio internazionale cateriniano-bernardiniano, Siena, 17–20 aprile 1980,* ed. Domenico Maffei and Paolo Nardi (Siena, 1982), pp. 89–120; the passage quoted is found on p. 92. See also Esch, "Die Zeugenaussagen im Heiligsprechungsverahren für S. Francesca Romana als Quellen zur Sozialgeschichte Roms im frühen Quattrocento," *Quellen und Forschungen aus italienischen Archiven und Bibliotheken* 53 (1973): 93–151.

33. For a concrete example, once again see Esposito, "S. Francesca e le comunità religiose femminili," p. 540.

34. Several examples are to be found in *Scrittrici mistiche italiane,* ed. Giovanni Pozzi and Claudio Leonardi (Genoa, 1988), part 1: "Dal Medioevo al Cinquecento."

35. See Marco Folin, "Procedure testamentarie e alfabetismo a Venezia nel Quattrocento," *Scrittura e civiltà* 14 (1990): 243–70.

36. In addition to the pioneering essay of Armando Petrucci, "Scrittura, alfabetismo, ed educazione paleografica nella Roma del primo Cinquecento: Da un libretto di conti di Maddalena pizzicarola in Trastevere," *Scrittura e civiltà* 2 (1978): 163–207, see the study of one *mulier religiosa* of late medieval Italy: Marcella Marighelli, "Spese di una terziaria domenicana, registrate in volgare dal 1449 al 1473," *Analecta Pomposiana* 16 (1991): 117–97. Unfortunately, this latter study does not provide a photographic reproduction of the woman's handwriting or analyze its characteristics.

37. See Anna Benvenuti Papi, "Devozioni private e guide di coscienze femminili nella Firenze del Due-Trecento," *Ricerche storiche* 16 (1986): 565–601, and now in her *"In castro poenitentiae,"* pp. 205–46, with the title "Padri spirituali."

38. Esch, "Tre sante ed il loro ambiente sociale," p. 103 n. 45, gives a general indication of the kind of books she read.

39. Mauro Tagliabue, "Francesca Romana nella storiografia: Fonti, studi, biografie," in *Una santa tutta romana: Saggi e ricerche nel VI centenario della nascita di Francesca Bussa dei Ponziani, 1384–1984,* ed. Giorgio Picasso (Monte Oliveto, 1984), p. 220, who refers the reader to Vittorio Bartoccetti, "Le fonti della visione di Santa Francesca Romana," *Rivista storica benedettina* 13 (1922): 13–40. The works in question were the Rule of St. Benedict, the Dialogues of Gregory the Great, the *Golden Legend* by the Dominican Jacobus de Voragine, and the *Lives of the Holy Fathers* by another Dominican, Domenico Cavalca. On the sources of the visions of female mystics, see also the works cited in note 63.

40. Giordano da Pisa, *Quaresimale fiorentino, 1305–1306,* ed. Carlo Delcorno (Florence, 1974), p. viii. See also Delcorno, "Cavalca, Domenico," in *Dizionario Biografico degli Italiani,* vol. 22 (Rome, 1979), p. 584, who notes that a *meschinella* —a "miserable little woman"—copied a Dominican miscellany (presently MS 46 in the Biblioteca Comunale of Verona) that contains fragments of sermons by Giordano of Pisa and works by his fellow Dominican Domenico Cavalca, while a manuscript of Cavalca's *Specchio di croce* (now MS 2102 of the Biblioteca Riccardiana in Florence) was copied by Sister Angelica of the Dominican convent of San Jacopo a Ripoli.

41. They were eventually published in Venice around 1515, as *Del modo del ben vivere,* with a declaration that this was an "Opera devotissima composta per el reverendo padre beato Bernardino da Feltre del sacro ordine de san Francesco: del modo del ben vivere de ogni religioso e religiosa: Et primo de la sancta Humiltà." See the bibliographical information in Roberto Rusconi, "Bernardino da Feltre predicatore nella società del suo tempo," in *Bernardino da Feltre a Pavia: La predicazione e la fondazione del Monte di Pietà,* ed. Renata Crotti Pasi (Como, 1994), p. 15 n. 74. For other sermons preached to nuns by Bernardino of Feltre and recorded by them, see the references in Vittorino Meneghin, "Due sermoni inediti del B. Bernardino da Feltre," *Studi francescani* 61 (1964): p. 212 n. 1. Similar sermons by another Observant Franciscan friar, Michele Carcano da Milano, have been published as *Cinque prediche a monache in lingua volgare di due celebri francescani del secolo XV,* ed. Marcellino da Civezza (Prato, 1881).

42. Rose of Viterbo is being studied by Darleen Pryds, whose essay, "Women Who Preached: The Proclamation of Sanctity through Proscribed Acts in Late Medieval Italy," is scheduled for publication in the forthcoming volume *Women's Preaching in the Christian Tradition,* ed. Beverly Mayne Kienzle and Pamela J. Walker. On Umiltà, see *I sermoni di Umiltà da Faenza: Studio e edizione,* ed. Adele Simonetti (Spoleto, 1995), and Simonetti, "I sermoni di Umiltà da Faenza: Storia della tradizione," *Studi medievali,* ser. 3, 33 (1991): 303–8.

43. For this and other references to women's preaching, see Adriana Valerio, " 'Et io expongo le Scripture': Domenica da Paradiso e l'interpretazione biblica, un documento inedito nella crisi del Rinascimento fiorentino," *Rivista di storia e letteratura religiosa* 30 (1994): 500–534, esp. pp. 508–9 and note 34. The passage mentioned is found in the same codex that contains a fifteenth-century vernacular translation of the thirteenth-century proceedings for the canonization of St. Clare of Assisi (see below, note 46).

44. See *Il Libro della beata Angela da Foligno,* ed. Ludger Thier and Abele Calufetti (Grottaferrata [Rome], 1985), and *Angela da Foligno, terziaria francescana,* ed. Enrico Menestò (Spoleto, 1992). On the sixteenth-century polemic surrounding the authorship of writings attributed to one nun, see Massimo Firpo, "Paola Antonia Negri, monaca Angelica, 1508–1555," *Studi Barnabiti* 7 (1990): 7–66, and now in *Rinascimento al femminile,* ed. Ottavia Niccoli (Bari and Rome, 1991), pp. 35–82. In the case of Maria Maddalena de' Pazzi (1566–1604), it was her fellow Carmelite nuns in the convent of Santa Maria degli Angeli at Careggi, near Florence, who laboriously recorded the visions she experienced in the course of her many ecstasies. The original manuscripts are still preserved in that convent: see Maria Maddalena de' Pazzi, *Le parole dell'estasi,* ed. Giovanni Pozzi (Milan, 1984), and *Tutte le opere di S. Maria Maddalena de' Pazzi, dai manoscritti originali,* 7 vols. (Florence, 1960–66).

45. Adriana Valerio, *Domenica da Paradiso: Profezia e politica in una mistica del Rinascimento* (Spoleto, 1992).

46. See, for instance, Balbino Rano, "Las más antiguas reglas conocidas de los agustinos/as seculares (Hermanos de la penitencia o terciarios)," *Analecta Augustiniana* 57 (1994): 35–109, and Giovanni Boccali, "Codice francescano nel Monastero delle Clarisse di Bressanone," *Archivum Franciscanum Historicum* 84 (1991): 491–98. What is thought to be a vernacular version of a poem by Francis of Assisi, "Audite poverelle," was recently found in a fourteenth-century miscellany belonging to the convent of Poor Clares in Novaglie (Verona): see the description of the codex in Giovanni Boccali, "Canto di esortazione per le 'Poverelle' di San Damiano," *Collectanea Franciscana* 48 (1978): 5–29. A similar codex in the Biblioteca Nazionale of Florence contains a vernacular translation of the canonization proceeding for St. Clare of Assisi, held in 1255: see Zeffirino Lazzeri, "Il processo di canonizzazione di S. Chiara d' Assisi," *Archivum Franciscanum Historicum* 13 (1920): 403–507 (though Lazzeri's description of the manuscript, on p. 438, does not indicate its contents). The reference to the Humiliate is found in Danilo Zardin, *Donna e religiosa di rara eccellenza: Prospera Corona Bascapè, i libri, e la cultura nei monasteri*

milanesi del Cinque e Seicento (Florence, 1992), p. 211. See also Zardin "Mercato librario e letture devote nella svolta del Cinquecento tridentino: Note in margine ad un inventario milanese di libri di monache," in *Stampa, libri, e letture a Milano nell'età di Carlo Borromeo,* ed. Nicola Raponi and Angelo Turchini (Milan, 1992), pp. 135–246.

47. See Gabriella Zarri, "La vita religiosa femminile tra devozione e chiostro: Testi devoti in volgare editi tra il 1475 e il 1520," in *I frati minori tra '400 e '500,* Proceedings of the Twelfth International Conference of Franciscan Studies, Assisi, 18–20 October 1984 (Assisi, 1986), pp. 125–68 (now in Zarri, *Le sante vive,* pp. 21–50), as well as the more recent essay by Katherine Gill, "Women and the Production of Religious Literature in the Vernacular, 1300–1500," in *Creative Women in Medieval and Early Modern Italy: A Religious and Artistic Renaissance,* ed. E. Ann Matter and John Coakley (Philadelphia, 1994), pp. 64–104.

48. See Pietro Bologna, "La stamperia fiorentina del monastero di S. Jacopo di Ripoli e le sue edizioni," *Giornale storico della letteratura italiana* 20 (1892): 349–78, and Susan Noakes, "The Development of the Book Market in Late Quattrocento Italy: Printers' Failures and the Role of the Middleman," *Journal of Medieval and Renaissance Studies* 11 (1981): 23–55, esp. pp. 43–48.

49. Zarri, "La vita religiosa femminile," p. 40.

50. Ibid., pp. 21 and 40.

51. Armando Petrucci, "Il testo prodotto: Dal libro manoscritto all'editoria di massa," in *Letteratura italiana,* directed by Alberto Asor Rosa, vol. 2, *Produzione e consumo* (Turin, 1983), p. 520.

52. See the remarks of Folin, "Procedure testamentarie e alfabetismo," p. 260 and the caption to fig. 10.

53. See, for instance, Mirella Ferrari, "Per una storia delle biblioteche francescane a Milano nel Medioevo e nell'Umanesimo," *Archivum Franciscanum Historicum* 72 (1979): 429–64, esp. pp. 457–64 (the manuscripts belonging to the convent of Santa Maria di Vedano as derived from a series of inventories).

54. Most of these manuscripts are now to be found in the Biblioteca Comunale Augusta of Perugia: see Ugolino Nicolini, "I minori osservanti di Monteripido e lo 'scriptorium' delle clarisse di Monteluce in Perugia nei secoli XV e XVI," *Picenum Seraphicum* 7 (1971): 100–130. Another convent particularly active in diffusing texts connected with the Observant reform of the Poor Clares was that of Montevergine in Messina: see Diego Ciccarelli, "Contributi alla recensione degli scritti di S. Chiara," *Miscellanea francescana* 79 (1979): 347–74, and "Volgarizzamenti siciliani inediti degli scritti di S. Chiara," *Schede medievali* 4 (1983): 19–51.

55. Roberto Rusconi, "Pietà, povertà, e potere: Donne e religione nell'Umbria tardomedievale," in Menestò and Rusconi, *Umbria: La strada delle sante medievali,* p. 28.

56. See, for instance, *Memoriale di Monteluce: Cronaca del monastero delle clarisse di Perugia dal 1448 al 1838,* ed. Chiara Augusta Lainati, with an introduction by Ugolino Nicolini (Assisi, 1983), and *Ricordanze del monastero di S. Lucia o.s.c.*

in Foligno, cronache 1424–1786, ed. Angela Emmanuela Scandella, with an appendix by Giovanni Boccali (Assisi, 1987).

57. See Serena Spanò Martinelli, "La biblioteca del 'Corpus Domini' bolognese: L'inconsueto spaccato di una cultura monastica femminile," *La Bibliofilia* 87 (1986): 1–23.

58. Daniela Mazzuconi, " 'Pauca quaedam de vita et miraculis beate Francisce de Pontianis': Tre biografie quattrocentesche di Santa Francesca Romana," in *Una santa tutta romana,* pp. 95–101. For the *vitae,* see now Alessandra Bartolomei Romagnoli, *Santa Francesca Romana: Edizione critica dei trattati latini di Giovanni Mattiotti* (Vatican City, 1995).

59. See Michele Catalano, *La leggenda della beata Eustochia da Messina: Testo volgare del sec. XV restituito all'originaria lezione* (Messina and Florence, 1950). For further information, see Zarri, *Le sante vive,* p. 130 n. 36, and the comments of Rudolph M. Bell, *Holy Anorexia* (Chicago, 1985), pp. 140–45.

The *Vita di Ludovica di Savoia, scritta in francese da una monaca clarissa del Monastero di Orbe coetanea della santa,* translated into Italian and published in 1840, was supposedly kept in that Piedmontese convent of Poor Clares for centuries after the death of Ludovica (1463–1503): Sara Cabibbo, "La santità femminile dinastica," in *Donna e fede: Santità e vita religiosa in Italia,* ed. Lucetta Scaraffia and Gabriella Zarri (Rome and Bari, 1994), p. 416 n. 2.

60. The *Miracula b. Dominici auctrice Angelica moniali, narrata a Caecilia moniali* was edited by Angelus Walz, "Die 'Miracula beati Dominici' der Schwester Cäcilia," *Archivum Fratrum Praedicatorum* 37 (1967): 5–45.

61. Giulia Barone, "Le due vite di Margherita Colonna," in *Esperienza religiosa e scritture femminili tra medioevo ed età moderna,* ed. Marilena Modica Vasta (Acireale [Catania], 1992), pp. 25–32.

62. On this, see Zarri, *Le sante vive,* p. 130 n. 36 and p. 131 n. 51.

63. See in particular Chiara Frugoni, " 'Le mistiche, le visioni, e l'iconografia: Rapporti ed influssi," in *Temi e problemi nella mistica femminile trecentesca,* Convegni del Centro di studi sulla spiritualità medievale, 20 (Todi, 1983), pp. 139–79 (translated in this volume as "Female Mystics, Visions, and Iconography"); Frugoni, "Su un 'immaginario' possibile di Margherita da Città di Castello," in Rusconi, *Il movimento religioso femminile in Umbria,* pp. 203–16; and more recently, Monica Chiellini Nari, "La contemplazione e le immagini: Il ruolo dell'iconografia nel pensiero della beata Angela da Foligno," in Menestò, *Angela da Foligno,* pp. 227–49. For a more general discussion of the relations between mysticism and iconography, see Elizabeth Vavra, "Bildmotiv und Frauenmystik: Funktion und Rezeption," in *Frauenmystik im Mittelalter,* ed. Peter Dinzelbacher and Dieter R. Bauer (Stuttgart, 1985), pp. 201–30.

64. See, for instance, Chiara Frugoni, *Francesco e l'invenzione delle stimmate: Una storia per parole e immagini fino a Bonaventura e Giotto* (Turin, 1993), pp. 401–4.

65. See Chiara Frugoni, "The Imagined Woman," in *A History of Women,* vol. 2, *Silences of the Middle Ages,* ed. Christiane Klapisch-Zuber (Cambridge, Mass., 1992), pp. 336–422 (an essay that is not limited to Italy); Dominique Rigaux, "La donna, la fede, l'immagine negli ultimi secoli del Medioevo," in Scaraffia and Zarri, *Donna e fede,* pp. 157–75; and Jacques Dalarun, "Hors des sentiers battus: Saintes femmes d'Italie aux XIIIe–XIVe siècles," in *Femmes, Mariages, Lignages, XIIe–XIVe siècles: Mélanges offerts à Georges Duby* (Brussels, 1992), pp. 79–102.

66. This point was also emphasized in the reviews of the Italian edition of this collection, *Mistiche e devote nell'Italia tardomedievale,* by Augustine Thompson, in *American Historical Review* 99 (1994): 885–86; Marjorie Reeves, in *Journal of Ecclesiastical History* 45 (1994): 174–75; and Ingrid Peterson, in *Catholic Historical Review* 80 (1994): 804–5.

67. Such was the title of an article by Ovidio Capitani, in *Studi medievali,* ser. 3, 8 (1967): 745–61.

68. On 27–28 September 1991, the University of Pennsylvania's Center for Italian Studies hosted a very stimulating conference, with the participation of a large group of Italian and American scholars, whose proceedings have recently been published under the title *Creative Women in Medieval and Early Modern Italy* (see above, note 47).

Simonetta of Perugia, 115
sodomy, 184, 188
Sofia (recluse of Trevi), 64
Soranzo, Antonio, 179n.40
Spanish *Alumbrados,* 252, 302n.205
Spanish chapel at Santa Maria Novella, 151
Spello, 63
spirituality, 3–4
stigmata, 237, 239–40, 287n.126, 302n.204
Sturion, Maria. *See* Maria of Venice
suits, 307

testaments, 310
Third Orders, 68–69, 89, 92–93, 135, 235
Thomas Aquinas, St., 139
three nails, 133–34
Tosti, Iacobella, 206
travel, 88
Tuscany: institutional affiliations in, 84–85; mendicants in, 85–86; monastic sanctity in, 86; preponderance of women in, 84; types of holy women in, 86–87

Ugolino Conti de Segni. *See* Gregory IX
Umiliana dei Cerchi, 3, 64, 85, 88–89, 91, 92, 94
Umiltà of Faenza, 86, 90, 97n.14, 157n.28

Vanna of Orvieto, 139
Vannozza (St. Francesca's granddaughter), 202
Vannozza (St. Francesca's sister-in-law), 199–200, 209
Vannozza (widow of Giacomo Santacroce), 202–3

Verdiana of Castelfiorentino, 85, 88, 102n.41
Veronica of Binasco, 226. *See also* living saints
Vigri, Caterina, 224, 232, 274n.79
Villana delle Botti, 95n.4, 97n.14, 134, 157n.28, 158n.31
Virgin of Humility, 151
Virgin of Mercy, 150–51
visions, 130, 131–32, 139, 179n.41, 238–39
visualization, 130, 131–32, 147–48
Vito of Cortona, 94
vows, 113–14

weaving, 99n.24
white Benedictines, 32, 33
widowhood, 86–87, 88, 184
wills, 310
witchcraft, 244, 246, 247, 291n.156
wives, 182, 186
women: authority of, 5; in confraternities, 309; contributions of, 222, 257n.18; domestic piety of, 4; dominant forms of life of, 10; editorial activities of, 314; forms of sanctity, 8–10; influence of, 6–7; literacy of, 312–13; meditations of, 136; Middle Ages religious movement of, 7–8; monastic spirituality of, 312; number of devout, in sixteenth century, 222; preaching by, 158n.37, 313; prominence in religious culture, 1; prophecies of, 234, 279n.89; religious culture of, 312; restrictions on, 1, 5; revelations to, 234, 281n.90; role models for, 5–6; spiritual guidance of, 19n.23; writings of, 312–15
work, 99n.24

Zorzi, Francesco, 227, 251, 265n.48